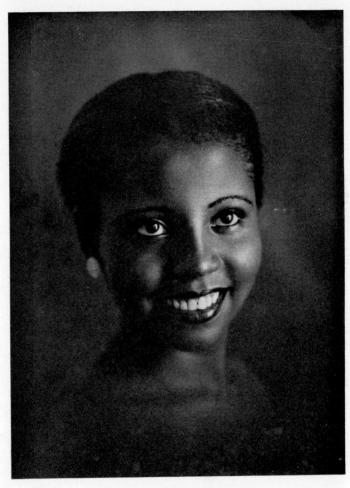

TYPICAL BAHIAN NEGRO GIRL

NEGROES IN BRAZIL

A Study of Race Contact at Bahia

By

DONALD PIERSON, Ph.D.

*Professor of Sociology, Escola Livre
de Sociologia e Politica de São Paulo*

THE UNIVERSITY OF CHICAGO PRESS
CHICAGO · ILLINOIS

THE UNIVERSITY OF CHICAGO SOCIOLOGICAL SERIES

THE UNIVERSITY OF CHICAGO SOCIOLOGICAL SERIES, established by the Trustees of the University, is devoted primarily to the publication of the results of the newer developments in sociological study in America. It is expected that a complete series of texts for undergraduate instruction will ultimately be included, but the emphasis will be placed on research, the publications covering both the results of investigation and the perfecting of new methods of discovery. The editors are convinced that the textbooks used in teaching should be based on the results of the efforts of specialists whose studies of concrete problems are building up a new body of funded knowledge. While the series is called sociological, the conception of sociology is broad enough to include many borderline interests, and studies will appear which place the emphasis on political, economic, or educational problems dealt with from the point of view of a general conception of human nature.

THE UNIVERSITY OF CHICAGO PRESS · CHICAGO
Agent: THE CAMBRIDGE UNIVERSITY PRESS · LONDON

PREFACE

ONE of the more significant consequences of World War I was a material reduction in the isolation of the United States, at least in so far as European peoples and European problems were concerned. Until very recently, however, our ignorance of almost everything south of Panama has been profound. In common with the other South American countries, Brazil has remained for us largely terra incognita. Even today, when tourists are discovering that Rio de Janeiro is one of the world's most beautiful cities, many intelligent and usually well-informed persons are surprised to learn, for instance, that Portuguese and not Spanish is the language of Brazil and that by reason of Brazil's European language-speaking population being greater than that of all other South American countries combined, or approximately equal to the population of France, Portuguese is the most-spoken language in South America.

This book, it is hoped, will contribute toward making better known and understood one aspect of Brazilian life, namely, the career of the Brazilian Negro. It makes no pretense of being a systematic and exhaustive inquiry into assimilation and acculturation as these processes operate in Brazil. It has rather the character of a general reconnaisance which conceivably might lay some of the groundwork for future investigation. It is designed to furnish at least a preliminary answer to the question: What has happened to the Africans who were imported in such large numbers into this part of the New World?

In 1934, while I was a Fellow in sociology at the University of Chicago, my attention was called by Dr. Herbert Blumer to the possibilities of Brazil as a locus for the study of racial and cultural contacts, and I subsequently received encouragement from Drs. Robert Redfield, Louis Wirth, and Ellsworth Faris to consider these possibilities seriously. As I subsequently went through the available literature in several languages, I became increasingly interested in Brazil, particularly as a locus for investigating, in an intimate and detailed way, what appeared to be a racial situation sufficiently distinct from that in India, for example, where the social order is based upon caste, or that in the United States, where the Negro is now escaping from a caste status and becoming a racial minority similar to the Jew in Europe and elsewhere, to constitute, along with, perhaps, the Hawaiian and certain other similar racial situations, a distinct type. At approximately this same time Dr. Robert E. Park returned from an extended world-tour, during which he had observed at first hand a number of the more important centers of racial and cultural contact, including Brazil, in which he also had for some time been particularly interested.

The outgrowth of these converging interests was a two-year period of field work in Brazil (from 1935 to 1937) as research assistant of the Social Science Research Committee of the University of Chicago, to which organization, together with the Rosenwald Fund, I am indebted for making this study financially possible. Twenty-two months of this period of residence were spent in intimate study of the social order of one city, the old seaport of Bahia.

This focusing of attention upon one particular locus is, in my opinion, an inescapable procedure, since the sentiments which determine human and personal relations are so in-

variably crystallized in the customs and habits of each lo-
cality that any portrayal of race relations which seeks to be
comprehensible must of necessity make some analysis of
local folkways and mores.

To name all the Bahian friends from whose characteristic
courtesy, so proverbial in Brazil, I profited during my field
work would be an exceedingly difficult task. For extensive
and continuous assistance I am under obligation particularly to Zacharias Pithon Barretto, João Canna Brasil, Ho-
sannah de Oliveira, Alfredo Gonsalves Amorim, Nestor
Duarte, Aloysio de Carvalho Filho, Laura Schlaepfer, João
da Silva Campos, Friars Tomaz and Protasius, Canon Manoel Barbosa, Francisco Sá, Euvaldo Diniz Gonçalves, José
Lourenço de A. Costa, Edison Carneiro, Edgar de Britto,
André Leon Achdjian, Martiniano, Mãe Anninha, and Zázá.
In addition, for other important contributions, I am in-
debted to Anisio Teixeira, Innocencio de Goes Calmon,
Theodoro Sampaio, Waldemar and Maria Lages, Braz do
Amaral, Oscar Caetano, Belfort Saraiva, Jayme Junqueira
Ayres, Elysio Lisboa, Pamphilo de Carvalho, Dantas Junior,
Pedro de Mello, Jorge de Menezes Berenguer, Alfredo Pi-
mentel, Francisco da Conceição Menezes, Oscar Cordeiro,
Ignacio Tosta Filho, João Mendonça, Edgard Matta, Cory-
pheu de Azevedo Marques, Antonio Barretto, Licia Barretto, Eliezer and Carmen Santos, Reginaldo Guimarães,
Enoch Torres, Silvio de São Paulo, Sergio Maranhão, Enoch
Carteado, Tharcicio Telles, João Varella, George Hassel-
mann, Socrates Marback, Frederico de Ferreira Bandeira,
Pedro Rodrigues Bandeira, Vicente Café, and Galba Araujo;
to a number of foreign residents at Bahia, especially the
vice-consul of the United States, Lee Worley, and his suc-
cessor, Robert Janz, Bruno Reitman, Margot and Gaby

Gleig, M. G. and Kate White, Peter and Irene Baker, Ralph and Catherine Varhaug, and "Slim" Jordan; and to a host of others, including Maria Bádá, Maria do Carmo, Pae Procopio, Pae Bernardinho, Pae Joazinho, Pae Manoel Paim, Mãe Minininha, Mãe Sabina, Dona Germania, Felisbertus, Hypolito, Bimba, Rodolfo, Marciano, Nestor, Edgar, Satyro, Estanislau, Antonio, Bábê, Angelo, Joanna, Dédé, Adalberto, and Eulalia.

For the clarification of several obscure points raised in reading, observation, or investigation I am grateful to such able interpreters of the Brazilian scene as Gilberto Freyre, Affonso de E. Taunay, Oliveira Vianna, Pedro Calmon, Rüdiger Bilden, and Lois Williams. Dr. Arthur Ramos, who is intimately acquainted with the Bahian Negro, and Dr. Hugh C. Tucker, who during fifty-four years' residence in Brazil has become acquainted with the country as have few North Americans, read the manuscript and offered pertinent comment. Drs. Robert Redfield, Herbert Blumer, Louis Wirth, Ellsworth Faris, and William F. Ogburn have from the inception of the study extended me many courtesies, the most important of which have been their unsparingly critical but always constructive suggestions. I am deeply indebted to Dr. Charles Johnson and Fisk University for the leisure to prepare the manuscript for publication and to Mrs. Martha Harris for patient and careful attention to manuscript detail. I am under perhaps the greatest obligation to Dr. Robert E. Park, whose seminal mind, long-range patience as a teacher, and rich research experience have contributed in fundamental ways to this study. My wife, Helen Batchelor Pierson, has been an invaluable assistant.

DONALD PIERSON

ESCOLA LIVRE DE SOCIOLOGIA E POLITICA
DE SÃO PAULO
October 1939

INTRODUCTION

DURING the years in which it has been a subject of discussion and investigation in the United States, the conception of what constitutes a race problem has undergone an extraordinary number of changes—one might say transfigurations. In recent years interest and research in the problematic aspects of race have centered about what is called technically "race relations." But new studies of race relations have invariably revealed new complexities in racial situations and have added new dimensions to the problem as originally conceived. The consequence is that with every new inquiry the conception of what constitutes race relations has steadily expanded until the term seems to include all or most human relations that have anywhere been defined and given formal recognition in the social sciences.

The most obvious and elementary of these relations are ecological and biological, that is, the territorial distribution of races and the inevitable miscegenation or interbreeding which changes in distribution inevitably bring about. The term also includes, by implication at least, all the special problems that emerge on every other level of social integration (i.e., economic, political, personal, or religious) as a consequence of the migration and mixture of races.

I say "personal" or "religious" because it is only within the fold of a family or of a religious society that human relations have anywhere assumed a character that can be described in any exclusive sense as personal and moral. Economic and political relations of individuals and of peoples are always relatively impersonal and external.

Meanwhile, a growing awareness of the complexities of the problem has been accompanied by a continuous expansion of what one may describe as "the racial horizon." As the world has grown smaller and our relations with other races and peoples more intimate, the race problem is no longer conceived either in the United States or elsewhere as a local problem or one that is limited to the Negro.

It is obvious today, as it possibly never was before, that race problems are neither a temporary nor an isolated phenomenon. On the contrary, it seems that, wherever European economic expansion has brought European peoples and the peoples or races of the world outside Europe into an association sufficiently intimate to produce a mixed-blood population, the resulting racial situation has inevitably constituted a race problem.

But race problems are not confined to colonial countries. Similar conditions, or at least conditions which make complete assimilation difficult or impossible, have produced in recent years, in Germany and elsewhere in Europe, a more conspicuous and more poignant instance of a race problem than the world outside of Europe has ever known. In fact, it is fair to say that if the race problem of the United States is pre-eminently the problem of Negroes, the race problem of Europe is and has been, ever since the Roman Empire first sought not only to conquer but to denationalize them, the problem of Jews.

Stated abstractly, and from the point of view of the Jewish people in Europe and the Negro people in the United States rather than from the point of view of the dominant majorities with whom they are associated, the race problem is that of a racial or cultural minority seeking to achieve, in a community in which it is regarded as in some sense and to some degree an alien, a status that is at once secure and unqualified by the stigma of any sort of inferiority. Elsewhere the race problem may take the form of a nationalistic struggle in which the native peoples, within the limits of an imperium where they have been conquered but not assimilated, are seeking, if not national independence, then some further measure of self-determination. This is the case of India. It may presently be, if the present German government succeeds in carrying out its program, the case of Europe.

The expansion of the racial horizon, which has changed and is changing current conceptions of the race problem in the United States and elsewhere, has brought about—and this is particularly true of sociology and social anthropology—something like a reorientation of the social sciences, with respect to the race problem and to all that is ordinarily included under race relations.[1]

Social anthropology is, apparently, no longer regarded, to the extent that it once was, as a purely historical science, interested mainly in unraveling and tracing to their sources the varied threads that make up the cultural patterns of primitive societies.

Anthropology, as it has become "functional," has become less interested in cultural diffusion and more interested in acculturation and in the processes by which cultural traits have been not merely diffused but integrated into those larger and more complex cultural patterns we call civilizations.

[1] Edgar T. Thompson (ed.), *Race Relations and the Race Problem* (Durham, N.C.: Duke University Press, 1939).

Anthropology has begun, also, in recent years to turn its attention to contemporary social problems, including that of education. In England anthropologists have become technical advisers in colonial administration.[2] In the United States they are beginning to study "marginal peoples," that is to say, peoples who, under the influence of European culture, are now in the process, sometimes slowly but more often rapidly, of being assimilated and incorporated into an emerging world-society—the society which the expansion of Europe has brought into existence.[3]

The race problem has assumed new dimensions and new significance, likewise, with the recent researches of sociologists in the field of race and culture and in areas of observation and research immediately contiguous. Probably nothing has been more influential than the publication of the monumental work by W. I. Thomas and Florian Znaniecki, *The Polish Peasant*, in directing the attention of sociological students to the possibility and the importance of studies in the field of race and culture. Thomas and Znaniecki were the first, or almost the first, to call attention to the fact that the situation of the European immigrant in the United States can be defined in terms that imply its logical relation to that of the Negro, even though the Negro, in the Americas, North and South and particularly in the West Indies, is not an alien or an immigrant but has become, in the course

[2] See G. Gordon Brown and A. McD. Bruce Hutt, *Anthropology in Action: An Experiment in the Iringa District of the Iringa Province, Tanganyika Territory* (London: International Institute of African Languages and Cultures; Oxford University Press, 1935). See also unpublished papers contributed to a symposium on "Education and the Cultural Process," in connection with the celebration of the Seventy-fifth Anniversary of Fisk University, April, 1941.

[3] See Robert Redfield, *The Folk Culture of Yucatan* (Chicago: University of Chicago Press, 1941).

of some three hundred years' residence, an indigenous race intimately related by blood to the Indian who preceded him.

Perhaps I should add, now that I have mentioned the *Polish Peasant*, that it was the rather elaborate "methodological note" with which the authors prefaced that study which first defined "social attitudes" and indicated the way in which that concept could be used in characterizing local cultures as well as in measuring, in some fashion, cultural and institutional changes.[4]

If I have ventured by way of introduction to this study of race relations in Brazil to sketch the outlines of an expanding though as yet very little integrated field of sociological and anthropological research, it has been less with the purpose of reporting on the state of knowledge in that field at the moment than of indicating the context in which this study had been conceived and the place it seems to have in the sequence of studies that have preceded and which will presumably follow it.

In suggesting the possibility of future studies to follow this one, I am reckoning with two facts: (1) that Brazil is one of the more conspicuous melting-pots of races and cultures around the world where miscegenation and acculturation are obviously going on and (2) that a comparative study of the problematic aspects of race and culture is likely to have a special importance at this time when the structure of

[4] William I. Thomas and Florian Znaniecki, *The Polish Peasant in Europe and America* (1st ed.; Boston: Richard C. Badger, 1918–20; 2d ed.; New York: Alfred Knopf, 1927). Herbert Blumer, *Critiques of Research in the Social Sciences. I. An Appraisal of Thomas and Znaniecki's "The Polish Peasant in Europe and America"* (New York: Social Science Research Council, 1939). As an illustration of how "attitudes" have been used in measuring fundamental institutional changes see Alfred Winslow Jones, *Life, Liberty, and Property: A Story of Conflict and a Measurement of Conflicting Rights* (New York and London: J. B. Lippincott Co., 1941).

the existing world-order seems to be crumbling with the dissolution of the distances, physical and social, upon which that order seems to rest.

It has become fairly obvious that, in a world which in the midst of wars is steadfastly seeking peace, a stable political order can be erected only on a moral order that does not terminate at the boundaries of national states. The problem that emerges is this: How is it possible to establish and maintain an effective social order in a more or less completely urbanized, industrialized, and cosmopolitan world?

In the past it has been, in the main, the task of religion and more especially of Christian missions to create within the limits of an expanding world-economy a moral order and moral solidarity commensurate with the economic and political interdependence which the expansion of European commerce has brought about. But the totalitarian states have now apparently seceded from the ecumenical councils of international Christianity, and the task of re-creating a moral order that includes all mankind has assumed an importance that it did not have when it was regarded not merely as a religious but as a religious denominational enterprise.

It is obvious that studies of race and culture are destined to assume increasing importance in a world in which the ancient local and tribal cultures, as an ineluctable incident of the rise of the so-called "great society," are visibly going into the melting-pot.

One thing that makes the racial situation in Brazil interesting is the fact that, having a Negro population proportionally larger than the United States, Brazil has no race problem. This is, at any rate, what might be inferred from the occasional and apparently disinterested reports of visitors to that country who have ventured to inquire into the subject. Among these visitors there are two—James Bryce and Theodore Roosevelt—whose knowledge of conditions in the United States make their reports upon the situation in Brazil peculiarly interesting.

Viscount Bryce, whose "observations and impressions" of South America were first published in 1912, remarked that in Brazil, in contrast to the United States, the color line is nowhere sharply drawn and that "the fusion of whites and blacks by intermarriage goes steadily on." Mr. Roosevelt—Theodore and not Franklin Delano—who visited the country a few years later, is more explicit. He says: "If I were asked to name the one point in which there is a complete difference between the Brazilian and ourselves, I should say it was in the attitude to the black man."

This attitude manifests itself in the fact that in Brazil "any Negro or mulatto who shows himself fit is without question given the place to which his abilities entitle him." However, the most conspicuous difference—the "one real difference"—is "the tendency of Brazil to absorb the Negro." This tendency is, however, not merely a historical and bio-logical fact; it is rather an expression of a national policy, in so far as Brazil can be said to have a policy with respect to the Negro.

Statistics of population, which are never very accurate in this matter of race and less so perhaps in Brazil than in the United States, indicate that the number of Africans of un-mixed blood is growing steadily less so that "with two or more racial crossings"—so say those Brazilians who are con-scious of the Negro or concerned about his future—"the Negro blood tends to disappear." This so-called Aryaniza-tion of the African, from the point of view of Brazilian national policy, is a thing, perhaps one should say *the* thing, to be desired. The policy of the United States, on the other hand, from the Brazilian point of view, particularly in so far as it counts every man a Negro who, to use the census definition, "is known to be a Negro in the community in which he lives," tends to perpetuate "a menacing element" —menacing not to the racial purity of the dominant race but to the political and cultural solidarity of the nation.

As a matter of fact the attitude of the Brazilian people to the race problem so far as concerns the Negro seems, on the whole, to be academic rather than pragmatic and actual. There is a certain ethnological and archeological interest in the survivals of the African fetish cults, the so-called *candomblés*, of which there seem to be an extraordinary number, especially in and about the cities of Bahia and Pernambuco. This archeological interest in the African is evidenced by two successive *Congressos Afro-brasileiros* which met in Recife and in Bahia in 1934 and 1937.

Since most of these *candomblés* are living and functioning forms of African religious practices, although obviously in process of assimilation to the ritual and mythology of local Catholicism, perhaps they should not be classed as survivals.

In any case it is a somewhat bizarre experience to a stranger in Bahia, walking along one of the ridges where *os ricos*, that is, the rich folk, live, to hear from the palm groves in the neighboring valleys where *os pobres*, the poor folk, live, the insistent boom of African drums. So narrow are the spatial distances that divide Europe on the ridges from Africa in the valleys that it is difficult to realize how wide the social distances are that separate them.

It is even more difficult for those of us whose conception of the Negro problem and of race relations generally has been formed in the United States to comprehend, in all its concreteness, the racial situation in a country with a different history and a different tradition. Comprehension in these matters is not something that can be achieved, it seems, through the medium of any formal statement. Insight and understanding come only with intimate and firsthand acquaintance—and not even then if those barriers which race consciousness invariably raises are not removed. That is why little children are likely in these matters of race relations to be wiser than their elders.

This observation seems pertinent here because, after reading the manuscript and proofs of this volume, I have come to the conclusion that the difference between Brazil and the United States in respect to race is due to the fact that the people of Brazil have, somehow, regained that paradisaic innocence, with respect to differences of race, which the people of the United States have somehow lost. I mention this fact, but I shall not attempt to explain it. The situation is complex and the explanations are only partial and not wholly convincing. One circumstance mentioned by the author, I am, however, disposed to underscore.

Brazil is a vast country and has been colonized, as has the United States, by a wide variety of peoples: Germans from northern Europe; Latins, particularly Italians, from southern Europe; not to mention the original settlers, the Portuguese. It has been colonized more recently by Orientals. There are now possibly some two hundred thousand Japanese in Brazil today. With the exception of the Italians, these different peoples have settled in more or less closed communities in widely separated parts of a vast territory. Dependent upon water transportation rather more than upon rail to maintain economic and political unity, Brazil has been haunted by the fear that the country would some day fall apart. Under these circumstances it has seemed that the security and the solidarity of the nation depended upon its ability to assimilate and ultimately to amalgamate its different immigrant populations. From this point of view the Negro has not constituted a problem.

The first task of this, as of every other attempt to study the race problem rather than to solve it, has been to define the racial situation in the country and in the culture in which the problem exists. But the author of this volume has done something more, it seems, than that. He has, as he puts it, given an account of "the career of the Negro in Brazil," and he has made this account a chapter in the life-history of the Negro outside of Africa, in what one might, to use a term that has been usually applied to the Jewish people, call the Diaspora.

The term "diaspora" was first used by the Greeks to designate a nationality, or some part of it, dispersed among other nations but preserving its own culture. The Negro outside of Africa is neither a nation nor a nationality, and, with the exception of Brazil, there is no country outside of Africa, so far as I know, where a people of African origin has sought to preserve African customs or African culture. Nevertheless, the attitude of Europeans has imposed upon peoples of African origin under European domination, either in or outside of Africa, a certain degree of race consciousness and racial solidarity. It has tended to make them a nationality.

Living thus, as Booker Washington once said of the Negro in the United States, as "a nation within a nation," the Negro has been subjected to extraordinary changes of fortune but changes that are nonetheless typical not merely of Negroes abroad but of other peoples who, in the interest of European commercial expansion, have been dispersed to widely separated parts of the world.

The diaspora, however, is no longer what it once was—an area of dispersion merely. It has become rather an area of integration, economic and cultural. It is in this sense that this history, I might better say natural history, of the career of the African in Brazil has sought to describe the processes by which the Negro has been assimilated and to measure the success he has had in finding a place in what was the diaspora but now is, to use Graham Wallas' term, *The Great Society*.

ROBERT E. PARK

TABLE OF CONTENTS

I. THE SETTING

II. SLAVERY

III. MISCEGENATION

IV. RACE AND SOCIAL STATUS

V. THE AFRICAN HERITAGE

VI. THE BAHIAN RACIAL SITUATION

APPENDIXES

SELECTED BIBLIOGRAPHY

INDEXES

LIST OF ILLUSTRATIONS

LIST OF TABLES

LIST OF TABLES

I

THE SETTING

CHAPTER I

THE SEAPORT OF BAHIA

JAMES BRYCE once wrote of the racial situation in Brazil: "It is a subject of study all the more interesting because the relations are . . . . different from those . . . . in the British colonies, in India, and in the United States."[1] Bryce might well have added that such differences constitute one of the more significant portions of any study of race relations. It is by investigating in intimate and concrete detail variant racial situations in different parts of the world and subsequently comparing and contrasting each set of conditions and circumstances that we are able to build up, case by case, a more complete knowledge of the race problem, its sources and nature. The more we see the United States and her problems through the perspective of a world-view—the more, in other words, we detach ourselves from the merely local and provincial—the more clearly will our own problems stand out.

If one looks about in Brazil for a door, so to speak, through which he may enter to examine at first hand the Brazilian racial situation, he may well choose the picturesque old seaport of Bahia,[2] known affectionately in Brazil as "A Mulata Velha." For here the processes of racial adjustment have perhaps gone on longest and most persistently, have involved large numbers from each of the three basic human

[1] *South America* (New York, 1912), p. 20.

[2] Bahia ("Bay") is pronounced *Bàh-ee'-uh* and is written, in "simplified" spelling, Baía. The city is also known as São Salvador or, more correctly, Salvador ("Savior").

races, and the ensuing termination is perhaps most clearly discernible.

Bahia lies in the tropics of the Southern Hemisphere, approximately thirteen degrees south of the Equator, her naturally warm and humid climate almost constantly tempered by the refreshing Southeast Trades. Located seven hundred miles above Rio de Janeiro, the Brazilian capital, and four hundred miles below the old sugar center of Pernambuco, Bahia marks approximately the mid-point of Brazil's four thousand miles of coast line which stretches from temperate Uruguay to the torrid Guianas. Some twenty-five hundred miles to the northeast lie the Gold and Slave coasts of Africa, once the home of the parents or grandparents of many present-day Bahians; directly to the east is Angola, another important source of the city's population.

In 1949 Bahia will celebrate her four hundredth anniversary. As cities go in the New World, she is an old city; in fact, one of the very oldest. Permanently founded fifty-eight years before Jamestown and thirty-five years earlier than St. Augustine, this outpost of Portuguese civilization was one of the world's richest ports long before New York had outgrown her swaddling clothes.

Here, shortly after 1500, set in the Portuguese transplantation, at first composed of adventurers, shipwrecked and deserting sailors; *degredados* banished from Portugal for criminal, political, or religious offenses; ambitious young men chosen for physical fitness and freedom from marital ties to serve in the colonial garrison; impoverished nobles seeking to recuperate fortunes squandered at the Portuguese court; a few officials, Jesuits, and secular clergy; Jews expelled by the Inquisition (who incidentally were to furnish a considerable portion of the much-needed capital for the

MAP OF SOUTH AMERICA SHOWING BAHIA AND SURROUNDING AREA

colony's development); gypsies destined to play a role in the subsequent slave trade and to bequeath their name permanently to the section of the city in which they settled; prostitutes and orphan girls sent over in limited numbers as wives by the Crown; and a few hardy peasant colonists, with their families, from Portugal, the Cape Verde Islands, and the Azores.

This incoming wave of European population met the indigenous Indians and eventually absorbed or expelled them from the coast. In and about Bahia they were the Tupinambás and the Tupiniquins, part of the earlier Tupí expansion from the south, and of very primitive culture. The wifeless soldiers and colonists took Indian or half-breed women, first for concubines and later for legally married wives, and soon a numerous mixed-blood population sprang up which was gradually absorbed into the dominant white. Indian males were annihilated in battle, died from the rigors of slavery, or were driven, together with their women and children, far back into the interior. When they put up too stubborn resistance, whole villages were deliberately exterminated, one of the most effective means being the planting of smallpox germs from the clothing of a recent victim of the disease. The Indians, previously strangers to this European malady, rapidly succumbed.

As early as the middle of the sixteenth century there began at Bahia extensive and prolonged Negro importation from Africa, and Bahia's Bay of All Saints subsequently served for generations as the principal port of entry into Brazil for this black commerce from the African coast. This involuntary population movement to Brazil eventually became what is, probably, the greatest intercontinental displacement of Negro peoples which ever occurred.

CITY OF BAHIA

At Bahia in 1807, 1809, 1813, 1816, 1826, 1827, 1828, and 1830, slave revolts broke out, terminating in the serious Malê uprising of 1835. There existed here, particularly in the nineteenth century, a well-established group of Negro disciples of the prophet Mohammed. Here Nagô was for a long time a Negro lingua franca (or, to use the corresponding Portuguese expression, a *lingua geral*), and Nagô is still occasionally to be heard among some of the older blacks. Here one might have encountered in the years just preceding abolition in 1888 an interesting paradox: while at home Bahia clung tenaciously to slavery, she was known abroad for the eloquence of her abolition orators.[3] Here, also, one might have observed the gradual fusion of Catholic belief and ritual with African mythology and religious practice, evidences of which may be seen today in *candomblés*, or fetish-cult centers, like that of Gantois, for example, whose ceremonies have been carried on in the same sacred place for many decades.

In the sixteenth and early seventeenth centuries Bahia became one of the world's great sugar centers where a small aristocracy, as is attested today by the pretentious edifices still standing, achieved great wealth. As early as 1587 there were forty-seven sugar *engenhos*[4] in and about Bahia, and

---

[3] See Luiz Anselmo da Fonseca, *A escravidão, o clero e o abolicionismo* (Bahia, 1887), *passim*. This book, although obviously written as abolition propaganda, cites names, places, and dates to support its contentions and does not overlook negative cases.

[4] Each *engenho* consisted of a sugar plantation and a mill for processing the cane. Those at Bahia often had a capacity of a thousand tons or more yearly. Each was largely a self-sustaining economic unit, dependent upon the labor of numbers of Negro slaves. H. Morse Stephens says (*Portugal* [New York, 1903], p. 228) that sugar cane was imported into Brazil from the Madeira Islands in 1548.

these, together with the plantations of Pernambuco, supplied a large part of the sugar for the tables of Europe.

By 1670 Bahia was a wealthy capital boasting that her flag was known upon the seven seas. Ships from the Portuguese empire in the East called regularly on their way back to Portugal. By the early eighteenth century Bahia had grown into a city of 70,000, her commerce protected by the cross-fire of fourteen forts. Six- and seven-story buildings were common; the possession of carved ebony furniture had become a symbol of social standing; silks, palanquins, and the finest porcelain were imported from China. In the surrounding cane fields toiled, it is estimated, ten times as many slaves as in Virginia. A century later, Lindley, an English smuggler, after admiring the abundance of gold jewelry worn by the women of Bahia, looked out over the shipping in the harbor and wrote of "a degree of wealth unknown in Europe."

Bahia continued to be the first commercial city of Brazil until about 1830,[5] when she finally yielded front rank to São Paulo, the rising young metropolis to the south. But during the entire colonial period (1549–1822), Bahia possessed the principal Brazilian firms and the largest Brazilian fortunes.

During the first two centuries of the colonial era, Bahia was the seat of Portuguese control in Brazil, the official residence of high functionaries representing the Portuguese crown. Even after the government was transferred to Rio (1763), Bahia continued to play a prominent role in the politics of the colony and, subsequent to independence

[5] In 1868, although the decline in sugar production was by that time well advanced, Bahia had 511 *engenhos* producing nearly 19,000 tons of sugar a year.

CAPE SANTO ANTONIO AT THE ENTRANCE OF TODOS OS SANTOS BAY

On the heights, the old church of Santo Antonio da Barra; below it, the ruins of the sixteenth-century fort by the same name

in 1822, in the politics of the Empire, a role similar to that
assumed by Minas Geraes, São Paulo, and Rio Grande do
Sul in the Republic following 1889. In fact, she has been
called "the Brazilian Virginia." Until 1907 Bahia was also
the religious center of the Brazilian nation. Her archbishop
was the head of the Roman Catholic church in Brazil, and
the religious orders maintained here their principal representatives. Thus in the economic, political, and religious
life of Brazil, Bahia boasts a long tradition of distinction
and prestige.

The present city is about the size of Indianapolis or Seat-
tle.[6] It nestles along the eastern rim of a huge bay, Bahia de
Todos os Santos. The bay is formed by the projection out
into the ocean of Cape Santo Antonio, which, on its western
side, breaks rather sharply almost at the water's edge, ex-
posing a bold promontory approximately three hundred feet
in height which parallels for some two to three miles the
rim of the bay. The city clings to the narrow shelf between
the bay and the cliff and then sprawls up over this sizable
barrier and spreads out along the ridges and into the valleys
to the east and north, where centuries of erosion have
carved a one-time flat plain into alternating crests and steep-
sloping depressions.

Bahia is thus divided by a natural barrier into a lower and
an upper city, into a Cidade Baixa and a Cidade Alta, as the
two parts are locally called; the one connected with the other
by steep, winding streets paved with cobblestones, by inclined planes and modern hydraulic elevators, or by numerous well-worn footpaths. In the lower city lies, of course,

---

[6] An estimate by the state government gave for the city of Bahia on
December 31, 1934, a population of 352,244 (*Annuario estatistico da Bahia,
1934*, p. 131). The federal census of 1920 gave for Bahia City 283,422 (*Recenseamento do Brasil, 1920*, Vol. IV: *População*, Book I, p. xxiv).

the port, with its customs, warehouses, shipping and consular offices, banks, the marine arsenal, the post office, the Association of Commerce, the principal public market, jewelry shops, hardware and cigar stores, and most of the men's shops of the city. Up on the promontory and extending out toward the suburbs are the public buildings and most of the churches, the convents and monasteries, hotels and movie theaters, the public library, museums, professional schools, primary and secondary institutions, hospitals, women's shops, photographic galleries, furniture and dry-goods stores, confectionary stalls, the "five and tens," physicians' and dentists' offices, clubs, the principal parks and *praças*, and the residential areas of the city.

Bahia the city is the economic and political capital of Bahia the state, whose area of 342,000 square miles makes it considerably larger than Texas. The region is composed in large part of a vast plain of gneiss formation which rises abruptly from the comparatively narrow coastal belt to heights varying from 600 to 1,200 feet in the interior. Upon this plateau and running north and south across the central portion of the state lie a series of low mountains composed principally of sedimentary rock, sandstone, or conglomerates and containing such minerals as iron, manganese, copper, lead, gold, and diamonds (including the black *carbonado* so essential for tool-cutting). This mountain barrier acts as a valuable condenser, gathering moisture for a land which otherwise might be virtually desert. In the extreme western part of the state the plateau is composed of sandstone overlying limestone, and thus it provides a natural sponge which assures perennial rivers in a region where light rains and near drought alternate in six-month periods.

Outside the city of Bahia and skirting the rim of All Saints Bay lies the Reconcavo,[7] some sixty miles long and varying from a few to thirty miles wide. Its soil is a cretaceous marl of great thickness, similar to the black gumbo of southern Arkansas and northern Texas, known locally as *massapé* or, in literal translation, "that which sticks to the feet." It is quite fertile and well watered and today appears only slightly impaired after nearly four centuries of cultivation. This is the cane and tobacco area upon which formerly both Bahia's commercial greatness and her need for reliable agricultural (hence slave) labor was based.

The Reconcavo was formerly a center of large landholdings, of a rural aristocracy, of a patriarchal system, and of slavery. Today, cane and tobacco are still cultivated, although the former, and to some extent the latter, languish by reason of the condition of the world-market and the persistence of primitive techniques of production. Although large landholdings are still common, the rural aristocracy is decadent, its prestige having suffered a gradual but persistent decline throughout the late eighteenth and the nineteenth centuries with the loss of the sugar monopoly, the growth of the coastal towns, and the accompanying increase in prestige of the urban professional classes. The abolition of slavery in the late nineteenth century was the final blow, and absentee ownership is now the predominating pattern. However, the present population is more dense in the Reconcavo than elsewhere in the state outside the city of Bahia and remains to this day markedly negroid in character.

[7] The literal meanings of the Portuguese word *reconcavo* are (1) a bay of semicircular shape and (2) the environs of a city. These two meanings appear to have fused in the Bahian use of the term.

As one moves interior from the Reconcavo into the
sertão, the Negro contribution to the population tends to
decrease and the Indian contribution, much mixed with
both white and Negro, to increase. Both on the moderately
watered plateaus and river basins, chiefly devoted to cattle-
raising and light farming and occasionally covered with virgin or second-growth timber, as well as in the sandy, dry,
and hot *caatinga* country of the semiarid zones, one finds a
frontier society which is relatively isolated and has been only
slightly modified during recent decades by contact with the
outside world.[8]

Thus, in this particular area of intimate racial and cultural contact where the Negro and his descendants have
been fated to work out a rather picturesque career, one
will find three distinct types of settlement and population.
In the *sertão*, or interior, is a highly mixed stock to whose
composition the Indian has contributed in greater proportion probably than either the Negro or the European. In
the Reconcavo, with its tradition of a departed rural aristocracy, a disintegrated plantation system, and a long
history of slavery, the population is still principally negroid.
While in the city of Bahia itself the people are largely of
mixed European-African origin, individuals of either pure
European or pure African descent being clearly in the minority.

In the city also, the social order is still relatively stable.
There has been in recent times little change. Bahia is, as we
have seen, a comparatively old city, conscious of its traditions and proud of them. Conventions originally developed

[8] Euclydes da Cunha's *Os Sertões* (12th ed.; Rio, 1933) gives a vivid and
dramatic account of life on the *sertão*. Although written in 1902, it is still
timely. R. B. Cunningham-Graham's *A Brazilian Mystic* (New York, 1925)
is based upon this more detailed account.

in response to the needs of colonial life still persist and direct life pretty much in the old familiar channels. Bahia has long been a relatively isolated city; and isolation has intensified personal intimacies and, by so doing, has promoted the growth of peculiarly local customs in response to peculiarly local conditions.

The character of Bahia's population, as might be expected, is also relatively stable. Virtually no immigration has come in from foreign lands in recent years, and little from other parts of Brazil. What population movement there is into the city comes largely from the interior of the state or from contiguous areas like Alagoas and Sergipe. Similarly there is little emigration.

Bahia is thus a "culturally passive" area[9] with a stability and an order reminiscent of Europe in the Middle Ages. In fact, Bahia is, in some respects at least, a medieval town. Every eminence of the city is dominated by a church or a cathedral. Until very recently there were no modern office buildings or industrial edifices to overshadow or to crowd out these symbols of a sacred order, and such as have in the past few years been erected only accentuate the dominance of the ecclesiastical structures. Over the habits of the female portion of the population in particular,[10] and to a con-

[9] Dr. Robert E. Park has used this phrase to describe an area "in which life continues, on the whole, to revolve in the same unbroken and traditional routine," where "population, natural resources, and the standard of living have achieved some sort of equilibrium and where custom and tradition provide for most of the exigencies of life." In such an area, "changes still take place, to be sure, but take place silently, continuously, and at an almost imperceptible pace" (see Robert E. Park, "Race Relations and Certain Frontiers," in Race and Culture Contacts, ed. E. B. Reuter [New York, 1934], p. 57).

[10] The ecclesiastical authorities have rigorously censured women's bathing suits which do not have sleeves to the elbow and knee-length skirts. Rarely is a woman other than a foreign resident or an occasional individ-

siderable extent over those of the male portion, the church exercises a substantial measure of control. Prestige of the military is high.

The large family, with its wide ramifications and its patriarchal organization, also bespeaks a preindustrial era. Social cohesion in the community is maintained by the close association of members of these large family groups, together with the intimate ties common to friends of long standing, the degree of whose intimacy is much greater than that ordinarily to be found in the cities of comparable size in industrial societies. One notes in Bahia a warmth of manner uncommon to the United States. Bahians, like most Brazilians, tend to be very affectionate in the family and warmhearted toward their friends. Characteristic of such primary relationships is a high order of courtesy and politeness and an almost limitless consideration for the convenience and comfort of relatives and friends. Religious affiliation and guild association weave further strands of solidarity, binding the urban community together as if it were merely an overgrown village.

In this stable society there is a comparative absence of most forms of conflict. In commerce and finance competition is comparatively slight and limited in considerable measure to foreigners. The economy is almost entirely extractive and industry is minimal. The few differences which arise between labor and capital often take the form of a

---

ual educated in Rio, to be seen on the beaches. Snug-fitting street dresses or those made of sheer or transparent material, and skirts which do not fall at least several inches below the knee, are subject to general criticism. At the exit of the principal churches and cathedrals is posted an official proclamation of the archbishop of Bahia specifying permissible dress. Failure to observe these regulations automatically bars the offender from the sacraments of the church.

struggle of native labor versus foreign capital and thus tend to unify rather than to divide the local group. Religious competition has not become severe enough to intensify self-consciousness on the part of rival adherents and thus evoke serious animosities. As far as national affairs are concerned, intense local loyalties had not, at least at the time this study was made, been seriously exacerbated by onerous control from without. A minimum of racial conflict will be evident throughout this account.

THE *ricos* OF THE RIDGES AND THE *pobres* OF THE VALLEYS

One of the things Darwin noted, when he visited Bahia in 1832, was that the city rested upon "a level plain of about three hundred feet in elevation, which in all parts has been worn into flat-bottomed valleys."[11] Today the scene is still much as Darwin saw it. Continuing erosion has merely emphasized the general characteristics of the landscape, transforming the once level plain somewhat more decidedly into alternating ridges, relatively steep declivities, and comparatively narrow valleys.

This physiography of the country has not been without significance in the cultural life of Bahia; for, in general, the distribution of the population by classes, and even to some extent by ethnic divisions, follows quite closely the lay of the land. Along the ridges, which wind with the changing terrain, ordinarily run the principal streets, bearing the chief lines of transportation, whether by streetcar, bus, or automobile. So far as accessibility to the center and other principal parts of the city is concerned, here are the more convenient residential locations. The elevation of the ridges,

[11] Charles Darwin, *The Voyage of the Beagle* ("Harvard Classics," Vol. XXIX [New York, 1909]), p. 521.

permitting as it does a full and unobstructed sweep of the cooling sea breeze, makes these heights more comfortable, more healthful, and, consequently, more desirable places of residence. One usually finds here the more modern and substantial buildings, the homes of the upper classes. Here ordinarily live the scions of the old aristocracy, the large landholders, the city's intellectuals, and the leaders of its "society"; the lawyers, physicians, engineers, and politicians; the officials of the army, the poets and journalists, the professors in the Faculdades, the few industrialists which Bahia has so far produced—in fact, nearly all those prominent in the intellectual, political, "social," and economic life of the city. These families possess considerable property and employ numerous servants. Their members are usually literate, and at least the males are *formados* (i.e., graduated from one of the Faculdades, either in law, medicine, or engineering), a distinction which in the Bahian society marks them off quite sharply from the rest of the population.

It is in these areas that the five newspapers published in the city circulate almost exclusively and the latest fashions from Paris or Hollywood are known and generally adopted. In recent years an occasional example of modernistic architecture and interior design has appeared. Here are to be found the owners of virtually all the city's 3,855 telephones, its 1,028 automobiles, its radios, and private libraries. Here live most of the 20,524 voters who cast ballots in the municipal election of 1936. Here attachment to the *candomblé*, or Afro-Brazilian fetish cult, is minimal and Catholic belief is least modified by elements from the more primitive religions. Here live that portion of the population which *o povo* ("the people") call the *ricos*, or the "rich."

THE *RICOS* OF THE RIDGES

The valleys, on the other hand, afford less comfortable, less healthful, less convenient, and, consequently, less expensive residential locations. Here the regularly laid out streets and paving disappear. The inhabitants get about by way of footpaths, the red clay of which becomes slippery after a tropical downpour and quite treacherous on the steeper slopes. Here live the lower classes. Dwellings are simple mud huts constructed of a sapling framework over which puddled clay has been spread and allowed to dry. If the owner's income has permitted, the rough exterior of the dwellings has been smoothed off and a lime wash in pale tints of pink, blue, green, or yellow added. The floor is commonly of earth, neatly sanded at regular intervals with fresh *areia* from the seashore. The roof of such dwellings is usually of palm fronds and may be slightly raised at the gable to permit the more ready exit of smoke from the housewife's fire. The furniture ordinarily consists of rude benches or stools, perhaps a cheap chair, a rough table, and cots, or, more commonly, straw mats for sleeping. A Standard Oil Company can whose top and bottom have been removed is used for a stove. Furnishings include an unpretentious niche with a small image of the family's patron saint, a candle, perhaps an almanac, and a rude iron support for washbasin and pitcher of water. Utensils are usually of baked clay and quite simple in design.

In respect to economic level, education, and, to some extent, religion, the inhabitants of these lower-class areas diverge widely from those of the ridges. They are usually illiterate, although some of the children are now being enrolled in government-sponsored schools. Communication is ordinarily by word of mouth, seldom by newspaper, book, or telephone. Conversation is carried on in the Portuguese

vernacular, with a limited vocabulary and numerous errors
in grammar. Many words of African or native Indian origin
are commonly heard. Transport is primitive. Here the fetish cult, and the attitudes, sentiments, and beliefs associated
with it, gains its most zealous and faithful devotees. Here,
cut off quite sharply from participation in the upper levels
of European culture, live that portion of the population
which the upper classes refer to as *o povo*, and who think of
themselves as *os pobres* ("the poor").

The social gulf between the *pobres* of the valleys and the
ricos of the ridges is wide and not easy to bridge. This is,
of course, to be anticipated in a society with an aristocratic
tradition whose upper circles still look somewhat askance
upon manual labor and have always regarded education,
family connection, and "good breeding" as indices of class.
Attitudes in this respect have changed little since the time
when the abolitionist Anselmo da Fonseca felt it necessary
to apologize for including the name of "a man of the people,"
a humble Negro shoemaker, among the prominent upper-
class abolitionists of Bahia, arguing that "intelligence, pa-
triotism, and truth are not the privilege of any one class"
and explaining that this particular individual had been more
useful to the abolition cause than many "more noble."

The upper classes habitually refer to members of the lower
classes as *trabalhadores* ("laborers"), *operarios* ("workers"),
or *o povo baixo* ("common people") and humorously carica-
ture them by a cartoon character known as Zé Povinho, an
illiterate, stupid, and unprepossessing lout. To their children they often direct such phrases as "não seja gentinha"
("don't be like common people"), "não tenha modos de
gentinha" ("don't take up the manners of common people"),
"não ligue a (or *para*) povo miudo" ("don't attach yourself

THE *POBRES* OF THE VALLEYS

to vulgar persons"), "não faça caso de gente baixa" ("don't
mind low people"), "não dê attenção á gentinha" ("don't
pay any attention to common people"), and "não se incom-
mode com a gente baixa" ("don't trouble yourself about
common people"). Of themselves, the upper classes use the
rather general expressions *as altas rodas* ("the upper circles"), *grand monde,* and the "élite."

The lower classes refer to the upper classes as *os "chefões"*
("the big shots"), *os donos da gente* ("the owners of the
people"), *os grandes graudos* ("the illustrious great"), *os
manda-chuvas da cidade* ("the rainmakers of the city"; i.e.,
those who can do anything), *ricaços* ("the plutocrats"), or
merely *os brancos* ("the whites").

Although this rather simple pattern in which ridges and
valleys appear as contrasted residential areas is, in general,
characteristic of the entire city, it is modified in a few minor
instances. The upper-class suburb of Barra, for example,
lies low on the seacoast, albeit well swept by the refreshing
sea breeze; while the ridges (as well as the valleys) in the
less accessible areas outside the main portion of the city are
covered with the huts of the lower class. In the old out-
moded four-to-seven-story buildings (relics of Bahia's former splendor), which hedge about the central portion of the
city and lie either on top, or well up toward the top, of the
central ridges, are crowded together in something approaching slum conditions hundreds of the city's poor.[12] But in
general the pattern of the city conforms quite closely to that
which has been described.

As one moves about the different residential areas, he

[12] For an intimate glimpse into the life of this latter area see Jorge Amado,
Suor (2d ed.; Rio, 1936). The locale of these interesting sketches is an old
building at No. 68 on the Pelourinho which fronts on the triangular *praça*
where the old slave whipping-post used to stand.

notes that this segregation by economic and educational classes conforms in a general way, although with certain important exceptions, to the differences in color in the population. In fact, Bahia on initial acquaintance seems not unlike a medieval city surrounded by African villages.[13]

Thus, in general, one may say that the whites and the lighter mixed-bloods ordinarily occupy the more comfortable, more healthful, more convenient, and hence more expensive ridges of the city; while the blacks and darker mixed-bloods usually reside in the less convenient, less healthful, hence cheaper, low-lying areas, and the outlying, less accessible regions called locally *suburbios*. In other words, the ridges of the *ricos* correspond in the main to the residential areas of the whites and of the lighter *mestiços*, while the valleys and the outlying sections of the *pobres* correspond in large measure to the residential areas of the darker portion of the population. On the outskirts of the city, such sections as Matta Escura, Engenho Velho, Federação, Garcia, Quintas da Barra, Retiro, Alto do Abacaxi, Alto das Pombas, Estrada da Liberdade, Estrada do Rodagem, Cabrito, Cruz do Cosme, Matatú Pequeno, etc., are all predominantly inhabited by blacks and darker mixed-bloods. The lighter *mestiços* are clearly in the minority and whites quite rare. On the other hand, the ridges of Vitoria, Canella, and Graça and the seaside *bairro* of Barra are almost entirely inhabited by whites, with only a limited number of the lighter mixed-bloods scattered among them. It is, however,

[13] An American resident who had spent five years at Lagos on the African West Coast once remarked, "When I go out into the suburbs of Bahia, I feel like I am back in Africa, the Negro huts and their surroundings are so similar."

true that one finds, on the slopes to the rear of the more pretentious houses of these areas and spreading into the valleys
beyond, a considerable number of simple huts whose occupants are blacks and darker mixed-bloods.

Nazaré is less predominantly an area of white residence,
there being in this *bairro* numbers of very light *mestiços* but,
except on the slopes toward the Baixa dos Sapateiros, on the
one hand, and the Dique, on the other, relatively few blacks.
The transitional sections of Santo Antonio, Barbalho, Bar-
ris, Tororó, and the peninsula of Itapagipe (which extends
more than a mile out into Todos os Santos Bay) are predominantly inhabited by mixed-bloods. Nevertheless, here
also a few whites and a considerable number of blacks, particularly in such subsections as Massaranduba in Itapagipe,
also live side by side with *mestiços*.

One soon discovers, however, that this ethnic segregation
is largely due to the circumstance that color and class, as
we shall soon see in detail, tend to coincide. This is, of
course, a situation to be anticipated, given the circumstances
and conditions of Negro importation and settlement and the
comparatively recent emergence of the darker race from a
servile status. The important consideration is that there is
in Bahia, it seems, no deliberate attempt to segregate the
races as a means of maintaining caste or class distinctions.

In fact, the spatial distribution of the races would appear
even on first sight to be an index of the racial situation, and
longer acquaintance with the city tends to confirm this hypothesis. The residential pattern suggests a gradually evolv-
ing, freely competitive society in which the Europeans
settled on the ridges, and the Africans and their descendants,
as propertyless slaves, or impoverished freedmen, were rele-

gated to the less desirable territory. Although the Europeans have still today, to a considerable extent, maintained
their original advantage, the blacks and darker mixed-bloods
have gradually pushed themselves up the slopes from their
less favored locations until now they have come, in some
cases, to share a portion of the Europeans' favored position.
One occasionally finds them living next to the homes of the
whites, symbolizing the fact that they now occupy those positions, social as well as spatial, which personal ability, occupational proficiency, and favorable circumstance have en-
abled them to achieve and to maintain. Thus the racial distinctions which one from the United States is so likely on
first acquaintance to note turn out to be, as we shall soon
see in more detail, not the things which are either so genuine
or so important as at first sight might appear.

It is significant, in this connection, that in what might be
called the intermediate residential areas of the city, where
the dwellings of those who are rising out of the lower classes
meet the dwellings of the upper classes, one finds the darker
and the lighter portions of the population meeting and mingling in close residential proximity. This is true, for example, along the Avenida Sete de Setembro.

The Avenida Sete de Setembro, from Jardim Suspenso on,
is the only artery into the "downtown area" from South
Bahia. It thus becomes the route of passage for processions
like those of Carnival, the "Micarêta,"[14] the Peruada,[15] and
the numerous religious *festas*, and the avenue of march for
the military during visits of political celebrities. Its streetcar line and constant flow of busses would make it less de-

[14] The "Micarêta" is the so-called "second Carnival" held the Sunday
following Easter.

[15] The Peruada is an annual students' parade with floats.

sirable as a seat of residence for one weary of the noises of an
industrial city, but for the Bahian wife and daughters, whose
world is still largely inside the doors of the home, these
characteristics seem to give it a peculiar charm. Hence, one
will see along this avenue, almost from Praça Castro Alves
out, the residences of many substantial families and, in Vitoria, just beyond the governor's palace, the more pretentious dwellings of the upper class.

TABLE 1

FAMILIES DWELLING ALONG THE AVENIDA SETE
DE SETEMBRO CLASSIFIED ACCORDING TO
ETHNIC COMPOSITION, BAHIA, 1936

	Number	Per Cent
Black.....................	19	7.6
Mixed-blood................	97	38.6
White.....................	128	51.0
Mixed-blood and white........	5	2.0
Black and mixed-blood........	2	0.8
Total..................	251	100.0

No Bahian house which boasts any pretension fails to
have a balcony, while nearly all possess large casement windows opening out on the street. From this vantage point
the family can while away many pleasant hours leaning on
elbows and "watching the *gente* (people) go by." Consequently, one can readily gain, especially during the passage
of processions when the balconies and windows are fully occupied, rather accurate information on the physical character of the population. It is possible at Carnival, for example, particularly just preceding the passage of the floats,
to take a census with respect to racial composition, as far

at least as color is an index of race.[16] On the first evening
of Carnival in 1936 an analysis into color categories of families dwelling along this avenue from Jardim Suspenso to the
Church of São Bento gave the distribution shown in Table 1.

That families of whites, of mixed-bloods, and of relatively
unmixed blacks dwell indiscriminately side by side on this
important street is even more clearly evident if one notes the
house-by-house distribution as he proceeds along the Avenida:

White	Mixed-blood	Mixed-blood
White	White	White
Mixed-blood	Mixed-blood (dark)	White
Mixed-blood	Mixed-blood (dark)	White
Mixed-blood	White	Mixed-blood
White	Mixed-blood	Mixed-blood
Mixed-blood	Mixed-blood	Black
White	White	Black
White	Mixed-blood	Mixed-blood
Mixed-blood (dark)	Mixed-blood	Mixed-blood
Mixed-blood	White	Mixed-blood
White	White	White

Of 142 white students to whom the question, "Do you dislike black neighbors?" was put, 120 responded "No." And
of 143 who responded to the question, "Do you dislike *pardo*
(brown) neighbors?" 129 replied in the negative. Among the
small minority who in each case appeared to be somewhat
troubled by the immediate proximity of darker neighbors,
subsequent inquiry developed that ordinarily the objection
arose out of apprehension that residence among black neighbors might imply residence in a lower-class (and hence less

[16] It is obviously likely that the actual residents were joined on this occasion by other persons, either relatives or friends. But since the object was
not to count faces but to test the ethnic composition of families dwelling side
by side, this possibility did not materially affect the enumeration. Only
seven cases were found of mixed ethnic composition, and it is reasonable
to assume in the light of the Bahian culture that some of these were so by
reason of ethnic mixture in the family itself.

desirable) neighborhood. The objection appeared to be not so much to the blacks *as such* but rather to those areas in which the darker portion of the population, being less secure financially (as we shall presently see in more detail), ordinarily dwell.

In this connection it is also significant to note that an occasional black resides in such upper-class sections as Canella or Vitoria without any question being made of the fact. He will ordinarily be a person of wealth, education, professional competence, and "good breeding"; in other words, a member of the upper classes. Similarly significant is the complementary fact that a considerable number of lower-class whites may be found living in the valleys or the outlying regions, scattered among the darker portion of the population, imbedded quite unconsciously in what might be called, if they were in the United States, the "Negro bottoms."[17] Sharing a common life with the other illiterate poor, these occasional white families visit about among their darker neighbors, eat, drink, work, play, and intermarry with them, and participate in a common body of ideas and sentiments, just as at the other end of the class scale an occasional black participates in the predominately white world of the élite.

Thus, although Bahia is divided quite definitely into upper- and lower-class residents who occupy rather distinct areas of the city, and these class and geographical divisions also tend to correspond rather closely to the color divisions in the population, one notes certain significant exceptions whose occurrence points rather clearly toward class rather than caste as the basis of social organization.

[17] An occasional well-to-do white upper-class family will reside in a lower-class area, the house and grounds ordinarily taking on the appearance of a spacious country seat surrounded by more humble dwellings.

II

SLAVERY

CHAPTER II

THE COMING OF THE AFRICANS

THE population of Bahia in 1585 included at least three to four thousand Negroes.[1] During the succeeding century the black portion of the city's inhabitants increased to such an extent that it is said a traveler "might have supposed himself in Negroland."[2] Frézier in 1714 estimated the proportion of blacks to whites in Bahia to be at that time twenty to one, which is probably an overstatement, although the preponderance of Negroes was undoubtedly considerable.[3] Approximately one hundred years later, in 1807, an *alistamento* for military service enumerated nearly twice as many blacks as whites, or approximately the same number of Negroes as both whites and mixed-bloods combined.[4] Twelve years later, in 1819, Conselheiro Velloso

[1] A. G. Keller, *Colonization* (Boston, 1908), p. 145. Gabriel Soares (*Roteiro do Brasil*, p. 126, quoted by Pedro Calmon, *Historia social do Brasil* [3 vols.; São Paulo, 1937-39, I, 179) puts the number of Negroes able to bear arms in Bahia in 1587 at four thousand. The Jesuit Anchieta estimated the population in 1583 to include three thousand Negroes, a figure thought by Vasconcellos to be an underestimation (see Salomão de Vasconcellos, "A escravatura africana em Minas Geraes," *Jornal do Commercio* [Rio], November 20, 1938).

[2] Robert Southey, *History of Brazil* (3 vols.; London, 1810), II, 674.

[3] At approximately the same time, Cook estimated the proportion in Rio de Janeiro to be seventeen to one (Calmon, *op. cit.*, p. 175). Each visitor may have been more familiar with the area immediately about the docks where a greater predominance of Negro workers would naturally be found. It is also probably true that the mixed-bloods were, in each case, included with the blacks.

[4] The totals were: blacks, 25,502; mixed-bloods, 11,350; whites, 14,260 (see João Pandiá Calogeras, "A politica exterior do imperio—as origens,"

de Oliveira estimated that there were then in Bahia province 147,263 unfree Negroes.[5]

The blacks were practically all introduced as slaves, Brazil being, until 1888, a slaveholding state.[6] Under the favorable conditions of a rich soil, intense tropical sunlight, and plentiful rainfall common to the Reconcavo, sugar cane thrived. Its cultivation and processing in a land of "open resources" demanded a constant and inexpensive labor supply which the Portuguese, by reason of insufficient numbers and imperfect acclimitization, were themselves unable to furnish. At first, as in the West Indies and the United States, the indigenous Indians were enslaved; and, after the limited supply on the littoral was exhausted, raiding expeditions penetrated deep into the interior. But the Indians, familiar with only the crudest forms of agriculture, seminomadic, and as unaccustomed to settled and ordered plan-

---

Revista do Instituto Historico e Geographico Brasileiro [tomo especial; Rio, 1927], p. 294).

[5] *Ibid.*, pp. 293 and 330.

[6] For detailed information on the slave trade and slavery see, especially, Perdigão Malheiro, *A escravidão no Brasil* (3 vols.; Rio, 1867); Percy A. Martin, "Slavery and Abolition in Brazil," *Hispanic American Historical Review*, Vol. XIII, No. 2 (1933); Louis Couty, *L'esclavage au Brésil* (Paris, 1881); Lawrence F. Hill, "The Abolition of the African Slave Trade to Brazil," *Hispanic American Historical Review*, Vol. XI, No. 2 (1931); Braz do Amaral, "Os grandes mercados de escravos africanos; as tribus importadas; sua distribuição regional," *Revista do Instituto Historico e Geographico Brasileiro* (special vol; Rio, 1927), pp. 437–96; Affonso Claudio, "As tribus negras importadas," *Revista do Instituto Historico e Geographico Brasileiro* (special vol., Part II; Rio, 1914), pp. 597–655; Mary W. Williams, "The Treatment of Brazilian Slaves in the Brazilian Empire," *Journal of Negro History*, Vol. XV (July, 1930); Evaristo de Moraes, *A escravidão africana no Brasil* (São Paulo, 1933); João Dornas Filho, *A escrividão no Brasil* (Rio, 1939); Roberto Simonsen, "As consequencias economicas da abolição," *Jornal do Commercio* (Rio), May 8, 1938; Affonso de E. Taunay, "Notas sobre as ultimas decadas do trafico," *ibid.*, July 24, July 31, August 7, 1938.

tation life as they were at home in the near-by bush, proved inefficient and undependable workers.

Just the reverse was characteristic of the Africans, with whom the Portuguese had for some time been acquainted. As early as 1433,[7] Negro slaves had been imported into Portugal to labor on the large estates of the military and religious orders, particularly in the Algarves. Moreover, the West Coast of Africa lay within easy reach of Brazil, directly opposite its central and northern coasts.

The exact date when African importation began is unknown, although it is thought that the fleet which Martim Affonso de Souza in 1531 encountered in the bay at Bahia was engaged in the transport of slaves.[8] Sometime later in this same century[9] the slave trade began to gather momen-

[7] Prado cites a statement from Georg Friederici (*Der Charakter der Entdeckung und Eroberung Amerikas durch die Europaer* [3 vols.; Stuttgart, 1925–36]) to the effect that the first Africans were imported into Portugal in 1433, instead of 1441, as commonly thought. See J. F. de Almeida Prado, *Pernambuco e as capitanias do norte do Brasil* (2 vols.; São Paulo, 1939–41), I, 250 n.

[8] Malheiro, *op. cit.*, III, 6; cf. Arthur Ramos, *As culturas negras no novo mundo* (Rio, 1937), p. 281.

[9] In a letter dated 1552 Padre Nobrega refers to having requested and received three slaves from Guinea. These arrived with others on orders from the king (see Ignacio Accioli de Cerqueira e Silva, *Memorias historicas e politicas da provincia da Bahia* [4 vols.; Bahia, 1919–33], I, 390). In another letter written June 5, 1559, Padre Nobrega refers to eight "Negros de Guiné" on the estate of one Andre Gavião at Bahia (see Amaral, *op. cit.*, p. 442). In 1583 a certain Salvador Correa de Sá made a contract with João Gutteres Valerio in which he agreed to purchase every slave brought from Africa in his ship (F. Borges de Barros, *Novos documentos para a historia colonial* [Bahia, 1931], p. 77). Pedro Calmon (*op. cit.*, p. 178) gives 1548 as the year in which the traffic began, and Arthur Ramos (*The Negro in Brazil* [Washington, 1939], p. 3) says that the first shipment of slaves direct from the Guinea coast is thought to have occurred in 1538 in a vessel belonging to one Jorge Lopes Bixorda.

tum, Bahia serving for at least two centuries as the principal
port of entry.[10] The traffic opened in Guinea and the island
of São Thomé, spread shortly to the Congo and Angola, and
finally to distant Mozambique. It continued uninterrupted-
ly for nearly three hundred years, assuming its largest proportions in the eighteenth and nineteenth centuries, when
first gold-mining and diamond-panning in Minas Geraes,
and then the development of coffee cultivation in São Paulo,
augmented the demand.[11] How many Africans were brought

[10] Often for transhipment to Rio or for overland delivery to Minas Geraes.

[11] Henry Koster, writing in the early nineteenth century, says of this
trade: "As the voyage from the coast of Africa to the opposite shores of
South America is usually short, for the winds are subject to little variation
and the weather is usually fine, the vessels which are employed in this traffic
are generally speaking small, and are not of the best construction. The
situation of captain or master of a slave ship is considered of secondary rank
in the Portuguese merchant-service; and the persons who are usually so
occupied are vastly inferior to the generality of the individuals who command
the large and regular trading vessels between Europe and Brazil. The slave
ships were formerly crowded to a most shocking degree; nor was there any
means of preventing this. But a law has been passed for the purpose of re-
stricting the number of persons for each vessel. However, I more than
suspect, that no attention is paid to this regulation. . . . . The slaves . . . .
are placed in the streets before the doors of the owners, ... lying or sitting
promiscuously upon the foot-path, sometimes to the number of two or three
hundred. The males wear a small piece of blue cloth round their waist,
which is drawn between the legs and fastened behind. The females are
allowed a larger piece of cloth, which is worn as a petticoat; and sometimes
a second portion is given to them, for the purpose of covering the upper parts
of the body. The stench which is created by these assemblages is almost
intolerable to one who is unaccustomed to their vicinity; and the sight of
them, good God! is horrid beyond anything. These people do not, however, seem to feel their situation, any farther than that it is uncomfortable.
Their food consists of salt meat, the flour of the manioc, beans, and plantain
occasionally. The victuals for each day are cooked in the middle of the
street in an enormous caldron. At night, they are driven into one or more
warehouses: and a driver stands to count them as they pass. They are
locked in; and the door is again opened at day-break on the following
morning. The wish of these wretched creatures to escape from this state of

in perhaps never will be known, but the number undoubtedly ran into millions.[12]

Angola furnished most of the importations during the late
sixteenth[13] and the seventeenth centuries; Guinea, during
the eighteenth and early nineteenth.[14] By 1710 Bahian to-

---

inaction and discomfort is manifested upon the appearance of a purchaser.
They start up willingly, to be placed in the row for the purpose of being
viewed and handled like cattle: and on being chosen they give signs of much
pleasure. I have had many opportunities of seeing slaves bought; for my
particular friends at Recife lived opposite to slave dealers. I never saw any
demonstrations of grief at parting from each other: but I attribute this to a
resigned or rather despairing sensation, which checks any show of grief, and
which has prepared them for the worst, by making them indifferent to whatever may occur: besides, it is not often, that a family is brought over together:
the separation of relatives and friends has taken place in Africa. It is among
the younger part of the assemblage of persons who are exposed for sale, that
pleasure is particularly visible at the change of situation; the Negroes of
more advanced age do whatever the driver desires, usually with an unchanged countenance. A species of relationship exists between the individuals who have been imported in the same ship. They call each other
malungos: and this term is much regarded among them. The purchaser
gives to each of his newly-bought slaves a large piece of baize and a straw
hat and as soon as possible marches them off to his estate. I have often in
travelling met with many parties going up to their new homes, and have observed that they were usually cheerful" (*Travels in Brazil, 1809 to 1815*
[2 vols.; Philadelphia, 1817], I, 205–9).

[12] Affonso de E. Taunay, "Numeros do trafico," *Jornal do Commercio*
(Rio), September 30, 1936. Estimates made by Brazilian writers range from
three to eighteen millions, although the latter figure would appear to be considerably exaggerated. Ramos believes the number did not exceed five millions (*The Negro in Brazil*, p. 6).

[13] Especially after the founding of São Paulo de Loanda in 1575 (Calmon,
op. cit., pp. 178–79). See also *Dialogos das grandezas do Brasil*, ed. Rodolfo
Garcia (Rio: Academia Brasileira de Letras, 1930), p. 143.

[14] In 1811 an agreement with England, actively enforced by the latter's
cruisers, cut off importations from north of the Equator. Angola once more
became the principal source of slave supply, and, between 1815 and 1850,
approximately a million Angola Negroes, it is estimated, came in (Calmon,
op. cit., p. 182).

bacco[15] was being shipped in quantity to "the Mina coast," which for more than a century thereafter absorbed a full third of Bahia's production.[16] A visitor early in the eighteenth century referred to Bahia as "New Guinea";[17] while the natives of Guinea were said at that time to have called the outer world "Bahia."[18]

In 1781 fifty vessels were engaged in the Brazilian traffic, "eight or ten with Angola and the rest with the Sudanese coast."[19] In 1800 twenty vessels were plying the trade from Bahia alone. According to custom-house records, 29,172 Negroes from "the Mina coast" and the islands of São Thomé and Principe entered Bahia during the decade from

[15] *Aguardente*, or *cachaça* (cheap rum), sugar, and manioc meal were also extensively used for trading purposes, as similarly were cowries (*buzios*) from the coast south of Bahia.

[16] Calmon, *op. cit.*, p. 180.

[17] Amadeu Francisco Frézier, *Relation d'un voyage à la mer du sud* (Paris, 1716); cf. Calmon, *op. cit.*, p. 185. The demand for slave labor in the gold fields of Minas Geraes so stimulated importations that La Barbinais, visiting Bahia in 1717, estimated that in that year 25,000 Africans were landed at Bahia. See Affonso de E. Taunay, *Na Bahia colonial* (Rio, 1925), p. 364.

[18] "It was principally to Bahia .... that the unfortunate sons of Lybia were brought, and it is for this reason that the natives of Guinea give the name of Bahia to Brazil, to America, and even to Europe" (Onesime Reclus, quoted by Manoel Querino, "A raça africana e os seus costumes na Bahia," *Annaes do quinto congresso brasileiro de geographia* [Rio, 1916], p. 626).

[19] Calmon, *op. cit.*, pp. 180–81. See letter of Silva Lisboa, *Annaes da Biblioteca Nacional*, XXXII, 504. From September 29, 1771, to September 22, 1772, nine slave ships with 2,307 Negroes entered the port of Bahia. One ship, "Nossa Senhora do Rosario," carrying 371 Africans "and two babies at the breast" had not had a single death on the voyage. Another vessel, "Nossa Senhora da Conceição da Ponte," sailing from the Mina coast with a call at São Thomé, landed 13 without casualty, July 11, 1772. But other ships lost, respectively, 111 out of 374, 17 out of 468, 17 out of 158, 29 out of 233, 11 out of 308, 44 out of 327, 20 out of 302—a total loss of 249 out of 2,554 leaving the African coast (from custom-house records; see Amaral, *op. cit.*, p. 458).

1785 to 1795, and in the last five of these years 17,409 Africans came in from Angola.[20] From 1797 to 1806 approximately 47,000 "Minas" and 11,000 "Angolas" entered Bahia.[21] In the Angola trade, ships plied directly between the Brazilian ports of Bahia,[22] Pernambuco, Rio de Janeiro, and Maranhão and the Angola ports of São Paulo de Loanda, Benguella, and, particularly, Novo Redondo, exchanging for Angola Negroes tobacco, *cachaça*, cotton prints, knives, glass beads, powder, and lead.[23] Thousands of Yorubas, Gêges (Ewes), Haussás, Fuláhs (Fulbis, Fulanins), Ashantis, Tapas, Effans, and Mandingas were imported from the ports of Lagos, Forte de El Mina, and São João de Ajudá (Whydah).[24] Felix de Sousa, better known as Cháchá,[25] a mulatto from Rio de Janeiro, played a prominent role in the trade in the early part of the nineteenth century.

In the sixteenth century a good slave is said to have been

[20] Calogeras, *op. cit.*, pp. 325–26.

[21] *Ibid.*, p. 322.

[22] Several slave warehouses existed in the area between Agua dos Meninos and the Dourado docks. Some slave merchants used their own houses as *depositos*. A certain Siqueira Lima had such a house in Vitoria on the present site of the governor's palace (Amaral, *op. cit.*, p. 70).

[23] Ferreira reports 8,037 Negroes imported into Bahia in the year 1807 (José Carlos Ferreira, "As insurreições dos africanos na Bahia," *Revista do Instituto Geographico e Historico da Bahia*, XXIX [1903], 96). In 1821, 21,199 Negroes entered Rio from Angola; in 1822, 24,934 (Maria Graham, *Journal of a Voyage to Brazil, 1821–1823* [London, 1824], p. 146).

[24] Braz do Amaral says there were also imported Africans known in Bahia as Macuas, Bambas, Jalos, Bechuanos, Balantes, Jingas, Krumanos, Timinis, Bengos, Jalofas, Bengalas, Cabindas, Congos, Manjocos, Sentys, Maguiscas, Benins, Queitos, and Bornûs. Numerically important were the Yorubas (Nagôs) and Gêges (Amaral, *op. cit.*, pp. 474–84). The Yoruba subgroups, the Egbas and Ige-shas, were apparently large.

[25] Calmon, *op. cit.*, p. 182; cf. Novas Calvo, *Pedro blanco el negrero* (Madrid, 1933), p. 69.

valued in Bahia at 40 milreis; in 1692, at 60 milreis; in 1703, at 100 milreis; and in 1800, at 140 milreis.[26] At Pernambuco, early in the nineteenth century, Negroes were valued at 32 pounds sterling; oxen at 31 pounds each, and horses the same; although "by management the two last may be obtained at lower prices," Koster informs us,[27] adding that "plantations of the first class ought to have eighty Negroes at least."

In addition to Bahia and Recife, there were two other centers of African importation on the coast, at Rio de Janeiro to the south and Maranhão to the north, and one interior region of concentration, the province of Minas Geraes. These five areas received the major portion of all importations and remain today the principal centers of Negro population in Brazil.

In 1831 a treaty with Great Britain sought to abolish the slave trade. But for a quarter of a century this agreement was so little enforced[28] that an estimated 500,000 additional

[26] Calmon, *op. cit.*, p. 182. A slave worth 100 milreis in 1830 was valued at five times this figure ten years later, and still more as the pressure of the British blockade continued (Amaral, *op. cit.*, p. 472).

[27] *Op. cit.*, II, 139.

[28] "At one time it appeared impossible to abolish the traffic. . . . . The planters declared that without Africans they would be absolutely unable to plant crops; that free labor was not to be had in sufficient numbers for the necessities of agriculture; that only by force could labor be obtained in this hot country; that the citizen, he who was a free man, possessed as his chief privilege 'não trabalhar' [the right not to labor], or at least to work only enough to enable him to eat and to live as 'Deus dará' [God will provide]; that since the 'gente rude' did not lack shelter, being content to live in palm-leaf huts, it was useless to attempt to obtain profitable labor from free men, who were always lazy and inclined to idleness; that the *fazendeiro* who used free labor was soon reduced to penury by the wages paid out and the poor quality of work so secured" (Amaral, *op. cit.*, pp. 472–73). On receiving news of the decree of 1831, the Bahian provincial assembly directed a petition to

Africans were brought into Brazil, many in United States ships, operated by English capital.[29] In 1846, 50,324 were imported; in 1847, 56,172; and, in the following year, 60,-000.[30] This traffic was completely suppressed only by 1852,[30a] Bahia being one of the areas in which it died hardest.[31]

In plant and animal communities different species come

---

the federal senate, demanding its repeal. At one time a *delegado de policia* in Bahia was dismissed from office for having apprehended a shipment of Africans, although such shipment was obviously illegal under the provisions of this law.

[29] Daniel P. Kidder, *Sketches of Residence and Travels in Brazil* (2 vols.; London, 1845), II, 96–97; Hill, *op. cit.*, pp. 179 ff.; Williams, *op. cit.*, p. 319. The most notorious slave-trade case involving a vessel from the United States was that of the "Mary E. Smith" of New Orleans. The ship was brought into Bahia by the Brazilian brig "Olinda" on January 29, 1856, with 370 slaves from fifteen to twenty years of age aboard. The "Mary E. Smith," despite efforts to detain her, had left Boston on the preceding August 24 and sailed to the Gold Coast, where she had picked up a cargo of nearly five hundred Africans. When captured, she had been attempting unsuccessfully for weeks to land her cargo on the Bahian coast. One hundred and six slaves died before the vessel was finally taken and those still alive upon arrival in Bahia were so weakened by starvation and disease that only a few survived.

[30] Calmon, *op. cit.*, II, 171. According to figures given by the British Anti-slavery Society, 221,800 Africans entered Brazil between 1840 and 1847 (Amaral, *op. cit.*, p. 495).

[30a] Percy A. Martin, *Argentina, Brazil and Chile since Independence* (Washington, 1935), p. 208. The last shipload into Bahia landed October 29, 1851. See Wanderley de A. Pinho, "O ultimo desembarque de escravos na Bahia," *Espelho* (September, 1936), pp. 13–16.

[31] Fonseca, *op. cit.*, p. 236. The *Argos Pernambucano* of January 30, 1850, says: "The way in which free Africans are imported into Bahia and reduced to slavery, with the obvious connivance of the government, is a notorious scandal." In the *Argos Sant'Amarense* appeared the following: "The Governor of the Province himself, at nightfall, on the twenty-first of October, 1849, unloaded in the city of Santo Amaro a large number of newly arrived Africans, which he had brought from the capital [Bahia] in a boat, and transported them to his *engenho*." See also Querino, *op. cit.*, p. 626.

to live together because they mutually support one another. Similarly, different racial stocks often occupy to mutual advantage the same habitat because each fits into a different niche in an interdependent symbiotic order. The fundamental problem is that of survival. The Portuguese at Bahia to a considerable extent resolved this problem by the development of an economy based upon plantation agriculture and slave labor.

A considerable number of Negroes died while being transported from Africa. Others subsequently perished from the ravages of cholera, yellow fever, and other epidemics. A few committed suicide or led religiously motivated uprisings against their masters. But the major portion were readily incorporated into the plantation system. Centuries of familiarity with the slave tradition of their African cultures and, in many cases, familiarity with the slave status itself probably made their adjustment to a slave system in the new land less difficult.

Most of the Negroes entering and remaining in the vicinity of Bahia were employed in the planting, cultivation, harvesting, processing, and marketing of sugar cane and tobacco. A limited number were engaged in cattle-raising. They also supplied the necessary artisan and domestic labor on the plantations.

Within the city of Bahia itself, as in other Brazilian ports, most of the slaves were engaged in domestic service. However, in addition, a modified form of slavery existed. Many blacks, known as *negros de ganho*, were employed as porters, stevedores, ironworkers, masons, carpenters, carriage- and cabinet-makers, printers, sign and ornamental painters, silversmiths, lithographers, sculptors in wood and stone, small shopkeepers, street merchants, etc. They were semi-inde-

pendent, lived apart from their masters, and arranged their
own employment. They were usually required to pay a stated sum weekly to their owners, after which they might re-
tain for their own use any balance remaining. In Bahia they
are reported to have been principally Yorubas, Gêges, and
Haussás.

These Negroes were reputedly strong, capable workers.
Almost all the Haussás were ardent Mohammedans, who in
Bahia seem to have converted to their faith many Yorubas,
Gêges, and other Africans. Shrewd and intelligent, they
were at times superior in cultural equipment to their masters. Many were literate, and some are said to have written
Arabic fluently. Often they banded together to mature
schemes of revolt, to buy the freedom of a favorite friend,
or to work under a leader for the liberation of all. The order
in which they secured their freedom was ordinarily determined by lot, the earliest liberated remaining with the group
until the last was purchased, after which they sometimes returned to Africa, paying their passage with what they had
earned.[32]

It was principally the Haussás who led the numerous
slave revolts[33] at Bahia during the early nineteenth century.
Although these uprisings were all unsuccessful and ordi-

[32] Daniel P. Kidder and James C. Fletcher, *Brazil and the Brazilians*
(Philadelphia, 1857), p. 135. Between 1850 and 1878 from four to six thou-
sand free Negroes from Brazil settled at Lagos and Whydah and a few in
Angola (Sir Harry H. Johnston, *The Negro in the New World* [New York,
1910], p. 98 n.). Repatriated Gêges are said to have founded on the African
West Coast a city with the name of a Bahian port, Porto Seguro.

[33] In the Archivo Publico at Bahia are four volumes of police documents
covering the revolts of this period. Each volume contains from a thousand
to twelve hundred sheets in long hand which, for their age, are fairly well
preserved.

narily ended in the death of their leaders, the Europeans lived throughout this period in a more or less constant state of alarm.[34] Arthur Ramos, following Nina Rodrigues, considers these disturbances to have been "nothing more or less than a continuation of the long and recurrent struggles of religious conquest carried on by the Mohammedan Negroes of the Sudan."[35] In support of this contention it has been pointed out that their animosity was directed not only at the Europeans but also at creole blacks and mulattoes who did not join the crusade.

In estimating the character of these revolts, one should give particular attention to the fact that the participants were either free Negroes or those slaves, like the *negros de ganho* and the field hands, whose relations with the whites were not the intimate relations which ordinarily arise out of close personal contact. It is highly significant that on the eve of revolt the whites always received timely warning from

[34] The following document, which was sent to the governor of Bahia by several *senhores de engenho*, shows the fear which at that time agricultural proprietors had of these disturbances (Silva, *op. cit.*, p. 346):

The undersigned owners of *engenhos*, considering the imminent peril in which by reason of the frequent slave revolts known to Your Excellency their persons and, in general, those of all the inhabitants of the Reconcavo and even perhaps of the entire Province [of Bahia] are placed, and considering that at every moment the property of each one of them is at stake, feel it an unavoidable duty to point out this situation to Your Excellency and to beg the actual placing of those Detachments which Your Excellency sometime ago ordered stationed at various points in the Reconcavo in keeping with the police plan of the 10th of December, 1828, the which, being included in the *Proposta* of the Provincial Counsel General, was approved along with other provisions and ordered put into effect, the expenses of its execution to be paid out of the public treasury.

It not being, however, the intention of the petitioners to load onto the Public Treasury the entire burden, they themselves offer to seek to raise a portion of this expense by means of a subscription.

The petitioners rest confident in the interest which Your Excellency has always taken in the preservation of public order, and are thereby assured that you will give ear to this urgent request which they have here set forth.

[35] Ramos, *As culturas negras*, p. 336; see also Nina Rodrigues, *Os africanos no Brasil* (São Paulo, 1932), pp. 61–107.

some slave,[36] and many Negroes repeatedly refused to participate in the uprisings.[37] The disturbances were ordinarily led, as we have seen, by Mohammedan Haussás, said to be exceedingly spirited and resolute individuals,[38] who were either free blacks or semi-independent *negros de ganho*. Moreover, they lived for the most part in the city where life was less arduous than on the plantations and where there was, at the same time, more leisure for brooding over grievances and perfecting schemes of revolt. Since all insurrectionists spoke the same or quite similar languages and shared

[36] Dantas Junior, in commenting on the revolt of 1807, repeats (*A Illustração* [Bahia], June, 1936) that on the night of the twenty-second of May (the revolt was set for 7:00 P.M. of the twenty-eighth) a "person of integrity" urgently sought out the governor at his palace and secretly informed him that "a Negro of mine told me that the slaves of the Ussá nation are plotting to revolt." Following the serious uprising of 1835, the provincial assembly rewarded (*Laws*, No. 344, August 5, 1848, and No. 405, August 2, 1850) the "free Africans," Duarte Mendes and his wife, Sabina da Cruz, with the cancellation of their taxes for having "informed on and thus prevented the success of the planned insurrection."

[37] "The Negroes of the warehouses belonging to Manoel Ignacio da Cunha and Francisco Lourenço Herculano did not wish to join the band" (Silva, *op. cit.*, p. 347). Wied Neuwied, who visited Bahia during the period of these uprisings, says that colored troops were used in suppressing them. See Prince Maximilian Wied Neuwied, *Viagem ao Brasil*, trans. from the German of *Reise nach Brasilien in den Jahren 1815 bis 1817* (2 vols.; Frankfurt, 1820), by Edgar Sussekind de Mendonça and Flavio Poppe de Figueiredo (São Paulo, 1940), pp. 450–51.

[38] Koster, noting that "Pernambuco has never experienced any serious revolt among the slaves; but at Bahia there have been several commotions," and convinced that "Bahia contains fewer free people than Pernambuco in proportion to the number of slaves," wrote, "I cannot avoid attributing the quietude of the latter in some measure to the circumstances of a few of the Gold Coast Negroes being imported into it, whilst at Bahia the principal stock of slaves is from that part of Africa. . . . . They are represented as possessing great firmness of mind and body, and ferociousness of disposition" (*op. cit.*, I, 214).

the same or similar religious beliefs and practices, they were able to act effectively together.

In 1806, following a raid upon a "conspirator's house," the imprisonment of a number of suspected plotters, and the confiscation of "four hundred arrows, a bundle of sticks, and quantities of cord for the making of bows, a large number of knives and pistols, a gun and a drum," orders were issued to arrest every slave found in the streets after nine o'clock at night "without a letter from his master or in his company."[39] The following year correspondence between African conspirators in Bahia and Santo Amaro (a sugar center in the Reconcavo) was intercepted, and the leaders thus exposed were subsequently tried, sentenced to death, and executed.[40] About the same time the governor of Bahia ordered destroyed two troublesome *quilombos*, or settlements of fugitive slaves, on the outskirts of the city near Cabula and Nossa Senhora dos Mares, and the *capitãomor* with eighty soldiers surrounded their huts and took prisoner seventy-eight blacks, some of whom were free Negroes.[41]

In 1809 a revolt about twelve miles from Bahia was put down after the Haussás had "committed all sorts of outrages."[42] In 1813 about five hundred Haussás revolted and fled into the surrounding country but were speedily pursued and disarmed and their leaders publicly hung on gallows erected in Praça Piedade, one of the principal squares of the city. Several others were deported to Africa.[43] In 1826 soldiers had to be sent to various points in the Reconcavo,

[39] Silva, *op. cit.*, p. 346.

[40] Alvares do Amaral, *Resumo chronologico da Bahia* (Bahia, n.d.), p. 111.

[41] Eduardo A. de Caldas Britto, "Levantes de pretos na Bahia," *Revista do Instituto Geographico e Historico da Bahia*, XXIX, 72.

[42] Alvares do Amaral, *op. cit.*, p. 6.

[43] *Ibid.*, p. 39. See also Ramos, *As culturas negras*, p. 337.

including Cachoeira, to put down an African insurrection, whose leader had been chosen a "king of the blacks" and when wounded and captured "carried a red flag, had on his head . . . . a crown, and over his shoulders an old-fashioned mantle of green velveteen on which had been embroidered a golden cock." An incident of this uprising was the successful resistance of a *quilombo* near Pirajá, a few miles distant from Bahia, to the attack of several *capitães do matto*[43a] who, in the mistaken belief that they had to deal with a small number of Negroes, sought without reinforcements to apprehend these fugitives and lost their lives in the attempt. A detachment of soldiers was required to dislodge the Africans.[44]

In 1827 a body of Yoruba slaves fled into the *matto* after sacking and setting fire to houses in the suburbs of the city. A police force sent in pursuit engaged the fugitives, killing or wounding eight of their number, but met with such resistance over a period of two days' skirmishing that it would have itself been wiped out had not a patrol of troops come to its rescue. The next year, following three separate revolts, slaveholders in the Reconcavo appealed to the governor for more effective police protection.

In 1835 the last and most serious revolt broke out, led again by Mohammedan Negroes, each of whom wore upon his person a *patuá*, or charm, presumed to protect the faithful against death in any form.[45] Bahia was at that time the

[43a] "Bush Captains" hired to track down fugitive slaves.

[44] Rodrigues, *op. cit.*, p. 76.

[45] Padre Etienne Ignace Brasil, "Os Malês," *Revista do Instituto Historico e Geographico Brasileiro*, LXXII, Part II (1909), 83. In São Salvador dos Campos, in the province of Rio de Janeiro, "restless slaves wearing plumes in their hats" were arrested, one of whom on being interrogated confessed that orders had been received from Bahia to revolt on the following Ash Wednesday (Alvares do Amaral, *op. cit.*, p. 91).

seat of the iman, or head in Brazil of all African disciples of the prophet Mohammed. Those who were resident in Rio, Ceará, and Pernambuco owed allegiance to him. Incidentally, it was a time of general social unrest not only among certain of the slaves but among the whites as well.[46] The aim of the conspiracy was "to set up a queen after exterminating all the Europeans." Extensive plans were laid, including the proposed participation of slaves from "every part of the Reconcavo," many of whom, immediately preceding the night set for the uprising, fled from their owners and came to Bahia. A banner was adopted and the robes worn at Mohammedan ceremonies selected as costumes of war. The time chosen for the uprising was during the popular festival of Nossa Senhora da Guia, when most of the European population would be gathered at Bomfim, outside the main area of the city, houses would consequently be deserted by white owners, and slaves might go in and out without arousing suspicion.[47]

The governor, forewarned by a faithful slave a few hours before the uprising actually occurred, doubled all police

[46] From 1831 to 1837 revolts against the Brazilian imperial government broke out in Pará, Sergipe, Pernambuco, and Rio Grande do Sul. In Maranhão three thousand slaves, led by an African named Cosme, had recently revolted.

[47] The report of the chief of police to the governor of the province of Bahia (republished from the *Diario da Bahia* in the *Jornal do Commercio* of Rio, February 10, 1835) said that the evidence indicated "the insurrection had been plotted for a considerable period of time with absolute secrecy. . . . . Almost all the leaders know how to read and to write in some unknown language, which appears to be Arabic. This is the same language which is used by the Ussás, who seem to be united today with the Nagôs. These Ussás are from the same tribe which has revolted on several occasions in this Province. . . . . Their leaders, among whom are many free and even wealthy Africans, stir up and organize revolts."

patrols which later, aided by foot soldiers and cavalry and favored by considerable confusion among the widely separated bands of blacks as to the actual hour of attack, scattered and broke up the Negro mobs, but only after a serious struggle.[48] The leaders of the revolt were tried,[49] given two hundred, five hundred, even one thousand lashes, or shot by a firing squad, or deported to Africa. Further importation of the *batá*, or African war drum, was forbidden.

The number and persistence of these slave insurrections may suggest that slavery in Brazil was unusually severe. The reverse seems to be the fact. Insurrectionists were unassimilated free Negroes and semi-independent slaves, morally isolated from the Europeans. Although the hardships incidental to a plantation system obviously existed, and atrocities occurred here as elsewhere, the slavery involved, as we shall see in detail in chapter iii, was ordinarily a mild form of servitude. In general, slavery in Brazil was characterized by the gradual and continuous growth of intimate, personal relations between master and slave which tended to humanize the institution and undermine its formal character.

[48] A letter from Bahia published in the *Jornal do Commercio* of Rio on February 10, 1835, and dated January 31, reads: "Business and commerce is completely at a standstill by reason of a Negro uprising which last Sunday suddenly upset public tranquillity in this city. The revolt, which had been planned for a long time, was very serious, but the armed forces managed to put it down."

[49] The police records deposited in the Archivo Publico at Bahia list 234 Negroes who, subsequent to the uprising, were brought to trial by the authorities. Among these, 165 are listed as Nagôs, 21 as Haussás, 6 as Gêges, and 6 as Tapas. Documents found in their possession, facsimiles of which may be seen in the above depository, were written in Arabic characters. See also the novel by Pedro Calmon, *Os Malês, a insurreção das senzalas* (Rio, 1933).

One advantage which Brazilian slaves had over bondsmen in the English colonies was the numerous holidays of which the Catholic religion enjoins the observance. Koster wrote:

These give to the slave many days of rest or time to work for his own profit; thirty-five of these, and the Sundays besides, allow him to employ much of his time as he pleases. Few masters are inclined to restrain the right of their slaves to dispose of these days as they think fit; or, at any rate, few dare, whatever their inclinations may be, to brave public opinion in depriving them of the intervals from work which the law has set apart as their own. . . . . The time which is thus afforded, enables the slave, who is so inclined, to accumulate a considerable sum of money.[50]

Among the small proprietors, parity of condition in many respects apparently obtained between master and slave, who worked together and fared much alike.[51]

It is, of course, true that cases of the most barbaric and extreme cruelty occurred, but apparently these were relatively rare and confined in large measure to frontier areas, where masters were very much a law unto themselves.[52] Public opinion was ordinarily opposed to such treatment, much of which has been attributed to Negro or mulatto owners or overseers who were notorious for their severity.[53]

[50] *Op. cit.*, I, 191.

[51] Southey, *op. cit.*, III, 782.

[52] However, Koster records as late as 1800 that, owing to the "abominable cruelty" with which they were treated in Rio de Janeiro, frequent murders were committed by slaves. Iron shackles, sharply pronged iron collars, stocks, and thumb screws were employed, and severe beatings to the point of death and even boilings in oil occurred. See also Thomas Ewbank, *Life in Brazil* (New York, 1856), pp. 116–17, 439.

[53] Joaquim Nabuco made public, and Conselheiro Dantas once referred in the federal senate to "a disgraceful tragedy" which occurred in Parahyba do Sul on July 29, 1886. A master who was an *homem de côr*, his *homem de côr* overseer and *algoz* "flayed and tortured" several slaves until they died

One must not overlook the fact, however, that during the first years of colonization the letters of the Jesuits contained numerous references to Indian slaves who were "tortured and branded in the face."[54] And later, the kings of Portugal, impressed by reports which had come to them concerning hardships inflicted on Negro slaves in Brazil, more than once wrote to their colonial representatives, exhorting them "to put a stop to such crying inhumanities."[55]

Most reports of cruelties, however, date from the abolition campaign and no doubt reflect the agitation and fervor of that movement. Thus, the able Bahian abolitionist, Anselmo da Fonseca, reports the case of a Negro in Rio Grande do Sul whose wrists were tied above his head and, after honey had been poured over his nude body, was left to the insects. Anselmo further reports the raping of small children, the use of stocks, the fracturing of teeth with a ham-

---

from the effects of their wounds (Fonseca, *op. cit.*, p. 145). Fonseca estimates that two-thirds of all the *feitores* (overseers), *capitães de matto*, and *corretores* (slave dealers) in Bahia were either mulattoes or blacks (*ibid.*, p. 151).

[54] Brazilian Indians, who before the coming of the Portuguese had killed their prisoners of war, changed this custom when it was discovered that they could sell their captives to the Europeans. Subsequently the latter organized raids into the interior in search of Indian slaves. The Jesuits fought this traffic, their struggles with the colonists lending a dramatic note to accounts of life in the sixteenth, seventeenth, and eighteenth centuries. Gradually their influence at the Portuguese court prevailed, certain restrictions were by royal decree put upon the enslavement of Indians, which, being disregarded by the colonists, led to further Jesuit protest and finally, in 1755, to a royal edict liberating all Indian slaves. Equal legal rights were subsequently granted the Indians, the University of Coimbra was opened to them, and they were even admitted, it is said, to the nobility.

[55] A writer cites three "royal letters" in support, dated, respectively, March 20, 1688, March 1, 1700, and April 27, 1719 (see the anonymous article entitled "Tradições bahianas," *Revista do Instituto Geographico e Historico da Bahia*, LVI [1930], 514).

mer, the filling of razor slashes with salt, the castration of males and the amputation of the breasts of females, and "murder at the slightest whim."[56] The custom of *novenas* and *trezenas* of slave beatings sometimes resulted in death.[57]

In 1887 a police sergeant in a village in the interior of Bahia Province reported to the governor: "Considering the number of crimes on slaves in this section which continually go unpunished, this town of Formosa is in great need of at least five soldiers to be stationed here at the disposal of the local police official."[58] The *Diario da Bahia* of July 21, 1887, reports the discovery of a slave woman bearing about her neck a pronged iron collar "weighing twenty-five pounds, from which were suspended heavy chains wrapped about her body like serpents."

Escapes were frequent, the fugitives being assisted by the character of the *matto*. They were hunted by hired *capitães do matto*, or "bush captains," usually Brazilian-born Negroes or mixed-bloods, whose trained dogs netted them a steady income.[59] Occasionally, fugitive slaves banded together in considerable numbers for mutual protection into *quilombos*.

[56] Fonseca, *op. cit.*, pp. 561–63. For illustrations of instruments used to punish slaves, see Arthur Ramos, "Castigos de escravos," *Revista do Arquivo Municipal* (São Paulo), XLVII (May, 1938), 79–104.

[57] "Each day at a certain hour . . . . the slave is stripped and tied to a post where he receives a certain number of blows which reopen wounds made on previous days. . . . . This is done for periods of nine to thirteen days in accordance with the practices [religious ceremonies extending over a period of nine to thirteen days] of the church" (*ibid.*, p. 43 n.).

[58] *Ibid.*, p. 673.

[59] Still played by children at Bahia is the game "Capitão do matto," a form of "hide and go seek" in which those hiding are presumed to be slaves and the hunter a "bush captain."

The present town of Orobó,[60] approximately a hundred and
fifty miles interior from the port of Bahia, is said to have had
its origin in such a settlement.[61] Even outlying areas of the
city of Bahia like Matta Escura and Estrada da Liberdade,
and the neighboring villages of Cabula, Armação, Pirajá,
and Itapoan, are said to have had their origin in *quilombos*,
dating from the colonial period. From these settlements
there were frequent sallies of Negroes into the city to rob and
to pillage. However, no *quilombo* in the state of Bahia

[60] The name has recently been changed to Ruy Barbosa.

[61] On September 23, 1796, an investigation was ordered of complaints
regarding the *quilombo* of Orobó. On April 6 of the following year this
report was made (Silva, *op. cit.*, III, 227):

ILLUSTRIOUS AND ESTEEMED SIR:

There having been repeated requests on the part of certain *senhores de engenho* and owners
of *fazendas* living in the vicinity of Orobó, district of the villa of Cachoeira, that there be destroyed a very old *quilombo* of fugitive slaves who have been wasting and destroying neighboring plantations and committing other excesses of great damage to the settlers, I ordered the
dezembargador, Juiz de Fora, of the same villa to find out if these reports were true, and if they
were, to seek by all means possible to destroy this *quilombo*, using all prudence and care to avoid
any fatal occurrence in the execution of the order, in view of the great distance between
Cachoeira and that district, as well as our ignorance of the size of the *quilombo* which,
according to some accounts, was not small. The necessity of collecting provisions, of enrolling
and arming men . . . . delayed for some time the execution of this order until, the complaints
continuing and the people themselves offering to lend some aid and assistance, I ordered the
capitão-mor of Entrados e Assaltos of the District of São José das Itapororocas, Severino Pereira, to organize an armed force and to destory the *mocambo*. This order was carried out in
December of last year, the two *quilombos*, or *mocambos*, known as Orobó and Andrah being
destroyed. At these places were found fields of manioc, *inhame*, rice, fruit, and a little sugar
cane, with all of which the inhabitants had easily been able to sustain themselves. Thirteen
slaves were apprehended, among them men, women, and children, all of whom were delivered
up to their respective masters. Previous to the arrival of the armed force, it is reported, a
great number of slaves living there fled, for apparently they suspected, or perhaps were even
aware of, the impending attack. As it appeared that they had fled to another *quilombo* called
Tupim, farther off, I ordered that it similarly be destroyed, but I have not yet had notice
whether such has been done. This is what I have to offer Your Excellency in reply to a letter
directed to me and received on the 23rd of September of last year, urging me to undertake the
most effective means of destroying the indicated *quilombos* and of relieving the settlers.

God guard Your Excellency.

Bahia, 6th of April, 1797. Most Illustrious and Excellent Sir, D. Rodrigo de Sousa Coutinho.

D. FERNANDO JOSÉ DE PORTUGAL

equaled in size or in importance the famed Palmares of Alagoas.[62]

It is a mistake, however, to conclude that humane and intimate relations between master and slave were by any means rare. In fact, they were in all likelihood, as we shall see in detail later, the general rule. The literature records numerous instances like that witnessed by John Codman in 1866, of which he says:

We drove up to the door of our Brazilian passengers. They were most boisterously welcomed by a troop of blacks. The pleasantest thing I had seen for some hours was the affection of these poor Negroes. Bright shone their eyes, and what a display was there of ivory! They fairly seized their mistress . . . . in their arms, and "toted" her off into the house, hugging and kissing her, screaming and dancing as they went.[63]

[62] The famous "Negroes of the Palmares" (or "Palm Forests") were slaves who had escaped from Pernambuco before and particularly during the struggles of the Portuguese with the Dutch. Constantly acquiring recruits, they set up a series of crudely fortified villages scattered over some sixty leagues (about two hundred and forty miles). From these they harried the neighboring regions, taking from outlying *fazendas* both mates and slaves, among the former of which white women were occasionally to be found. They became so strong and so difficult to dislodge, that numerous expeditions sent out by the Dutch and later by the Portuguese served only to check for a time their growth—were unable for seventy years to destroy them completely. Only in 1697 were they finally subdued by an army from Recife led by a Paulista famed for success in such fighting and especially imported for this service, and then only after he had at first encountered serious reversals at their hands and their resistance had subsequently been broken by a failure of the food supply (Southey, *op. cit.*, III, 23–29). This Negro group had at times carried on trade with the whites, exchanging agricultural products for articles of manufacture. That they were seriously treated as an alien but respected group is attested by an exchange of peace commissioners during the governorship of Ayres Souza e Castro and the subsequent signing of a treaty of peace. (Incidentally, this treaty was never kept by the whites.) For a critical examination of the exaggerated reports of this erroneously labeled "Negro Republic" see Rodrigues, *op. cit.*, pp. 111–43.

[63] John Codman, *Ten Months in Brazil* (Boston, 1867), p. 125.

The first recorded protest in Brazil against slavery as an institution was that of the Jesuit Manoel de Nobrega, who, shortly after Bahia was founded, sent a letter to the superior of his order in Lisbon protesting against the importation of Africans into the new settlement.

In 1758 Manoel Ribeiro da Rocha, who had been educated at Coimbra, published in Lisbon a book entitled *Ethiope resgatado, empenhado, sustentado, corrigido, instruido e libertado*, in which the abolition of the slave trade was advocated. Sixty-five years later, in 1823, José Bonifacio de Andrade e Silva unsuccessfully proposed in parliament a measure designed to end importation by 1828. But on November 7, 1831, the regent, Padre Diogo Antonio Feijó, signed a resolution drawn up by Costa Carvalho, Lima e Sousa, and Basilio Muniz, which declared free all Africans subsequently brought into Brazil.

Manumission existed from the first. Apparently early in the colonial period it became customary for masters to accept remuneration for original cost.[64] Public opinion demanded that an owner set at liberty any slave requesting his freedom and offering the price of his purchase.[65] The requirement was later made legally binding and enforced by law.[65a] Other slaves were given their freedom either during their master's lifetime or upon his death. The fathers of illegitimate offspring often freed their children at the baptismal font. From 1864 to 1870 large numbers of slaves were granted their freedom on agreeing to serve in the Para-

[64] The wearing of shoes or slippers became a symbol of freedom.

[65] R. Walsh, *Notices of Brazil* (2 vols.; London, 1830), II, 391.

[65a] National Law No. 2040, September 28, 1871. See Manoel Joaquim do Nascimento e Silva, *Synopsis da legislação brasileira* (Rio, 1874), p. 460.

guayan war.[66] The law eventually provided that Negro women, after rearing ten children, should be automatically liberated.[67] In 1871 the so-called "law of Rio Branco" freed offspring of slaves born subsequent to its adoption[68] and set up a fund for the purchase and liberation of Negroes by the government. By 1880 a widespread emancipation movement was under way.[69] Thousands were freed by will, by payments from emancipation funds,[70] or by outright gift.[71] For instance, in 1883, in the towns of Baturite, Aca-

[66] On March 30, 1867, the monastery of São Bento in Bahia, which had already freed eleven slaves for service in the war with Paraguay, liberated six more Negroes and "presented them to the Governor for the same purpose."

[67] Koster, however, wrote from Pernambuco in the early nineteenth century: "A slave who has brought into the world, and has reared ten children, ought to be free, for so the law ordains. But this regulation is generally evaded" (op. cit., I, 195).

[68] This law was, however, in some cases ineffective. Sixteen years after its passage the Bahian Diario Official, of June 4, 1887, reported the following auction of slave property at the fazenda Concordia: "Alberto, 10 years of age, one conto of reis; Vicente, 13 years, one conto of reis; Felix, 14 years, 800 milreis; Flauzinha, 13 years, 600 milreis, Simplicio, 14 years, one conto of reis" (Fonseca, op. cit., p. 587 n.)

[69] Among the prominent abolitionists mentioned by Anselmo da Fonseca were: José do Patrocinio, Joaquim Nabuco ("the great and illustrious head of the abolition movement"), Senator Dantas, Ferreira de Menezes, Andre Rebouças, Quintino Bocayuva, Joaquim Serra, Ennes de Souza, Getulio das Neves, Nicolau Moreira, José Mariano, Celso Junior, Senator Jaguaripe, Luiz de Andrade, João Clapp, Beaurepaire Rohan, Aristides Spinola, Ruy Barbosa, Escragnole Taunay, Franco de Sá, Antonio Pinto, Leopoldo Bulhões, and "a writer using the pseudonym of Clarkson" (ibid., p. 23).

[70] These funds were sponsored by emancipation societies, private individuals, and municipal, state, and national treasuries.

[71] The Provinciano, a newspaper of Parahyba do Sul, listed in 1884, among others, the following emancipations: "Dona Anna S. José, 16 slaves liberated and a farm given them for their use; Condessa do Rio Novo, 200 slaves

rapi, and São Francisco, a *Sociedade Libertadora* freed 122
slaves in one day. Scores of these societies operated
throughout Brazil.[72]

Dr. João Garcez dos Santos was the first Bahian *fazendeiro*
(planter) to exchange slave labor for free. After spending
some years in Europe studying agriculture, he returned to
Brazil and, in 1864, bought an *engenho* called Pimental, in
the *termo* of São Francisco. He freed all the slaves except
eight domestic servants and paid these freedmen wages, re-
taining a portion of their earnings until he had been recom-
pensed for their original cost. During the subsequent year
he produced with free labor two hundred boxes of sugar.
Three years later, he "freed the womb" of his eight female
domestic servants, and, on his death in 1874, he set at liberty
all the slaves which he had inherited from his father (a total
of about sixty persons) on condition that they continue
working for wages on the *engenho* for five years.[73]

In 1868 the Senhoras Condessa de Barral and Pedra

---

liberated by will, and the Cantagallo plantation given them for a home;
Barão de Dias, 163 slaves liberated, who remain established on his plantation as laborers." In 1887 Anselmo da Fonseca wrote: "As to the *cartas de
alforria* granted by slaveholders themselves, it is well known that these have
always appeared in greater or lesser number in the country, and that from
1880 on they have multiplied greatly and have now become quite numerous,
thanks to the powerful influence of that propaganda which has contributed so
much to the elevation of the moral sentiments of the Brazilian people."

[72] On September 7, 1869, an emancipation society was organized in Bahia
"with the noble purpose of ending slavery in Bahia," and by March 1, 1874,
it had conferred 267 "Letters of Liberty," 89 of which were "granted gratui-
tously in its name," and 178 by means of its own funds, the amount thus
employed totaling 58,289 milreis (Alvares do Amaral, *op. cit.*, p. 181). This
organization was named A Sociedade Libertadora Sete de Setembro ("The
Seventh of September Liberation Society") in honor of the day on which the
independence of Brazil was declared.

[73] Fonseca, *op. cit.*, pp. 220–22.

Branca while sojourning in France "freed the womb" of the slave women on their *engenhos*, São Pedro and São João, in Santo Amaro, and continued gradually to manumit all their slaves. In the same year the friars of the Order of São Bento "freed the womb" of their slave women and announced that all their slaves would be free within three years, or by September, 1871.[74]

The first Bahian abolitionist to raise his voice to "a shout loud enough to be heard throughout the entire country" was Conselheiro Jeronymo Sodré Pereira, a state deputy and professor in the local Faculty of Medicine. In an address to the Bahian *camara* on March 5, 1879, he declared: "We who represent the democratic ideal, we who earnestly desire the liberation of the citizen through the vote and through instruction, ought to proclaim to our fellow-countrymen throughout the land that all Brazilians are citizens, all are free." This speech was favorably reported by several Bahian newspapers, including the *Gazeta de Noticias* and the *Gazeta da Tarde*, which at this time were becoming organs of the abolition movement. Although the ideas they were advancing had been at first considered "antipatriotic, subversive of the social order, and incendiary," they gradually spread.[75]

The clergy as a group did not support abolition, and many padres who possessed slaves were accused by the abolitionists of "the same cruelty toward the victims, the same outspoken hostility, the same fury toward abolition, the same hypocritical and ridiculous insistence upon the rights of property, the same lack of respect for justice and the true interests of Brazil." Occasionally a priest, like João Manoel,

---

[74] *Ibid.*, pp. 227–28.   [75] *Ibid.*, pp. 18–21.

became known throughout the country as an opponent of abolition, and, further, in 1791, a bishop of Pernambuco, José Joaquim da Cunha de Azevedo Coutinho, published a book in Lisbon entitled *A analyse sobre a justiça do commercio do resgate dos escravos da costa d'Africa*,[76] in which he upheld slavery as having "existed since the beginning of the world and in the lap of all religions."

Nevertheless, some noted ecclesiastics did from time to time take up the slave cause. Padre Antonio Vieira, although he later became more cautious under "the necessity of furthering the Jesuit determination to free the Indians, even at the expense of the Negroes," delivered a sermon as early as the middle of the seventeenth century in which he said: "The fact that whites dominate blacks is due to force and not to either reason or nature." On another occasion, he said:

O inhuman traffic in which the merchandise is men! Few masters, many slaves; masters richly dressed, slaves despised and naked; masters banqueting, slaves dying of hunger; masters swimming in gold and silver, slaves loaded down with irons; masters treating their slaves like brutes, slaves in fear and awe of their masters as if they were gods; masters present at a whipping, standing like statues of might and tyranny, slaves prostrate, their hands strapped behind their backs, like debased emblems of servitude.

Peradventure these men are not our brothers?

Were these souls not redeemed with the blood of the same Christ? Are not these bodies born and do they not die like ours? Do they not breathe the same air? Does not the same sky cover them? Are they not warmed by the same sun?[77]

An archbishop of Bahia, the Marquis of Santa Cruz, in an address to the *camara* in 1827, vigorously opposed slav-

[76] This book went through two editions and was translated into both French and English.

[77] *Sermões* (15 vols., 1679–1748), Vol. X, Sermon 27.

ery.[78] As early as Independence Day, 1851, the Benedictine friar, Francisco da Natividade Carneiro da Cunha, preached a sermon in the Bahian Cathedral in which he urged Bahians "to complete Brazilian independence by gradually emancipating the slaves."[79] Monsenhor Joaquim Pinto de Campos attacked slavery in sermons as early as 1856, in one of which, preached before the Sociedade Ypiranga, he said: "Humanity is one, and all of its parts have equal rights. The public conscience, which is the voice of God re-echoing in the souls of the people, is always repelled by favoritism in the distribution of liberty."

Canon Rodrigo de Souza Menezes, in the columns of *O Horizonte* as early as 1872, and in a sermon preached in the Cathedral on July 2, 1883, vigorously attacked slavery and advocated its abolition throughout Brazil. Another Bahian canon, Dr. Romualdo Maria de Seixas Barroso, wrote many abolition articles for the newspapers, among them one addressed especially to Bahian women; and in his will, probated in 1886, he declared: "I have always considered it a crime to draw up a contract for the buying and selling of any human being—he who is my own brother and who may be redeemed, as I, by the blood of the Savior of mankind."[80]

The bishop of Olinda, on March 25, 1887, wrote a pastoral letter urging his clergy to free immediately their

[78] *Ibid.*, p. 35. The archbishop said: "I have always been persuaded that the word 'slavery' calls up images of all vices and all crimes; and that the word 'liberty' calls out the ideas and the sentiments attendent upon all virtue and all good. Always I have maintained that slavery is a harmful condition which destroys the spirit, weakens the faculties of understanding, and perverts the heart."

[79] "Public opinion was aroused against the words of Friar Carneiro. Upon his descending from the pulpit, one of his relatives asked him if he had lost his reason" (Fonseca, *op. cit.*, pp. 382–83).

[80] *Ibid.*, pp. 384–88.

slaves so that "on the next birthday of the Holy Father, Leo XIII, there may be laid next his throne a declaration saying: 'The clergy of Olinda no longer own slaves.'" A similar suggestion was shortly thereafter made to the bishop of São Paulo by several of his priests. On July 29 the archbishop of Bahia issued a pastoral letter in which he referred to slavery as "a cruel injustice practiced on many of our brothers . . . . a blot which stains the Brazilian flag alone among the banners of civilized nations." The archbishop further declared that, while the church had previously feared that abolition would disrupt public order, the consequences of recent manumissions had entirely dispelled this apprehension.

The proposal of the bishop of Olinda was supported by the bishop of Maranhão, who agreed that "one can do nothing which would honor the august head of the great Christian family more than to grant liberty to those who are our brothers and children of our church." The proposal was also supported by the bishop of Rio Grande do Sul, who closed his pastoral letter with the strong declaration that "slavery is a corpse in need of being interred;"[81] and by the bishop of Diamantina, who proposed "a decree written in letters of gold abolishing slavery in Brazil by the thirty-first day of December, 1887." The bishop of Mariana also advocated general abolition, referring to slavery as an obstacle to the spread of "the great principles planted by our Master Jesus Christ" and reminding the priests of his bishopric that

[81] *Ibid.*, pp. 513–19. Although the enumeration in accordance with the law of September 28, 1871, listed 99,401 slaves in Rio Grande do Sul, the census which was completed June 12, 1885, gave only 27,242, or less than one-third of those returned fourteen years earlier. The enumeration of March 30, 1887, listed only 8,436 (*ibid.*, p. 520). It appears that attempts to emancipate by entire provinces originated in this province.

"slavery is extinct in all other countries of America to the shame of Brazil."

Beginning about 1862 a Bahian professor of mathematics, the mixed-blood, Dr. Francisco Alvares dos Santos, whose classes were said to be attended by two-thirds of the students of mathematics in the city, began carrying on abolition propaganda, and during the subsequent quarter of a century he each year gave a banquet to former students and invited as a special guest a slave whose liberty had been purchased on that day with funds supplied by a "patriotic battalion" composed of his students and organized in honor of the independence of Brazil. Out of his teaching arose the Sociedade Libertadora Dois de Julho, which freed several slaves.

By 1875 the Sociedade Libertadora Sete de Setembro, organized in 1869, had freed approximately five hundred slaves, and twenty-four numbers of a periodical, *O Abolicionista*, had been published. At a bazaar held by the Society in that year, Castro Alves, Bahia's "glorious poet of liberty," addressed a letter to Bahian women in behalf of the slaves, and Barão de Macahubas, resident at the imperial court, sent several gifts. The Society at that time numbered five hundred and twelve members, of whom fifteen were women.[82]

The Sociedade Humanitaria Abolicionista was organized in 1869, and the Sociedade Libertadora Bahiana in 1883.

[82] Among the more prominent members were: Frederico Marinho de Araujo, Victor Isaac de Araujo, Lourenço Gomes de Araujo e Silva, Abilio Cezar Borges, Conselheiro José Luiz de Almeida Couto, Dr. Francisco José da Rocha, Conselheiro Manoel Pinto de Souza Dantas, Conselheiro Salustiano Ferreira Santo, Dr. Augusto Guimarães, Dr. Antonio Ferreira Garcez, Bellarmino Barretto, Julio Alves Guimarães, Constancio José dos Santos, Major Antonio de Souza Vieira, Dr. Frederico Augusto da Silva Lisboa, Conselheiro Carneiro da Rocha, and Major Antonio Ferreira de Barros.

Four years later the latter changed its name to Sociedade Abolicionista Bahiana. In that time it had purchased the freedom of about fifty slaves, "including those whose liberty was demanded by reason of illegal servitude." The treasurer of the Society was a Negro shoemaker, Manoel Roque, "a man of the people," who carried on abolition propaganda among the free Negroes and "made several converts to the cause."

Abolitionists in other parts of the province of Bahia were similarly active. In 1884 an emancipation society was organized at Cachoeira, where two "out-spoken abolition newspapers," the *Jornal da Tarde* and *Planeta Venus*, were keeping the slave issue before the public. Another emancipation society, under the leadership of Pedro Alves de São Boaventura, operated at Camisão. Abolition sentiment and activity were also reported from Ilheos, Cannavieiras, Santo Antonio da Barra, and Feira de Sant'Anna, said to be "a strong pro-slave center."

In 1862 a Bahian student published an antislavery article in a local publication, *O Estudante*. In 1869, after the Liberal party had adopted emancipation as a party policy, the *Diario da Bahia* began to support the antislavery cause. On March 20, 1872, five of the six newspapers then printed in the Bahian capital agreed "not to give publicity from this day forth to advertisements of any kind relative to the flight, purchase, sale, or placement of any slave."[83]

[83] Signed by Francisco José da Rocha for the *Jornal da Bahia*, Innocencio Marques de Araujo Goes Junior for the *Correio da Bahia*, Manoel Pinto de Souza Dantas for the *Diario da Bahia*, Carvalho Gama for the *Diario de Noticias*, and José Marques de Souza and Aristides Ricardo de Sant'Anna for the *Alabama*. This agreement was renewed nine years later (in 1881), and the resolution was then taken "to urge the adhesion to it of all the press of the Empire." Only the *Gazeta da Bahia* refused to sign (Fonseca, *op. cit.*, pp. 276–79).

In 1872 Dr. Frederico Lisboa advocated in *O Horizonte*
"the right of all men to natural liberty" and, in keeping with
this sentiment, liberated several slaves which had been presented to him on the occasion of his marriage. Subsequently
he bought and freed some thirty Negroes belonging to
others. In nine months Bahian abolitionists secured the release of approximately two hundred slaves illegally imported
after passage of the law of 1831.[84] To make less difficult the
transition from a slave to a free status, the courts appointed
lawyers as *curadores* ("guardians") of the freedmen.[85]

In 1880 Pamphilo da Santa Cruz founded a newspaper
called *Gazeta da Tarde*, in whose first issue he stated a frankly
abolitionist program. He was assisted in its publication by
the journalist, Raymundo Bizarria, and by Conselheiro
Luiz Alvares dos Santos, a professor at the Faculty of
Medicine. In 1881, on the anniversary of the death of Castro Alves, "the immortal poet," author of the antislavery
Gonzaga and *Poema dos escravos*, the public was invited
through the columns of the *Diario da Bahia* "eloquently to
affirm our irrevocable adhesion to the cause of abolition."

[84] For instance, Eduardo Carige demanded the liberation of an African
woman whose owner, Antonio Alves Fernandes, had registered her in 1872 as
forty years of age. Dr. Amphilophio Botelho Freire de Carvalho, "the first
Bahian judge to comply with this law," whose decisions "were widely
publicized and attracted the attention of the whole province," freed her on
February 10, 1887. One irate master appealed from a decision of Botelho,
charging that the judge was incompetent. The Superior Tribunal denied the
appeal (see *Diario da Bahia* for March 15, 1887; Fonseca, *op. cit.*, pp. 319–23).

[85] Among Bahian lawyers accepting this charge were: Dr. Affonso do
Castro Rebello, Dr. Elpidio de Mesquita, Dr. Arthur de Mello e Mattos,
Dr. Mauricio Francisco Ferreira da Silva, Dr. José Heraclides Ferreira, Dr.
Francisco Moncorvo de Lima, Dr. Adolpho Carlos Sanches, Dr. Alexandre
Galvão, Dr. Severino dos Santos Vieira, and Dr. Izaias Guedes de Mello. Dr.
Raymundo Mendes Martins "rendered important services to the cause of
the captives" as *curador geral* of orphans (Fonseca, *op. cit.*, pp. 324–26).

At the ceremony Bahia's most famous citizen, the statesman, jurist, and orator, Ruy Barbosa, read from *Gonzaga:*
"No more slaves! No more masters! Liberty to all hands,
liberty to all heads," and himself added, "Abolition is an
expression of the most inflexible of social necessities." Antonio Augusto de Mendonça, one of several Bahian poets
then active in the antislavery cause, wrote and recited a
poem dedicated to the Sociedade Libertadora Sete de Setembro. In the following year the *Gazeta da Tarde* inaugurated
a series of abolition lectures to be given in the Lyceu de
Artes e Officios and invited as the first speaker the well-known
abolition orator, José do Patrocinio.[86] In 1885 a pamphlet
entitled *A incoherencia da escravidão n'um paiz christão* was
published in Bahia by Antonio Pereira de Araujo. When
the news arrived (June 30, 1887) that the cabinet had secured the dissolution of "the pro-slave" *camara* a celebration was held at the offices of the *Diario da Bahia*, on the
initiative of the *Libertadora Bahiana* and the *Gazeta da
Tarde*.

In 1872 the province of Bahia freed the twenty-two slaves
which it owned and had employed as gardeners, laundry
women, and grave-diggers, either at the Hospital dos Lazaros or the cemetery of Quintas. In 1880 Joaquim Nabuco
presented a project to the Pernambuco legislature calling for
the extinction of slavery within ten years, and three years
later he published a stirring abolition treatise entitled *O
Abolicionismo.*[86a] In 1885, and again in 1887, he was elected
federal deputy on an abolition platform. In 1881 the Bahian

[86] Other lectures were given by Dr. Aristides Spinola, Dr. José de Oliviera
Campos, Paula Ney, Conselheiro Luiz Alvares dos Santos, Ennes de Souza,
Salles Barbosa, Elpidio de Mesquita, and Dr. Arthur Ferreira Vianna.

[86a] London, 1883.

provincial assembly created an emancipation fund "to free slaves in this province."[87] On March 25, 1884, slavery was abolished in the province of Ceará, the culmination of fifteen months of municipal emancipation.[88] Similar action was taken by the provinces of Amazonas and Maranhão later in the same year. In 1885 all Negroes over sixty years of age were liberated by edict of the Brazilian emperor.[89] In 1886

[87] Law No. 2146 of May 14, 1881, sponsored by Deputies Marcolino Moura, Alexandre Herculano, Frederico Lisboa, and Virgilio de Carvalho. Articles 2 and 3 read as follows:

ARTICLE 2.—This Emancipation Fund shall be derived:

SECTION 1. From each and every provincial tax relative to slaves, including the inheritance and legacy stamps.

SEC. 2. From the returns of an annual lottery of 100 contos.

SEC. 3. From the donations of individuals and of philanthropic associations.

SEC. 4. From legacies left or set up for the benefit of the fund.

SEC. 5. From the payment of a tax obligatory for this purpose by every dramatic and musical company which shall play in the Theatro Publico.

ART. 3.—The distribution of this Emancipation Fund shall be in the hands of each *municipio* in accordance with Article 26 of Statute 5135 of the thirteenth of November, 1872.

The seventh apportionment from this fund, made by act of Governor Theodoro Machado on May 13, 1886, amounted to 59 contos, 723$244 (Fonseca, *op. cit.*, p. 233).

[88] The *Rio News* of April 5, 1884, reported a week's festival being at that time held in Rio in celebration of emancipation in Ceará. Large sums were realized from donations and bazaars, several slaves were liberated, and a movement set on foot to secure complete emancipation in Rio also. On September 28, 1887, there was held at Belem a "redemption celebration" to which flocked "the press, the abolition societies, the Masons, leaders of the city's commercial life, many women, and the people." One hundred and nine *Cartas de Liberdade* were distributed. On the following day, the *Provincio do Pará*, one of the leading abolition journals of Brazil, published an editorial suggesting a *liga redemptora*, whose program would be that of seeking to secure complete emancipation in the Belem *municipio* by the following December 31 (Fonseca, *op. cit.*, p. 548).

[89] The provisions of this law freed slaves from sixty to sixty-two years of age on the condition that they serve three additional years without remuneration. Slaves sixty-three years of age were to serve two additional years; those sixty-four, one additional year.

the municipal *camara* of Bahia, following the initiative of other Brazilian cities, authorized a *Livro de Ouro* ("Golden Book") in which the names of persons contributing toward the emancipation of slaves in the *municipio* were to be inscribed. On April 19 of the following year a project was presented to the municipal *camara* by its president, Dr. Augusto Guimarães, authorizing the setting-up of a commission to study means of extinguishing slavery throughout the *municipio*.

On the eve of nation-wide abolition, or in 1887, a number of emancipation projects were presented to the Bahian *camara*. Two were presented in the state senate: one by Senator Taunay and one by Senator Dantas, the former setting Christmas, 1889, as the date of final abolition for the province of Bahia, and the latter naming December 31 of the same year. Slaves in various parts of Brazil, "learning that they are men and will one day be citizens," were by this time deserting the plantations.[90] Police and the soldiery often refused to aid in their recapture.

In 1887, "as a significant manifestation of abolition senti-

[90] In 1887 Fonseca mentions the "recent flight" en masse of slaves from several *fazendas* in the province of São Paulo. For instance, in Piracicaba, a hundred slaves fled from Barão de Serra Negra. In the *municipio* of Campos fifty slaves fled from the *fazenda* of Becco and, joined by other Negroes who were deserting the *fazenda* of Penha, turned upon the police sent out from Itu to apprehend them and caught, stripped, and beat them. That year the following advertisement appeared in the *Gazeta da Bahia:*

Fled from the owner whose signature appears below the following slaves: Maria dos Neves, *cabra* [offspring of Negro and mulatto], short, stocky, round faced, with prominent cheek bones, milk-white teeth, straight hair, parted in the middle; speaks very rapidly. Antonio (who sometimes calls himself Maria da Piedade), dark *cabra*, short, fat, with good teeth, and large scars on breast and one arm (these scars are from burns). Was last seen in Rio Vermelho.

Whoever recovers and brings these slaves to my office at Rua do Julião, No. 1, or to No. 125 Ribeira in Itapagipe, will be well rewarded.

DR. JOSÉ ALVES CARDOSO E SILVA

(Fonseca, *op. cit.*, pp. 595, 602–3, 161).

ment," a picture of José Bonifacio was hung in the salon of
the Gremio Litterario at Bahia, in the presence of "the principal civil and military authorities, representatives of the
press, and several delegations from other organizations."
The Sociedade Libertadora Bahiana took advantage of the
occasion to present six "Letters of Liberty." As these were
being distributed,

a young slave girl, so covered with rags as to look like an abandoned
beggar, forced her way into the assemblage and, falling upon her knees,
begged and pleaded for her liberty. The pitiful aspect of this girl, the
recently spoken words of Sr. Carige, and, above all, the sentiments
evoked in contemplation of the sacrificial heroism of José Bonifacio,
produced a profound effect. . . . . A citizen arose and said, "In honor
of the memory of José Bonifacio, I contribute one hundred milreis
toward the liberation of this woman."

Finally, in 1888, the imperial government at Rio, through
a decree signed by Princess Isabel, abolished slavery entirely, freeing the last six hundred thousand Negroes in bondage
throughout the country.

The extinction of the institution of slavery in Brazil thus
came about gradually by means of a progressively increasing and finally irresistible popular movement, aided, it seems,
by the decay of the sugar industry,[91] by the arguments of
the economists who held that the slave was an expensive
workman, by the example of the United States in freeing
her slaves (which left Brazil the only slaveholding American
nation), and by the "strain for consistency" exerted upon
the institution by the philosophy of the French Revolution[92]

[91] Silvio Romero, "O Brasil social," *Revista do Instituto Historico e Geographico Brasileiro*, LXIX (1906), 111.

[92] In 1883 Joaquim Nabuco wrote: "Slavery has now endured in Brazil
almost a century after the French Revolution taught the world to know and
to love liberty."

and the doctrines of Christianity. The normal development of the emancipation process was never checked or seriously hampered by a wave of fear like that which swept over slave areas in the United States following the Haitian revolution and the consequent annihilation of Haitian whites and the slaughter of thousands of mulattoes and blacks.

Resistance to abolition was apparently never strong or well organized. It was not confined to any one section of the country but even in slaveholding centers like Bahia was, as we have seen, constantly being undermined by local criticism. An occasional newspaper "persisted in being a slave organ" or appeared "timid and acquiescent with reference to slavery,"[93] but the overwhelming majority of the press increasingly supported the antislavery cause.

It is, however, true that commercial leaders like Ramalho Ortigão, president of the Bahian *Centro* of Commerce and Agriculture, "tenaciously opposed" the abolition movement. Anselmo da Fonseca says that Portuguese immigrants, many of whom engaged in trade and commerce, were, with rare exceptions, "decided partisans of slavery" and not only became "the greatest and most audacious slave traders of Bahia" who offered most of the opposition to the cessation of the slave traffic but also energetically opposed the abolition of slavery itself.[94] However, the prestige of this group,

[93] Fonseca, *op. cit.*, p. 25.

[94] "The Portuguese cannot comprehend a Brazil without slaves. We hear daily from them, 'The Negro is peculiarly created by nature for the cultivation of sugar' " (*ibid.*, pp. 155–56). The Portuguese are said to have been the principal violators of the law of 1831, several of the more powerful of whom Euzebio de Queiroz felt impelled to deport when, some twenty years after the passage of this law legally abolishing the slave trade, he sought effectively to suppress the traffic. However, immigrant laborers, since they were in competition with slave laborers, ordinarily opposed slavery. See Henry K. Norton, *The Coming of South America* (New York, 1932), pp. 103–4.

from early colonial times on, seems not to have been very great, and the upheaval which in 1822 culminated in Brazilian independence seems to have buried most of the vestiges of Portuguese prestige. Even today the Portuguese are the constant butt of vaudeville jokes.

Many of the free *homens de côr* (men of color), especially those who possessed slaves, either were indifferent to the slave question or openly opposed abolition.[95] Most of the large plantation owners and their spokesmen in the provincial legislature and national parliament opposed the abolition campaign, and their forces at one time dominated the Liberal party.[96] However, many of the slaveholders appear to have increasingly accepted abolition as inevitable and merely to have asked remuneration for the financial loss involved. Apprehension that the plantation system would utterly collapse if free labor were substituted for slave

[95] The abolitionist, Anselmo da Fonseca (*ibid.*, pp. 137, 142–43), complains of the persistent opposition to abolition on the part of *homens de côr*. In 1884, out of thirty candidates for the Bahian *camara*, "the only one who in a published document had the audacity to ask election in the name of slavery" was the *homem de côr*, Conselheiro Domingos Carlos e Silva. In 1887 an *homem de côr* canceled his subscription to the *Diario da Bahia* for its refusal to publish an advertisement regarding a fugitive slave. Fonseca regarded this man as "one of the most intolerant slaveholders in Bahia."

[96] On hearing of the program presented by the imperial cabinet on June 6, 1884, "almost all the leaders of the liberal party in Bahia, the owners of large business and commercial houses, and the sugar aristocracy" lodged a protest in which they declared: "The slave is more than a portion of a private fortune; he is a social institution, a labor supply, a necessity to production, an asset of the national life. Above the immediate interests of planter and merchant . . . . are the permanent . . . . interests of society, the benefits which accrue to thousands of human beings living or yet unborn—the necessities of public order, and the development of national wealth" (Fonseca, *op. cit.*, p. 283).

and that the sudden liberation of large numbers of subjected blacks would subvert public order gradually melted away as the numbers of emancipated Negroes increased and these freedmen gave evidence of their ability and willingness to become an orderly part of the free population and to labor as effectively, if not more effectively, for wages as when impelled by physical force.

The free people of color (who by 1872 largely outnumbered the slaves)[97] were, Southey says, "an industrious and useful part of the population: most of the maize, manioc and pulse, with which the towns were supplied, was raised by them upon small pieces of ground, which they rented of the great proprietors at a low rate."[98] Freedmen were also employed as laborers on the large estates, where they lived as squatters on the land of their employers, erecting mud and palm-leaf huts for their families, and looking to the planter for protection from any who would do them harm.[99] In the towns they were employed principally as artisans, porters, messengers, barbers, street merchants and small shopkeep-

[97] Johnston, *op. cit.*, p. 97.

[98] Southey, *op. cit.*, III, 787. Cf. also: "The masters who freed slaves often gave them, with their liberty, a piece of land to insure their subsistence. The Negroes who have inherited these small holdings are to-day (1911) the best element of the black agricultural population" (Pierre Denis, *Brazil*, trans. from the French by Bernard Miall [New York, 1911], p. 322).

[99] Koster writes: "The Negroes in my possession could not perform what ought to be done in proper time; and therefore I collected free laborers for the purpose, and in a short period between thirty and forty men, some of whom brought their families, removed on to the lands of the plantation; and most of them erected hovels of palm-leaves, in which they dwelt; but a few of them were accommodated with huts of mud. . . . . Many of these fellows would have committed almost any crime under the impression that my protection would screen them" (*op. cit.*, I, 295, 297).

ers; some of them accumulated considerable sums of money. Occasionally, as we have noted, they owned slaves[100] or invested their savings in the slave trade, sending money, arms, and trade goods to some convenient individual in Africa to "get up raids in their old homes or amongst neighboring tribes."[101] In Minas Geraes free black laborers came to own mines like Encardideira and Palacio Velho.[102] In Bahia they maintained their own regiment,[103] fraternal orders, and religious brotherhoods, each limited in membership exclusively to Negroes of pure African descent.[104] Many made sustained efforts to educate their children, and a few even had sons in the priesthood who, since the bishops of Brazil did not confer them, took their orders in São Thomé.[105]

But the free Negro, in competition with the European

[100] Walsh, a visitor to Brazil in the early nineteenth century, writes: "Next came an old free Negro woman, with a young slave of her own sex and color carrying her bundle. . . . . Her young slave was her only property, and she made a good livelihood by hiring her out as a beast of burden, to whoever wanted her, and for whatever purpose" (*op. cit.*, II, 18).

[101] Johnston, *op. cit.*, p. 90.

[102] Gilberto Freyre, *Sobrados e mucambos* (São Paulo, 1936), p. 73.

[103] "There are two of these regiments for the province of Pernambuco . . . . distinguished from each other by the names Old Henriques and New Henriques. . . . . I have seen some portion of one of these regiments, in Recife. . . . . They were dressed in white cloth uniforms, turned up with scarlet: and they looked very soldier-like. They were in tolerable discipline. . . . . They acted with an appearance of zeal and the desire of excelling. Those of which I speak formed a finer body of men than any other soldiers which I had an opportunity of seeing in that country. . . . . These men receive no pay, so that their neat appearance on such occasions bespeaks a certain degree of wealth among them" (Koster, *op. cit.*, II, 182–83).

[104] See, in this connection, *Compromisso da Irmandade do Senhor Bom Jesus das Necessidades e Redempção* (Bahia, 1929); Joventino Silvino da Costa, *Relatorio da Sociedade Protectora dos Desvalidos, 1832–1932* (Bahia, 1934).

[105] Affonso de E. Taunay, *Na Bahia de João VI* (Bahia, 1928), p. 173.

and his descendants, was faced with a difficult struggle. Even though he might cease to speak Nagô and to scarify his face and body; even though his wife might discard her distinctive African costume, and both no longer identify themselves with African fetish beliefs and practices but give instead allegiance to Catholic forms; nevertheless, the free Negro could not escape the fact that he was sharply differentiated from the ruling class in color, hair texture, and facial characteristics. He could not readily discard a highly visible badge of his former slave status. Wherever he went he would be known, if not for a slave, at least for the descendant of slaves.

The occupations of the free Negroes, or at least those of their immediate forebears, had been employments commensurate with servile status and had ordinarily consisted in hard, sordid, manual labor. The common saying, "Trabalho é para cachorro e negro" ("Work [i.e., hard manual labor] is for Negroes and dogs"), reflects this fact. To work with one's hands has been in Brazil long considered debasing for a white man. As Monteiro has said, "Even if in Portugal he had been a servant with a hoe in his hands, upon setting his foot upon Brazilian soil, he cared not to work."[106] That artisan labor was not a white man's job was long a tradition in Brazil.[107] To be a white was identical with being noble,[108] and "there was a common root of plebeian origin: it was African descent."[109] Government employ was for a long time

[106] Vahia Monteiro, quoted by F. J. Oliveira Vianna, *Evolução do povo brasileiro* (2d ed.; São Paulo, 1933), p. 153.

[107] Freyre, *op. cit.*, p. 105.

[108] Vianna, *Populações meridionaes do Brasil* (3d ed.; São Paulo, 1933), p. 139.

[109] "A côr significava nobreza; havia uma comum origem plebéia—o tronco africano" (Calmon, *op. cit.*, I, 24).

denied to the black.[110] In colonial Brazil marriage into upper-class white families was zealously restricted to individuals of pure European descent,[111] and at least one case is on record of an Indian being seriously rebuked for having married a Negro woman.[112]

[110] There was "a separate justice" in colonial Brazil for cases relating to "Indians, mulattoes, and Negroes" (Vianna, *Populações meridionaes do Brasil*, p. 140).

[111] "It was this preoccupation with purity of lineage and white blood in their prospective sons-in-law which, in those provinces whose development was more irregular, like that of Minas, made the problem of marriage so difficult. In Pernambuco and São Paulo the problem was resolved by marrying cousins with cousins: a custom which gradually made of the early families almost a single strain" (Freyre, *op. cit.*, p. 152).

[112] The eighth vice-*rei*, Marques de Lavradio, in an order dated August 6, 1771, removed an Indian from the post of *capitão-mor* for having married a Negro woman and, as the order said, "thus tarnished your blood and shown yourself unworthy of office" (Freyre, *Casa grande e senzala* [2d ed.; Rio, 1936], p. 290).

CHAPTER III

CASA GRANDE AND *SENZALA*[1]

EVEN as late as the second quarter of the nineteenth century a visitor to Brazil wrote: "Again and again, while travelling in the interior, I have seen troops of new slaves of both sexes, who could not speak a single word of Portuguese, varying from twenty to one hundred individuals, marched inland for sale, or already belonging to proprietors of plantations."[2] These newly imported Africans were known as *negros novos*, or "new Negroes."[3]

Since the major portion of African importations into Bahia came from contiguous territory in Africa, the Negroes ordinarily brought with them closely related dialects and, consequently, could more easily communicate among themselves in African tongues. Gradually there came into general use, especially among the influential semi-independent *negros de ganho*, an African language known as Nagô,[4] which by facilitating intercommunication intensified the Negroes' moral isolation from the white world and retarded the whole acculturation process. Nagô continued for a long time to

---

[1] The "Big House" and the "slave quarters."

[2] George Gardner, *Travels in the Interior of Brazil, 1836–1841* (London, 1849), p. 12.

[3] Nina Rodrigues, *Os africanos no Brasil* (São Paulo, 1932), p. 187.

[4] "Like the French, we in Bahia call Nagôs all Negroes from the Slave Coast who speak the Yoruba language. Of this group we have received slaves from all the smaller subdivisions, from Oyó the capital of Yoruba, from Ilorin, Ige-sha, Ibadan, Ifé, Iebú, Egba, Lagos, etc." (*ibid.*, p. 157).

be the *lingua geral*, or general Negro language.[5] The ritual
of the more important fetish-cult centers was, and still is,
carried on in this language. Inscriptions in Nagô were occasionally to be seen not only on cult buildings but also in small commercial establishments owned and operated by Negroes, like the meat stall on the Baixa dos
Sapateiros over whose entrance Nina Rodrigues in 1895
noted the inscription "Kosi oba Kan afi Olorun."[6] So important did Nagô become, and so widespread its use that,
although Nina Rodrigues early in the twentieth century
estimated that there were only approximately five hundred
Africans still living in the city and they were at that time
dying at the rate of a hundred and fifty to two hundred a
year,[7] one still today, more than three decades later, finds

[5] Nina Rodrigues, intimately acquainted for many years with Bahian
Negroes, commends the accuracy of the Visconde de Porto Seguro when he
says, "The best known Negroes in Brazil were those coming from the *Costa
da Mina*, whence arrived the greater portion of those imported into Bahia;
so that in this city many slaves learned little Portuguese but instead com-
municated among themselves in Nagô." About 1900 he himself wrote:
"The Nagô dialect is commonly spoken in Bahia by almost all the old Africans from the various tribes and by a great number of creoles and mulattoes"
(*op. cit.*, p. 197).

[6] Rodrigues translates the phrase: "There is no God but Olorun" (principal deity of the Nagô cult). A photograph of the entrance to the shop
showing this inscription may be found in *ibid.*, opp. p. 202.

[7] *Ibid.*, p. 154. In the seven years from 1896 to 1902, 1,282 Africans died
at Bahia. The distribution was as follows:

Year	Total	Male	Female
1896	110	55	55
1897	258	156	102
1898	200	96	104
1899	209	110	99
1900	151	87	64
1901	152	74	78
1902	202	136	66
Total	1,282	714	568

Nagô at times spoken in Bahia and an occasional individual whose command of this language is comparable to his command of Portuguese.

The nature of Negro settlement at Bahia favored to a considerable extent the preservation of African cultural forms. Tribal units were not deliberately broken up, as in Jamaica and the United States, and the Negro was thereby able to preserve and to transmit to his children a considerable portion of his African heritage. Even on the plantations the distribution of newly imported Africans among the old-established Negroes seems not to have occurred.[8] The concentration in the city of Bahia over a long period of time of large numbers of semi-independent *negros de ganho*, around whom there gradually accumulated a considerable number of relatively unassimilated free Negroes, also favored the persistence of African cultural elements.

It is likely that Nagô was not maintained in a pure form but came to be a patois containing numerous elements from other African dialects as well as from Portuguese. A Catholic missionary, Padre Coquard, visiting Bahia in 1899 to solicit funds, spoke to the colored population in Nagô. But the sermon, preached in the ancient church of Sé, was wholly ineffective.[9]

Other African languages were spoken in Bahia.[10] Rodrigues believed that Gêge (or Ewe) was used throughout the eighteenth century and until at least the middle of the nine-

[8] Henry Koster, *Travels in Brazil, 1809 to 1815* (2 vols.; Philadelphia, 1817), I, 229 n.

[9] Rodrigues, *op. cit.*, pp. 200–201. Perhaps another reason for this ineffectiveness was that the Negroes who were most able to understand Nagô were unassimilated Africans who, out of loyalty to the religion of their fathers, deliberately absented themselves from this ceremony of the Catholic church.

[10] *Ibid.*, pp. 197–230.

teenth. Tapa and Haussá were spoken during the entire nineteenth century, and the latter perhaps long before 1800. Although the Haussás were relatively few in number, their influence was considerable. The slave revolts of the early nineteenth century were, as we have seen, led by this reputedly "most intellectual element" among the imported Africans, many of whom could read and write Arabic characters. Kanúri, spoken in Bahia by the Bornús, and Grúnce, the tongue used by the slaves known as Gallinhas, are included, along with Haussá, Gêge, and Tapa, in the limited vocabularies which Rodrigues collected from Bahian Negroes near the beginning of the twentieth century.[11] Tshi (or Odji), Gá (or Acrá),[12] and Mandê (or Mandinga) were also employed to a limited extent.

As late as 1900, Negro laborers in Bahia continued to wear "white vestments of coarse cotton cloth," which reminded Rodrigues of "the Nagô *camisús.*"[13] The *Bahiana* costume,[14] of partial African origin, was extensively used by the Negro women. It was also customary for them to carry their babies bound to the back with a large cloth. African dishes, in the preparation of which *azeite de dendê* (oil of the *dendê* palm) and *pimenta da costa* (pepper from the West Coast) prominently figured, formed a considerable portion of the Negro diet.

At that time, also, African music might be frequently heard, particularly in the ceremonies of the *candomblé.* African musical instruments, like the *atabaque,* the *agê,* the *canzá,* the *marimba,* the *agôgô,* the *caxixi,* and the *xáque-xáque*[15] were commonly employed. The fetish cult drew alle-

---

[11] *Ibid.,* pp. 217–21.

[12] Spoken in Bahia by the Ashantis.   [13] *Op. cit.,* p. 181.

[14] The *Bahiana* costume is described in detail in chap. ix.

[15] These instruments are described in chap. ix.

giance from numerous and zealous devotees. African dances
still invaded the popular festivals of the Europeans to such
an extent that vigorous protests on the part of the white
citizenry appeared in the newspapers.[16] Numerous images
employed in the fetish worship were imported from Africa,
and others were made by Negro sculptors in Bahia.

One occasionally encountered Negroes who in Africa had
been chiefs or other dignitaries of considerable power and influence. Although in Brazil they shared the fortunes of a
slave with their former subjects, they nevertheless often received allegiance and great reverence from them. On a
chance meeting in the street these personages were, we are
told, "saluted respectfully, their hands kissed, and a blessing requested of them." Even their masters were reported
to have paid them, in several cases, considerable respect.

Slaves who were in close contact with their masters,
especially the house servants, soon became, by the very
necessities of the situation, at least to some extent bilingual.
And their offspring, reared in close contact with the children
of their masters, acquired little, if any, African vocabulary and came almost exclusively to speak Portuguese. Thus,
about 1800, Koster wrote from Pernambuco, "Portuguese

[16] In the *Jornal de Noticias* for February 12, 1901, a white citizen wrote:
"I wish to protest against the way in which this great civilized festival
[Carnival] is being Africanized." Three days later the following was published: "These infamous Africanized groups *de canzás* and *buzios* which, far
from adding to the brilliance of our Carnival festival, bring shame upon the
name of Bahia . . . . have since yesterday been keeping up their infernal
tumult." Immediately preceding the opening of Carnival the following year
there appeared in the *Jornal de Noticias* (February 5, 1902) the following
note: "If during these former Carnival festivals when the popular enthusiasm
has been greatly aroused by the passage of the victorious floats . . . . these
groups of *Africanos* have been repugnant, what will the Carnival of 1902 turn
out to be, unless the police take effective measures to prevent our streets from
looking like *terreiros* where fetish practices reign amid a retinue of *ogans* and
their *canzás* and tambourines?" (Rodrigues, *op. cit.*, pp. 236–38).

.... is spoken by all the slaves; and their own dialects are allowed to lie dormant until they are by many .... quite forgotten."[17] With the acquisition of the master's language went quite naturally other European habits and customs, and the group of assimilated Negroes, known as *ladinos*, grew in numbers relatively rapidly.

Although the hardships incidental to a plantation system continued, the circumstances under which this gradual assimilation went on were ordinarily those imposed by a mild form of slavery in which the natural and continuous growth of intimate personal relations tended to further humanize the institution and to modify its formal and legal character to such an extent that the widely traveled Richard Burton, enamored as he was of the customs of the East, could in the middle of the nineteenth century say, "Nowhere, even in oriental countries, has the 'bitter draught' so little of gall in it."[18]

Symbolic of the intimate character of these personal relations is a custom recorded in detail and with some sense of the humor of the situation by the able French artist Debret.[19] The head of a Brazilian household is depicted setting out with his family, all in gala attire, for a customary Sunday promenade. The entire group is in single file, the two

[17] *Op. cit.*, p. 200.

[18] Sir Richard F. Burton, *Explorations of the Highlands of the Brazil* (2 vols.; London, 1869), I, 270.

[19] Invited to Brazil at the request of the Brazilian emperor, Debret subsequently published three volumes of drawings and comment which together furnish a highly illuminating record of the life of Rio de Janeiro in the early part of the nineteenth century (see J. B. Debret, *Voyage pittoresque et historique au Brésil, 1816–1831* [3 vols.; Paris, 1835]). A similar record was made by another competent artist, Maurice Rugendas. See his *Voyage pittoresque dans le Brésil*, trans. from the German by de Colbery (3 vols.; Paris, 1835).

From a painting by J. B. Debret

A BRAZILIAN FAMILY OF THE EARLY NINETEENTH CENTURY

daughters immediately behind the father, then the mother, followed by her mulatto *femme de chambre*, next the family *ama*, or Negro nurse, and the latter's female assistant, then the father's Negro body servant, and last a young slave in training for domestic service.[20] On such occasions it was a matter of considerable pride to dress the slaves as well as the family's station would permit. As late as 1852 a visitor to Rio recorded:

Though less generally the custom than formerly, it is still the habit of some of the *bourgeosie* . . . . at least on Sundays and great holidays, to promenade to and from church, by whole families, parents and children, from adults to infants, with a retinue of servants in their best dresses . . . . bringing up the rear, and, whether male or female, ... usually as elaborately, if not as expensively, dressed as the rest of the family; and often, in the case of the women, with an equal display of laces, muslins, and showy jewelry.[21]

In the cities domestic slaves ordinarily lived in the same houses as their masters, occupying the lower floor; or, where the buildings were only of one story, "a sort of cellar" underneath.[22] Since the mistress of the household and her daughters lived a very secluded life in the interior of the home,[23] they were in almost constant contact with domestic slaves and the slave's children. Debret has sketched[24] one such intimate scene in which two Negro women are at work,

[20] *Ibid.*, Vol. II, Pl. 5 ("Un Employé du gouvernement sortant de chez lui avec sa famille").

[21] C. S. Stewart, *Brazil and La Plata* (New York, 1856), p. 295.

[22] Maria Graham, *Journal of a Voyage to Brazil, 1821–1823* (London, 1824), p. 145.

[23] Until recent years, women from the upper classes in Bahia were rarely seen on the public thoroughfares and then only in the company of a male escort.

[24] Debret, *op. cit.*, Vol. II, Pl. 6 ("Une dame brésilienne dans son intérieur") and p. 33.

seated on the floor at the feet of their mistress and her
daughter, while two little Negro babies play near by.[25] Koster wrote of an estate near Recife that the "Great House"
was full of young Negro children. "They were quite naked,
and played with each other, and with some large dogs which
were lying at full length upon the floor. These ebon cupids
were plainly great favorites, and seemed to employ the
greater part of the thoughts of the good ladies, the youngest
of whom was on the other side of fifty; and even the priest
laughed at their gambols."[26] Visiting in the interior of Rio
de Janeiro province in 1823, Maria Graham noted that "the
female in-door slaves . . . . have been mostly . . . . brought
up in their mistress' house." She saw "children of all ages
and colors running about, who seemed to be as tenderly
treated as if they had been of the family," and commented
that, under these conditions, slavery was "more like that
of the patriarchal times, where the purchased servant became to all intents one of the family."[27] "How many times,"
writes Lacerda, "have we not seen masters who did not hesitate to bring their little mulatto slaves to the family
table?"[28] Relations within these households became so intimate that, as sometimes also occurred in our South, white
women took to their breasts colored babies whose mothers
had died in childbirth.[29]

In the home, on the plantation, along the roads of the

[25] Debret writes (*ibid.*, p. 39): "A Rio de Janeiro et dans toutes les autres
villes du Brésil, il est d'usage, pendant le tête-à-tête d'un *diner marital*, que
le mari s'occupe silencieusement de ses affaires, et que la *femme* s'amuse de
ses *petits* négrillons, qui remplacent la famille presque éteinte des petits chiens
carlins en Europe."

[26] *Op. cit.*, pp. 258–59.   [27] *Op. cit.*, pp. 279–80.

[28] Jean Baptiste de Lacerda, "The *Metis*, or Half-breeds, of Brazil,"
Papers on Inter-racial Problems, ed. G. Spiller (London, 1911), p. 379.

[29] Gilberto Freyre, *Casa grande e senzala* (2d ed.; Rio, 1936), p. 327.

From a painting by J. B. Debret

A DOMESTIC SCENE IN COLONIAL BRAZIL

rural areas, or in the streets of the cities, on the hunt, at parties, or at church, black and white were constantly to be seen in each other's company. And since human beings, wherever they come into close and uninterrupted contact upon an intimate personal basis, sooner or later tend to lay personal claims upon one another, it is not surprising to find that ties of enduring sentiment arose, which tended gradually to break down the formal barriers between the races and to modify the nature of slavery.

It is, of course, probably true that the Mohammedan conception of the slave exercised considerable influence over the original form of African slavery in Portugal itself. The Arabian prophet, it is said, while unable to do away with an ancient institution, "did his utmost to soften the rigors of slavery." After conceding to his importuning followers that "God hath ordained" the slave institution, Mohammed added: "Therefore, him whom God hath ordained to be the slave of his brother, his brother must give him of the food which he eateth himself, and of the clothes wherewith he clotheth himself, and not order him to do anything beyond his power. . . . . A man who ill-treats his slave will not enter into Paradise." Thus

there is no more commendable action in Mohammedan morals than to free slaves, and such enfranchisement is enjoined by the Prophet especially as an atonement for an undeserved blow or other injustice. In Andalusia, the slaves upon the estates that had passed . . . . into the possession of Moslems were almost in the position of small farmers; their Mohammedan masters, whose trade was war, and who despised heartily such menial occupations as tilling the soil, left them free to cultivate the land as they pleased, and only insisted on a fair return of products.[30]

[30] Stanley Lane-Poole, *The Story of the Moors in Spain* (New York and London, 1886), p. 48. Cf. also: "The Mohammedan slave was rarely

Mild though its original form may have been, slavery in Brazil was not, as we have already seen, without at least occasional evidences of brutality. The fact is that slavery in Brazil was *both* mild *and* severe. But as an institution continuing over centuries it became more and more mild. Cases of brutality ordinarily occurred under conditions of absentee ownership or in fear of slave insurrection, or arose in dealing with recalcitrant and unsubjected individuals, many of them at the hands of mixed-blood or Negro overseers who in this way unconsciously compensated for otherwise limited social effectiveness.[31] Moreover, the relatively few cases which did occur were so ably used by such prominent political and intellectual leaders as Ruy Barbosa and Joaquim Nabuco that they have probably left behind in the Brazilian mind of today an exaggerated notion of the cruelties of slavery. The important point to note is that, under circumstances of intimate, personal contact, the institution of slavery, with its occasional cases of harsh treatment, gradually lost its character as a political, and assumed that of a patriarchal and familial, institution.

Obviously, there is inherent in slavery an economic consideration which has little regard for the interests of the slave himself. But wherever human beings live together in close proximity for any period of time there also tend to grow up *personal relations* which humanize whatever formal institutions have been set up. The opportunities in Brazil

---

abused. . . . . His acceptance of the faith of Islam rendered his manumission easy. No stigma attached to his (subsequent) condition" (S. P. Scott, *History of the Moorish Empire in Europe* [Philadelphia, 1904], p. 660.

[31] Koster, reflecting over the fact that mulattoes, especially those who had formerly been slaves, "make bad masters," concluded that "the change of situation would lead to the same consequences in any race of human beings" (*op. cit.*, II, 177–78).

for these relations to develop, particularly in the case of
domestic servants, were extensive. Cooper states a fact long
characteristic of the upper classes in Brazil when he says:
"As in the East, the houses are . . . . filled with . . . . servants, and these servants partake of the character of their
Eastern prototypes in their . . . . willingness to perform the
many small and menial acts of personal service which the
Brazilian requires, but which would hardly be expected of
servants in the United States."[32]

Symbolic of the intimate nature of these relations was the
common form of etiquette which grew up and became customary between Brazilian master and slave. It is said to
have been a practice observed in all well-regulated families
that slaves, "of both sexes and of every age," requested
each morning and evening a blessing from their master. According to Stewart, the words used in the middle of the
nineteenth century were, "I beseech your blessing [or
"Grant me a blessing"], in the name of our Lord and Savior
Jesus Christ!" To which the master replied, "Jesus Christ
bless you forever!"[33] As João Ribeiro has aptly said, "Agru-
pavam-se em familias, senão no sentido da lei, ao menos da
religião."[34]

Debret, who spent several months at Rio in the early part
of the same century, says[35] that it was there customary for

[32] Clayton S. Cooper, *The Brazilians and Their Country* (New York, 1917),
pp. 61–62. Cf. also Gilberto Freyre, "Social Life in Brazil in the Middle of the
Nineteenth Century," *Hispanic American Historical Review*, V, No. 4 (November, 1922), 607.

[33] *Op. cit.*, p. 408.

[34] "They were united into families, if not by law, at least by religion."

[35] *Op. cit.*, III, 130. Cf. also the account of Maria Graham regarding a
fazenda in the province of Rio de Janeiro: "I attended the weekly muster of
all the Negroes of the *fazenda;* clean shirts and trousers were given to the

slaves, on repeating the evening Ave Maria, to present themselves before the master with a "Boa noite, meu senhor,"[36] in reply to which, as a sign of approbation, the master made a simple movement of the head. It was also customary for a Negro who by chance met a white acquaintance on a public thoroughfare to bow his head, extend his right hand, half-opened, and to request a blessing, to which the white replied, "Deus te faça santo,"[37] or simply "Viva!"

These forms of etiquette, together with their religious implications, although they became in time highly conventionalized and occasionally were reduced to "the shortest possible abbreviation" and repeated with "all manner of intonations of voice and every mood of humor,"[38] still symbolized the recognition on the part of the master of a common human bond with his slaves. "I can call to mind," writes Codman, "many touching incidents of the kind feelings of masters and servants towards each other."[39]

Relationships of this character were undoubtedly advantageous to the Negro, not only during his period of subjection as a slave but also after his enfranchisement. Koster says of Brazilian neighbors in Pernambuco who possessed a considerable number of slaves:

These excellent women and the good priest [intend] eventually to emancipate all of them; and that they may be prepared for the change, several of the men have been brought up as mechanics of different

men, and shifts and shirts to the women, of very coarse white cotton. Each, as he or she came in, kissed a hand, and then bowed to Mr. P. saying either, 'Father, give me blessing,' or 'The names of Jesus and Mary be praised!' and were answered accordingly, either 'Bless you,' or 'Be they praised!' This is the custom in old establishments: it is repeated morning and evening, and seems to acknowledge a kind of relationship between master and slave" (*op. cit.*, p. 196).

[36] "Good night, my master."
[37] "God make thee a saint."   [38] Stewart, *op. cit.*, p. 408.
[39] John Codman, *Ten Months in Brazil* (Boston, 1867), p. 201.

descriptions; and the women have been taught needle-work, embroidery, and all branches of culinary knowledge.[40]

In 1822 an observer in Rio noted:

When the Emperor had received the public bodies, he came and led the Empress into the great receiving room, and there, both of them standing on the upper step of the throne, had their hands kissed by naval, military and civil officers, and private citizens. . . . . It was curious, but it pleased me, to see some Negro officers take the small white hand of the Empress in their clumsy black hands, and apply their pouting African lips to so delicate a skin; but they looked up to *Nosso Imperador* (Our Emperor), and to her, with a reverence that seemed to me a promise of faith *from* them, a bond of kindness *to* them.[41]

"There is evidently," commented another visitor, "a sincere wish to make the liberated slave a useful citizen, if possible."[42]

Custom came gradually to grant the slave, as Burton has pointed out, many of the rights of a freeman:

He may educate himself, and he is urged to do so. He is regularly catechised, and in all large plantations there is a daily religious service. If assailed in life or limb he may defend himself against his master, or any white man, and an over-harsh proprietor or overseer always runs considerable risk of not dying in bed. He is legally married, and the chastity of his wife is defended against his owner. He has little fear of being separated from his family: the humane instincts and the religious tenets of the people are strongly opposed to this act of barbarity. He has every chance of becoming a free man: manumission is held to be a Catholic duty and priestly communities are ashamed of holding slaves. . . . .[43]

[40] *Op. cit.*, I, 258: "The owners said that all their own immediate relations were rich; . . . . and that therefore these their children had no right to work for any one else."

[41] Graham, *op. cit.*, p. 319.   [42] Codman, *op. cit.*, p. 203.

[43] *Op. cit.*, pp. 271–72. Some cases undoubtedly occurred in which the master refused to manumit a slave upon his presenting the cost price, but these were probably rare. Koster (*op. cit.*, I, 192–94) says that, although

The two days in seven which according to custom the master allotted the slave for the cultivation of a plot of land[44] was as early as 1700 sanctioned in law.[45] His right in property could be transferred to his children.[46] He could

"a great deal depends upon the inclinations of the master, he will, however, be very careful in refusing to manumit, owing to the well-known opinion of every priest in favor of this regulation, to the feelings of the individuals of his own class in society, and to those of the lower orders of people; and likewise he will be afraid of losing his slave. He may escape with his money; and the master will then run much risk of never seeing him again, particularly if the individual is a creole slave. . . . . The master might indeed deprive the slave of the fruits of his labor, but this is never thought of; because the slave preserves his money in a secret place, or he has entrusted it to some person upon whom he can depend, and would suffer any punishment rather than disclose the spot in which his wealth lies concealed."

[44] "This day [Sunday] . . . . is the Negroes' own; after morning mass they are free to do their own will; and then most of them run to the hill to gather their coffee or maize, or prepare the ground for these or vegetables. They were just beginning to return from the wood, each with his . . . . basket laden with something of his own, something in which the master had no share; and again and again as they passed me, and displayed with glistening eye the little treasure, I blessed the Sabbath, the day of freedom to the slave" (Graham, *op. cit.*, p. 288).

[45] João Ribeiro, *Historia do Brasil* (3d rev. ed.; Rio, 1909), p. 255.

[46] However, if the slave died childless, his property reverted to the master. Note the following account given by Maria Graham regarding a slave on an estate in the province of Rio: "He was a mulatto boatman, the most trusty servant on the estate, and rich, because he is industrious enough to have earned a good deal of private property, besides doing his duty to his master. In his youth, and he is not now old, he had become attached to a creole woman, born, like him on the estate; but he did not marry her until he had earned money enough to purchase her, in order that their children, if they had any, might be born free. Since that time, he has become rich enough to purchase himself, even at the high price which such a slave might fetch; but his master will not sell him his freedom, his services being too valuable to lose, notwithstanding his promise to remain on the estate and work. Unfortunately, these people have no children; therefore on their death their property, now considerable, will revert to the master" (*op. cit.*, pp. 197–98).

take his master's name.[47] Slaves who desired to change masters had the right to request transfer, and the master was expected to acquiesce.[48] Intercession in behalf of a fugitive slave, or even of one about to be punished for some other offense, is said seldom to have been in vain.[49] The master guilty of inhuman treatment toward his slave was liable to the police or tribunals.[50] Some masters preferred to have

[47] Ribeiro, *op. cit.*, p. 256; cf. also Freyre, *op. cit.*, p. 327: "Hence, the many Cavalcantis, Albuquerques, Mellos, Mouras, Wanderleys, Lins, Carneiro Leãos, etc., who possess none of the illustrious blood which their names imply."

[48] Ribeiro, *op. cit.*, p. 256. Koster (*op. cit.*, I, 194) records that "for this purpose a note is given, declaring that the bearer has leave to enter into the service of any one, upon the price which the master demands being paid by the purchaser. With this the slave applies to any individual or property whom he may wish to serve; owing to having heard a good report of his character toward his slaves, or from any other cause. This is a frequent practice." The following interesting case was observed: "A Negro woman applied to a planter to be purchased; for which purpose she had brought a note from her master. She was accepted; and a bargain was concluded between the two persons. However, the day after she had taken up her abode upon the estate of her new master, she came to him, and falling down upon her knees, said that she had a fellow-slave who wished likewise to serve him; and she begged him to purchase her companion. The new master spoke to the owner of the slave in question of the subject; but he refused to sell him, and the matter rested in this manner. But on the third day, he received a visit from the owner, offering the slave for sale, adding, that the man had refused to work, and had threatened to hang himself; and as he was a Gabão Negro (noted for the resolute manner which, on occasion, they committed suicide), he much feared that he might put his threat into execution. The price was soon fixed, and on the following morning the man made his appearance. He proved to be a most excellent slave" (*ibid.*, p. 203 n.).

[49] Codman, *op. cit.*, p. 201. Cf. also: "Costumes belissimos instituem-se entre os senhores; como o de *apadrinhar* os remissos ou fugitivos, o que impede o castigo, e nunhum senhor viola" (Ribeiro, *op. cit.*, p. 255).

[50] J. B. von Spix and C. F. von Martius, *Travels in Brazil, 1817–1820*, trans. H. E. Lloyd (2 vols.; London, 1824), I, 179.

their slaves, on the payment of a small sum, punished by
the civil authorities.[51] Gardner remarked that "many of the
crimes for which only a few lashes are awarded, are of such
a nature that in England would bring upon the perpetrator
either death or transportation."[52]

It was customary each week to grant slaves, in addition
to their regular food, an allowance of tobacco.[53] On the large
estates certain hospital facilities,[54] and nurseries for Negro
children were maintained.[55] Accounts of white mistresses
who themselves attended to the sick among their slaves are
numerous.[56] The *amas* (nurses) were often "emancipated as
soon as their work was over, and nearly always continued to
live in freedom under the same roof with their masters and
to have various privileges."[57] "The aged Negroes were only
employed in light occupations; during the remainder of their
time they chatted with the master's young children, telling

[51] Gardner, *op. cit.*, p. 14.

[52] *Ibid.*

[53] Prince Adalbert, *Travels of Prince Adalbert of Prussia*, trans. from *Aus
meinem Tagebuche, 1842–1843* (Berlin, 1847), by Robert H. Schomburgk
and John Edward Taylor (2 vols.; London, 1849), II, 37. Prince Adalbert
noted on the coffee plantation Aldea, near Novo Friburgo, that "every evening, when their work is done, the slaves light fires in the rooms set apart for
them, around which they sit for hours, even after the severest day's work, all
talking and smoking, women as well as men."

[54] *Ibid.*, p. 36. "In the hospital, the hall and rooms for the two sexes
were separated. A Negro woman was lying on a mat, with her little "negrinho' at her breast, to which she had given birth only the night before. 'In
a few days she will be able to resume work,' said the Doctor to Count Bis-
marck. In the men's room, there were four or five patients, suffering from
accidents of various kinds" (coffee plantation Aldea, near Novo Friburgo).

[55] C. C. Andrews, *Brazil, Its Condition and Prospects* (2d ed.; New York,
1889), p. 164.

[56] Note, e.g., Gardner, *op. cit.*, p. 14.

[57] Lacerda, *op. cit.*, p. 379.

them odd stories which were calculated to strike their imagination."[58]

Public opinion expected of masters the acceptance of an offer made to manumit an infant on the occasion of his baptism.[59] It also became customary, when marriages were being solemnized in the master's family, to free one or two favorite slaves.[60] Masters frequently declined the money proffered by a Negro for his purchase and granted his freedom without payment.[61] Slaves of the religious orders, it is said, considered themselves to belong to the saints themselves and were never sold.[62] The law adopted in 1809 to protect the property of sugar planters against attachment for debt also provided that slaves need not be sold separately from an estate to satisfy a creditor's claims. Thus the master could not be forced to dispose of his slaves, unless the debt amounted to the value of the entire estate; and, as Koster has pointed out,[63] the slave in this way was advanced, in some degree at least, toward the condition of a serf.

[58] *Ibid.*

[59] "Another custom which was advantageous to the slave was that of *alforrias na pia*, which was accomplished with the insignificant amount of 5 to 50 milreis and never was refused; this custom became very common, especially when the child had a light skin" (Ribeiro, *op. cit.*, p. 255). Koster gives the price in Pernambuco early in the nineteenth century as £5 and says that "in this manner, a considerable number of persons are set at liberty; for the smallness of the price enables many freemen who have had connections with female slaves to manumit their offspring; and instances occur of the sponsors performing this . . . . act. Not infrequently female slaves apply to persons of consideration to become sponsors to their children, in the hope that the pride of these will be too great to allow of their godchildren remaining in slavery" (*op. cit.*, I, 195–96).

[60] Frank Bennett, *Forty Years in Brazil* (London, 1914), p. 111.

[61] Ribeiro, *op. cit.*, p. 256.   [62] *Ibid.*   [63] *Op. cit.*, I, 229 n.

In the light of these customs which gradually grew up and
ameliorated the lot of the bondsman, it is not surprising that
neither Brazil nor the mother-country ever felt it necessary
to adopt a "Black Code." The Englishman Dent says "I had
certainly opportunity of seeing something of the treatment
of slaves, being thirteen months in the country; but I never
came across any other than considerate kindness from master to slave, sometimes even far greater benevolence and
consideration than is exercised towards servants in our own
country."[64] Dent mentions an old Negro woman who "had
received her liberty sometime ago, but seemed to be much
attached to the family and never to have thought of leaving
them."[65] Numerous other visitors to Brazil remark that the
slaves appeared to be treated with kindness, to be well cared
for, and happy. In 1821 Mathison noted that Negroes on an
estate near Rio "showed by their cheerful looks and bodily
condition that they were well taken care of."[66] "He who has
had occasion to observe the happy songs and dances that are
sung and danced after sunset by great groups of Negroes in
the streets of Bahia," wrote the German scientists, Spix and
Martius, "can with difficulty be convinced that these are the
same slaves which one had thought, according to the exaggerated accounts of certain writers, had been pulled down to
an animal existence."[67]

[64] Hastings Charles Dent, *A Year in Brazil* (London, 1886), p. 285. Compare the remarks of another English traveler, Bennett (*op. cit.*, p. 10): "I
want to say that, although some slaves may have been (and undoubtedly
were) badly treated, a great many of them were better off than some free-
born people here in England in the present day."

[65] *Op. cit.*, p. 120.

[66] Gilbert Farquhar Mathison, *Narrative of a Visit to Brazil, Chile, Peru,
and the Sandwich Islands, 1821–1822* (London, 1825), pp. 93, 121.

[67] Spix and Martius, *op. cit.*, p. 90.

Wells, journeying three thousand miles through the interior of Brazil a few years before abolition, thought that "many a poor laborer at home [in the United States] would enjoy their lot."[68] Gardner, who during five years' residence "saw more than has fallen to the lot of most Europeans," said:

I have conversed with Negroes in all parts of the country, and have met with but very few who expressed any regret at having been taken from their own country, or a desire to return to it. On some of the large estates at which I have resided for short periods, the number of slaves often amounted to three or four hundred, and but for my previous knowledge of their being such, I could never have found out from my own observations that they were slaves. I saw . . . . contented and well-conditioned laborers turning out from their little huts, often surrounded by a small garden, and proceeding to their respective daily occupations, from which they returned in the evening anything but broken and bent down with the severity of their tasks.[69]

Codman wrote:

It is the result of my observation, and I believe that of every one who has investigated the subject, that the Brazilians are generally kind and indulgent masters, treating their slaves with much greater leniency than has been practised by any other people among whom the "institution" has existed in modern times.[70]

[68] James W. Wells, *Three Thousand Miles through Brazil* (2 vols.; Philadelphia, 1886), II, 187.

[69] *Op. cit.*, p. 14.

[70] *Op. cit.*, p. 201. Absentee ownership, however, occasionally resulted, as on the estate of Prince Dom Rodrigo visited by Mawe, in a "system of management . . . . so bad that the slaves are half starved, almost destitute of clothing, and most miserably lodged" (John Mawe, *Travels in the Interior of Brazil* [Philadelphia, 1816], p. 115). Note also Mathison, *op. cit.*, p. 114. Nor is it to be supposed that the field hands always fared as well as the house servants. Compare the conclusion of Stewart (*op. cit.*, p. 296): "House servants in Rio [1852] are said to have easy times, and to do very much as they please; but to judge from the incidents I have seen of field laborers, I fear such have but a sad and wearisome life."

The "wide spread of gentle manners in Brazil,"[71] which impressed some commentators as contributing to the favored treatment of Brazilian slaves, was an integral part of a social order in which the large family was the principal unit of cohesion. Under such conditions the network of personal relations arising out of the intimate contact of master and slave not only tempered but, over a period of time, tended to destroy the formal barriers between them. "The Negro is everywhere among the Brazilians," wrote Codman, "and they understand him thoroughly."[72]

It was usually among the newly arrived Africans, the field hands, or those blacks like the semi-independent *negros de ganho*, all of whom were not in intimate contact with the whites, that escapes and insurrections occurred. Some of these Negroes at times affected scorn and contempt of whites.[73] But those who were in close contact with the Europeans over a period of time developed sentiments of "belonging together," of loyalty and affection. Under such cir-

[71] "One afternoon I sat in a street car of the Copacabana line running to and from the heart of Rio de Janeiro city. As we approached the Avenida and paused at a sharp turn at the regulator's signal, a small boy poorly clad in cotton clothes got onto the front platform with a dinner pail in his hand. He set it down, removed his cap, bent his knee as the motorman, with a swift smile at the child, extended his right hand. The boy respectfully kissed it, replaced his cap, and jumped down. The little incident was typical of the wide spread of gentle manners in Brazil; it is here usual enough to see elderly bankers kiss the hands of their parents, but courtesy is not confined to the upper classes. . . . . Brazilian men meeting each other in the street a dozen times a day, lift their hats every time to each other" (L. E. Elliott, *Brazil, Today and Tomorrow* [New York, 1917], p. 76).

[72] *Op. cit.*, p. 202.

[73] Bennett (*op. cit.*, p. 9) mentions the following incident from Pernambuco: "One evening when we were walking along the Rua Nova, a black woman who was passing us suddenly drew aside with a lofty air, exclaiming: 'O meu Deus, os brancos perto de mim!' (Oh, my God, whites near me!)"

cumstances they gradually lost their African customs and traditions and took over more and more European ideas, attitudes, and points of view.

This loyalty and devotion, as well as even deeds of heroism, on the part of Negro slaves quite naturally evoked corresponding sentiments of appreciation and affection in masters and their children. Mrs. Louis Agassiz, visiting, together with her husband, the Academy of Fine Arts in Rio in 1865, noted with particular interest the portrait of a Negro

who, in a shipwreck off the coast, had saved a number of lives at the risk of his own. When he had brought several passengers to the shore, he was told that two children still remained in the ship. He swam back once more and brought them safely to the beach, but then sank down exhausted, and was seized with a hemorrhage. A considerable sum was raised for him in the city of Rio, and his picture was placed in the Academy to commemorate his heroism.[74]

There hangs today in the Pinacotheca at Bahia a famous painting of the *māe preta*, or "black mother." "We children," recently remarked a prominent Bahian banker, "respected our *māe preta* as much as, or perhaps even more than, we did our own parents. I'm sure we feared her more and obeyed her more readily."

Henrique Dias, a Pernambucan slave, materially and somewhat spectacularly aided the Portuguese when they were engaged, during the seventeenth century, in driving the Dutch out of Pernambuco. Captured, he was shortly released, the Dutch thinking that "because he was a Negro slave he wasn't worth the cost of feeding." He returned to fight effectively for the Portuguese and was once wounded in battle. Following the expulsion of the Dutch, he was given many honors, commissioned in the local militia, and put in

[74] Professor and Mrs. Louis Agassiz, *A Journey in Brazil* (Boston and New York, 1888), p. 478.

command of a Negro regiment. As a Bahian *preto* recently remarked with pride, "His contribution to his country was an honored one."

Negros novos were required by law to be baptized into the Christian religion on penalty of forfeiture to the state. Those from Portuguese Angola were baptized in lots before they left their native shores.[75] The mark of the royal crown upon their breasts signified that they had undergone this ceremony and also that the king's duty had been paid. With slaves from other parts of Africa, the master was allowed a year for the instruction requisite for baptism.[76] Debret noted that elderly Negroes acquainted with African languages were often used to catechise the candidates, ordinarily the oldest and "most virtuous" slaves being chosen for this purpose.[77] One of the first things taught was the threefold sign of the cross accompanied by the words, "The sign of the cross delivers us from our enemies." Slaves were not considered, we are told, "members of society, but rather brute animals," until they could "lawfully go to mass, confess their sins, and receive the sacrament."[78] Participation in these ceremonies made them fellow human beings.

On the plantations slaves were regularly instructed in Catholic ritual and belief, chaplains often being retained on the larger estates for this purpose as well as to conduct the public religious ceremonies in the chapel attached to the plantation. Mawe, visiting the estate of Prince Dom Rodrigo near Rio in the early years of the nineteenth century, noted that it was customary "to have prayers publicly read

[75] Koster, *op. cit.*, I, 198.

[76] Koster (*ibid.*) writes that "the law is not always strictly adhered to as to time, but it is never evaded altogether."

[77] *Op. cit.*, III, 129.   [78] Koster, *op. cit.*, I, 199.

to slaves morning and evening, at the commencement and close of their day's labor."[79] Mathison noted that "on Sunday large numbers of slaves may be seen in the churches, particularly females."[80] For the exclusive worship of the Negroes, certain saints—Nossa Senhora do Rosario, São Benedito, and Santa Efigenia—were set aside, and their images were often, and still are today, painted black. Numerous *irmandades* composed entirely of Negroes were organized, usually under the patronage of São Benedito and Nossa Senhora do Rosario,[81] and in Bahia, at least, these all-Negro organizations persist to the present day. Koster, writing about 1800, tells us:

The ambition of the slave very generally aims at being admitted into one of these Irmandades, and at being made one of the officers and directors of the concerns of the brotherhood. Even some of the money which the industrious slave is collecting for the purpose of purchasing his freedom, will often times be brought out of its concealment for the decoration of a saint, that the donor may become of importance in the society to which he belongs.[82]

In 1848 Henry Bates noted that on an estate called Caripí, near Pará, the Christmas festival "was celebrated by the Negroes of their own free will, and in a very pleasing manner."

The room next to the one I had chosen was the *capella*, or chapel. It had a little altar which was neatly arranged, and the room was furnished with a magnificent brass chandelier. Men, women, and children were busy in the chapel all day on the 24th of December, decorating the altar with flowers and strewing the floor with orange leaves. They invited some of their neighbors to the evening prayers; and when the simple ceremony began, an hour before midnight, the chapel was

[79] Mawe, *op. cit.*, p. 115; cf. also Mathison, *op. cit.*, p. 157.

[80] *Op. cit.*, pp. 156–57.

[81] Cf. Ribeiro, *op. cit.*, p. 255.　　[82] *Op. cit.*, I, 199–200.

crowded. They were obliged to dispense with the mass, for they had no priest; the service therefore consisted merely of a long litany and a few hymns. There was placed on the altar a small image of the infant Christ, the "Menino Deus" as they called it, or the Child-God, which had a long ribbon depending from its waist. An old white-haired Negro led off the litany, and the rest of the people joined in the responses. After the service was over they all went up to the altar, one by one, and kissed the end of the ribbon. The gravity and earnestness shown throughout the proceedings was remarkable.[83]

Slaves were often married according to the forms of the Catholic church, and the banns were published in the same manner as for free persons.[84] Debret has preserved a visual impression of such a ceremony being performed in the house of wealthy Brazilians.[85]

As Freyre has pointed out,[86] priests continually urged upon white masters the advantage of conceding to the Negroes their African pastimes. A Jesuit, writing in the eighteenth century, advised slaveowners not only to permit but even to encourage the *festas* of the blacks, saying: "You should not make it difficult for them to choose their king, and to sing and dance as they desire on certain appointed days of the year, and legitimately to enjoy themselves on Sunday afternoons when in the morning they have executed the ceremonies in honor of Nossa Senhora do Rosario, São Benedito, or the guardian-saint of the chapel." Slaves were granted permission to use during public festivals—at first the Vespers of Reis, later Christmas, New Year's, and Carnival—

[83] Henry W. Bates, *The Naturalist on the River Amazons* (reprint, London, 1892), p. 88.

[84] Koster, *op. cit.*, I, 202. The consent of the master was required and the ceremony could not be performed until "the requisite prayers have been learned, the nature of the confession . . . . understood, and the sacrament can be received."

[85] *Op. cit.*, Vol. III, Pl. 15.   [86] *Op. cit.*, p. 264.

African costumes, songs, and dances.[87] The Catholic church was never in haste, it seems, to assimilate the Brazilian Negro but adopted instead a patient and tolerant policy which in the end was eminently successful. Early in the nineteenth century Koster wrote from Pernambuco, "No compulsion is resorted to, to make the Negroes embrace the habits of their masters; but their ideas are insensibly led to imitate and adopt them."[88]

As might be expected, the transition from fetish-cult ideas and practices to Catholic ritual and belief was marked by intermediary stages in which elements of both religions co-existed in the Negroes' thought and practice, and the objects of one cult were identified with objects of a similar nature in the other. Hence, the extensive identification, for instance, of several African *orixás* with certain Catholic saints (as we shall later see in greater detail) and the coexistence of African and European forms in the principal religious and popular festivals.

Thus, in 1852, a visitor wrote from Rio de Janeiro:

For many nights past, Gloria Hill . . . . has echoed till a late hour with the songs, the wild music, and the tread of the dance in the Negroes' favorite amusements; and yesterday afternoon, I accidentally became a spectator of a grand gathering of this kind. It was "Twelfth" or "King's Day," as sometimes called—being that commemorative of the adoration of the Magi in the stable of Bethlehem; and it is a chief festival with the Negroes. . . . . When about half way up the Larangeiras . . . . my attention was arrested by a large gathering of Negroes within an enclosure by the wayside, engaged in their native dances, accompanied by the wild and rude music brought with them from Africa. . . . . Many of the principal performers, both among the dancers and musicians, were dressed in the most . . . . grotesque manner. . . . . A majority, if not all the performers, were baptized

[87] *Ibid.*   [88] *Op. cit.*, I, 200.

members of the . . . . church. . . . . Exhibitions of this kind are far
from being limited here to extraordinary holidays, or to the seclusion
of by-places. I have seen them in open daylight, in the most public
corners of the city, while young [white] females . . . . hung over the
surrounding balconies as spectators.[89]

The festival here witnessed was probably that of the Rei
do Congo ("King of the Congo"). Throughout Brazil,
Africans were permitted on occasion to select a king and a
queen and to celebrate their coronation with extensive ceremonies. This festival came to be held at the same time as
that of the Catholic celebration of Epiphany and to be confused in the minds of the Negroes with it.[90] Of the king and
queen, Koster records:

The personages . . . . fixed upon may either actually be slaves, or
they may be manumitted Negroes. These sovereigns exercise a species
of mock jurisdiction over their subjects, which is much laughed at
by the whites. But their chief power and superiority over their coun-
trymen is shown on the day of the festival. The Negroes of their nation . . . . pay much respect to them. The man who had acted as their
king in Itamaraca (for each district has its king) for several years,
was about to resign from old age, and a new chief was to be chosen. He
who had been fixed upon for this purpose was an old man and a slave,
belonging to the plantation of Amparo. The . . . . queen would not
resign, but still continued at her post. The old Negro who was this
day to be crowned, came early in the morning to pay his respects to
the vicar, who said to him in a jocular manner, "Well, sir, today I
am to wait upon you, and to be your chaplain." About eleven o'clock
I proceeded to the church with the vicar. We were standing at the
door when there appeared a number of male and female Negroes,
habited in cotton dresses of colors and of white, with flags flying and
drums beating; and as they approached, we discovered among them
the king and queen, and the secretary of state. Each of the former
wore upon their heads a crown, which was partly covered with gilt

[89] Stewart, op. cit., p. 293.

[90] Cf. Ribeiro, op. cit., p. 256: ". . . . festa que eles faziam coincidir e
confundir com a catolica dos Tres Reis."

paper, and painted various colors. The king was dressed in an old fashioned suit of divers tints, green, red, and yellow: coat, waistcoat, and breeches. His sceptre, which was of wood and finely gilt, was in his hand. The queen was in a blue silk gown, also of ancient make; and the wretched secretary had to boast of as many colors as his master; but his dress had evident appearances of each portion having been borrowed from a different quarter; for some parts were too tight, and others too wide for him. The expense of the church service was . . . . provided for by the Negroes . . . . and . . . . the vicar . . . . and his assistant priests were to chant high mass. . . . . At last their Majesties knelt down at the railing of the principal chapel, and the service commenced. As soon as this was over, the new king was to be installed. But as the vicar who had not breakfasted, though it was now midday, was hungry, he dispatched the matter without much ceremony. He asked for the crown, then went to the church door—the new sovereign presented himself, and was requested, or rather desired, to kneel down. The insignia were given to him; and the vicar then said, "Agora, Senhor Rei, vai te embora" (Now, Sir King, go about thy business). As the king belonged to Amparo, the eating, drinking, and dancing were to be at that place.[91]

Koster did not witness the subsequent ceremony, but Burton has left an account of a similar one in Minas Geraes:

A score of men, after promenading through the settlement, came to the *Casa Grande*. They were dressed, as they fondly imagined, after the style of the Agua-Rosada House,[92] descended from the great Mani-kongo and hereditary lords of Congo land. But the toilettes, though gorgeous with colored silks and satins, were purely fanciful, and some wore the Kanitar or plumed head-gear, and the Arasira or waist fringe, and carried the Tacape or tomahawk belonging to the red man. All were armed with sword and shield, except the king, who, in sign of dignity, carried his sceptre, a stout and useful stick. The masked old man, with white beard, trembling underjaw, *chevrotante* voice, and

[91] *Op. cit.*, II, 25–28.

[92] An interesting account of this African dynasty is given, according to Burton, in M. Valdez, *Six Years of a Traveler's Life in West Africa* (London, 1861), Vol. II, chap. ii.

testy manner, was clearly represented by a young black from Sabará.
On his right sat the captain of war, the Premier; on his left the young
Prince, his son and heir. Of course the buffoon of the Dahomean court
was there, and the fun consisted in kicking and cuffing him as if he
were one of our clowns. . . . . The "play" was a representation of . . . .
a slave hunt; the march, accompanied with much running about and
clashing of swords, which all handled like butcher's knives; the sur-
prise, dragging in prisoners, directions to put to death recreant ministers and warriors, poisonings and administering antidotes. . . . . His
Majesty freely used his staff, threshing everybody right regally. The
speeches were delivered in a singsong tone; the language was Hamitico-
Lusan, and there was an attempt at cadence and rhyme. Slaughtering
the foeman and drinking his blood were the favorite topics, varied
by arch allusions to the Superintendent and his guests.[93]

But the "Kings of the Congo," says Koster,

also worship Nossa Senhora do Rosario; and are dressed in the dress
of white men. They and their subjects dance, it is true, after the manner of their country; but to these festivals are admitted Africans of
other nations, creole blacks, and mulattoes, all of whom dance after
the same manner; and these dances are now as much the national
dances of Brazil, as they are of Africa.

Shortly after 1800 Maria Graham, visiting a plantation in
the interior of Rio de Janeiro Province, wrote:

While we were sitting by the sugar-mill presses, Dona Mariana
(mistress of the *engenho*) desired the slave women, who were supplying
the canes, to sing, and they began at first with some of their own wild
African airs, with words adopted at the moment to suit the occasion.
She then told them to sing their hymns to the Virgin; when, regularly
in tune and time, and with some sweet voices, the evening and other
hymns were sung.[94]

[93] Burton, *op. cit.*, I, 237–38. For further information see Mario de An-
drade, *"Os Congos," Lanterna Verde*, No. 2 (February, 1935), pp. 36–53;
Francisco Augusto Pereira da Costa, "Rei do Congo," *Jornal do Brasil* (Rio),
August 25, 1901.

[94] *Op. cit.*, p. 282.

The dances *dos Congos* became attached to the Catholic festivals of São Benedito and Nossa Senhora do Rosario. In Bahia the annual *lavagem* ("washing") of the church of Bomfim became "a Yoruba religious ceremony" and, as late as 1900, was "a living cult, O Senhor do Bomfim[95] being for the Africans, the creole Negroes and the mixed-bloods of the Nagô *seita*,[96] Obatalá[97] himself."[98] The Cucumbys[99] became attached in Bahia to the Catholic festivals of Epiphany and Christmas.

[95] The saint to whom the Church of Bomfim (in Itapagipe) is consecrated is known as O Senhor do Bomfim, and his image is prominently displayed in the church. To evaluate more fully the important role of this famous church to which pilgrimages are still regularly made from long distances, see Carlos Alberto de Carvalho, *Tradições e milagres do Bomfim* (Bahia, 1915); João Varella, *Na Bahia do Senhor do Bomfim* (Bahia, 1936); and Manoel Raymundo Querino, *A Bahia de outrora* (Bahia, 1922), pp. 117–30, 222–31.

[96] The fetish-cult is sometimes called the *seita* (sect).

[97] Obatalá is one of the more important *orixás*, or deities, of the fetish cult. See chap. x.

[98] Rodrigues, *op. cit.*, p. 270.

[99] Moraes describes the Cucumbys of Rio as follows: "After a sumptuous meal of *cucumbe*, which is a dish eaten by the Congos and Munhambanas on the days of the circumcision of their sons, a group of Negroes set out to take to the Queen her new vassals who have just passed through this species of savage baptism. The procession, made up of princes and princesses, soothsayers and magicians, interpreters of foreign languages, and a host of other people, and conducting between two lines of gay celebrants the *mametos*— those who have just been circumcized with the bamboo splinter—is attacked on the way by an enemy tribe and the King's son killed by an arrow. When the procession finally reaches the King's dwelling-place, they find that the King, having heard of his son's death from a messenger, has already sent for a famous diviner, the most celebrated *feiticeiro* (witch-doctor) of the kingdom, of whom he demands, immediately upon his arrival, the resuscitation of the dead prince. To the divinations of this magician, the youth finally responds and gets to his feet. The dances then continue for some time, until the noisy ceremony ends with the Cucumbys singing the *Bemdito* and other popular refrains" (Mello Moraes Filho, *Festas e tradições populares* [Rio, 1888], p. 157, quoted in Rodrigues, *op. cit.*, pp. 272–73).

In the time of Nina Rodrigues, African "carnival clubs"
were still active in Bahia.[100] A Embaixada Africana ("The
African Legation") and Os Pandegos da Africa ("The African
Clowns") were the more prominent. Of lesser importance
were A Chegada Africana ("The Arrival of the Africans")
and Os Filhos da Africa ("Children of Africa"). A common
theme portrayed on the floats prepared by these Negroes was
"primitive Africa brought to Brazil a slave." Certain African traditions were also represented. Thus, for the Carnival
of 1899, Os Pandegos da Africa prepared a float representing
the river Zambesi "on one of whose banks might be seen the
King Labossi reclining in an immense seashell and surrounded by his ministers Auá, Oman, and Aboto." A second
float carried "two individuals representing the powerful
ministers of the King's court—Barborim and Rodá"; and a
third showed "the hut of Pae Ajou, his wife and the magical
caboré[101] which brings good fortune to one and all." Rodrigues was impressed with the enormous crowd of Negroes
and mixed-bloods which accompanied the floats, "singing
African songs, dancing African dances and applauding the
images on the magician's float." The scene was one of "a
colossal *candomblé* traversing the streets of the city,"[102]
although police regulations at that time forbade the public
appearance of the cult.

Much enjoyed by Brazilian Negroes were certain dances
like the *lundú* and the *batuque*, evidently of at least partial
African origin, although they perhaps also contained certain
Portuguese and native Indian elements.

[100] Rodrigues, *op. cit.*, p. 270.

[101] The *caboré* is a nocturnal bird.   [102] Rodrigues, *op. cit.*, p. 271.

Wells, visiting in Minas Geraes in the latter part of the nineteenth century, witnessed the *batuque* and records that it is usually danced by two couples, sometimes more, who face each other. Two tinkling . . . . guitars on this occasion commenced a thrum-thrum, thrum-thrum, and the head man of the estate . . . . advanced and marshaled the dancers, two women and two men; thrum-thrum, thrum—three or four voices suddenly commenced a loud, high-pitched, wild, rapidly delivered, impromptu refrain, con- taining allusions to the *patrão*[103] and his merits, the incidents of the daily work mingled with the loveliness of ideal Marias; the other men present joined in the chorus, each taking a second or third, a falsetto, or a bass. With rhythmic songs accompanied by clapping of hands and shuffling of feet, the dance commences, at first a slow measure that is maintained for some time, then gradually it increases in rapidity, the dancers advance and retreat, the women swaying their bodies and waving their arms, the men clapping time with their hands at every chorus. The measured tones rise and fall, then again increase in time, the songs and shuffling steps become fast and furious, hands and feet and voices all keep time; and there is much pantomimic action between the couples. . . . . The surroundings were a bright fire that burned and flickered on the earth floor. A single-wick castor-oil lamp was hung on a post. The forms of men and women, lightened by the up- ward glow of the fire, figured prominently against the dark obscurity of the interior of the shelter.[104]

Certain customs of the whites were taken over completely by the Negroes. Especially was this true (with a few excep- tions which we shall see later) of dress. Stewart recounts of

[103] Employer.

[104] *Op. cit.*, pp. 198–99. The *samba*, a form of the *batuque*, is today in a modified form the favorite popular music of Brazil. For information on the African contribution to Brazilian music see especially Mario de Andrade, "O samba rural paulista," *Revista do Arquivo Municipal de São Paulo*, XLI, 37–114; Flausino Rodrigues Valle, *Elementos de folk-lore musical brasileira* (São Paulo, 1936), particularly chap. iii; Luciano Gallet, *Estudos de folklore* (Rio, 1934).

Rio in 1852 that "two black African women, richly and fashionably attired, came sauntering along with the most conscious air of high-bred self-possession. They were followed by a black female slave, also in full dress, carrying a black baby three or four months old, and decked out in all the finery of an aristocratic heir—an elaborately wrought, lace-frilled and rosetted cap, and long flowing robe of thin muslin beautifully embroidered, and ornamented with lace."[105]

A fashion which in the early part of the nineteenth century served "to mark the high rank of those (of either sex) who adopted it" was that of "permitting the nails of the fore-finger and thumb to grow to a great length . . . . [and be] cut to a sharp point."[106] Today, while the whites in Bahia no longer follow this fashion, one occasionally sees individuals of prominence in the Negro group—for instance, Mãe Anninha of the *candomblé* of São Gonçalo—with long fingernails.

However, assimilation is not a process in which the individuals of only one of the races in contact are modified thereby while members of the other race remain unchanged. Circumstances in Brazil were such as to favor the taking-over by the whites of certain African elements. One rarely found a white child, especially during the slave period, who had not been reared by a Negro *ama*. She "gave him of her own milk, rocked him in his cradle or hammock, taught him his first words of halting Portuguese, his first Padre Nosso, his first Ave Maria, his first 'vôte!' or 'oxente'; she put into his mouth the first *pirão* with meat and

---

[105] *Op. cit.*, p. 295.

[106] Andrew Grant, *History of Brazil* (London, 1809), p. 234.

molho de ferrugem."[107]   From her and from the *mucama*
(maid), as much as, if not more than, from his father and
mother, the white child learned to speak. And almost without exception, he was given a *muleque companheiro de brin-
quedo,* a little Negro slave of his own age and sex, to be his
playmate and his almost constant companion.[108] José Veris-
simo says that during slavery there was "no house which did
not have one or more *muleques,* one or more *corumins,* little
victims consecrated to the caprices of *nhônhô:*[109] his horse,
his *leva-pancada,* his servant, his companion, his friend."[110]
In 1821 Mathison saw on an estate near Rio "a number of
fine Negro children playing in front of the house, and in the
midst of them a younger brother of the proprietor, a lad
about fourteen years of age, who had been brought up in this
manner . . . . like the Negroes."[111] Freyre has suggested that
"very likely many a Brazilian child took for his first hero,
not a white physician, nor a navy official or a lawyer, but a
slave acrobat who knew how to execute the difficult pirou-
ettes of the impromptu circuses and of the *bumbas meu bois*[112]
of the *engenhos;* or a Negro player of the trombone or the
flute."[113] Under these conditions it is not surprising that

[107] Freyre, *op. cit.,* p. 247. *Pirão* is made of manioc meal and meat broth;
molho de ferrugem is oil of the *dendê* palm.

[108] Lacerda, *op. cit.,* p. 379.

[109] Slave rendering of *menino* (male child).

[110] *A educação nacional* (Rio, 1906), quoted in Freyre, *op. cit.,* p. 248. A
leva-pancada is one who "takes the beatings."

[111] *Op. cit.,* p. 93.

[112] The *bumba meu boi* is still to be seen in the Bahian interior. It is a folk
drama in which a man dressed to represent an ox plays a prominent role
(see Arthur Ramos, *O negro brasileiro* [Rio, 1934], pp. 259–68; see also his
O folk-lore negro do Brasil [Rio, 1935], pp. 103–14).

[113] Freyre, *op. cit.,* p. 292.

Koster found the masters and their families taking over many of the customs of their slaves.[114]

Grant, visiting Bahia about 1800, noted that the principal amusement engaged in at private gatherings of the upper class was a dance of African origin:

It is performed by an individual of each sex moving their bodies to the monotonous tones of an instrument, always in one measure, and with scarcely any action of the legs or feet. The spectators seem delighted with the performance, and cheer the dancers by the most clamorous marks of approbation. This national dance . . . . is indulged in by all ranks of the citizens. . . . .[115]

Numerous changes in the whites' speech occurred. Especially was this true on isolated fazendas where *senhores* and their families were semiliterate or even illiterate. The *r* and the *s* disappeared as final consonants from many words, *fazer* becoming *fazê; mandar, mandá; comer, comé;* and *lh* was often reduced to *l, mulher* becoming *muler; colher, coler;* etc. In 1798 the bishop of Recife urged the teachers in a local *recolhimento* to try to correct "certain errors of speech" in the young ladies there studying, especially that of inverting certain letters and saying, for instance, *breço* instead of *berço, cravão* instead of *carvão;* of omitting letters in the middle of a word and saying, for example, *teado* instead of *telhado, fio* instead of *filho;* of dropping the final letter of the plural or of words ending in a harsh sound and saying, for instance, *muitas florê* for *muitas flores*, and *Portugá* for *Portugal.*[116] Freyre says that these dialectical modifications were particularly noticeable among isolated families in the rural areas, where Negro slaves were "constantly within the

[114] *Op. cit.*, I, 200–201.   [115] *Op. cit.*, pp. 232–33.

[116] Freyre, *Sobrados e mucambos* (São Paulo, 1936), p. 103.

house like persons of the family." Freyre adds that "still to-day the members of certain illustrious families *de engenho* can be identified by their peculiar vices of pronunciation which were originally learned from Negroes within their homes," as, for example, the Wanderleys of Serinhaem and Rio Formosa.[117]

The use, among certain slaveholding families, of a "slow and heavy manner of speaking," which gave "an appearance of affectation, fatigue, and illness," is also ascribed by Freyre to African influence. Numerous African words were adopted, especially into the common speech of the lower class, and a few have become good usage even among the educated minority. Freyre writes:

What Brazilian, at least from the North, feels any strangeness about such words as: caçamba, canga, dengo, cafuné, lubambo, mulambo, caçula, quitute, mandinga, muleque, camondongo, mugan-ga, quibêbe, quengo, batuque, banzo, mucambo, banguê, bozó, mocotó, bunda, zumbí, vatapá, carurú, banzé, mucama, quindim, catinga, mugunzá, malungo, birimbau, tanga, cachimbo, candomblé? Who prefers to say "mal cheiro" instead of "catinga"; or "garoto" instead of "muleque" or "moleque"; or "trapo" instead of "mu-lambo"? These are terms which correspond better than Portuguese words to our experiences, our palates, our understanding, and our emotions.[118]

[117] *Ibid.*, pp. 101–2.

[118] *Casa grande e senzala*, p. 245. For further information on words and phrases of African origin commonly used today in the predominately Portu-guese speech in large areas of Brazil see, particularly, Renato Mendonça, *A influencia africana no português do Brasil* (2d ed.; São Paulo, 1935); Jacques Raymundo, *O elemento afro-negro na lingua portuguesa* (Rio, 1933); Mario Marroquim, *A lingua do Nordeste* (São Paulo, 1934), especially pp. 155–59; Dante de Laytano, *Os africanismos do dialeto gaucho* (Porto Alegre, 1936). The author himself collected approximately three hundred words of African origin commonly used today in Bahia.

In the speech of very young children the doubling of a tonic syllable became common. Hence, *nhônhô* replaced *menino; titio* and *titia* were used for *tio* and *tia; dodoe* for *doe; dindinho* for *padrinho; vôvô* for *avô*, etc. Proper names "lost their solemnity, dissolving in a delicious manner in the mouths of the slaves." Little Antonia came to call herself, and to be called by her parents and other relatives, "Dondon" or "Toinha" or "Totonha"; Thereza became "Teté"; Manoel became "Mané," "Mandú," or "Nezinho"; Francisco became "Chico," "Chiquinho," or "Chicó"; Pedro became "Pepé"; and Alberto became "Bebeto" or "Betinho."[119]

In addition to the "hard and imperative" *diga-me, faça-me, espere-me*, of Portugal, another method of placing the pronoun came into use in Brazil. The slave and the lower classes developed *me-diga, me-faça, me-espere*, a manner of speaking which Ribeiro describes as of "great suavity and sweetness."[120] Freyre says "*faça-se* is the master speaking, the father, the patriarch; *me-dê* is the slave, the woman, the child."[121]

The Negroes in Brazil are said to have been assiduous story-tellers. Many free *pretas*, mostly older women, made their living by wandering from *engenho* to *engenho* recounting tales to the women slaves which eventually found their way, transmitted especially by the *mãe preta* and the *mucama*, into the ears of the master's children. Particularly common were stories of animals possessing human characteris-

[119] Freyre, *Casa grande e senzala*, p. 243.

[120] João Ribeiro, *A lingua nacional* (São Paulo, 1921), quoted in Freyre, *Casa grande e senzala*, p. 246 n.

[121] *Casa grande e senzala*, p. 246.

tics, as similarly were tales of the tortoise.[122] Boisterous children were quieted with stories of the Kibungo, a terrifying creature, half-man, half-animal, with an enormous hole in the middle of its back which opened ominously when the creature lowered its head.[123] The Kibungo was especially fond, it is said, of visiting the houses in which naughty boys lived, announcing his presence with:

> De quem é esta casa?
> auê
> como gérê, como gérê
> como érá.[124]

Max Schmidt observed in Matto Grosso that many of the local practices connected with cattle-raising were of African origin, as similarly were the iron instruments in use there. Eschwege contends that ironworking was learned in Brazil from imported Africans.[125]

[122] See Rodrigues, *op. cit.*, pp. 282–83.

[123] *Ibid.*, pp. 301–3.

[124] Whose is this house?
> *auê*
> I eat *gérê*, I eat *gérê*
> I eat *érá*.

[125] Freyre, *Casa grande e senzala*, pp. 220–21. It is also probable that certain microbes were unwittingly brought to Brazil in the bodies of imported Africans. See Octavio de Freitas, *Doenças africanas no Brasil* (São Paulo, 1935).

III

MISCEGENATION

CHAPTER IV

RACE MIXTURE AND THE CRUMBLING
OF THE COLOR LINE

URING at least the first century of colonization relatively few European women emigrated to Brazil.[1] Incoming Portuguese were predominantly males whose adventurous natures had led them to sever more or less completely family ties in the homeland. The soldiers of Thomé de Souza's first permanent garrison, who constituted no inconsiderable portion of Bahia's early population, had been specially chosen, we are told, because they were unincumbered by family ties. The few women, principally prostitutes or girls from orphanages, sent out from Lisbon by the Crown at the insistent request of Padre Nobrega[2] were insufficient to provide the necessary mothers of a new generation.[3] So great at one time was the demand for European women that the king of Portugal issued a decree denying girls permission to go from Brazil to Portugal to be trained as nuns unless they themselves on their own volition expressed an unalterable desire to remain unmarried.

[1] Gilberto Freyre, *Casa grande e senzala* (2d ed.; Rio, 1936), p. 60.

[2] Francisco A. de Varnhagen, Visconde de Porto Seguro, *Historia geral do Brasil* (3d complete ed., 4 vols.; São Paulo, n.d.), I, 308.

[3] As late as 1731 Captain-General D. Lourenço de Almeida wrote from Minas Geraes: "Em todas estas minas não ha mulheres que hajam de casar, e quando ha alguma (que são raras) são tantos casamentos que lhe saem que se ve o pai da noiva em grande embaraço a escolha que ha de fazer do genro" (*Revista do Arquivo Publico Mineiro de 1933*, I, 350, cited by Pedro Calmon, *Historia social do Brasil* [3 vols.; São Paulo, 1937–39], I, 95).

At the same time, if the colonizing venture in Brazil was to succeed, a sufficient population, either European or closely identified with the European, was a necessity.[4] But a shortage of man-power existed in the mother-country. A small number of Portuguese were seeking to establish themselves on a widely extended and constantly expanding frontier. The colonial ventures in India and other areas of the East, where the Portuguese held an irregular coast line fifteen thousand miles long,[5] were draining the mother-country of her quite limited population, depleted as it already was from centuries of war with the Moors. The inhabitants of Portugal at the beginning of the reign of Dom Manoel the Venturesome (1495) are given as only one million.[6] During the thirty years from 1497 to 1527, three hundred and twenty ships are said to have transported to India, "between soldiers and passengers," eighty thousand persons.[7] Some of these returned to Portugal, but most of them remained. Still, Albuquerque complained of the insufficient number of men furnished for his conquests in the East.[8]

The general movement of rural population into Lisbon, drawn by the expansion of overseas trade, had at that time so depleted the supply of agricultural laborers in Portugal, particularly in the southern provinces, that Africans were being imported in considerable numbers to supply the short-

[4] In 1612 Diogo de Vasconcellos in a letter to the Portuguese king complained that without increased population "mal se poderá remediar nem povoar tão larga costa" (Manoel Bomfim, *O Brasil* [São Paulo, 1935], p. 11).

[5] Albert G. Keller, *Colonization* (Boston, 1908), p. 108.

[6] Calmon, *op. cit.*, p. 159.

[7] Fidelino de Figueiredo, *Estudos de historia americana* (São Paulo, n.d.), p. 21, quoted in Calmon, *op. cit.*, p. 159.

[8] F. C. Danvers, *The Portuguese in India* (2 vols.; London, 1894), I, 305–6.

age.[9] Such migration to Brazil as did occur so seriously affected Portugal that in 1720 King Dom João V issued a royal proclamation prohibiting further emigration.[10]

An indication of this population scarcity is the fact that seventeenth-century Portuguese law recognized "common-law" marriage (*casamento Conhoçudos*) as legally binding. There grew up throughout Portugal "a great tolerance for every kind of union from which there might result an increase in population." Even the church came to recognize *de juras* marriage, if consummated by sexual intercourse.[11]

A scarcity of European women in the East led Francisco d'Almeida not only to accept the fact that a considerable degree of intermixture was already taking place in the Indies but also deliberately to foster as a matter of administrative policy Portuguese unions with native women. "In every Portuguese settlement the married men rapidly became a class to themselves with special privileges; all petty offices were reserved for them, and in Goa all the lands belonging to the King—a very large part of the area—were divided among them."[12] This policy of encouraging unions with na-

[9] H. Morse Stephens (*Portugal* [New York, 1903], p. 182) says that the population of Lisbon trebled in eighty years.

[10] The decree stated as its purpose the prohibition "of yearly migrations from this country to the *capitanias* of Brazil of so many people . . . . chiefly from the province of Minho, which from once being the most populous now finds itself without a sufficient number of people to cultivate the soil or to perform necessary services" (J. de A. Corvo, *Estudos sobre as provincias ultramarinas* [4 vols.; London, 1883-87], I, 15, quoted in Keller, *op. cit.*, p. 152 n.).

[11] Freyre, *op. cit.*, p. 179. *De juras* marriage was a simple ceremony "in which the mutual consent of both parties was affirmed on oath before a representative of the church without, however, the sacrament being given." See Alexandre Herculano, *Casamento civil* (Lisboa, 1907), pp. 30 ff.

[12] R. S. Whiteway, *The Rise of Portuguese Power in India, 1497-1550* (Westminster, 1899), p. 177; cf. Danvers, *op. cit.*, p. 217.

tive women was similarly sponsored by the Dutch during their colonizing ventures in South Africa and in Java and later by the English in India—a policy which emerged in each case as a natural response to the actual conditions of settlement.

The first Dutch settlers in South Africa and in Java were, almost without exception, males who, in order to establish themselves on a racial and cultural frontier, took up with native women. The mixed-blood progeny of these unions was treated with tolerance and consideration and often sent to the Netherlands to be educated. It was only with the arrival of the Dutch housewives, after Cape Colony had been fairly established, that the attitude of the Dutch toward the mixed-bloods changed. Today there are probably few people in the world who oppose intermixture more vigorously than do the Boer descendants of these Dutch settlers.[13]

During the early years of English penetration in India intermarriage between the English and native Indians not only extensively took place but was encouraged as a deliberate policy by the English authorities. In 1678 the court of directors of the British East India Company wrote the president of Madras that

the marriage of our soldiers to the native women of Fort St. George is a matter of such consequence to posterity that we shall be content to encourage it with some expense, and have been thinking for the future to appoint a *pagoda* to be paid to the mother of any child, that shall hereafter be born of any such future marriage, upon the day the child is christened, if you think this small encouragement will increase the number of such marriages.

This policy in all probability did not so much initiate interracial crossing as recognize its existence in an informal

[13] Robert E. Park, "Race Relations and Certain Frontiers," in *Race and Culture Contacts*, ed. E. B. Reuter (New York, 1934), pp. 67–68.

state. Unions were not confined to the lower classes but extended into even the upper social ranks, not only of the English, but of other European nationalities as well.[14]

Miscegenation and interracial marriage are perhaps always incidental to the expansion of a racial frontier. As Park has pointed out: "Transplanting a people, like transplanting any other organism, is a ticklish business, and interbreeding is one way of successfully accomplishing the transition."[15]

Thus, the Brazilian society of the sixteenth and early seventeenth centuries came to be founded largely upon families in which Indian or part Indian women were the consorts and mothers.[16] At least this was generally true of the lower classes, but it was by no means limited exclusively to them.[17]

These *de facto* unions were gradually "regularized by the church into Christian marriage," thus lending the powerful sanction of the ecclesiastical authority, chief guardian of the mores in a sacred society, to interracial crossing. The church was joined in this policy by the state, which legalized mixed unions. Thus, neither church nor state injected any "strain for consistency"[18] into the colonial mores which had grown up quite naturally in response to the exigencies of colonization but instead themselves offered support to the "definitions of the situation"[19] already laid down in the prevailing attitudes.

[14] See Cedric Dover, *Half-caste* (London, 1937), pp. 117 ff.

[15] *Op. cit.*, p. 57.

[16] Freyre, *op. cit.*, p. 60.

[17] E.g., the *mameluca* descendants of Caramurú married into prominent families.

[18] See William Graham Sumner, *Folkways* (Boston, 1906), p. 5.

[19] See W. I. Thomas, *Primitive Behavior* (New York and London, 1937), pp. 8–9.

The mating in Brazil of Portuguese men with native women was probably facilitated by the fact that many early colonizers were Moçarabes from southern Portugal, who had long been acquainted with the darker peoples and in whom "consciousness of race" was reputedly weak.[20] In fact, in some cases at least, African blood may have flowed in their veins.

It is possible that the first experience of the Portuguese with a darker race was the experience of a conquered people with their more swarthy conquerers. For the Moors, whose occupation of Portugal extended over more than five hundred years (711–1244), were perhaps darker in pigmentation than the Iberian peoples among whom, as lords of a conquered land, they settled. At least we know that their advance into the Iberian peninsula was led by the Berbers of northern Africa, whom Ripley describes as possessed of a slightly concave nose which in profile suggests the Negro, with hair varying from wavy to curly, beards rare, and body hair seldom heavy.[21] Ripley attributes their resemblance to the Negro to admixture with negroid tribes south of the Sahara.

If it is true that the Moors were of darker pigmentation than the Portuguese among whom they settled, men of dark hue had, at the time Brazil was colonized, been for centuries men of prestige in Portugal. They had brought in with them

[20] Freyre, *op. cit.*, p. 60. From the fifteenth century onward, Negroes were common even in Lisbon. Nicolau Clenard, French tutor of the (at that time) crown prince Dom Henrique, once wrote in a letter: "I believe there is in Lisbon a greater number of Moors and Negroes than of whites. There are nests of slaves in every house" (quoted from Domingos de Magalhães, *Os indigenas do Brasil*, by Luiz Anselmo da Fonseca, *A escravidão, o clero e o abolicionismo* [Bahia, 1887], p. 165).

[21] William Z. Ripley, *Races of Europe* (New York, 1899), pp. 277–78.

a superior culture; were more learned in the arts and sciences. They had become the wealthy class who occupied the towns or lived in the principal castles and on the great estates. Consequently, it came to be considered an honor for Portuguese women to mate with them, and we know that such marriages often occurred, even among members of the royal family.[22] Thus, the Portuguese, long before the discovery of Brazil, were "accustomed to mixed unions and their offspring."[23]

If the Portuguese came to look upon the dark Moors, and the somewhat negroid Berbers among them, as objects of prestige and eventually as marriageable individuals, the importation into Portugal of African Negroes (who from 1433 on were introduced in considerable numbers,[24] particularly as agricultural laborers in the Algarves at that time almost depopulated by the long wars of the Moorish expulsion) would have found the Portuguese accustomed to associating on a basis of social equality with, or even being inferior to, people of dark color. Even a royal prince is known to have had intimate Negro associates, for King Affonso VI's chief delight as a boy, it is said, was to roam the streets of Lisbon "at the head of a troop of mulattoes and Negro slaves."[25] Traces of African descent are still today unmistakable in the population of Lisbon.[26]

In the Jesuit schools at Bahia in the sixteenth and seven-

[22] Stephens, *op. cit.*, p. 23; Stanley Lane-Poole, *The Story of the Moors in Spain* (New York and London, 1886), pp. 48, 55, 247.

[23] Keller, *op. cit.*, p. 104.

[24] African slaves became so numerous that, by the middle of the sixteenth century, they were said to outnumber the free men of Lisbon.

[25] Stephens, *op. cit.*, p. 330.

[26] Noted by Dr. Robert E. Park on a recent visit to Lisbon.

teenth centuries, mixed-blood, pure Indian, and Portuguese
children were accepted with equal favor and educated together. "The chronicles of the time reveal no segregation or
any other form of discrimination inspired by prejudice
against the Indian; the program adopted by the padres appears to have continually fostered friendly intermingling of
the races."[27]

By the time the relatively small numbers of Indians at
Bahia had been absorbed into the dominant population
group, African women had been imported in sufficient numbers to continue extensively the process of race mixture.
The scarcity of white, or near-white, women, at least as
mates for men of the upper classes, was not now so acute as
formerly; consequently, most of the sexual unions with
African women were extra-legal,[28] comparable in some measure to interbreeding in our South, except that in the case
of Brazil the extent of intermixture was perhaps greater.[29]
Padre Nobrega wrote from Bahia in the early days of the
colony: "Among the people here there are none who do
not possess several *negras* from whom they have many
children."[30] By 1819 the number of *mestiços* in Brazil was
given as 628,000—a figure not greatly inferior to that of the
whites, who were estimated at 843,000.[31] The pure Negro, it

[27] Freyre, *op. cit.*, p. 120.

[28] Marriages with Negroes were at first frowned upon. Thus an *alvará*
of 1755 which referred to marriages of white men with Indian women as
"convenient and noble" condemned "staining one's self" by marrying
Negroes or Jews (Calmon, *op. cit.*, p. 156).

[29] See Freyre, *op. cit.*, esp. chaps. iv and v.

[30] Manoel de Nobrega, *Cartas do Brasil, 1549-1560* (Rio, 1886), quoted
in Freyre, *op. cit.*, p. 302.

[31] Alcide d'Orbigny, *Voyage dans les deux Amériques* (Paris, 1836), p. 155,
quoted in Calmon, *op. cit.*, p. 155.

is said, did not usually exist in Brazil much longer than the third generation.[32] In Minas Geraes, in 1835, while importations from Africa were still large, there were 170,000 mulattoes to 305,000 blacks.[33]

Thus miscegenation has gone on in Brazil in an unobtrusive way over a long period of time. In few places in the world, perhaps, has the interpenetration of peoples of divergent racial stocks proceeded so continuously and on so extensive a scale.[34]

One circumstance in Bahia still favorable to miscegenation is the system of household service universal in upperclass, principally white, families. Whereas no inconsiderable portion of the domestic labor in the United States, at least in northern areas, is white, consisting largely of peasant immigrant women from Europe, household labor in Bahia is almost invariably black or dark mulatto. For example, of 250 servant women noted, 197 were black, 47 were mulatto (predominantly dark), 4 were *cafuso*,[34a] and only 2 were white. In other words, only 0.8 per cent appeared to be of unmixed white descent. For this reason, interbreeding between males in white upper-class families and servant girls leads almost always to black-white, or at least mulatto-white, crosses.

The disposition to tolerate intermixture with the African

---

[32] Calmon, *op. cit.*, p. 163.   [33] *Ibid.*

[34] Calmon writes (*ibid.*, p. 158): "Nenhum outro povo tão ligeiro marchou para a estabilização de um tipo procedente dos mais opostos fatores; principalmente em nenhum outro as propriedades unitivas do idioma, da religião, do meio físico, se conjugaram tão intimamente para uniformizar, num imenso territorio (Luc Durtain disse que o Brasil é um dos cinco países verdadeiramente cosmicos) a descendencia de inumeros troncos, celtico, negroide, aborigene."

[34a] Indian-Negro mixed-blood.

grew up during slavery, and no circumstance has subsequently arisen to change it. In the United States, on the other hand, the spread of contraceptive practices[35] and the increasing race consciousness of the Negro have led to a decided decrease in miscegenation. Traditional behavior in Bahia is, in this respect as in many others, well defined. The sanction of custom has become, as it always does eventually in any case, moral sanction.

Race mixture is further favored in Bahia today by the widespread custom of *mancebia*,[36] or those conjugal unions outside marriage in which there is some degree of permanency. In many cases the women involved are mulattoes, rarely blacks. The man agrees to pay for rent and food; the woman, to care for the house and children. The man may have, at the same time, a legal family, although informal unions are often entered into by young men previous to marriage.

Miscegenation is also favored in Bahia today by the prestige which ordinarily attaches to the so-called "whiter" child. Dark mothers who bear "whiter" children consider themselves especially favored and are so looked upon by their immediate associates. A black mother proudly showed her light child and said, "Estou limpando a minha raça" ("I am cleansing [i.e., I am 'whitening'] my race"). One also

---

[35] In Bahia there is not the fear of venereal disease common to this country. Its contraction is regarded by young men as an indication of sexual coming-of-age and perhaps enhances their prestige among their associates (cf. Freyre, *op. cit.*, pp. 49 ff.).

[36] This term is used only in more polite conversation. The woman involved is called *manceba*, the verb is *mancebar*, and the participle *mancebado*. The popular expression, however, is *amasia*, or *amiga* (the feminine form of "friend"), or *amante*, or *comboso*, for the woman; the verb is *amasiar* or *amigar*, the participle *amasiado* or *amigado*.

often hears in Bahia the expression *melhorando a raça* ("improving the breed").[37]

The attitude here inferred arose during slavery, when it became a distinct privilege for a Negro woman to bear a child to her white master; for she and her progeny were thereby placed in a more advantageous position, especially as far as material benefits, and even freedom, were concerned.

João Varella, in a booklet entitled *Da Bahia do Senhor do Bomfim*, reproduces the figure of a Negro woman bearing a young child bound to her back by a wide cloth. "When the child was black and ugly," Varella writes, "he was usually carried in this fashion. If, however, he was a *coisa mais limpa* (literally, 'a cleaner thing'), he was borne in front, in his mother's arms, so that all the world might the more readily see him."

This desire "to marry whiter" is not limited to the female portion of the black population. Successful males here, as in Haiti and the United States, generally seek to insure further their status and that of their children by marrying lighter-

[37] Of twenty-four babies delivered at the free maternity ward of Santa Isabel Hospital from Negro and mulatto mothers, four, an obstetrician thought, would grow up relatively "white," while only two appeared to be completely negroid. Although pigmentation apparently is not fixed at this early period, the appearance of *manchas* (or deeply colored "stains," called in popular speech *genipapo* after a common Brazilian fruit of a similar coffee-brown color), on either the back or buttocks is, in Bahia, commonly considered an index of subsequent dark pigmentation over the entire body. Three of the babies from dark mulatto women and one whose mother was a light mixed-blood showed no evidence of *manchas*. One dark mulatto mother, when requested, removed her child's clothing and proudly displayed his back free from these marks. The obstetrician, with a smile and a friendly pat on the mother's shoulder, inquired, "It's father was white, wasn't he?" The colored mother, pleased, replied, "I have five other children like him, all without *manchas*."

colored women. A common expression heard in this connection is: "I don't want to go back to Africa."

Race mixture is further favored in Bahia today by the economic and social position of the occasional immigrant, usually from Portugal or Spain. Ordinarily from the lower class,
he arrives unattached, poor, and with little or no education.
He meets a rigid class line and, at least during the first years,
before he gains some measure of economic competence, is
ordinarily cut off from a better class marriage. Moreover, in
many cases he conceives of his stay as temporary. Many
immigrants, especially among the Spanish, have left families
in Europe to whom they expect to return once they have
accumulated a sizable competence.

In his struggle to gain a footing, the immigrant soon discovers that the lower-class black or mixed-blood woman is a
valuable assistant. She may become his cook and house-
keeper, supplement his income by taking in washings or by
preparing and peddling food delicacies, and ordinarily demands little in return. So frequently do such unions occur,
especially among Portuguese immigrants, that the Portuguese have come to be popularly regarded, not only in Bahia
but throughout Brazil, as peculiarly attached to Negro
women.

· However, as we have indicated, not all immigrant men living *amancebados* with Negro women are from Portugal. A
number of the *vendas*, or small grocery stores, scattered
about Bahia are owned by Spanish immigrants, many of
whom live with Negro women, as similarly does occasionally
an Italian, an Englishman, an American, or a German.[38]

[38] A German who had been manager of a nail factory in Bahia returned a
few years ago to Germany. For sometime thereafter a Negro woman with
whom he had lived and their son received 200 milreis regularly each month

One reason why race mixture in Bahia is more extensive than in the United States is that in Bahia it goes on by legal intermarriage in a less restricted way than with us. Although interbreeding between individuals from extreme ends of the color scale is largely extra-legal, intermarriage becomes more frequent as the colors approach along this continuum.

The general tendency is for the predominantly European portion of the population to absorb the lighter mixed-bloods while the mulattoes in turn absorb the blacks. This means that the Brazilian population is constantly becoming more European, less negroid, in appearance, a tendency which is referred to by local intellectuals as "progressive Aryanization." As Oliveira Vianna has said: "Podemos já assignalar . . . . uma tendencia que cada vez mais se precisa e define: a tendencia para a aryanização progressiva dos nossos grupos regionaes. Isto é, *o coefficiente da raça branca eleva-se cada vez mais em nossa população.*"[38a]

Family ties are, as we have noted, tenacious. Loyalty to the clan still today transcends loyalty to the state, the church, or any other institution. There is strong personal attachment between white parents and colored offspring, both legitimate and illegitimate, and these ties obviously place the mulatto in an advantageous position for social advancement.

It is commonly thought in Brazil that the Brazilian

---

from Germany. The man also sent money to a second Negro woman, her two girls and a boy, for whom he, while still in Brazil, had built a comfortable home.

[38a] "A progressive whitening of our population is clearly evident. In other words, the proportion of white blood is constantly increasing" (*Evolução do povo brasileiro* [2d ed.; São Paulo, 1933], p. 172). See also João Pandiá Calogeras, *Formação historica do Brasil* (3d ed.; São Paulo, 1938), p. 36.

mixed-blood is superior in vitality to both ancestral stocks.[39]
The mulatto, being a "native plant," is popularly considered
to have been better acclimated than either the European
or the African.   The Indian-white mixed-blood, concluded
Colonel Artur Lobo da Silva of the Brazilian Army Health
Service on the basis of a study which he made, is physically
superior to both the white and the native Indian.[40]

There is some evidence, however, that the Brazilian
mixed-blood is less resistant than the European and the
black to certain diseases, for example, tuberculosis. Comparative statistics given for Bahia some years ago by A. Pacifico
Pereira support this hypothesis. Although the percentage of
mestiços in Bahia in 1904 was given as 35.1 per cent, the percentage of mixed-bloods among those dying from tuberculosis in that year was 49.0 per cent; while the whites, presumably 31.4 per cent of the population, furnished only 21.4
per cent of the deaths from this disease; and the blacks, who
were 26.3 per cent of the total population at that time,
furnished 26.9 per cent.[41] To resolve the problem of the vitality of the Brazilian mixed-blood in comparison with his
parent-stocks would seem to require more extended research.

The most obvious effect of miscegenation is to reduce
physical differences between the races. In Bahia intermixture has now, for more than four hundred years, been breaking down physical barriers and reducing that visibility which

[39] See, e.g., Calmon, *op. cit.*, p. 163.

[40] "A anthropologia do exercito brasileiro," *Archivos do Museu Nacional*
(Rio), XXX (1928), 33.

[41] A. Pacifico Pereira, *A tuberculose na Bahia* (Bahia, 1904), p. 15. The
remaining 7.2 per cent of the population were resident aliens, who accounted
for 2.7 of the deaths from tuberculosis.

in the United States always serves to call out the traditional responses long associated with variations in social status.

Today there exists in Bahia the belief that the population is gradually but persistently "whitening," a conviction difficult to understand, given the heavy preponderance of Africans among the population which originally migrated to this area and the negligible number of European immigrants in recent times.

The probable greater mortality of blacks may in part account for this change. According to a recent unpublished study, the infantile death rate among the lower classes in Bahia, which, as we have seen, are principally black and dark mulatto, is approximately twice that of the upper classes; and, in 1932, deaths under five years of age constituted nearly one-third of all deaths for that year (1,698 out of 5,407). At the same time there does not seem to be any marked difference in fertility between the races.

At any rate, Bahians frequently comment on an appreciable change in the color of the population within their memories. One continually hears remarks like that of a mixed-blood citizen who said:

Formerly, the *pretos* (blacks) were the most numerous group in Bahia, the *pardos* (browns) next, and the *brancos* (whites) last. Today, the *pardos* are in the majority, the *brancos* next, and the *pretos* last. I am convinced that before long the *pretos* will have completely disappeared. The *brancos* will soon overtake and, in the course of time, completely absorb the *pardos*.

The mixed-bloods tend to look upon themselves as transition points in an inevitable whitening process. Pride in the present advanced stage is common, and the end result is eagerly anticipated. From the mulattoes, as from the whites, one frequently hears the declaration: "We Brazilians are rapidly becoming one people. Some day not far distant there will be only *one* race in our country."

On visiting Brazil, Theodore Roosevelt once wrote: "Perhaps the attitude that the Brazilians, including the most intelligent among them, take is best symbolized by a picture which we saw in the Art Museum in Rio. It portrayed a black grandfather, a mulatto son, and a white grandchild, the evident intention of the painter being to express both the hope and the belief that the Negro was being absorbed and transformed so that he would become a white man." Quoting a Brazilian statesman, Roosevelt continued: "You speak of Brazil as having a large Negro population. Well, in a century there will not be any Negroes in Brazil, whereas you will have twenty or thirty millions of them. Then for you there will be a real and very uncomfortable problem, while for us the problem in its most menacing phase will have disappeared."[42]

It is difficult to check this general impression that the population is constantly becoming more and more European in appearance. Reliable statistics on the present distribution of the various ethnic groups are not available. No adequate data of this sort have recently been compiled by any agency. The last Brazilian census to include racial categories was taken a half-century ago, in 1890. At that time the racial division in Bahia was given as: *brancos*, 32.0 per cent; *pretos*, 26.4 per cent; and *mestiços*, 35.1 per cent.[43]

Vital statistics, however, are still recorded in the city by

[42] *Outlook*, CVI (February 21, 1914), 410–11.

[43] *Caboclos* were given as 6.5 per cent. It is difficult to understand how so large a number of Indians, or Indian mixed-bloods (the term is variously used at different times and in different places in Brazil), could have at that time existed in the city of Bahia.

color categories, three being officially recognized: *branco*, *preto*, and *pardo*. These classifications are based upon physical appearance, the principal criteria being pigmentation and hair texture. Racial intermixture has now proceeded to the point where public officials say no attempt is made to indicate ethnic distinctions. Thus the *branco* category includes many light mulattoes and the *preto* category many dark mixed-bloods.

These official color divisions directly reflect popular distinctions. It is therefore important to note that their usage indicates a shift in criterion from racial descent (as in the United States) to physical appearance; and physical appearance is a characteristic which miscegenation tends continually to modify. Whereas in the United States one drop of Negro blood, if it be known, makes a man a Negro, in Bahia many individuals are listed in the census as white (and, one might add, are so considered by their friends and associates) whose grandmothers were Negroes of pure African descent.

For instance, the grandmother of a *branco* politician who holds a responsible position in the Rio government, and who himself shows no noticeable traces of Negro ancestry, is said to have been a black woman who wore on Bahia's streets "a *saia grande* and a *panno da Costa*."[44] The *branco* wife of a prominent physician, fair and blue eyed, similarly had an African grandmother. A former governor, to all appearances white and so considered throughout the community, is only two generations removed from an African forebear. Cases might be cited indefinitely similar to that of a Bahian who, referring to a prominent local woman invariably con-

[44] Elements of the distinctive costume, partially African in origin, which is worn in Bahia by Negro women (see chap. ix.).

sidered white, casually commented: "I learned the other day that she has a Negro grandmother. Someone who knew her family twenty years before she was born showed me a picture of the woman. The grandmother was as black as coal."

That such discovery led, and will lead in all similar cases, to no alteration in the social standing of the individual involved, to no modification in the social esteem in which he or she is held, is a significant indication of the character of the Brazilian racial situation as compared with that in the United States, for example, where a similar revelation would create a scandal. "We never go very far into a person's past," explained another Bahian. "That would be impolite."

The meaning of the term *branco* (white) in Bahia is, as we have indicated, a significant index of the racial situation. A recent comparison of the classification of the first five hundred individuals listed as *brancos* in the files of the Gabinete de Identificação with the photographs (one, sometimes two, occasionally three) attached to the individual's identification record,[45] indicated that the racial probabilities were as given in Table 2.[46]

It is clear that many individuals are considered white at Bahia who not only have Negro ancestors but whose physical characteristics definitely attest this fact. The old saying, "Quem escapa de branco, negro é" ("Who can't be a white

[45] An identification card is required of all students, travelers, applicants for licenses, etc.

[46] Considering the means employed, one must allow perhaps for some error in the result. But the photographs had received no "retouching." And even if color distinctions were still somewhat subject to misinterpretation, hair texture and facial characteristics were rather readily distinguishable. It is quite probable that what error did occur was in the form of an understatement rather than of an exaggeration.

man is a Negro"), has now been largely replaced by, as Freyre says, the "more Brazilian saying": "Quem escapa de negro, branco é" ("Who isn't a Negro is a white man").

With due regard, then, to such qualifications regarding the precise meaning of *branco* as these facts suggest, we may note that the classification of births in Bahia in 1932 indicated the color distribution to be as given in Table 3.

TABLE 2

PROBABLE ETHNIC ORIGIN OF THE FIRST FIVE
HUNDRED INDIVIDUALS LISTED AS *Brancos* IN
THE FILES OF THE GABINETE DE IDENTIFI-
CAÇÃO, BAHIA, 1937

Probability	Number	Per Cent
Whites......................	340	68.0
Mulattoes*..................	95	19.0
Indian-white mixed-bloods†.....	39	7.8
Indian-white-Negro mixed-bloods†....................	26	5.2
Total....................	500	100.0

* Individuals with the following physical characteristics were noted: (1) nose very broad, lips very full; (2) dark skin, hair almost kinky, lips thick; (3) skin *café com leite* ("coffee with milk"), hair exceedingly curly; (4) hair almost kinky; (5) lips full, nose broad, considerable prognathism.

† Ordinarily only slight traces of Indian ancestry evident in each case.

Since the total registration of births for each of these years averages slightly in excess of five hundred in a city of an estimated 360,000, the records are obviously incomplete. Many midwife deliveries go unrecorded; and, since these births occur usually among the lower classes, which are largely black and dark mulatto, the relative color percentages are probably skewed toward the white pole.

Deaths are less likely to go unrecorded. But since deaths

occur to a considerable extent among the older generation, they throw no light on the extent of miscegenation in recent times. Consequently, their relative frequencies do not ac-

TABLE 3*

BIRTHS ACCORDING TO COLOR, BAHIA, 1932

COLOR	CITY PROPER		OUTLYING VILLAGES		TOTAL	
	Number	Per Cent	Number	Per Cent	Number	Per Cent
Branco..........	1,482	33.3	65	11.0	1,547	30.7
Preto...........	659	14.8	114	19.3	773	15.3
Pardo..........	2,314	51.9	411	69.7	2,725	54.0
Total.......	4,455	100.0	590	100.0	5,045	100.0

*Source: City records deposited in the Secretaria de Saude e Assistencia Publica da Bahia.

TABLE 4*

DEATHS ACCORDING TO COLOR, BAHIA, 1932

COLOR	CITY PROPER		OUTLYING VILLAGES		TOTAL	
	Number	Per Cent	Number	Per Cent	Number	Per Cent
Branco..........	1,375	25.4	79	9.8	1,454	23.4
Preto...........	1,310	24.2	191	23.7	1,501	24.2
Pardo..........	2,722	50.4	536	66.5	3,258	52.4
Total......	5,407	100.0	806	100.0	6,213	100.0

*Source: City records deposited in the Secretaria de Saude e Assistencia Publica da Bahia.

curately reflect the present racial distribution in the *total* population.

Bearing in mind these qualifications, we may note the color distribution among deceased at Bahia in 1932 (Table 4).

Short of a racial census, an adequate statistical statement of the racial composition of Bahia would probably require an extended sampling of the population in various parts of the city—a procedure not feasible under the limits of this study. Samples readily obtainable at the numerous festivals such as Segunda Feira do Bomfim, Conceição da Praia, the Vespers of Reis, etc., are not practical for the reason that participation of one or another of the ethnic components is ordinarily out of proportion to its size in the general population. But at Carnival, when nearly the entire population frequents the public thoroughfares, this difficulty disappears. A new obstacle arises, however, in the form of a considerable infiltration of population from surrounding areas. And since the whites are ordinarily from the upper-income groups and consequently more able to travel, the white percentage of the city's population is probably at that time swollen beyond its normal proportion. The "Micarêta," or second Carnival, held one week after Easter, avoids this latter disadvantage. Of five thousand people noted among the participants in the "Micarêta" for 1936, the racial percentages appeared to be those given in Table 5.

Thus one can perhaps confirm the common-sense judgment of Bahian citizens to the effect that at least half, and perhaps more, of the population is now noticeably mixed, that both biologically "pure" whites (but not "whites" in the social sense) and biologically "pure" Africans are relatively few in number.

Some notion of the change in physical characteristics by generations, at least among members of the lower classes, may be had from a study of five hundred cases of mothers and their offspring applying at Bahia's free children's

clinic.[47] The offspring of 221 black and 200[48] mulatto mothers appeared to vary from their mothers as indicated in
Table 6.

Since cases in which only obvious variations appeared
were recorded as differing, the data would indicate a rather
noticeable variation by generations. At least this is true in
so far as mothers are concerned. Accurate information on
fathers is difficult to obtain, since, in the section of the popu-

TABLE 5

ETHNIC ORIGIN (AS DETERMINED BY INSPECTION)
OF FIVE THOUSAND PARTICIPANTS IN THE
"MICARÊTA" FESTIVAL, BAHIA, 1936

Racial Identity	Number	Per Cent
European	1,585	31.7
Negro	900	18.0
Mulatto	2,495	49.9
Cafuso*	20	0.4
Total	5,000	100.0

* The term *cafuso* is employed to designate an individual of mixed
Indian and Negro descent.

lation whence these cases come, one finds extensive cohabitation without formal marriage, either civil or religious.

So widespread has the dispersion of African blood in the
predominantly European group now become that relatively
few families in Bahia are of undiluted European origin,
without African strain somewhere in the lineage. This mixture of the races in Bahia is in some respects similar to the

[47] Since pigmentation, it is presumed by local physicians, does not become "fixed" until approximately six months after birth, children under one
year were eliminated from the tally.

[48] Seventy-nine children were white of white mothers.

mixture of the nationalities in the United States, where old families of pure English descent have for some time been mingling their blood with that of Germans, Scandinavians, Slavs, and the Mediterranean peoples. "Even if one marries a person who does not himself possess some African blood," said a young lady of the upper class, "this same individual

TABLE 6

VARIATION IN PHYSICAL CHARACTERISTICS BETWEEN
CHILDREN AND THEIR MOTHERS,* BAHIA, 1936

CHILD	MOTHER			
	Black		Mulatto	
	Number	Per Cent	Number	Per Cent
Color lighter, hair "straighter".....	55	24.9	45	22.5
Color lighter.....................	12	5.4	34	17.0
Hair "straighter".................	12	5.4	20	10.0
Color lighter, hair more kinky......	0	0.0	2	1.0
Color darker, hair "straighter".....	0	0.0	1	0.5
Color darker.....................	0	0.0	3	1.5
Hair more kinky..................	0	0.0	3	1.5
Color darker, hair more kinky......	0	0.0	1	0.5
No noticeable variation............	142	64.3	91	45.5
Total......................	221	100.0	200	100.0

* As determined by inspection.

will have cousins or other relatives of African descent. Somewhere there will be a connection."

"It is very hard to say a man doesn't have some Negro blood coming from somewhere in his recent or remote past," said a prominent *branco* lawyer and politician. "Take myself, for instance. I can't say for certain that my grandparents didn't have African connections. 'Quando não vem de perto, vem de longe' ['If it isn't close, it's distant']."

The widespread dispersion of Negro blood in the *branco* group obviously makes it difficult for its members to draw sharp, clear-cut racial distinctions. Relatively few pure Europeans, as we have seen, exist. And if rigid distinctions were made between those individuals who appear to be European and those who in their color and features indicate some African lineage, the dividing-line would in many cases pass directly through family groups. The natural ties which ordinarily grow up between parents and offspring, and between brothers and sisters, constantly militate against such invidious distinctions. In like manner, similar ties in the United States tend to undermine nationality distinctions and to fuse together in sentiment and attitude individuals of, for example, English, Danish, French, Czech, and Italian origin. "It's difficult to keep the colors distinct in Bahia," said a *branco* educator. "Look at this boy of mine; he's white! And this girl; she is, you might say, a bit of a *mulata!*" A prominent political figure who is commonly considered white but shows slight traces, especially in his hair, of African ancestry, has a wife who also is considered white but similarly possesses slight indications of African origin. Of their nine children, all except three, possibly four, could readily "pass" in the United States. Each of the others shows slight evidences of African lineage. Said the father playfully, as he caressed a small daughter, "Here's a typical *mulata*." The sense of this remark seemed similar to that of a father in the United States saying, "Look at my little blue-eyed girl," or "Here's a real brunette."[49]

Thus miscegenation, whether by way of legally consti-

[49] Occasionally, children are more negroid than either parent. For instance, the daughter of a Portuguese immigrant and a Brazilian-born *branco* wife has a "yellowish complexion," lips somewhat thick, and nose strongly suggesting the Negro. But the myth of the so-called "throwback," or black child born to near-white parents, is apparently unknown.

tuted marriages or otherwise, extends personal relations to the point where they inhibit the rise of caste prejudice. Natural ties, personal and familial, grow up to cement with common bonds of sentiment individuals from both racial stocks.

"Racial intermixture has had a long history, a history older than civilization itself," commented Theodoro Sampaio, a prominent Bahian mixed-blood.

Wherever the conquering Romans went, mixture occurred. Spain and Portugal for centuries interbred with the Moors; Italy, Greece, and the Mediterranean isles, all early mingled their blood with that of Africa. In Crete—that old center of ancient civilization—are statues of men with crinkly (*crespo*) hair. The Gothic hordes which overran Europe as the Roman Empire was crumbling were themselves much mixed; and wherever they went they added their blood to that of the peoples whom they conquered. Race-crossing is obviously no new thing; it has been common the world over wherever races have come together. How natural, then, that Brazil should blend her races into one, and that we Brazilians should become *one* people.

Among the mixed-bloods there is still a wide range of variation in physical type. The distribution, however, is probably skewed toward the Caucasian pole. Indian traits have virtually disappeared, the native element having been almost completely absorbed into the predominantly European population. The occasional traces of Indian characters which are still discernible are usually found in combination with Negro characters and are probably a consequence of the recent migration into the city from the *sertão* of predominantly negroid individuals of partial Indian descent.

To designate some of the intermediate types which extensive intermixture has now produced, a number of popular expressions have arisen. These terms describe the variations more accurately than do the official categories. The latter, as we have seen, are limited to three: *branco*, *preto*, and

pardo; but common speech adds *cabra* (or *caibra*), *Cabo Verde*
(*Cape Verde*), *sarará*, and *moreno*.

The *cabra*, or *caibra*, is slightly lighter in pigmentation
than the *preto* and has hair a little less kinky. The *Cabo
Verde* is very dark, with Caucasian features and black,
glossy, "straight" hair. The infrequent *sarará* is light in col-
or, with hair red (or sandy) and kinky. The *moreno*, many
Bahians say, is the new physical type which Brazil is developing.

Quite significantly, the *morena* (or feminine *moreno*) is
the "ideal type" of Bahian femininity. She is in many cases
an individual of remarkable beauty. Typically, she has
dark-brown eyes and dark hair, quite wavy, perhaps even
curly, and Caucasian features; her color is *café com leite* (literally, "coffee with milk"; i.e., like that of one "heavily
tanned"), and she has a healthy appearance. The term
morena is seldom mentioned to a Bahian male without there
appearing an instant change in his expression. His face
"lights up," and a smile breaks on his lips. He pronounces
morena with a tone indicative of admiration, affection, desire.[50] He seems pleased, happy in the contemplation of an
agreeable object. Poets, both professional and amateur,
pour out passionate stanzas in her honor,[51] songs are sung

[50] The *morena* has the reputation of being more desirable than lighter
Brazilian women; she is commonly described as "more *ardente*" (passionate),
"more *adstringente*" (clinging).

[51] As, for example, the following:

Elsa . . . .
Number One girl,
Pretty little "paca" [small Brazilian
    animal]
Caboclo-colored butterfly,
Splendidly "morena." . . . .

I danced the "catêrêtê" *samba* with Elsa,
Her warm flesh quivering,
Her breasts full, almost exploding,
Inside her little white blouse.

And then she fell into my arms willing-
    ly, voluptuously,
Her eyes like burning coals,
Her ruby lips
Glued to mine in delirious pleasure.

Ah! Ah! mad girl!
"Bamba" girl!
Devilish girl!

to her,[52] romances written.[53] Of 146 male students responding to the query, "All things being equal, whom would
you prefer to marry, a *branca*, a *morena*, a *parda*, a *preta*,"
117, or 80.1 per cent, replied "a *morena*." Similarly, of 93
white female students responding to a like question, 80, or
86 per cent, preferred a *moreno* for a mate.

The *morena* may, or may not, have African blood.[54] But
at least in Bahia this category includes many individuals of
partial African descent. For instance, a study of five hundred women classified as *morenas* in the Gabinete de Identificação indicated the probable distribution given in Table 7.

It is the opinion of Arthur Ramos[55] that, although "the
charms of the *morena* exert a profound sexual attraction"
and the regard in which she is held "has a sexual base in the
Freudian sense," the present attitude toward the *morena*
"grew out of the enthusiasm and the sentimentalism of the
abolition campaign. The *morena* expresses in a symbolic way
the union of the two races—the black and the white—and
the absence of [caste] prejudice."

The *morena* probably constitutes a decided bond be-

[52] As, for example, the following:

Beautiful morena,
Morena,
Morena who makes me suffer!
The full moon, so bright,
Is not as luminous as your eyes.
You are a *morena*,
A wonderful girl.
There's not a *branco* who hasn't
    fallen for you.

Often,
When you pass by,

Men quarrel over you;
Everyone eagerly anticipates
Your smile.

Your heart is a boarding-house,
A family hotel
Along the seashore.
Oh, *moreninha*, do not rent all!
Leave at least a corner
For me to live in!

[53] A rock on the island of Paquetá in Guanabara Bay at Rio de Janeiro
very popular with young lovers, has been dedicated to the *moreninha*.

[54] Pronouncing the word *morena* (or *moreno*) with a certain emphasis or
changed inflection indicates darker color.

[55] Stated in personal correspondence with the author.

tween the races, serving at once as a symbol and as a means of white-Negro union. When, as often happens, marriage occurs between a *branco* and a *morena* some of whose ancestors were Africans, the resulting offspring obviously make it more difficult for white fathers to consider African blood prejudicial—an attitude intensified in the new generation, which actually possesses some African blood.

TABLE 7

PROBABLE ETHNIC ORIGIN OF THE FIRST FIVE HUNDRED WOMEN CLASSIFIED AS *Morenas* IN THE FILES OF THE GABINETE DE IDENTIFICAÇÃO, BAHIA, 1936

Probability	Number	Per Cent
Whites........................	131	26.2
Mulattoes.....................	308	61.6
White-Indian mixed-bloods.......	28	5.6
Negro-Indian mixed-bloods.......	15	3.0
Negro-White-Indian mixed-bloods.	18	3.6
Total.....................	500	100.0

The term "Negro" is seldom heard in Bahia. It is a *palavra pesada*, a harsh, even offensive, term. Its actual meaning is "African," i.e., "foreigner." In this respect it is a term somewhat similar to "Wop," "Dago," "Sheeny," "Greaser." It also implies slave status and hence calls up memories of the harsher aspects of slavery of which the blacks do not like to talk and the whites are ashamed. Its use is therefore "not good form," and one hears it ordinarily employed only in anger, as an epithet. If otherwise used, it must be "with a smile." *Mulato* is coming to have a somewhat similar connotation, and, as a white Bahian put it, "the better people are beginning to use *moreno* instead."

At the same time, *meu negro* ("my Negro"), with its variation *meu nego*[56] and diminutive *meu negrinho*, all spoken in soft tones, are terms of endearment used even by whites in speaking to other whites, especially in cases of great intimacy as, for instance, between lovers. Their use constitutes, as a Bahian put it, "um modo de tratar bem" ("a way of being nice"). Occasionally one hears these expressions on the lips of a beggar asking alms of a white and, if he appears well to do, of a mulatto as well. Clerks sometimes employ them in addressing a customer. They appear to call up tender memories of intimate, personal relations like those existent, for example, between Mammy and Scarlett O'Hara in Margaret Mitchell's *Gone with the Wind*.

The term *branco da Bahia* ("Bahian white") is also heard, although it is ordinarily employed *outside* Bahia. It has reference to the local custom of including many light mixed-bloods in the *branco* category. The phrase *branco por procuração* ("white by proxy") is occasionally used in Bahia but never when speaking to such an individual directly or in his presence. Light mixed-bloods are sometimes referred to as *bem areiadas* ("well sandpapered"); very dark young Negro boys as *pregos* ("nails"); very dark blacks as *pretos retintos* (literally "black blacks," or "black as coal"), and *reclames do pixe* (literally "shouts of tar," i.e., "black as pitch"). The phrase *ele tem genipapo* refers to the possession of *manchas*, as previously noted. Of a person who shows slight traces of Negro ancestry, it is said, "Ele tem dedo na cozinha" ("He has a finger in the kitchen"). Additional descriptive words or phrases include: *de côr escura* ("of dark color"), *de côr*

---

[56] The feminine forms are *minha negra*. *minha nega*, and *minha negrinha*.

morena, de côr branca, de côr parda, de côr preta, mestiço
("mixed-blood"), and *moleque.*[57]

In the Bahian interior four categories are in common use:
branco, moreno, roxo ("purple"),[58] and *preto. Pardo, mulato,*
and *negro* are seldom employed. Occasionally, *curiboca* is
used in referring to a cross between a *preto* and an Indian.

Indicative of the (as yet) somewhat indeterminate character of these categories are the variations in meaning which
several of these terms seem to have for different individuals.
For example, *moreno,* an upper-class lady of European descent said, "might for all practical purposes be considered as
identical with *branco,*" an opinion concurred in by numerous
other individuals from the upper class. But a lower-class
preto thought of *moreno* as "almost identical with *pardo*"; a
lower-class *parda* considered a *moreno* more negroid than a
pardo; while other individuals made a distinction between
two classes of *morenos: morenos claros* ("light *morenos*"),
and *morenos escuros* ("dark *morenos*").

In classifying a given individual, hair texture is much
more important than color of skin. One often hears in Bahia
the expression, "Ele é um pouco escuro, mas o cabello é
bom" ("He is a bit dark, but his hair is good").

[57] Also spelled *muleque.* The word is of African origin and was originally
used to refer, as we have seen, to a small Negro boy. It is now occasionally
employed in Bahia, without regard to color, in the sense of "street urchin."

[58] The purple tinge of the skin of black individuals under the bright rays
of the tropical sun is probably responsible for this expression.

CHAPTER V

INTERMARRIAGE

AS WE have already seen, the first Portuguese settlers in Bahia were almost exclusively males and, like the Dutch under similar circumstances in South Africa and in Java, the English in India, and the English and Americans in Hawaii, took native women for wives. It is reported that when Thomé de Souza dropped anchor in Todos os Santos Bay, he found in and about the site on which the city was subsequently founded "more than forty" Portuguese men living with native women.[1] According to legend, De Souza was much indebted to the Indian spouse of one of these adventurers, "the comely Paraguassú," daughter of chief Itaparica of the local Tupinambás, for the eventual success of the settlement.

Paraguassú had been living with a Portuguese sailor, Diogo Alvares Correia, who, some years earlier, either was shipwrecked or had deserted ship at this point. He had since that time lived with the Indians on what is now known as Graça Hill, which lies within the present limits of the city, and had founded an extensive half-breed family. With the passing of time he has become a legendary figure to whom living descendants proudly trace their lineage. As given by Alvares do Amaral,[2] the legend appears more plausible than Southey's account[3] and is as follows:

[1] Francisco A. de Varnhagen, Visconde de Porto Seguro, *Historia geral do Brasil* (3d complete ed., 4 vols.; São Paulo, n.d.), I, 300. Based on a *Carta* by Nobrega.

[2] *Resumo chronologico da Bahia* (Bahia, n.d.), p. 201.

[3] Robert Southey, *History of Brazil* (3 vols.; London, 1810), I, 30–31.

Diogo Alvares Correia, or Caramurú . . . . was a native of Vianna do Minho, in Portugal. While still a young lad, overcome with the desire to see new lands, he shipped with a vessel bound for India. But the ship was buffeted by contrary winds and finally, lashed by a severe storm, was broken in pieces and cast upon the coast of Brazil at the mouth of the Rio Vermelho near a place called by the Indians *Mairaguiquity* and now known as Mariquita. This was in 1510. The shipwrecked sailors who escaped being eaten by fish served as choice morsels for men, for they were all made prisoners and subsequently devoured by the savage Tupinambás with the exception of Diogo Alvares Correia, who was saved by a young Indian girl, by name Paraguassú, the daughter of Itaparica, the chief of the tribe, who implored her father not to kill this man since she had at first sight become very fond of him; to which appeal the chief was attentive and presented her with Diogo, who then aided the Indians in recovering the spoils of the wreck among which were several kegs of powder and ball, and some muskets. Of the latter he prepared one and began to fire it, shooting down some birds. The flash of fire, the noise of the discharge, and the death of the birds caused great terror among the natives, for they had never before known firearms. Thenceforth they treated Diogo with great veneration, giving him their daughters for concubines, and the chief offering his daughter for a wife. Diogo was given the name of Caramurú-Assú, which in their idiom means "sea-dragon." He was also called "man-of-fire."[4]

In this savage state Diogo Alvares lived for some time, dwelling in a village later called Villa Velha, today the site of Graça until, some eight years later, in 1518, a French ship arrived in Bahia, and he decided to sail back in it by way of France to Portugal. When the ship, filled with a fresh cargo of Brazilwood, set sail again, he and the gentle Paraguassú were on it. Several of his Indian concubines, seeing him leave, swam out after the ship . . . . , among them the charming

[4] Antonio Alexandre Borges dos Reis (*Chorographia e historia do Brasil, especialmente do estado da Bahia* [Bahia, 1894], pp. 161–62) records a variant account of Caramurú's rescue: "Paraguassú, chancing upon him hiding in a pocket of a reef into which he had crawled to escape detection, and taking him under her protection, saved his life, he gaining afterwards, thanks to his qualities as a civilized man, the influence which he came so effectively to exercise."

Moema, who, exhausted, perished in the billows of the sea. This unhappy Indian maiden is still today sung by the poets. . . . .

On returning from Europe, Cathcrina Paraguassú, endowed with
a beauty that was first among her people, performed the duty of a true
heroine by receiving as her guest the first Governor-general, Thomé de
Souza. She and her husband made the native Indians, without the
least hesitancy, subject themselves to the Portuguese dominion. And
it is from Diogo Alvares Caramurú and Catherina Paraguassú that
the ancient and noble house of Garcia d'Avila, so celebrated for its
wealth and civic services, is descended.

Subsequent to the arrival of Thomé de Souza, Diogo had
been legally married to Paraguassú. And the church soon
saw to it that most, if not all, of the similarly informal unions
between European men and native Indian women were
"regularized in Christian marriage."

Although incoming Portuguese colonists and adventurers
had readily entered into informal unions with native women,
they appear at first to have hesitated before actual marriage.
It was the Jesuits, we are told, who "managed to conquer in
the early colonists the repugnance which they originally held
toward marriages with Indian women."[5] "Most of them [the
Portuguese] here," wrote Padre Nobrega from Pernambuco
in 1551, "have for a long time kept Indian women from
whom they have had children; but to marry them was considered a scandalous thing (grande infamia). They are now
marrying and assuming a proper life."[6] At any rate, intermarriage eventually became a firmly established custom,
sanctioned by both church and state.

Although the scarcity of European women, so notable
during the first century of colonization, had by the early

---

[5] Gilberto Freyre, Casa grande e senzala (2d ed.; Rio, 1936), p. 302.

[6] Padre Manoel de Nobrega, Cartas do Brasil, 1549–1560 (Rio, 1886),
quoted by Freyre, op. cit., p. 302.

seventeenth century largely disappeared, Zacharias Wagner at that time observed that unions of Portuguese men with Indian or mixed-blood women were still of frequent occurrence.[7] Capistrano de Abreu records the desire of native women to have children "belonging to the superior race, since, according to the ideas current among them, parentage was important only on the paternal side."[8] Freyre, following Varnhagen, thinks "a decided sexual preference" was involved.[9]

Intermarriage assures to the family relationships of the mixed-blood a relative permanence and continuity not always characteristic of informal unions. Although human beings are responsive to the natural claims of paternity, illegitimate offspring are often denied the regular presence of a father in the family and the relative security in other respects of legitimate children.

Among the Africans imported into Bahia were numerous individuals possessed, as we have seen, of a cultural equipment superior not only to that of the native Indian but also "to that of the majority of the white colonists . . . . many of whom were illiterate and the greater portion only semiliterate."[10] In the eighteenth and early nineteenth centuries there was so little literacy among the Europeans that "not rarely rich *fazendeiros* in the interior requested their friends on the coast to arrange a son-in-law who, although he had no

---

[7] Alfredo de Carvalho, "O Zoobillion de Zacharias Wagner," *Revista do Instituto Archeologico, Historico e Geographico de Pernambuco*, Vol. XI (1904), quoted by Freyre, *op. cit.*, p. 59.

[8] Capistrano de Abreu, *Capitulos de historia colonial* (3d. ed.; Rio, 1934), quoted by Freyre, *op. cit.*, p. 59.

[9] *Op. cit.*, p. 59.   [10] *Ibid.*, p. 212.

other possessions, did know how to read and write."[11] Incidentally, some of these men were light mulattoes.

The Negro women known in Bahia as "Minas" were famed for their fine physiques, their proud, dignified bearing, and their culinary skill.[12] They were probably Fulahs and Ashantis who were called "Minas" after the name of the Portuguese slave factory on the West Coast known as Forte de el Mina,[13] whence they were imported into Brazil. They approximated the whites in color and features perhaps more closely than any other imported Africans. Araripe Junior writes that they made "excellent companions." "Healthy, ingenuous, and affectionate, it was inevitable," he concludes, "under the precarious conditions of the first and second centuries, that they should dominate the situation."[14] It is probably among these women that the first legal marriages of Europeans with Negro women occurred. In 1730 the governor of Rio de Janeiro, Luis Vahia Monteiro, stated that "there is no Mineiro [gold miner] who can live without a Mina Negro woman. They say that only with them are they lucky."[15] The Minas became not only *amigas* and *mancebas* of the Europeans but eventually *donas de casa* ("housewives").

[11] Henry Koster, *Travels in Brazil, 1809 to 1815* (2 vols.; Philadelphia, 1817), II, 178–79.

[12] Braz do Amaral, "Os grandes mercados de escravos africanos," *Revista do Instituto Historico e Geographico Brasileiro*, tomo especial, *Congresso Internacional de Historia de America* (1927), V, 481.

[13] Arthur Ramos, *As culturas negras no novo mundo* (Rio, 1937), pp. 324–25.

[14] Araripe Junior, *Gregorio de Mattos* (Rio, 1894), quoted by Freyre, *op. cit.*, p. 220.

[15] F. J. Oliveira Vianna, *Evolução do povo brasileiro* (2d ed.; São Paulo, 1933), p. 149.

Dampier, who visited Bahia in the seventeenth century, knew several Europeans living in common-law marriage with Negro women. By this time the relations were not merely casual affairs. "Many an African woman," we are told, "had managed to gain the respect of her white mate; some through the fear inspired by their *mandingas* (black magic); others, like the Minas for example, by their affectionate natures and womanly qualities."[16] "At least a minority of these women had by this time achieved for themselves . . . . positions as housekeepers to the whites; no longer were they kept in the *senzalas* merely for the physical pleasure of their masters and the increase of his human capital." By the early nineteenth century the marriage of white men with *mulheres de côr* were, we are told, not rare.[17] The women involved, like the Osage Indian women of the United States, for instance, whose oil lands have increased their desirability as wives for white men,[18] often possessed considerable property. Such cases were "commented upon in intimate circles but without acrimony, especially when the excuse proved to be the dowry of the bride."

Other marriage partners of the whites were mixed-bloods, men as well as women. Gradually, we are told, marriages with mulattoes came "no longer to be disdained as they formerly were, now that the high position of the mulatto

[16] Freyre, *op. cit.*, p. 302.

[17] Koster, *op. cit.*, II, 178.

[18] "The white demand for Osage women, who are rich in oil land, is now so great that the Indian agent requires every prospective husband to give a bond, submit to a physical examination, and present character references. White husbands have become so easy to get that they are now considered somewhat less desirable than even Indian men of other tribes" (Ralph Linton, "An Anthropological View of Race Mixture," *Publications of the American Sociological Society*, XIX [1924], 76).

and the proof of his moral qualities have led people to overlook the evident contrast of his physical characters, and his black origin is lost sight of in the approximation of his moral and intellectual qualities to those of the white."[19]

In Bahia today people neither think nor talk very much about interracial marriage. It is of no more consequence, perhaps, than interclass marriage or marriage between different nationalities in the United States. Few marriages of any kind cross class lines. Marriages between a member of the upper class, on the one hand, and an individual who has climbed up out of the lower class into an intermediate position, on the other, or between the latter and a member of the lower class, do occasionally take place. But they occur very rarely between individuals from the upper and the lower strata.

It is the impression of competent residents well acquainted with the social structure of Bahia that marriages cross race lines more often than class lines; that is, that marriages between individuals from different occupational and income levels within each racial group are less frequent than marriages between members of the different racial groups in the same class. Unfortunately, reliable statistical data upon this important point are not available.

According to the official records, 42 cases of intermarriage occurred at Bahia out of a total of 1,269 marriages during the year and four months from September 1, 1933, to December 31, 1934. Although this figure represents only 3.3 per cent of the marriages recorded, it does not include those cases in which one of the participants, although classified according to local categories as a *branco* or a *branca*, actually

---

[19] Jean Baptiste de Lacerda, "The *Metis*, or Half-breeds of Brazil," in *Papers on Inter-racial Problems*, ed. G. Spiller (London, 1911), p. 382.

has some degree of color in his ancestry. In other words, the white–*branco da Bahia* marriages are omitted.[20] It represents, therefore, the number of intermarriages from the local point of view, but, as a government official pointed out, it does not accurately reflect the amount of actual race-crossing.

Among the whites of the upper classes a definite line is drawn at intermarriage between individuals from the extreme limits of the color scale, just as a line is drawn, and perhaps for the same reason, at marriage between individuals from the lower and upper limits of the class scale. Although such marriages do occasionally occur, they are ordinarily frowned upon. Thus, of 149 students classifying themselves as *brancos* and responding to the query, "Do you object to marrying a *preto?*" 139, or 93 per cent, replied "Yes." Of 140 similar students, 93, or two-thirds, even objected to dancing with a black.

The brother of a former governor of Bahia, scion of a family which traces its lineage back through a long line of colonial and European aristocracy, had never married but had lived all his life with a lower-class Negro mistress. When, on his deathbed, he desired to marry the woman and thus legitimize the children, his family objected so strenuously that the attempt was abandoned. However, opposition was not only on color but also, and more importantly, on class grounds.

Hence, white-Negro *consorcios* which involve a member of the upper class are ordinarily extra-legal, outside marriage. In the upper circles intermarriage becomes more pronounced as the colors approach along the white-black continuum.

[20] It is also true, of course, that *branco da Bahia–pardo* marriages are included.

No effective opposition appears to an individual with *um pouco da raça* ("a little color"), provided he also possesses the requisite characteristics of upper-class standing.

As we have indicated, marriages between individuals of different colors, like marriages between individuals from the same race, ordinarily take place within class lines. Thus, of twenty-four marriages at Bahia in which one partner was a *branco* or a *branca* and the other a *preto* or *preta*, all the individuals, with the possible exception of one couple, were from the same class. When such marriages occur outside class lines—that is, between individuals from different occupational or income levels—the economic and social advantage, as might be anticipated, will ordinarily be in favor of the white.[21] A *preto*, speaking of the marriage of a certain white woman on the Ilha de Mare to a black, explained, "She got more out of it than he did ['foi mais para ela']. He had money and she didn't."

Of 72 cases of intermarriage upon which it was possible to secure accurate and relatively complete information, 61, or 85 per cent, were contracted by individuals from the same occupational level. Of the 11 remaining cases in which people married across class lines, in 8, or 73 per cent, the social and economic advantages accrued to the white partner. In the remaining 3 cases, in which white individuals married a spouse from a lower occupational level, the whites were all women, a circumstance probably to be expected, given a social order wherein women are ordinarily at a disadvantage socially and at the same time under pressure to avoid spinsterhood.

Of 35 cases on which reliable information regarding financial condition was available, only 8 were from the same eco-

[21] To some extent this is also true of intermarriage *within* the same class.

nomic level. Of the 27 others, in 21, or 80 per cent, of the cases the financial condition of the white was less favorable than that of the colored partner. Of the 6 other cases, in which monetary advantage was in favor of the darker individual, 3 of the whites involved were males, and 3 were females.

One of the males had married the daughter of a respected and widely revered mixed-blood educator, an "authority" on Portuguese grammar, with whom many Bahians of the upper classes had studied and into whose family, by reason of the father's prestige, anyone in Bahia would deem it an honor to be accepted. Moreover, the difference in economic level between the two families was slight. A second had married a "beautiful *morena*" whose physical charm, it is said, readily compensated for the difference in economic status.

In 19 cases of intermarriage on which information was obtained from a town in the interior (Itaquara), 15 were from the same occupational level. In the 4 cases in which one spouse came from a lower social stratum than the other, the social advantage was in each case in favor of the white. Thirteen of the 19 couples came from the same economic level.

One may say that the frequency of intermarriage at Bahia varies inversely with class level. In other words, intermarriage takes place readily in the lower circles, occasionally among whites who are climbing in the class scale, and rarely with whites in the upper class.[22]

When intermarriages involving upper-class individuals do occur, however, "society" does not completely close its doors

[22] This generalization does not hold for *brancos da Bahia*, or those mixed-bloods who have passed over into the white category.

on the couple. "Some people feel sorry for them and try to treat them as usual; but, especially if the black is from the lower classes, there is always a difference," commented a member of the upper class. If someone marries a person a great deal darker than himself, one hears the phrase "Ele não tem vergonha na cara" (literally, "He does not have shame in his face").

"But it would be different," added a white upper-class woman, "with Dr. Raul Calogeras,"[23] naming a prominent *preto*, a man of considerable personal charm, with the poise and bearing of a "gentleman," an able engineer for six years in charge of the sanitary service at Bahia and for twenty years at the head of a similar service for the city and state of São Paulo, once a federal senator and friend of the former president of Brazil, Washington Luiz. He is also nationally regarded as the principal Brazilian "authority" on the Tupi language. For years he has been president of an important intellectual and social institution in Bahia among whose membership, principally white, are to be found many of the leading intellectuals of the city. "Several white women whom I know would feel themselves honored to be his wife."

The implications of this remark are highly significant, if one would understand the actual racial situation at Bahia. It indicates rather clearly that opposition to marriage with a black is more importantly on class than on racial grounds. When black color comes no longer to identify an individual as a member of the lower class, opposition to him tends to disappear. Virtually no opposition attaches to the marriage of light mixed-bloods into even the upper class, especially if they do not show in their features or color too obvious evidence of Negro origin.

[23] The name is, for obvious reasons, fictitious.

In 1914 Theodore Roosevelt wrote of Rio de Janeiro: "In the lower ranks intermarriages are frequent, especially between the Negroes and the most numerous of the immigrant races of Europe. In the middle class these intermarriages are rare, and in the higher class almost unknown so far as concerns men and women in whom the black strain is at all evident. But even in the higher ranks there is apparently no prejudice whatever against marrying a man or girl who is, say, seven-eighths white, the remaining quantity of black blood being treated as a negligible element."[24] Although the Bahian aristocracy has maintained itself as endogamous as any similar group in Brazil, or perhaps even more endogamous, individuals possessing at least some Negro blood are now marrying into its ranks.

A dark mixed-blood at Bahia, a prominent and relatively wealthy commercial figure, courted and married a girl from a distinguished white family. A common expression heard in connection with this case of intermarriage and which perhaps sums up in a pithy statement the racial situation at Bahia is: "Negro rico é branco, e branco pobre é negro" ("A rich Negro is a white man, and a poor white man is a Negro"). This is merely another way of saying that class (one criterion of which is wealth), not race, is the primary consideration.

A prominent medical specialist, a dark mixed-blood, has a blond German wife whom he courted and married while a student in Germany. Because of his professional competence, intellectual ability, and personal charm, he occupies a high position in the community. He is a member of the most exclusive social club, membership in which is an infallible index of social status. Since his professional practice is extensive

[24] "Brazil and the Negro," *Outlook*, CVI (February 21, 1914), 410.

and his clients are drawn largely from the élite, he is well to do financially. His wife, it is said, is envied by other white women.

A woman of the upper class when asked if a woman's social standing declined after her marriage to a black or dark mulatto said: "This depends largely on the man. It may; but if he is cultivated and refined, it may not. A woman marrying Dr. Raul Calogeras would not lose caste."

Obviously, then, a distinction must be made between interclass and intraclass marriages. The following reasons given by whites responding affirmatively to the query, "Do you object to marrying a *preto?*" indicate that their objection was basically on class, rather than on racial, grounds:

Because *pretos* seldom have social standing.
Because they are ordinarily lower in the social scale.
Because they are usually crude and stupid.
Because they belong to a low class.
Because it would lower me.
Because I think both should be on the same social level.
Because black color usually lowers one's social position.
Because I think social equality is indispensable for marriage.

These statements all reduce perhaps to one general statement: The Negro ordinarily lacks class.

A distinction must also be made between those individuals who are noticeably negroid and those who are *branqueados*, who have only *um pouco da raça*. As an upper-class white woman remarked: "It's different with the lighter shades. You can't easily draw the line between the pure whites and those with only *um pouco da raça*. Race mixture has now become so extensive that there wouldn't be many left to choose among." Very light mixed-bloods often marry whites without any question whatever arising. For instance, the four sons and two daughters of a family which shows slight traces of African ancestry all married white spouses, *brancos finos* ("genteel whites"), as a friend put it. One married the daughter of a distinguished physician and professor at the Faculty of Medicine. Another married into a prominent upper-class family. A third married a young man whose family possesses considerable wealth and lives in a palatial home in one of the select residential areas. The fourth married a descendant of the colonial aristocracy, now a state deputy, an able lawyer, and professor at the Faculty of Law.

A seventeen-year-old white girl "of good family," after replying in the negative to a query whether she would marry a *preto*, was asked, "How dark a man would you be willing to marry"? After reflecting a moment, she replied, "One about like Reginaldo," naming a light mixed-blood with *bom* ("good") hair.

An important commercial figure shows slight traces of Negro lineage, particularly in his hair. He is intelligent, capable, "dynamic." His wife is white, handsome, of gracious bearing. Their daughter, beautiful, of "charming personality," would pass easily for white anywhere. Her fiancé is almost white, but shows a few traces of Negro lineage.

The rate of interracial marriage is probably increasing, although positive data are not available. As the black and the mixed-blood rise in class, one would expect this to take place. Several individuals from different class levels were quite certain that intermarriage is more prevalent today than formerly. "The races used to stay apart much more than they do now," commented a *preta* cook. "Once in a while a dark person and a white would marry, but it was rare. The whites used to say he was *uma mosca dentro do leite* ('a fly in the milk'). There wasn't so much mixture then."

One may perhaps say, then, that black color, although an undeniable handicap to marriage into the upper classes at Bahia (at least when sufficiently obvious to be readily observable) is not an absolute bar and may be overcome with the aid of such advantages as wealth, intelligence, occupational proficiency, beauty, and personal charm. The individual involved will be accepted more on the basis of his mental and social qualities than on racial descent.

However, since a Negro cannot escape his color but, on the contrary, constantly carries with him this indelible badge of low status, he tends to be catalogued by one meeting him for the first time as a member of the lower status group. Only as he simultaneously or subsequently gives evidence of other characteristics ordinarily associated with upper-class standing, such as economic competence, professional skill, educational achievement, "gentlemanly bearing," etc., is this original conception modified; and even then the fact of his being in appearance like a lower-class man remains one of the criteria of him and is undoubtedly a handicap.

It is in the light of this distinction that one perhaps best understands what at first sight appears to be discrimination on the basis of race. Since to a large extent discrimination follows color lines, one is likely to assume its similarity to that which we know in the United States and naïvely posit an automatic relationship between race and discrimination. But if one focuses his attention on those *homens de côr* who have risen in class and who for this reason are no longer subjected to the same prejudices as others of their fellows who have not yet risen, he sees that the connection between race and discrimination is not direct but *indirect;* that not necessarily discrimination on the basis of *race* is involved but discrimination on the basis of *class*, involving in most cases, quite expectedly, individuals of color, owing to the concentration of the darker portion of the population for centuries in the lower status ranks.

Race has undoubtedly been a factor in Brazil in fixing classes and making them, to some extent at least, hereditary. But race as a criterion of class is breaking down, increasingly, as more and more individuals of dark color give evidence of the possession of, or the ability to achieve, other characteristics indicative of superior status. The significant fact is that a black or dark mulatto *can* overcome the handicap of color, *can* overbalance this liability by means of other assets. His social position is not fixed and rigid. It is always subject to change.

IV

RACE AND SOCIAL STATUS

CHAPTER VI

THE RISE OF THE MIXED-BLOOD

EARLY in the colonial period race mixture resulted in an intermediate population group in more favorable position for social advancement. Mulatto slaves, because they were ordinarily chosen by their masters and mistresses for the more delicate and exacting household tasks, to be *mucamas* (maids), *amas de crear* ("mammies"), and other *pessoal de casa* (house servants), early developed into a distinct group apart from the field hands.[1] They were baptized, received the master's name, and often were married in accordance with the prescribed legal and religious practices, thus establishing legitimate families and adding to the social security of their offspring by building up a family tradition.

Many *mulatinhos*, illegitimate children of the *senhor*, learned to read and to write even more quickly than white, legitimate children, outstripping them in preparatory and even advanced studies. The Reconcavo of Bahia yields a number of such cases.[2] Particularly fortunate, we are told, were the children of priests. Their fathers, being ordinarily from upper-class families and possessing money and prestige, transmitted to their offspring, colored as well as white, ad-

---

[1] F. J. Oliveira Vianna, *Evolução do povo brasileiro* (2d ed.; São Paulo, 1933), p. 157; Jean Baptiste de Lacerda, "The *Metis*, or Half-breeds of Brazil," in *Papers on Inter-racial Problems*, ed. G. Spiller (London, 1911), p. 379.

[2] Gilberto Freyre, *Casa grande e senzala* (2d ed.; Rio, 1936), pp. 324–25. The author throughout this chapter is greatly indebted to Freyre's *Sobrados e mucambos* (São Paulo, 1936), esp. chap. vii.

vantages of ancestry, social position, intellectuality, and
wealth. The professions were readily open to them, and
"marriages into the bosom of the most exclusive families"[3]
sometimes took place. "More fortunate even than the son
of a priest" and "A child of a priest is never unhappy" are
expressions still heard at Bahia.[4]

Significant also was the widespread system of *creação*,
whereby colored children who were being reared within the
master's house, the so-called *crias, irmãos de creação, malungos, muleques de estimação*, gained position as "persons of
the house," somewhat comparable to poor relations in the
households of medieval Europe. Often they were seated at
the patriarchal table as if members of the family. Some even
rode in the family vehicle with their masters.

Owing to the peculiar personal associations in which the
mulattoes grew up, they tended to develop certain traits
favorable to their advancement. They were usually more intelligent, we are told, more aggressive, more dexterous, and
more cunning than the pure blacks. Consequently, they
were often assigned to the more skilled occupations, such as
shoemaking, carpentry, and tailoring, where they developed
occupational skills symbolic of greater personal worth than
ordinarily attaches to unskilled labor.

Because they were liberated in preference to the blacks,
the mixed-bloods, early in the colonial period, began to
enter the free classes.[5] The disproportion between black

[3] Freyre, *Casa grande e senzala*, p. 324.

[4] "The social ascension of children of priests, both white and light mixed-
blood, has always occurred with great facility" (*ibid.*, pp. 323–24).

[5] In addition, the king of Portugal in 1773 intervened in their behalf,
denouncing those persons "so lacking in the sentiments of humanity and of
religion" that they still keep in slavery persons "whiter than they are"
(Freyre, *Sobrados e mucambos*, p. 327).

and mulatto slaves noticeable even before 1800, had by the end of the first quarter of the nineteenth century become great. In 1822, for instance, the free blacks in Maranhão were reckoned at 9,308; the free mulattoes, at 25,111. Only 6,580 mulattoes were still in bondage as compared with 77,954 blacks. Thus, in this important center of Negro concentration, over three-fourths of the mixed-bloods had by 1822 been emancipated, whereas approximately only one-eighth of the blacks had been liberated. Walsh in 1828 reports that there were at that time in Brazil approximately 160,000 free blacks and 400,000 free mulattoes. In 1835, among a total of 170,000 mulattoes in Minas Geraes, only 40,000, or less than one-fourth, were reported to be slaves; while 250,000 out of an estimated 305,000 blacks, or approximately five-sixths, were still in bondage.[6] Although no figures are available for Bahia, it is likely that similar proportions held here also.

These numerically important liberated mulattoes began their rise in social rank by becoming small farmers (*lavradores, sitiantes*), or artisans (both rural and urban), street merchants, small shopkeepers, etc., taking their places beside those lower-class whites who either had not yet risen or did not possess the requisite ability to rise.

Free blacks, as well as free mulattoes, were able to establish themselves in manual occupations more readily than their brothers in the United States because the descendants of Europeans in Brazil have ordinarily looked down upon manual labor, as attested by the common saying: "Trabalho é para cachorro e negro" (work [that is, hard manual labor] is for Negroes and dogs). "Whatever may have been the en-

[6] Maurice Rugendas, *Voyage pittoresque dans le Brésil*, trans. from the German by de Colbery (3 vols.; Paris, 1835), p. 27.

ergy exerted by their immigrant fathers, creoles [native Bra-
zilians] ordinarily imbibed the colonial prejudice against labor, and assumed the airs of gentlemen." Free men of color
entering agricultural or artisan employment "in no way
aroused the jealousy of Europeans."[7]

The mobility of the Brazilian population in the colonial
period, both vertically and horizontally, facilitated climbing. Changes in status during the lifetime of a given individual were common phenomena and at times even precipi-
tous, a condition reflected in the common saying "Pae taber-
neiro, filho cavalheiro, neto mendicante" ("Father an inn-
keeper, son a squire, grandson a beggar"). Endogamy
among the rural aristocracy, even in such *fidalgo* centers as
Bahia and Pernambuco, was never absolute. Clerks and
small merchants in the cities, immigrant peddlers in the interior, modest proprietors of small farms, owners of small
herds of cattle—all aspired to, and some succeeded in attaining, the ranks of the rural aristocracy.[8]

Similarly significant was freedom to move in space. For
in areas distant from those of their birth, light mulattoes of
slave origin often managed to pass for individuals born of
free parents. They were thus able readily to strip from themselves the social stigma of servile origin. One of the functions of the *bandeiras* and the *monções*[9] was to assist ambitious individuals to whom migration and the freedom of
the frontier appeared to offer the most rapid and successful
means of social advancement. Many mixed-bloods sought
out new homes and became settlers, stock-raisers, small

[7] H. A. Wyndham, *The Atlantic and Slavery* (London: Oxford University
Press, 1935), pp. 249–50.

[8] Vianna, *op. cit.*, p. 153.

[9] The *bandeiras* (also called *monções*) were groups of hardy explorers and
frontier fighters who explored the interior or raided Indian villages for
slaves.

senhores de engenho, fazendeiros, etc.[10] Often they were run-away slaves.[11] In the cities they became masons, cobblers, tinsmiths, soldiers, actors, and at times reached even the small bourgeosie.[12]

The mulatto, owing to his closer approximation in physical characteristics to the European, was better able than the Negro to appropriate certain symbols of status—the small shoe and the little boot, for instance, the wearing of which was an important index of social standing in colonial and imperial Brazil.[13] Small feet, particularly among women, were for a long time, and still are, fashionable.

As the mulatto rose in class, he came to occupy something

[10] Freyre, *Sobrados e mucambos*, pp. 190–91, 205, 238.

[11] "I heard of a mulatto slave who ran away from his master; and in the course of years had become a wealthy man, by the purchase of lands which were overrun with cattle. He had, on one occasion, collected in pens great numbers of oxen which he was arranging with his herdsmen to dispatch to different parts for sale, when a stranger who came quite alone, made his appearance, and rode up and spoke to him, saying that he wished to have some private conversation with him. After a little time they retired together; and when they were alone the owner of the estate said, "I thank you for not mentioning the connection between us, whilst my people were present." It was his master, who had fallen into distressed circumstances, and had now made this visit in hopes of obtaining some trifle from him. He said that he would be grateful for anything his slave chose to give him. To reclaim him, he well knew, was out of the question—he was in the man's power, who might order him to be assassinated immediately. The slave gave his master several hundred oxen, and directed some of his men to accompany him with them to a market, giving out among his herdsmen, that he had thus paid a debt of old standing, for which he had only now been called upon" (Henry Koster, *Travels in Brazil, 1809 to 1815* [2 vols.; Philadelphia, 1817], I, 244–45).

[12] Vianna, *op. cit.*, p. 143. In 1774 a law opened to *homens pardos* access "to all offices, honors and dignities, without discrimination on account of difference in color" (*Annaes da Biblioteca Nacional*, XXXVII [1913], 85). See also Pedro Calmon, *Historia social do Brasil* (3 vols.; São Paulo, 1937–39), I, 168.

[13] "The use of shoes and little boots, which was at first almost entirely limited to persons recently arrived from Portugal, spread among those men

analogous to a middle position distinct from either that of the dominant European or that of the subject African. In the colonial period, "to appease the repugnance felt by whites at being put on the same level with mulattoes,"[14] the latter were segregated for military duty. Thus separate battalions were organized at Bahia and elsewhere for whites, for *pardos*,[15] and for *pretos*.[16] Similarly, separate church organizations arose for *pardos* (Palma, Guadaloupe, Boqueirão) as well as for *pretos*.[17]

In the Brazilian rural society of the colonial period Oliveira Vianna identifies three distinct social strata: the predominantly white *senhores* of the upper rank, the predominantly mixed-blood free artisans, *rendeiros*, and petty

---

and women of the Brazilian aristocracy who were blessed with small feet. The difficulties of the blacks, even when serving as pages, to adjust themselves to this new European and aristocratic style so ill adapted to their large and flat feet, can be easily understood. The mulattoes, on the other hand, who possessed smaller feet, well formed according to the European standard, could adapt themselves more readily to a practice which Handelmann observed constituted in nineteenth-century Brazil one of the marks of class distinction" (Freyre, *Sobrados e mucambos*, pp. 329–30).

[14] Vianna, *op. cit.*, p. 164; see also his *Populaçoes meridionaes do Brasil* (3d ed.; São Paulo, 1933), p. 140.

[15] In Bahia, the Regimento dos Pardos. See Luiz dos Santos Vilhena, *Cartas*, edited and annotated by Braz do Amaral (2 vols.; Bahia, 1922), pp. 253–54.

[16] In Bahia, as elsewhere, Os Henriques.

[17] In Bahia, Rosario de João Pereira, Barroquinha, Corpo Santo, Rosario "at the foot of the Pelourinho." Cf. also: "The cemetery for Africans was located next to the Misericordia Cemetery, as one can see from the map made of the city of Salvador and its suburbs by Carlos Augusto Weyll" (J. B. von Spix and C. F. P. von Martius, *Através da Bahia* [excerpts from the larger work, *Reise in Brasilien* (3 vols.; München, 1823–31)], trans. Pirajá da Silva and Paulo Wolf [3d ed.; São Paulo, 1938], pp. 141–42 [translators' note]).

officials of the middle tier, and the predominantly black slaves of the lower stratum.[18]

The duration of this particular organization was, however, brief. As the color line bent further under pressure of the rising mulatto, certain of the more able or more successful mixed-bloods broke through into the upper tiers.

The development of the cities increased the possibilities for economic advancement to individuals who, like the mulattoes, were noted for their skill as artisans and—what was more important—for their intellectual ability.[19] The rise, after independence in 1822, of the *academias superiores* offered to the more able mixed-bloods possibilities not previously attainable. Since by reason of their mental alertness the mulattoes often excelled, it is said, in those pursuits wherein intellectual ability is an essential for success, the development of these centers of advanced study opened, at least to the ambitious and favored ones among them, ready access to the rising professional classes, especially as *doutores* or *bachareis*.[20] Many promising young mulattoes were aided to a professional training by indulgent white fathers or other relatives and friends among the dominant class.

Of a prominent Brazilian intellectual, Raul Calogeras, whose father was a Bahian planter and whose mother was a Negro slave, we are told:

Raul was very intelligent, and showed remarkable ability in his studies. It is said that when a very young boy at Santo Amaro, he used to slip away late at night, after his mother's master had gone to bed, to study by the street lamp on the corner near the house. When his father discovered this, he was much impressed, and other signs

[18] Vianna, *op. cit.*, pp. 72–73.

[19] *Ibid.*, p. 151; Freyre, *Sobrados e mucambos*, pp. 160–61, 190.

[20] Physicians, lawyers and engineers.

of Raul's intelligence and his ability to apply himself multiplied the interest which his father took in him, and he supplied all his needs. When his father left the Reconcavo to come to Bahia, he brought Raul with him, and here, under his tutelage, Raul went to primary school where he had as white playmates his father's nephews and others. And later, when his father went to Rio, he took Raul with him. The boy never left his father's company as long as his father lived.[21]

Raul was a very dark mixed-blood with kinky hair. He came to be a prominent citizen and was noted not only for his fine figure, distinguished bearing, poise, and personal charm but also for his intelligence and professional competence. At one time he was a much-loved confidant of a recent president of Brazil.

Significant also, so far as the rise of the mulatto is concerned, is the fact that early in the nineteenth century the return of young professional men who had been trained in Europe—in Coimbra, Montpelier, Paris, and other centers— enhanced the prestige of the rising professional classes. These young lawyers and physicians, among whom were a number of quite capable mulattoes, were returning to Brazil after an education abroad, ordinarily more traveled, better informed, and more urbane than their brothers or half-brothers on the plantations, in the army, or among the clergy. They were especially attractive, we are told, to the upper-class ladies of the time. The importation of fashionable articles from the Continent—Parisian haberdashery, perfumes, hair-dressings, and English shoes—with the use of all of which these returning young men were quite familiar, enhanced their standing among the élite. The increasing

[21] From a letter to the author from a man reared in the same community as the individual in question and long acquainted with him. For information on the later life of this mixed-blood see Appen. A.

prestige of youth, accelerated by the popular rule of young King Dom Pedro II, together with the increasing dominance of the cities in which the young graduates located, also contributed to their rise in social esteem.

The disruption of the old order based upon slavery, owing to the loss of the sugar monopoly, the increasing dependence of rural *senhores* on their urban agents and commission merchants, and the progress of the abolition campaign, eventually leading as it did to widespread desertion of slaves from the *engenhos*, also facilitated the rise of the professional classes. There was under way a gradual transfer of prestige from the rural aristocracy,[22] which had been almost exclusively European, to the urban intelligentsia, which increasingly included mulattoes, particularly of the lighter shades; for example, Gonçalves Dias, Natividade Saldanha, José do Patrocinio, Machado de Assis, Barão de Cotegipe, Olavo Bilac, Domingos Caldas Barbosa, Salles Torres Homem, Nilo Peçanha, Domicio da Gama, Dom Silvero Gomes Pimenta, Dom Luiz Raymundo da Silva Brito, Tobias Barretto, Antonio Vieira, José Mauricio, Auta de Souza, Francisco Gé Acabaya de Montezuma, the Rebouças brothers, and "hundreds of other Brazilians," as João Dornas Filho says, "whose great mental capacity has brought resounding fame to Brazil."[23]

Dom Pedro II elevated to the nobility a prominent mixed-blood who was subsequently known familiarly as "Barão do Chocolate."[24] The Count do Gobineau speaks of meeting

[22] For a sketch of the *rise* of the Brazilian aristocracy see Alan K. Manchester, "The Rise of the Brazilian Aristocracy," *Hispanic American Historical Review*, XI, No. 2 (May, 1931), 145–68.

[23] *A escravidão no Brasil* (Rio, 1939), p. 228.

[24] Freyre, *Casa grande e senzala*, p. 190.

three mulatto ladies-in-waiting to the Brazilian empress, one "marron," one "chocolat eclair," one "violette."[25] Montezuma became a viscount and sat in the national senate, as did also Salles Torres Homem. The best elements of the aristocracy attended the receptions for the noted engineer, Andre Rebouças.[26] His brother Antonio, a federal deputy, on requesting a representative on the crown council for the *população mulata* was heard attentively by the *camara*.[27] Domicio da Gama and the Barão de Cotegipe were long prominent in political and diplomatic circles. Dom Silvero Gomes Pimenta became an archbishop. No musician is said to have been more distinguished at court than the mixed-blood, José Mauricio. Domingos Caldas Barbosa, the son of a Negro woman from Angola, acquired considerable fame in the salons of Rio de Janiero and of Lisbon as a singer of popular songs. The eighteenth-century sculpture of Antonio Francisco Lisboa, better known as Aleijadinho, which may still be seen today in the old churches of Ouro Preto, Sabará, São João d'El Rei, and other cities of Minas Geraes, attracted much favorable comment. José Basilio da Gama, whose *Uruguay* is said to be the best epic poem of the colonial period, the writer, Machado de Assis, and the lyric poet, Antonio Gonçalves Dias, were universally accorded high rank in Brazilian letters. Tobias Barretto was honored as a poet but even more as a jurist and annotator of German philosophical works which he had translated. José de Natividade Saldanha, an able poet, was one of the leaders of the revolt in Recife in 1824.

[25] Freyre, *Sobrados e mucambos*, p. 354.

[26] Visconde de Taunay, *Homens e cousas do imperio* (São Paulo, 1924), p. 145, noted by Calmon, *op. cit.*, II, 112.

[27] Antonio Pereira Rebouças, *Recordações da vida parlamentar* (2 vols.; Rio, 1870), I, 524, noted by Calmon, *op. cit.*, II, 113.

José do Patrocinio became an able editor and wielded a powerful influence in the abolition movement. Joaquim Manoel was a violinist of considerable talent. A number of Francisco Braga's musical compositions achieved acclaim, and he was later invited to teach composition in the National Institute of Music. The Bahian mulatto, Francisco Chagas, better known as "Cabra," carved images with such skill that at least five of them ("Nossa Senhora do Carmo," "São Benedito," "São João e Magdalena," "Nossa Senhora dos Dores," and "Senhor da Redempção") may still be seen in the Igreja do Carmo. Valentim da Fonseca e Silva, popularly known as "Master Valentim," achieved fame as a skilled worker in gold and silver. The mulatto, Jesus, was a notable figure in an influential school of painting which flourished in Bahia in the eighteenth century. Crispim do Amaral, better known by his pseudonym "Falstaff," and Pedro Americo were accepted as among the most competent Brazilian painters of the nineteenth century. Antonio Gonçalves Teixeira e Sousa, Laurindo Rabello, and Gonçalves Crespo, all won acclaim in the Brazilian world of letters, and at least the latter of these three in the Portuguese world of letters as well. The psychiatrist, Juliano Moreira, became director-general of the hospital for the insane in Rio de Janeiro and was elected an honorary professor of the Faculty of Medicine in Bahia. The name of the Hospital João de Deus in Bahia was, in 1936, changed in honor of him to the Hospital Juliano Moreira. Theodoro Sampaio became widely known and respected throughout Brazil as an able engineer, intellectual figure, and linguistic scholar. José Ferreira de Menezes, Monteiro Lopes, Cardoso Vieira, Eliseu Cesar, Evaristo Ferreira da Veiga, and (in more recent times) the Bahian brothers, João and Octavio Manga-

beira, have all been influential politicians with national repu-
tations. Luiz Gama, mulatto journalist and lawyer, born a
slave in Bahia, became exceedingly popular not only in São
Paulo, where he came to reside, but throughout Brazil. At
least one president of the Republic, Nilo Pecanha, had African ancestors.[28]

It is said the royal family set the example of social acceptance of the darker Brazilians and gently rebuked those
whites inclined to be hesitant in the matter. Dom João VI,
in his audiences at São Cristovão, cordially received men of
all stations, and the two Pedros (Dom Pedro I and Dom
Pedro II) continued the tradition. Once, at a court ball,
Princess Isabel, noting that a lady had declined to dance
with André Rebouças, herself offered to dance the subsequent waltz with him, "to compensate for the affront to this
illustrious man."[29]

The range of acceptance was at that time broadening.
Formerly only the exceptionally able mixed-bloods, or those
most similar to the Europeans in color, had been incorporated into the upper circles. But "the prestige of the title
'doutor' began to overcome much of the prejudice which had
been so active and apparently so invincible during three previous centuries."[30] Similarly, an army uniform, "especially

[28] For information in some detail on prominent Brazilian mixed-bloods see
Arthur Ramos, *The Negro in Brazil* (Washington, 1939), *passim*.

[29] Calmon, *op. cit.*, II, 114. Affonso de E. Taunay (in a letter to the
author) reports the incident thus: "At a court ball the Princess Isabel,
Countess of Eu and heir to the throne of Brazil, insisted on dancing with
André Rebouças, a mulatto who was almost black (albeit a man of great
mental and moral worth), in order to censure the attitude of certain ladies
of the court who had objected to him as a dancing partner."

[30] Vianna, *Evolução do povo brasileiro*, p. 145.

the gold braid of an officer, Aryanized and 'aristocratized' many mulattoes into whites."[31]

The rise of the mixed-bloods was also facilitated by the conviction which, since at least the late eighteenth century, had been crystallizing in the minds of Brazilian intellectuals to the effect that the Negroes, whose strong arms and backs had long furnished the country's labor supply, were to a considerable extent the actual builders of Brazil. In prose and poetry not only the toil of the slave but also the creative energies of the free people of color came to be exalted.[32] This appreciation of the African contribution to Brazilian civilization increased with the progress of the abolition campaign. Especially were the *amas* extolled.[33] Much of the abolition sentiment had its sanction in the affectionate gratitude of young aristocrats whom they had reared.

The rise of the mulatto, as also that of the black, was further favored by the gradual, rather than catastrophic, character of the emancipation process which in Brazil released most of the lower stratum of society from servile status gradually and as individuals, under circumstances favorable to the continuance of those intimate personal ties so highly advantageous to a "new freeman." Moreover, final emancipation was not, as in our South, brought about as an incident of civil strife, and the normal relations which had

[31] Freyre, *Sobrados e mucambos*, p. 318.

[32] See Borges dos Reis, "Colonos indigenas e escravos," *Revista do Instituto Geographico e Historico da Bahia*, XXVIII (1902), 61. Note also Alvarengo Peixoto's stanza:

". . . . homens de varias accidentes
pardos, pretos, tintos e tostados
. . . . os fortes braços feitos ao trabalho."

[33] Freyre, *Sobrados e mucambos*, p. 128.

grown up naturally between the races were never threatened, let alone destroyed, by a program of reconstruction originating from without and imposed by armed conquest. Individual ability, personal ties and family solidarity, instead of external pressure, were the levers of social advancement. The rise of the mixed-blood and of the black in Brazil has always had effectively in its favor those sentiments and personal attachments which primary relations tend normally to develop.

Such political upheavals as did occur tended to advance the mixed-bloods not as a group but as individuals. Thus the overthrow of the monarchy and the rise of the republic marked a definite break with the rural aristocracy and accelerated the rise of a new class, that of the *bachareis* and the *doutores*, among whom were many mulattoes. And, more recently, the recrystallization of the political structure following the "revolution of 1930" found many Bahian mixed-bloods in positions of trust and responsibility, since the new political "ins," who were diligently seeking to solidify their gains and to establish themselves firmly in power, found it expedient to accept such support as was readily at hand. Again the mixed-bloods figured prominently, not as a group per se but as individuals belonging to an eligible professional class.

The role of sex and of romantic love should not be overlooked. The sexual attraction which the mulatto male exerted upon daughters of rich and influential European families led quite often to elopement or, occasionally and increasingly, to marriage with parental consent.[34] Similarly,

[34] "The daughters, the *yáyás* of the *sobrados*, the *sinhás* of the *casas grandes de engenho*, let themselves be kidnaped by these Don Juans, even by such as were plebeian and of color. . . . . Sellin noted the large number of young ladies eloping . . . . during the latter half of the nineteenth century. They were girls whose parents, for reasons of blood or of social position, had

the mulatto women profited by the myth of the sexual potency of the hybrid,[35] the high mortality of white women (especially during the nineteenth century), and the consequent successive marriages of elderly patriarchs who sought an increasing degree of sexual stimulation. Cases of "marriages of elderly white men from illustrious families, descendants of barons and well situated in life, with beautiful octoroon, quadroon, or mulatto women who carried themselves like fine ladies and gave evidence of a sexual ardor beyond the ordinary,"[36] increasingly occurred.

Today, the mixed-bloods are gaining a constantly increasing measure of social recognition. Among them are to be found prominent lawyers, jurists, physicians, engineers, politicians, diplomats, priests, educators, business and commercial magnates, musicians, painters, poets, novelists, journalists, planters.[37] In other words, the mulattoes have now penetrated to the top of the class scale.[38]

---

not consented to their marriage with men for whom they had come to feel a sentimental or sexual predilection" (*ibid.*, pp. 156–57). Note also the novel *O mulato* (3d ed.; Rio, 1889), by Aluisio de Azevedo, whose hero is a mixed-blood *bacharel* educated in Europe and enamored of a white girl from a family "full of prejudices of white purity." Gilberto Freyre calls this book "a human document warm with the life of the time."

[35] A popular saying commonly heard in Bahia is: "A white woman for marriage, a Negro woman for work, a *mulata* for sexual intercourse."

[36] Freyre, *Sobrados e mucambos*, p. 337.

[37] See Lacerda, *op. cit.*, pp. 381–82; Manoel de Oliveira Lima, *The Evolution of Brazil Compared with that of Spanish and Anglo-Saxon America* (Palo Alto, 1914), p. 39; Rudiger Bilden, "Laboratory of Civilization," *Nation*, CXXVIII (January 16, 1929), 73; Thomas Ewbank, *Life in Brazil* (New York, 1856), p. 267; Professor and Mrs. Louis Agassiz, *A Journey in Brazil* (Boston and New York, 1888), p. 124; Theodore Roosevelt, "Brazil and the Negro," *Outlook*, CVI (February, 1914), 409.

[38] To accelerate his social climbing, the mixed-blood has developed certain characteristic personality traits: "a pleasant smile and manner, a cordial

In all probability, the movement was at first largely vertical. When, however, the mixed-blood had gained some economic or professional competence, had definitely established his personal worth, he tended to be recognized as an "exceptional" individual; that is, as a person rather than as a member of a group. As the numbers of these "exceptional" individuals multiplied, the social conventions were subjected to constantly increasing pressure, since it is difficult to treat "exceptional" individuals in situations of intimate social intercourse differently from the way they are treated in intellectual, commercial, or political circles. This "strain for consistency" tends in time to modify conduct.[39]

Thus, as the mixed-bloods rose in class, this upward movement was accompanied by what might be called "horizontal progression." The individual who was rising in rank and establishing himself in the upper intellectual and economic circles began actually to penetrate the "inner sanctuaries" of the more exclusive social groups, breaking down marriage and familial taboos. The class tradition, in so far as it had been fixed by race, gradually began to give way under the irresistible pressure exerted upon it by the rising mulatto group.

This rise was accompanied by the personal stresses and strains which an individual in the process of moving from one class to another ordinarily experiences. The first mulattoes to penetrate the upper tiers reflected in their personal

---

show of hospitality, the use of diminutives as a means of being both respectful and intimate at the same time" (Freyre, *Sobrados e mucambos*, pp. 357–58).

[39] Moreover, class interests tended to become more and more important and eventually to bind members of the same class with common bonds of sentiment, attitude, and idea, and thus to cut across lines of color or of racial descent.

lives participation in two different, and to some extent antagonistic, worlds which met and fused, so to speak, in their
own personalities. They were perhaps, to some extent at
least, "marginal men."[40]

The Brazilian mixed-blood was marginal, however, in the
cultural rather than in the racial sense. Often he had moved
during his lifetime from the lower rungs of the class ladder to
the middle or even upper tiers. He had achieved some measure of recognition and was enjoying certain of the advantages of the upper classes. At the same time he was deeply
sensitive to his servile origin and to the fact that he in-
escapably carried with him in his physical characteristics a
mark of low status. Thus, Gonçalves Dias was, we are told,
throughout his life a melancholy soul. "A wound always
bleeding, although hidden under the cloak of a *doutor*. Sensitive to his inferior origin, to the stigma of his color, to his
negroid features always shouting at him from his mir-
ror, 'Remember you are a mulatto!' "[41] The mixed-blood
became noted for an extravagant use of perfume which
seems to have been an overcompensation for the body odor,
the so-called *catinga*, or *budum*, reputedly characteristic of
the African. At home the mulatto sought to keep out of sight
the "*tira-teima* of the family," the relative whose dark color
or negroid features too clearly betrayed his "less noble"
origin. In an attempt to convince himself and others of his
identity with the upper strata, he often developed an "em-
phatic Aryanism" and became, like Machado de Assis or
Olavo Bilac, "a champion of the white against the black."[42]

[40] See Robert E. Park, "Human Migration and the Marginal Man,"
American Journal of Sociology, XXXIII (May, 1928), 881; Everett Stone-
quist, *The Marginal Man* (New York, 1937).

[41] Freyre, *Sobrados e mucambos*, p. 320.

[42] *Ibid.*, pp. 335, 355, 363; Freyre, *Casa grande e senzala*, p. 324.

It should be noted that, although the light mulattoes have ordinarily set the pace in this struggle to rise and have contributed the bulk of the advancing individuals of color, they have not completely monopolized the advance.[43] They have been followed, and in some notable cases even outdistanced, by individuals from the darker portions of the population. For example, Henrique Dias, the black hero of the expulsion of the Dutch from Pernambuco, was made a member of the nobility and granted membership in the Ordem de Christo.[44] A black is today president of an important intellectual and social institution at Bahia. Another is a member of the most exclusive club. But the appearance of black individuals among the upper classes is still today quite rare. In the attempt to achieve higher standing in the social order, the blacks have had to contend even more decidedly with the handicaps of starting on the bottom and of bearing constantly with them a physical badge of slave ancestry and a symbol of low status.

It is perhaps also true that individuals of African descent, mixed-bloods as well as blacks, have risen in class more slowly than has the Negro in the United States. Being less under the stigma of racial inferiority, the Brazilian blacks and mixed-bloods have naturally had less incentive to demonstrate to a hostile white world their personal competence and ability to achieve. Hence, it is likely that they have been less ambitious, less aggressive, than their northern brothers, and consequently have risen *as a group* less rapidly.

[43] See Manoel Querino, "Os homens de côr preta na historia," *Revista do Instituto Geographico e Historico da Bahia*, XLVIII (Bahia, 1923), 353–63; see also Augusto Victorino Alves Sacramento Blake, *Dicionario bibliographico brasileiro* (Rio, 1893), II, 452–55.

[44] Heinrich Handelmann, *Historia do Brasil* (Portuguese trans. by the Instituto Historico e Geographico of *Geschichte von Brasilien* [Berlin, 1860]; 2 vols.; Rio, 1931), I, 381.

CHAPTER VII

THE PRESENT ETHNIC COMPOSITION OF THE CLASSES IN BAHIAN SOCIETY

TODAY one finds at Bahia a freely competitive order in which individuals compete for position largely on the basis of personal merit and favorable family circumstance. Individual competence tends to overbalance ethnic origin as a determinant of social status.

However, the darker portion of the population, as we have already noted, have had to contend with the serious handicap that their parents or grandparents or other immediate ancestors began on the bottom as propertyless slaves of the white ruling class and now bear constantly with them, by reason of color and other physical characteristics, indelible badges of this slave ancestry, ineradicable symbols of low status. It is not surprising, therefore, to find that the relatively unmixed blacks are still concentrated in the low-pay, low-status employments and that they gradually disappear as one ascends the occupational scale, until in the upper levels they are seldom to be found.

But the mixed-bloods, especially the lighter mulattoes, evidence a strong tendency to climb the occupational ladder. Although the darker individuals still occupy very largely the low-pay employments, the lighter mulattoes tend to be concentrated in the middle tier; while a considerable portion, especially of very light mixed-bloods, or *brancos da Bahia*, as they are sometimes called, have penetrated into the upper strata.

The whites, as might be anticipated, are concentrated in the upper levels. Their numbers, both absolute and relative, diminish sharply as one descends the occupational scale, and they appear only in small percentages in the lower tiers.

TABLE 8

RACIAL DISTRIBUTION IN THOSE EMPLOYMENTS AT
BAHIA IN WHICH BLACKS APPEAR TO BE
PREDOMINANT, 1936

EMPLOYMENT	SAMPLE	PERCENTAGE				
		Black*	Mulatto	White	Cafuso§	Total
Carregadores†	100	93.0	7.0	0.0	0.0	100
Laundresses	200	89.5	9.5	0.0	1.0	100
Carroceiros‡	100	83.0	15.0	0.0	2.0	100
Masons	125	82.4	16.8	0.0	0.8	100
Stevedores	125	81.6	15.2	1.6	1.6	100
Truck helpers	250	81.2	18.0	0.8	0.0	100
Domestics	250	78.8	18.8	0.8	1.6	100
Street laborers	225	78.3	21.2	0.5	0.0	100
Candy-peddlers	100	77.0	21.0	1.0	1.0	100
Cobblers	70	74.4	22.8	2.8	0.0	100
Venders	200	68.5	28.0	3.5	0.0	100
Newsboys	100	68.0	31.0	1.0	0.0	100
Shoe-shiners	50	66.0	32.0	2.0	0.0	100
Streetcar motormen....	80	60.0	32.5	5.0	2.5	100
Truck-drivers	150	44.7	43.3	10.7	1.3	100

* It is, of course, possible that individuals with some degree of mixture are included in this category. Color and hair texture were the differentials particularly noted.

† *Carregadores* operate at the port, discharging the functions of porters and baggagemen.

‡ Individuals who own a mule and a two-wheeled cart and transport goods about the city are known as *carroceiros*.

§ Indian-Negro mixed-blood.

Of the employments in which relatively unmixed blacks and mulattoes were found to predominate, those in which there appeared to be more blacks than mulattoes (together with the corresponding percentages) were as indicated in Table 8. The mulattoes in each case were predominantly dark mixed-bloods.

Of the same employments (in which blacks and mulattoes were found to predominate), those in which there appeared to be more mulattoes than unmixed blacks were as indicated in Table 9.

TABLE 9

RACIAL DISTRIBUTION IN THOSE EMPLOYMENTS AT
BAHIA IN WHICH MULATTOES APPEAR TO BE
PREDOMINANT OVER BLACKS, 1936

EMPLOYMENT	SAMPLE	PERCENTAGE				
		Mulatto	Black	White	Cafuso	Total
Barbers*	150	74.0	20.0	6.0	0.0	100
Band musicians†	98	68.4	23.5	8.1	0.0	100
Street-sweepers	75	62.7	34.7	2.6	0.0	100
Streetcar *fiscais*‡	50	62.0	24.0	10.0	4.0	100
Streetcar conductors	80	58.8	22.5	16.2	2.5	100
Firemen†	100	58.0	32.0	9.0	1.0	100
Bus *cobradores*§	90	54.5	30.0	12.2	3.3	100
Taxi-drivers	85	54.1	31.8	9.4	4.7	100
Police*	150	54.0	32.6	13.4	0.0	100
Bus-drivers	90	50.0	27.8	17.8	4.4	100
Soldiers†	750	48.1	40.5	11.1	0.3	100

* These mulattoes were predominantly light.
† These mulattoes were predominantly dark.
‡ Individuals who check streetcar conductor's records.
§ *Cobradores* are fare-collectors in some cases, changeboys in others.

Of the employments in which whites and mulattoes appear to be predominant, those in which there appeared to be more mulattoes than whites were as given in Table 10.

Of the same employments (in which whites and mulattoes were found to predominate), those in which there appeared to be more whites than mulattoes were as indicated in Table 11.

Thus, the occupational groups found to be composed probably three-fourths or more of relatively unmixed blacks included: *carregadores*, laundresses, masons, stevedores, truck helpers, *carroceiros*, unskilled laborers, domestic servants, and candy-peddlers; those found to be composed perhaps two-thirds or more of blacks (in addition to the foregoing): cobblers, street venders, newsboys, and shoe-shiners; and those composed half or more of blacks (in addition to the above): streetcar motormen.

TABLE 10

RACIAL DISTRIBUTION IN THOSE EMPLOYMENTS
AT BAHIA IN WHICH MULATTOES APPEAR TO
BE PREDOMINANT OVER WHITES, 1936

EMPLOYMENT	SAMPLE	PERCENTAGE			
		Mu-latto	White	Black	Total
Army officers:					
Superior*......	33	57.6†	42.4	0.0	100
Inferior.......	38	47.4	34.2	15.8	100‡
Clerks..........	350	55.1§	44.6	0.3	100

* The range was from lieutenant upward.
† There were only two dark mulattoes.
‡ *Cafuso*, 2.6 per cent.
§ These mixed-bloods were predominantly light.

The occupational groups which appeared to consist half or more of mixed-bloods, included: clerks, barbers, band musicians, army officers (superior), police, firemen, streetcar conductors, streetcar *fiscais*, taxi- and bus-drivers, bus *cobradores*, and street-sweepers. Approximately two-thirds of the band musicians appeared to be mulattoes, and about three-fourths of the barbers.

Among those occupational groups which are composed probably three-fourths or more of whites were found priests, bank employees, and businessmen;[1] among those two-thirds white (in addition to the above): professors in the Faculdades, lawyers, politicians, and cabaret entertainers;[2] and among those half or more white (in addition to the groups

TABLE 11

RACIAL DISTRIBUTION IN THOSE EMPLOYMENTS AT BAHIA IN WHICH WHITES APPEAR TO BE PREDOMINANT, 1936

EMPLOYMENT	SAMPLE	PERCENTAGE				
		White	Mulatto	Black	Branco da Bahia	Total
Bank employees.......	125	84.0	2.4	0.0	13.6	100
Priests..............	50	76.0	8.0	0.0	16.0	100
Businessmen..........	40	75.0	7.5	0.0	17.5	100
Cabaret entertainers...	26	73.1	11.5	0.0	15.4	100
Professors (Faculdades).	232	70.3	14.2	0.0	15.5	100
Lawyers..............	413	67.1	9.7	1.7	15.2	100*
Politicians...........	60	66.7	11.6	1.7	18.3	100†
Physicians...........	100	63.0	20.0	1.0	16.0	100
Teachers (secondary)...	58	57.0	24.1	3.4	15.5	100
Commercial employees.	325	54.8	27.4	1.6	15.3	100‡
Government *funcionarios*	250	45.2	32.8	5.6	16.0	100§

* Indian-white descent, 0.7 per cent; Indian-Negro descent, 0.7 per cent; white-Negro-Indian descent, 0.5 per cent; incomplete records, 4.4 per cent.

† *Mameluco* (white-Indian mixed-blood), 1.7 per cent.

‡ *Mameluco*, 0.6 per cent; *cafuso*, 0.3 per cent.

§ *Mameluco*, 0.4 per cent.

just named): physicians, commercial and government employees, and teachers in the secondary schools.

Of the first 500 *brancos* applying in 1935 at the Gabinete

[1] If *brancos da Bahia* are included in the white group, one would have to add cabaret entertainers, professors (advanced schools), politicians, lawyers, and physicians.

[2] If *brancos da Bahia* are included, one would have to add physicians, teachers in the secondary schools, and commercial employees.

de Identificação for cards of identification, 292 were males. Of these, 213 were classified as students, 17 as businessmen, 11 as salesmen, 8 as government clerks, 8 as commercial employees, 5 as soldiers, 4 as teachers, 4 as hucksters, 3 as peddlers (a Rumanian Jew, a Pole, and a Spaniard), 3 as bus *cobradores*, 2 as engineers, 2 as house servants, and 1 each as carpenter, printer, auto mechanic, sailor, ship's engineer, tailor, musician (instrumental), vocalist, magistrate, laborer, farmer, and *proprietario* (one whose income is derived from rentals). Of the 208 females, 170 were classified as students, 24 as teachers, 7 as government clerks, 5 as housewives, 1 as vocalist, and 1 as typist.

Of the first 500 *pardos*, 244 were males. Of these, 90 were classified as students, 44 as peddlers, 25 as soldiers, 13 as commercial employees, 9 as mechanics, 7 as operators of bakeries, 7 as *carregadores*, 7 as shopkeepers, 6 as farmers, 4 as shoemakers, 3 as orchestra players, 3 as teachers, 2 as barbers, 2 as gardeners, 2 as house servants, 2 as beggars,[3] 2 as masons, 2 as bus *cobradores*, 2 as sailors, 2 as shoe-shiners, and 1 each as salesman, painter, carpenter, ironworker, tinsmith, vulcanizer, tailor, butcher, waiter, and truck-gardener. Of 256 females, 214 were classified as students, 30 as teachers, 4 as housewives, 2 as dressmakers, and 1 each as embroidery worker, designer, house servant, and beggar.

Of the first 155 *pretos*, 125 were males. Of these, 17 were classified as students, 51 as hucksters, 17 as *carregadores*, 8 as soldiers, 4 as bus *cobradores*, 3 as farmers, 4 as bakers, 2 as mechanics, 2 as masons, 2 as shoemakers, and 1 each as commercial employee, small shopkeeper, government clerk, decorator, hairdresser, pianist, jazz orchestra player, ironworker, leather worker, cabinet-maker, *carroceiro*, house

[3] *Mendicantes.*

servant, sailor, farmer, and shoe-shiner. Of the 30 females, 23 were classified as students, 2 as teachers, 2 as housewives, and 1 each as street peddler, domestic servant, and government clerk.

Inferences based upon this occupational distribution, together with certain other indices (such as tax returns, automobile ownership, the purchase of different-priced seats at cinemas and sport events), indicate that blacks and the darker mixed-bloods ordinarily occupy the lower economic levels, the medium and light mulattoes the middle position, and the whites (including the *brancos da Bahia*) the upper stratum.

A Bahian official engaged in income-tax collections knew of no rich blacks in the city,[4] but he did know of several well-to-do mixed-bloods, among whom were a few dark mulattoes. Most incomes in the upper brackets, however, are those of whites.

Of 116 cars being driven along the central thoroughfare, the Rua Chile, during a popular festival, in 90, or 77.6 per cent of the total, only whites were riding; in 26, or 22.4 per cent, mixed-bloods were among the occupants;[5] while no cars were occupied by blacks. However, on a similar occasion, of 50 cars noted, 2 were occupied exclusively by blacks.

At a cinema performance, of 63 persons occupying *poltronas* at 2$200 a seat, 73 per cent were whites, 20.6 per cent

---

[4] Although at Ilhéos in the rich cocoa area south of Bahia a few blacks and dark mulattoes are quite well to do. For a sketch of life in this region see Jorge Amado, *Cacau* (Rio, 1933).

[5] The 6 cars in which only mulattoes were riding constituted 5.2 per cent of the total (only 1 car was occupied by dark mulattoes); the 19 cars in which both whites and mulattoes were riding constituted 16.3 per cent of the total (3 cars were occupied principally by *brancos da Bahia*, 16 by whites, with only one or two light mulattoes in each case); 1 car (0.9 per cent of the total) contained one black and five dark mulattoes.

were mulattoes, and only 6.4 per cent were relatively un-mixed blacks; while, of 30 occupants of general admission seats at one-half this price, only 20 per cent were whites, 40 per cent were mulattoes, and 40 per cent were blacks. Among spectators at a Sunday-afternoon soccer game, one noted the distribution as given in Table 12.

Of five hundred mothers applying for aid at the state's free children's clinic, only 9.2 per cent were white, 40.6 per

TABLE 12

RACIAL DISTRIBUTION OF SPECTATORS AT A
SPORTS EVENT,* BAHIA, 1936

SEATS	PRICE (IN MIL-REIS)	OCCU-PANTS	PERCENTAGE			
			Blacks	Mulat-toes	Whites	Total
Reserved............	10	143	2.1	23.8†	74.1	100
Grandstand..........	7	267	4.1	29.4†	66.5	100
General admission.....	3	519	51.1	39.9‡	9.0	100

* *Futebol* (soccer), Campo da Graça, March 22, 1936.

† Chiefly light mulattoes, many of whom were very light with only slight traces of Negro lineage.

‡ Principally dark mulattoes.

cent were mulatto, predominantly dark, and 44.5 per cent appeared to be relatively unmixed blacks.[6] Of 1,511 photographs displayed in eleven photograph galleries, 73.2 per cent were probably of white individuals, 24.9 per cent of mixed-bloods, and only 1.7 per cent of unmixed blacks.[7]

In interpreting this ethnic distribution in the occupations and according to financial means, one might point out that

[6] The remaining 5.7 per cent were *cafuso* (21 individuals), *branco da Bahia* (2 individuals), *mameluco* (2 individuals), and of Indian-white-Negro descent (1 individual).

[7] In addition, 0.2 per cent were *cafuso*.

the present social order at Bahia results, as it probably does in a free class society anywhere, from the tendency of the more advantaged and the more able to rise to, or to maintain themselves at, the top. Since the Africans began in Brazil at the bottom, the present distribution of color through the class scale obviously indicates the extent to which the Negroes (either pure or diluted) have been able to survive and to rise in competition with the Europeans and their descendants, who in the main began at the top. The present distribution is therefore that probably to be expected, even in a freely competitive society, given the original slave status of the Negro, his relatively disadvantaged position upon receiving freedom, the consequently limited opportunities for economic advancement, and the comparatively brief time he has enjoyed a freely competitive status.

One might also note that racial distribution in the occupations and with reference to economic status is not greatly dissimilar at Bahia to that in the United States. In other words, the Negro, either pure or mixed with the white, has slowly but steadily advanced both in Brazil and in this country, until today he is represented there and here in all the professions and in many, if not most, of the occupations. Even the relative numbers in the different levels of the occupational and economic scales are somewhat similar in the two cases.

The differences, however, are profound. Whereas in the United States the rise of the Negro and of the mixed-blood has been principally within the limits of the Negro world, in Brazil the rise has been with reference to the total community; that is, the Negro in Bahia not only competes freely with all others of his own color but can and does compete with all aspirants to the same class; and, if he has ability and gives evidence of definite personal worth, he will be accepted for what he is as an individual, and his racial antecedents will, at least to a considerable degree, be overlooked.

The extent of participation of the different ethnic units in the total life of the community may be indicated by analyzing racial participation in such institutions as exclusive clubs, schools, labor unions, and churches.

One of Bahia's most exclusive clubs, membership in which is definitely indicative of advanced social status, is composed of Bahian "society," including most of the leading officials and many of the more prominent citizens. Numerous receptions for visiting celebrities are held at this club, and its dances are considered to be among the principal social functions of the year. No blacks have yet been admitted, although several mixed-bloods, including a number of *brancos da Bahia* and even a few dark mulattoes, are regular and honored members. Whites, of course, predominate.

Among the members is a dark mixed-blood, with Caucasian hair and features, a prominent citizen, an able eye, ear, nose, and throat specialist trained in Europe, and husband of a white wife. Of him a Bahian of undiluted European descent once commented, "You know when I went to see him about my eyes the other day, I never once thought of him as colored. I needed professional advice and I simply recalled that he, like his father before him, was the best eye specialist in Bahia." Another member of this club is a dark mixed-blood, a wealthy exporter, prominent in Bahian commercial circles, and husband of a white wife, upon whose visits into the interior, it is said, all those with whom he has business dealings (including whites) feel deeply honored when he visits them in their homes.

Not listed among the members is a dark mixed-blood of distinguished bearing, probably Bahia's leading colored citizen, son of a white planter and a black slave, able engineer, once federal senator, president of an important intellectual and social organization, and "authority" on the Tupi language. However, an officer of the club, a white banker from one of the leading families whose aristocratic lineage, general competence, and recent contribution of a governor to the state and a federal senator to the national *camara* unquestionably admits its members to the most exclusive circles, once remarked that "if this distinguished colored citizen should sometime apply for membership, there would be no doubt that a man of his intelligence, refinement, and professional competence would be accepted without serious question."

In the schools there is no segregation in any form. Students, however, are predominantly white and light mulatto. The participation of blacks is somewhat limited, and there is a progressive elimination of the darker shades as one climbs the educational ladder. Illiteracy is high, especially in the lower class, in which, as we have seen, blacks and dark mulattoes predominate.

Table 13 indicates more equable participation of the blacks in the elementary schools, especially in those which are state supported, attendance at which is free and hence more accessible to Negro children, concentrated as their parents are in the lower economic levels.

In a parade of school children celebrating Emancipation Day (the thirteenth of May) twelve elementary schools participated, each group being dressed in its distinctive uniform. For example, the boys of one school wore light gray suits with a blue stripe down the trousers, blue belts, and gray caps with blue bands; while the girls wore light gray dresses with blue belts, blue collars, and blue cuffs. Of approximately 325 pupils in the parade, about two-sevenths were black, two-sevenths white, and three-sevenths mulatto, indiscriminately mingled. In eight schools, the proportions were not greatly dissimilar. Two schools, however, were

TABLE 13

COMPARATIVE SCHOOL ATTENDANCE OF THE
ETHNIC UNITS AT BAHIA, 1936

School	No. of Schools Sampled	Black	Mulatto	White	Others	Total
Elementary:						
Public............	22	438	496	385	16*	1,335
Private............	8	40	97	175	3†	315
Parochial..........	6	31	88	318	13‡	450
Secondary...........	5§	34	99	390	2‖	525
Superior (Faculties of Law, Medicine, Engineering)...........	3	12	88	424	6¶	530
Trade..............	3	88	122	123	2**	335
Normal.............	1	45	83	157	0	285

* *Cafuso,* 9; *mameluco,* 7.   ‖ *Cafuso,* 2.
† *Cafuso,* 2; *mameluco,* 1.   ¶ *Cafuso,* 2; *mameluco,* 4.
‡ *Cafuso,* 5; *mameluco,* 8.   ** *Cafuso,* 1; *mameluco,* 1.
§ One public, 2 private, 2 ecclesiastical.

principally black and mixed-blood (in one of which there were 16 blacks, 34 mulattoes, 8 whites); and two schools were largely white (in one of which there were 25 whites, 8 mulattoes, and 5 blacks).

During the 1936 Peruada, which is an annual *festa* held by students at the Faculdades, of 168 individuals participating in a parade, 3 per cent were black, 10 per cent were mulatto, and 87 per cent were white.

At the graduating exercises of one of the Faculdades, no

black families were present. The guests were principally white, including a number of *brancos da Bahia*. A few mulattoes, principally light, also attended. A dark mixed-blood assisted with the ushering, in the course of which he led two of his relatives (young light mulatto ladies) to excellent seats well to the front. Later, as the room became crowded, he was seen to request two white men to give up their seats to two other mulatto ladies. The request was courteously complied with. When, during the subsequent formal ceremonies, this dark mixed-blood received his diploma, he was given by his fellow-students (chiefly whites) a vigorous round of applause, he being one of the few so honored. "He is a fine man with a brilliant mind," remarked a white colleague.

A number of teachers, particularly in the elementary and secondary institutions, are mixed-bloods, but the greater number are whites. Although 120 of 148 white students responding to an inquiry regarding the matter did not object to being taught by a *preto* teacher, black instructors are rare and are limited, with few exceptions, to the elementary ranks. This is, in all probability, largely due to the fact that comparatively few blacks have so far received educational advantages equal to the whites.

For instance, of 232 instructors at the four Faculdades (Law, Medicine, Engineering, and Economics), none was black; 163, or 70.3 per cent, were white; 36, or 15.5 per cent, were *branco da Bahia;* and 31, or 13.4 per cent, were mulatto.[8] Of 69 *professores cathedraticos*, 54, or 78.3 per cent, were white; 10, or 14.5 per cent, were mulatto; 5, or 7.2 per cent, were *branco da Bahia;* and none was black. Of 5 profes-

[8] One was an Indian-Negro mixed-blood, and one was of Indian-white descent.

sors honored as *paranymphos*,[9] all were white. Of 21 faculty members honored with *homenagem*,[10] 6 were mulattoes (2 quite negroid), 1 was *branco da Bahia*, 14 were whites, and none was black.

In a prominent secondary institution, of 18 instructors, 1 was a black, 5 were mulattoes, 3 were *brancos da Bahia*, and 9 were whites. In another secondary school, of 33 instructors, 7 were mulattoes, 6 were *brancos da Bahia*, and 20 were whites. While of 30 elementary teachers noted in state schools, 3 were blacks, 10 were mulattoes, 6 were *brancos da Bahia*, 1 was a *mameluco*, and 10 were whites.

In educational circles one often hears of a dark mixed-blood of distinguished bearing with snow-white hair and beard who organized some years ago one of the present secondary institutions and whose two sons are well-known and widely respected educators. Several whites now prominent in local and national circles speak with pride of their schooling under this distinguished man.

A similar attitude is not infrequently manifested with reference to other colored teachers or professors; for instance, a prominent medical specialist and noted lecturer at the Faculty of Medicine; a legal "authority" and author of textbooks in law, now associate justice of the Brazilian supreme court; a prominent nerve specialist; a noted surgeon; and the city's ablest and most quoted literary critic.

In a private elementary school a class of boys ranging in age from seven to eleven years were being taught by a Negro teacher. Among the group were two whites, one *branco da*

[9] Each graduating class in the secondary and professional schools selects one of its more popular teachers or professors for special recognition as *paranympho*.

[10] Graduating classes also select, besides a *paranympho*, several teachers or professors to be honored with *homenagem*.

Bahia, one mulatto, and three blacks. Several substantial white citizens had received their early training under this man.

The public library is patronized indiscriminately by members of all ethnic groups. Blacks, however, appear among its frequenters only in rather limited numbers. For instance, of 560 individuals using the library facilities on different days and at different hours during the day,[11] only 9.6 per cent were blacks, while 35.9 per cent were mulattoes and 52.7 per cent were whites.[12]

In labor unions organization definitely follows class lines, and ethnic differences are largely lost sight of in the pursuit of common ends. Leadership, however, tends to be white or near-white, even in those unions composed predominantly of blacks and dark mixed-bloods. For instance, at a "solemn assembly" for the installation of new officers in a local labor union whose membership, limited to 550, is overwhelmingly Negro (as indicated by a detailed check of the members with the aid of the union secretary), the retiring president was a *branco da Bahia* and the incoming president a light mulatto. Only eleven *brancos* (probably all, or nearly all, of whom are *brancos da Bahia*) and relatively few mulattoes are to be found among the membership.[13]

[11] Samples were taken for each hour from 9:00 A.M. to 4:00 P.M., with the exception of 12:00 noon to 2:00 P.M., when the institution was closed.

[12] Also 7 (1.2 per cent) *cafusos*, 3 (0.5 per cent) *mamelucos*.

[13] Of the speakers, 6 were blacks, 5 were mulattoes (2 quite light), 1 was a *branco da Bahia*, and 1 was a white. Among the themes presented were: "Solidarity! All Workers Are Brothers!" "Since the Revolution of 1930 Workers Are No Longer Slaves"; "Viva Getulio Vargas, the God, the Jesus, and the Senhor do Bomfim [patron saint of Bahia's poorer classes] of the Workers!" "Remember the Chicago Workers Who Died for Liberty!" "Save Brazil's Wealth from Exploitation by *Norte-Americanos* Who Hope To Seize Her Mines and Her Waterfalls and Make Slaves of Her People!" "Look to the World's Greatest Socialist and Sociologist, Jesus Christ."

In the churches, both Catholic and Protestant, one notes the side-by-side, unsegregated worship of all ranges of the color scale. For instance, out of 927 worshipers present one Sunday morning[14] at the Matriz Nossa Senhora de Sant' Anna, 277 were blacks, 327 were mulattoes, 312 were whites, 9 were *cafusos*, and 2 were *mamelucos*. At the ancient and historic Igreja do Carmo on another occasion,[15] of 227 persons attending Mass, 34 were blacks, 109 were mulattoes, and 84 were whites. At the famed São Francisco Church one Sunday morning,[16] of 470 worshipers, 124 were blacks, 187 were mulattoes, and 159 were whites. At Santo Antonio da Barra on another Sunday,[17] of a total of 177 persons present, 74 were blacks, 52 were mulattoes, and 48 were whites. One of the best-dressed audiences in the city, at the Convento de Piedade, numbered,[18] among a total of 285, 52 blacks and 64 mulattoes.

Of a total of 7,396 worshipers in thirty-eight Catholic churches, cathedrals, and chapels scattered throughout the city, including (in addition to the foregoing) the Matriz da Vitoria, the Mosteiro de São Bento, the Cathedral, the Matrix de Nazaré, the Basilica do Bomfim, Conceição da Praia, Campo Santo, Rosario de João Pereira, Barroquinha, Palma, Ajuda, Pillar, Conceição do Boqueirão, and the Matriz do Rio Vermelho, 25 per cent were blacks, 33.3 per cent were mulattoes, and 40.8 per cent whites,[19] the various ethnic groups being in each case indiscriminately represented throughout the audience. A similar distribution was

---

[14] July 26, 1936, 9:00–10:30 A.M.

[15] August 2, 1936, 8:30 A.M.　　　[17] August 16, 1936, 8:15 A.M.

[16] January 5, 1936.　　　[18] January 12, 1936, 9:00 A.M.

[19] Absolute numbers: black, 1,846; mulatto, 2,462; white, 3,019; *cafuso* 50; *mameluco*, 19.

noted in two Protestant churches, one Baptist, the other Presbyterian. Of a total of 157 worshipers, 27.4 per cent were blacks, 29.9 per cent were mulattoes, and 42.7 per cent were whites, seated indiscriminately, in each case.

Although 104 of 130 white students responding to an inquiry regarding the matter did not object to receiving the sacrament from a black priest, priests and pastors are usually white, only occasionally mulatto (ordinarily light), and very rarely black. For instance, of 43 priests officiating at Mass, 42, or 98 per cent, were white, and 1 was a mulatto, quite light. Of 60 novices at the Seminary of Santa Thereza, only 7 were mulattoes, 1 very dark.[20] Of the 2 Protestant pastors, 1 was white, the other a dark mulatto. In the latter's audience were over a score of whites.

Altar boys are often mulattoes, occasionally blacks. For instance, of 70 altar boys seen assisting with Mass, 35, or 50 per cent, were whites; 3 were *brancos da Bahia;* 20, or 28.6 per cent, were mulattoes; and 11, or 15.7 per cent, were blacks.

A similarly mixed participation may be noted in meetings of the spiritualist cult. At a session of the União Espirita Bahiana, for instance, of 73 persons present, 20 were blacks, 26 were mulattoes, and 27 were whites.[21] Among the leaders gathered about a table in front of the audience, 2 were whites, 2 were *brancos da Bahia*, 1 was a mulatto, and 2 were blacks.

In noting the circumstances under which the Brazilian racial accommodation has taken and is taking place, one ought not to overlook the fact that Catholic ideas and practice, permeating as they do very largely the whole moral order at

[20] One *mameluco*, 52 whites.   [21] Also 1 *cafuso*.

Bahia, tend to implement and to support the Brazilian racial policy. For the Catholic church, by emphasizing ritual, centers attention *outside the individual* upon common objects; while the Protestant churches, by emphasizing belief, center attention *upon the individual*, thus tending to increase self-consciousness and, consequently, awareness of difference which, in so far as the self and its distinguishing characteristics are identified with a group, automatically increases *group*-consciousness.

The Catholic conceptions tend to lay emphasis upon the community, upon the totality of individuals. For it is through his participation in the community that the individual in the Catholic view gains recognition as a person. The Protestant churches, on the other hand, tend to emphasize the individual. It is by reason of his inherent worth that the community in which he participates gains meaning in the Protestant ideology.

The Catholic procedure thus tends to unify the community, while the Protestant procedure tends to divide it into separate groups, each of which emphasizes its points of difference with all the others and tends to be divisive in its attitude toward the others. Obviously, a sect (which is by its very nature a conflict group) can in no other way live. The Catholic procedure lays a premium upon solidarity, while the Protestant lays a premium upon diversity.

Indicative of race relations among the younger generation at Bahia is the behavior of three groups of children who were observed playing together in Campo Grande. Aged approximately four to fifteen years, they were hilariously enjoying themselves. When first noted, there were at the "giant stride" 4 blacks, 5 mulattoes, and 2 whites. At the teeter-totter were 1 black, 9 mulattoes, and 15 whites. At the garden swing were 11 blacks, 8 mulattoes, and 7 whites. There was considerable moving about from group to group. In the garden of the governor's palace a similar band, aged about seven to thirteen years, were laughing and shouting together around another teeter-totter. Among them were 3 blacks, 5 mulattoes, and 4 whites. "Beginning with his earliest years," wrote a white student, "a child in Bahia is accustomed to associating with all racial types without any distinction being made between them."

In Campo da Graça[22] 6 whites and 5 mulattoes (one of whom was quite dark) composed the team of the Faculty of Law in a soccer game with the Faculty of Medicine (among whom were 7 whites, 3 mulattoes, and 1 black). In the subsequent professional contest 9 whites, 4 mulattoes, and 4 blacks composed the visiting team from São Paulo, coached by a *cafuso*. Bahia's colors were upheld by 2 whites, 5 mulattoes, 9 blacks, and 1 *cafuso*. The referee was a *branco da Bahia*.

At an informal basketball game played on an outdoor court at the Fortress of São Pedro, a black and 4 mulattoes composed one team; a black, 2 mulattoes, and 2 whites, the other. The referee was a black.

At a tea dance given at Bahia's most exclusive club in honor of Getulio Vargas, president of Brazil, the city's most distinguished citizens and their families, to an approximate total of 600, were present. No blacks were among the guests, and only 28 individuals were noticeably negroid, 6 of whom were dark mulattoes. At a banquet subsequently given the President, all individuals seated at his table were white. A number of mixed-bloods, however, principally light mulattoes, were among the guests. Two of the six speakers at the

[22] On March 22, 1936.

dedicatory exercises for the newly constructed Instituto de Cacau on the following day were *brancos da Bahia* (each with only slight indications of Negro ancestry), and four were whites.

During the visit of a neighboring governor, a procession formed in the Avenida Sete de Setembro to escort the distinguished visitor, together with the Bahian governor, Juracy Magalhães, to the latter's palace. Riding in the procession, alighting in front of the palace, and following the two chief executives into the spacious rooms of the governor's mansion, were presumably the city's political élite, all in formal attire. Of a total of 99 persons, 70 were whites, 22 were very light mulattoes with only slightly noticeable traces of Negro lineage, 7 were dark mulattoes, and none was black. Of the escort of 23 army officials dressed in appropriate uniform, 9 were whites, 12 were very light mulattoes, 2 were dark mixed-bloods.

Of 46 members of the state legislature, 69.4 per cent were whites, 15.2 per cent were *brancos da Bahia*, and 11.0 per cent were mulattoes.[23] Of 14 aldermen, 8 were whites, 4 were *brancos da Bahia*, and 2 were mulattoes (both very light).

In legal proceedings no discrimination is at all evident. Colored individuals appear not only among the defendants but also among those engaged in the defense or the prosecution, as well as among the jury itself. Whites, however, predominate.

Of the officers of the medical association, 6 were whites, 3 were *brancos da Bahia*, and 3 were mulattoes. Of 18 members of an elective supervisory body for the legal profession, 14 were whites, 3 were *brancos da Bahia*, and only 1 had noticeable evidence of mixed ancestry and that principally

---

[23] One deputy was a black, and there was also 1 *mameluco*.

in pigmentation. An able lawyer, with an extended period of practice in Bahia, he was well regarded by his associates.

At a formal dinner given by *A Tarde*, probably the most influential Bahian daily, in honor of a noted journalist and poet, 15 whites, 4 *brancos da Bahia*, 3 light mulattoes, and 6 medium or dark mixed-bloods sat down together at the banquet table. Among the guests, according to the account on the subsequent day, were "all the editorial writers and collaborators of this newspaper, together with a few specially invited friends and admirers of the honored guest [a white]."

Among the members attending a session of the Bahian Academy of Letters were 5 whites, 1 *branco da Bahia*, and 3 mulattoes. One of the latter is an able poet, quite dark, with kinky hair.

Present at a tea dance given by Bahia's Girl Guides at the exclusive club previously mentioned were the city's social élite, including the governor. *A Tarde*, in reporting the event, said, "As was to be expected, there was present our best society—all of it, almost—making the occasion one of elegance and distinction." Of the 414 guests, 346 were whites, 64 were very light mulattoes (exhibiting only slight traces of Negro ancestry), and 3 were dark mixed-bloods. One of the latter, with kinky hair but Caucasian features, was accompanied by a light mulatto wife, almost white, and two light mulatto daughters. One of the latter danced once during the afternoon—with a white youth. Of 30 Girl Guides serving the guests, 3 showed slight traces of Negro origin. The only blacks present were the members of the jazz orchestra (composed of 3 blacks and 6 dark mulattoes) and 2 maids who had accompanied white families.

The president of a literary, semiscientific, and social organization which numbers about 345[24] of the city's intellectual élite, is a dark mixed-blood, the able engineer and Tupi scholar previously mentioned. The secretary of the organization is white, but during his absence on federal appointment in Rio the assistant secretary, a dark mulatto educator, discharges the secretarial duties. Of the 30 officers and committeemen of this institution, 24 are whites, 2 are *brancos da Bahia*, and 4 are mulattoes. Among the whites are several scions of the old aristocracy.

At a dinner of the Rotary Club, which numbers among its members some of the city's most prominent businessmen, 42 whites, 5 *brancos da Bahia*, and 1 very light mulatto (a visitor) were present. The guest speaker was white. Of 55 members, 47 are whites, 6 are *brancos da Bahia*, and 2 are very light mulattoes.

Of 28 citizens assuming prominent roles in a community organization designed to erect a mausoleum to Castro Alves, 15 were whites, 5 were *brancos da Bahia*, 7 were light mulattoes, 2 were dark mulattoes, and 1 was a black, the latter an able engineer and local historian. At a public meeting in honor of Castro Alves, the speaker was a white politician with a national reputation, an able man of letters, and scion of the old aristocracy. Of 200 individuals in the audience, only 18 were colored (15 mulattoes, mostly very light mixed-bloods, and 3 blacks).

At a recital given by a noted Brazilian pianist, where there were present, according to a newspaper account, "the most select of Bahia's artistic and social circles,"[25] the audience was composed of 116 whites, 14 mulattoes, predominantly light, and 2 blacks.

[24] According to the secretary of the organization.

[25] *Estado da Bahia*, January 22, 1937.

Celebrating the one hundredth anniversary of the birth of Carlos Gomes, famed Brazilian composer of the operas *Guaraný* and *Fosca*, 389 Bahians gathered in the Instituto Geographico e Historico. Of these, 316 were whites, 61 were mulattoes (predominately light), 11 were blacks, and 1 was a *cafuso*. With the governor of Bahia (white) on the platform were 12 citizens in formal dress, all whites[26] except the governor's bodyguard, a light mulatto in army uniform. Two young ladies in formal dress, both white, sang and declaimed. Of the 3 subsequent speakers, 2 were whites and 1 was a *branco da Bahia*. The military police band, which furnished instrumental music for the occasion, was composed of 9 blacks, 26 mulattoes, 2 whites, 3 *cafusos*, and 1 *mameluco*, under the direction of a mulatto bandmaster. Fifty students from the Instituto de Musica da Bahia sang one of Gomes' compositions. All were whites, except 2 light mulattoes.

Twenty-one women, aged eighteen to forty, were present at a cooking school sponsored by a foreign resident. A novel experience in Bahia, where for generations Negro servants have prepared the food, this school had assumed somewhat the character of a fad. The group included several ladies from upper-class families, well to do, educated and traveled. The wife of the governor occasionally attended. Present were 18 whites and 3 light mulattoes, among the latter a *morena*, perhaps the best-dressed lady of the group. Her father is deceased, and her mother is a dressmaker in moderate circumstances. The girl's beauty, pleasant manner, and constant well-tailored appearance have secured for her admittance into the upper circles. She is often invited into the "best" homes. Another of the mixed-bloods present was

[26] Including one *branco da Bahia*.

very light. Her mother is a *sarará*, her grandmother is a
dark mulatto with kinky hair, and her husband is also a dark
mixed-blood. Her family, it is said, has gradually risen from
the lower class by reason of constantly taking advantage of
every educational opportunity, by increasing their economic
competence, and by deliberately cultivating "good manners."

At a "night club," where there were gambling, liquid refreshments, and partners for dancing, of 128 guests,[27] 62
were whites, 40 were *brancos da Bahia*, 21 were mulattoes
(several quite dark), 1 was a *cafuso*, and 4 were blacks. Of
the 26 female entertainers (dancers and singers), 19 were
whites,[28] 4 were *brancas da Bahia*, and 3 were mulattoes (all
very light). None of the darker patrons danced during the
evening.

In the main gambling-room the group about the table
were principally whites, with a few light mulattoes and an
occasional dark mixed-blood. In the hallway near the entrance, however, was another gaming-table where stakes
were lower. It was patronized principally by dark mulattoes, together with an occasional black, a few *brancos da
Bahia*, and very few whites.

Carnival at Bahia lasts three days and is perhaps the most
popular festival of the year. At the close of one celebration
plans are immediately set on foot for the next. From time to
time throughout the ensuing twelve months, newspapers
carry reports of the development of these plans, and, beginning about a hundred and fifty days before Carnival, a regular daily feature appears, the time before the big event being
checked off, day by day, much as United States newspapers
sometimes check off the days preceding Christmas; except

[27] On September 26, 1936.   [28] Including a very swarthy Syrian girl.

that the period of time involved is much greater in the case of Carnival.

In 1936, as for some years previously, three clubs competed in presenting floats on the opening and closing evenings of Carnival. The rivalries, especially between Cruz Vermelha and the Fantoshes, are intense, the Innocentes em Progresso appearing to be rather generally admired.

Preceding, during, and following the parade, Negro *batucadas* and *cordões* pass through the milling crowds. The *batucadas* are usually composed of fifteen to twenty young men, invariably blacks or dark mulattoes, who carry small drums, *cuicas*, and *xaque-xaques*,[29] and parade in single file. The music is one toned and monotonous, reminiscent of the *candomblé* ritual. A *cordão* consists of fifty or sixty people of both sexes and all ages, invariably blacks and dark mulattoes, inclosed within a roped quadrangle, some marching, rather informally, some constantly whirling and dancing, all singing African songs and beating their palms. A banner, usually of silk and velvet, bears the group's name. It may be Outum Obá de Africa, Ideal Africano, Onça,[30] or some similar designation. The group also includes from ten to fifteen musicians with brass instruments, a few blacks in African costume, and a dancer bearing an animal's head (tiger, lion, *onça*, etc.). The women and the small children are usually dressed in the *Bahiana* costume, to be described in detail in a subsequent chapter.

In a spirit of levity common to the Carnival season, one will occasionally see a group of whites and light mulattoes burlesquing the *cordão*. Encompassed by a rope, they pass through the crowd, singing, dancing, and beating their palms. In one of these *blocos*, as they are called, 16 of the

[29] See chap. ix.   [30] The *onça* is the Brazilian jaguar.

participants were whites and 12 were mulattoes, all light except one. There were no blacks. Whereas in a *cordão* noted, 24 were blacks, 19 were dark mulattoes, and none were whites. In 9 *batucadas*, of a total of 157 young men, 113, or 72 per cent, were blacks; 40, or 25.5 per cent, were mulattoes, all dark except one (who, although light of skin, had kinky hair); 3 were *cafusos*, and only 1 was white.

In the milling, dancing, singing crowd one ordinarily sees whites with whites, blacks and dark mulattoes with blacks and dark mulattoes, the exceptions being that a white occasionally accompanies a group of dark mulattoes and blacks, while *brancos da Bahia* and light mulattoes are often to be seen with whites. For instance, three young men, abreast, arms over each other's shoulders, danced past, singing their way into, and through, the crowd. One was a light mulatto, one a *branco da Bahia*, one a white. About twenty girls in single file danced past, each with her hands on the shoulders of the one in front, all singing, the line weaving in and out of the crowd. Among them whites and light mulattoes were indiscriminately mingled; the leader of the group was a light mulatto.

If one notes carefully the individuals who perform various functions in the Carnival parade, he is likely to find the blacks principally occupied with the menial task of guiding the horses which pull the floats, although occasionally they act as escorts or musicians. The "queen" of the Carnival and the "queens" of the Carnival clubs are all whites, the heralds are whites, as also, with rare exceptions, are the girls on the floats. For instance, of 168 young ladies from Bahia's "best" families on the floats in the Carnival parade of 1936, all were whites except 2, and these were very light mulattoes (see Table 14).

The entire racial and cultural situation at Bahia is thus symbolized in the Carnival celebration. The *cordão* points to the persistence of African survivals, adherence to which still isolates to some extent the darker portion of the population. The young blacks and dark mulattoes who parade solemnly, quite self-consciously in the long files of the *batucadas*, represent those youths who, although they have in large measure

TABLE 14

PARTICIPATION BY ETHNIC UNITS
CARNIVAL PARADE, BAHIA, 1936

	Black	Mulatto	White	*Cafuso*	Total
Club sponsors (in autos)............	13	67	73	1	154
Heralds.............	....	....	3	....	3
Horsemen..........	14	47	42	....	103
Horsewomen........	....	....	16	....	16
Trumpeters.........	13	....	1	....	14
Bandsmen..........	45	51	5	....	101
Squires.............	111	5	1	....	117
Girls on floats......	....	2	166	....	168
Men on floats.......	....	4	14	....	18
Queens.............	....	....	3	....	3
Pages..............	5	14	8	....	27
Escorts............	6	....	4	....	10
Truck-drivers.......	1	....	....	....	1
Total..........	208	190	336	1	735

broken with the African cultural forms of their parents or grandparents, have not yet been entirely incorporated into the European world. Whites and light mulattoes dance together and sing their way through the milling crowds. While most of the blacks and dark mulattoes, neither identified with the African tradition to the extent of participating in the *cordões* nor yet sufficiently established in class to move freely in the white world, merely mill about.

This is the general pattern. The exceptions, however, are significant. One occasionally notes, for instance, a darker person participating, apparently without any inhibition or the slightest show of self-consciousness, in the fun of the lighter groups. He ordinarily is an able individual, as evidenced by general appearance, bearing, and speech. Occasionally a white, in appearance and dress evidently of lower-class identity, will be celebrating with black or dark mulatto companions. Among the directing personnel, mulattoes appear in limited numbers, assisting the whites in planning and executing the various activities.

In like manner, the upper social circles at Bahia remain today predominantly white. Only the lighter mixed-bloods, with few exceptions, have penetrated the upper tiers. The darker mulattoes, and particularly the blacks, have only in rare instances gained admittance.

But it is just these few individuals who indicate most clearly the actual racial situation at Bahia. The Negroes began on the bottom. The acceptance, then, of an occasional black, a few dark mulattoes as well as numerous light mixed-bloods into the upper circles points conclusively to the fact that if a person has ability and general competence, the handicap of color can be, and is constantly being, overcome. While it is undoubtedly true that status continues extensively to coincide with color, the fact that certain individuals who are quite dark and otherwise possessed of negroid traits have nevertheless been admitted into exclusive clubs and otherwise have attained positions of trust and responsibility in the community demonstrates quite clearly that in Bahia color is subordinate to other indices of class identification. Individual competence overbalances racial descent in the final determination of status. Color is undoubtedly a handicap. But it always tends to be discounted if the individual in question possesses other characteristics of upper-class identity, such as professional competence, intellectual ability, educational achievement, wealth, an "engaging" manner, personal "charm," poise, "breeding," and, especially with the females, beauty. All these are characteristics which define status in a society based upon class rather than upon caste distinctions.

In this connection, an incident in Brazil noted by Edschmid is illuminating:

The conductor [of the street car] passed all the men wearing collars into the first-class compartment whether they were white, yellow, brown, or black. He relegated all men without collars, regardless of their pigmentation, to the second class. He only looked for a collar. He sent a black-boy with a collar but without boots or shoes into the first, and he relegated a handsome English lad in a low-cut jersey to the second class.[31]

[31] Kasimir Edschmid, *South America* (New York, 1932), p. 370.

CHAPTER VIII

RACIAL IDEOLOGY AND RACIAL ATTITUDES

IN RECENT years there has grown up in Brazil a lively interest in the African and his descendants. This has resulted, among other things, in the holding of two *Congressos Afro-brasileiros*, the first of which met in Recife in November, 1934, and the second in Bahia in January, 1937. Composed of intellectuals having a common interest in the Brazilian Negro, their agenda indicate that such interest is confined almost entirely to three fields: (1) the history of African importation and slavery; (2) problems of acculturation, with especial attention to the survivals of African cultural forms; and (3) anthropometric variations. Generally absent is any concern with problems of racial conflict or accommodation, implying quite definitely the comparative absence of these problems in the social order as well as the comparative absence of any race consciousness answering to them on the part of the Negro or any other ethnic group.

The participants in the 1937 *Congresso*, which met in Bahia, visited fetish-cult centers, witnessed *capoeira*[1] and *samba*[2] presentations, studied the material relics of fetish-cult ceremonies available in Bahian museums, honored the memory of Nina Rodrigues (who some forty years ago pioneered in studies of the Afro-Brazilian cults in Bahia),[3] and

---

[1] See chap. ix.

[2] The *samba*, probably of African origin, is a dance with vocal accompaniment (see chap. ix), as well as a musical form.

[3] See Nina Rodrigues, *L'Animisme fétichiste des nègres de Bahia* (Bahia, 1900) and *Os africanos no Brasil* (São Paulo, 1932).

passed resolutions protesting police interference with the *candomblé* and demanding full religious liberty in the exercise of its rites.

Papers presented to this congress by Brazilians dealt with such subjects as "Slave Insurrections in the Province of Espirito Santo during the Nineteenth Century," "Old Documents concerning the Negroes of the Palmares," "Castro Alves and Brazilian Poetical Treatment of the Negro Slave," "The *Africano* in Bahia," "Chapters in Afro-Brazilian Ethnology in Rio Grande," "Bantú Contributions to Religious Syncretism in Brazil," "A Revision of Afro-Brazilian Ethnology," "The *Africano* and His Culture in Brazil," "The *Orixá*[4] of the Poor," "The School of Nina Rodrigues," and "The Negro and the Problem of Acculturation in Brazil." Only one paper was not concerned with ethnological or historical problems; and it, although it took account of ethnic differences, did not treat of any form of racial conflict. It dealt with "The Negro Criminal in Bahia."

Similar questions were discussed in the first *Congresso Afro-brasileiro*, which met in Recife, sponsored by Gilberto Freyre, a social historian whose *Casa grande e senzala* and *Sobrados e mucambos* throw significant light upon the Negro in colonial and imperial Brazil.[5] This gathering was, because of its informal character and the attempt to present factual data, "something new in Brazil."[6] As Freyre describes it:

There was lacking both formality and a consciousness of class. Around a table, at the head of which different individuals took turns

[4] *Orixá* is a Yoruba word meaning "deity."

[5] An interesting estimate of Freyre's work by Dr. Lewis Hanke appears in the *Quarterly Journal of Inter-American Relations*, July, 1939, pp. 24–44, under the title "Gilberto Freyre: Brazilian Social Historian."

[6] Gilberto Freyre, "O que foi o primeiro Congresso Afro-brasileiro no Recife," in *Novos estudos afro-brasileiros*, ed. Freyre *et al.* (Rio, 1937), p. 348.

presiding in accordance with the varying subjects under consideration, were seated erudite *doutores* from lecture-room and laboratory; huge *filhas de santo;*[7] aged Negro cooks who brought from . . . . the crude kitchens of their mud huts recipes of . . . . Afro-Brazilian dishes; Negroes from the cane fields (like Jovino, whose paper was as full of errors in Portuguese as of *saudades* of the time of the *almanjarras*);[8] . . . . *babalorixás*[9] like Pae Anselmo; queens of the *maracatú*[10] like Albertina de Fleury, whose name reminded José Lins do Rego[11] of the heroine of a romance by Proust; certain others who, although illiterate or semiliterate, had such intimate knowledge of Afro-Brazilian matters as to be able to make an appreciable contribution to the Congress; students of law, engineering, and medicine . . . . ; elderly folklorists like Rodrigues de Carvalho, who never missed a session . . . . ; individuals like Nobrega da Cunha, who knew intimately the ritual of the *macumba;*[12] psychiatrists of the ability and reputation of Ulysses Pernambucano, who was acclaimed with all justice Honorary President; artists like Luis Jardim and Cicero Dias; intellectuals, journalists, and special representatives of Rio newspapers; the teacher, Ernani Braga, who collected for the Congress a number of invocations to Xangô[13] sung by the young ladies of the Conservatorio on the closing day of school to the enthusiastic applause of the best people of Recife. Individuals

[7] *Filhas de santo* are ceremonial dancers of the fetish cult (see chap. x).

[8] On the sugar plantations of colonial Brazil the beam to which animals were hitched to turn the millstone and crush the cane was called the *almanjarra*.

[9] Priests of the fetish cult are sometimes called *babalorixás*. The word is formed from the Nagô words *bábá* ("father") and *orixá* ("deity").

[10] The *maracatú* was an organization of Negroes which formerly participated in Carnival at Recife (see Mario Sette, *Maxambombas e maracatús* [São Paulo, n.d.], pp. 339–41).

[11] José Lins do Rego is a noted Brazilian novelist whose realistic accounts of lower-class life, particularly in the state of Pernambuco, have helped to reveal a level of culture about which little had previously been written. See, e.g., his *Banguê* (Rio, 1934); *Menino de engenho* (2d ed.; Rio, 1934); *Usina* (Rio, 1936); *Historias da velha Totonia* (Rio, 1936); *Pureza* (Rio, 1937); *Pedra Bonita* (Rio, 1938); *Doidinho* (Rio, n.d.).

[12] The Afro-Brazilian fetish cult is known in Rio de Janeiro as the *macumba*.

[13] Xangô (pronounced "Shàn-go") is a deity of the fetish cult (see chap. x).

who at last had seriously taken up "these Negro things" and had found them to be something more than merely picturesque, ... to be, in fact, a great living part of the genuine Brazilian culture.[14]

Before this democratic gathering were read such papers in history and ethnology as the following:[15]

England and the Slave Traffic
Three Centuries of Slavery in Parahyba
The Negro in the History of Alagôas
The Negro during the Dutch Occupation
Unusual Slaves
Physical Deformities of Negro Slaves
The Republic of the Palmares
The Negro Laborer in the Time of the *Banguê*[16] Compared with the Negro Laborer in the Time of the Sugar Factories
The Diet of Brazilian Slaves
Abolition and Its Causes
African Diseases in Brazil
Negro Music in Africa and Brazil
The Negro in the Folklore and Literature of Brazil
The Drama among Early Brazilian Negroes
The Contribution of the Negro to Brazilian Culture
A List of Nagô Words
Xangô
The Legend of Xangô and Its Corruption in Brazil
Invocations to Xangô Heard in Recife
African *Seitas*[17] in Recife
Notes on the *Catimbó*[18]

[14] *Op. cit.*, pp. 348–52.

[15] In several cases titles have not been translated literally; instead, an effort has been made to indicate more definitely the actual subject matter discussed.

[16] The primitive sugar mill used in colonial Brazil, often called the *engenho*, was also known as the *banguê*.

[17] A fetish-cult center is often referred to as a *seita*.

[18] *Catimbó* is a word commonly used in northeast Brazil to designate the fetish cult, which is also known as the *candomblé* (in Bahia) and the *xangô* (in Recife).

Ohum Eniadúdú[19]
Recipes for Afro-Brazilian *Quitutes*[20]
The *Calunga*[21] of the Maracatús
The "People's Library" and the "Modern Collectanea"[22]

Obviously, there is implied in these titles no interest other than in history and ethnology. But in the following ten papers, although there again appears to be no concern with problems of racial accommodation, one does note an awareness of physical differences and an interest in their measurement.

Some Anthropological Measurements of the Population of Recife
Some Data on the Physical Characteristics of the Population of Recife
Some Physical Measurements of Brazilian Negroes and Mulattoes
A Study of Cephalic Indices and Color Variation among Mulattoes in Pernambuco
A Contribution to the Study of Lapicque's Index
Physical Measurements of Negro Students
Comparative Heights and Weights of Newborn *Branco*, *Pardo*, and *Preto* Babies
A Statistical Study of Longevity in *Brancos*, *Pardos*, and *Pretos*
The Comparative Incidence of Tuberculosis in *Pretos* and *Brancos*
Mental Disease among the Negroes of Pernambuco

[19] Under this title two topics were considered: (1) legends from Dahomey and (2) Anamburucú (an Afro-Brazilian deity [see chap. x]).

[20] *Quitutes* are food delicacies.

[21] The *calunga* referred to here was a richly adorned female image representing a water deity. It was carried by the "Dama do Passo," a female dancer of the Maracatú.

[22] The "Modern Collectanea" and the "People's Library" are two sets of inexpensive leaflets containing ballads and other folklore, historical sketches, anecdotes, prayers, recipes, etc. See, in this connection, Jorge Amado, "Literatura dos negros e mulatos da Baía," *Revista do Arquivo Municipal de São Paulo*, XLVIII (June, 1938), 179–82.

Quite exceptional in their subject matter are the following three papers:

Race Mixture in Brazil as a Eugenic Factor
The Mixed-Blood and the Problem of Degeneracy
The Social, as Opposed to the Racial, Causation of Degeneracy

These three papers, concerned as they obviously are with the oft-considered question of the relation of race mixture to degeneracy, indicate some concern in Brazil with this problem and thus appear at first sight to imply an interest in race relations in the North American sense of that expression. The question at issue turns out to be, however, largely an academic one, evoked perhaps by foreign literature and concerned with supporting arguments of white superiority and of Negro inferiority originating in Europe and the United States. At any rate, it is true that certain scholars, at a loss to account for the persistence in twentieth-century Brazil of African cultural forms, have seriously come to question the cultural capacities of the black race and to believe the future of Brazil prejudiced by the infusion of African blood.

Thus, about 1900, Nina Rodrigues, intimately acquainted with a number of Africans in Bahia and impressed with the slow rate at which they and their descendants were sloughing off African cultural forms and being assimilated into the white world,[23] and also influenced to a considerable degree by foreign writers,[24] raised very earnestly the question of "the capacity of the Negro to accommodate himself to the civilization of the superior races."[25] Doubting specifically the ability of the Negro to take on European civilization,[26]

[23] *Os africanos no Brasil*, pp. 407–9; see also *ibid.*, chaps. v–vii.

[24] *Ibid.*, chap. vi, esp. pp. 388–98.

[25] *Ibid.*, p. 385.　　　　　[26] *Ibid.*, p. 391.

he identified the "Negro problem" with the question of "the cultural capacity of the Brazilian Negro; the means of increasing it or of compensating for its deficiencies; the actual value of the African's contribution in acclimating Europeans to the tropical zone; and the advisability of diluting the black population with a preponderance of white blood which would then control the country."[27]

The significant facts about these conclusions of Nina Rodrigues are (1) that they in no way challenged the commonly accepted Brazilian assumption of the inevitability of race mixture and (2) that, when this inquiry into the Negro's native capacity to assimilate European culture was published (posthumously) for the first time in 1932, it immediately aroused a storm of protest, to allay which such zealous but scientifically minded disciples of Nina Rodrigues as Arthur Ramos thought it necessary to remind Brazilians that "the Bahian master" had been influenced by "certain postulates of the epoch in which he labored" and that his followers are well aware that "the science of our days challenges the accuracy" of such conclusions.[28]

Restating, then, the "Negro problem" as far as Brazil is concerned, Arthur Ramos considers it "first of all a historical problem, a question of the slave traffic, of the different tribes imported, of the history of slavery, etc." He continues:

It is further a problem in anthopogeography, a question of the physical characteristics of the various Negro stocks both in the areas of their origin and in Brazil, and of the variations occurring by reason of the change in their environment. It is an ethnographic problem, a question of the habits, traditions, etc., of the Negro in the countries of his origin, and their modification in the new habitat. It is a biological problem, a question of racial heredity and race mix-

[27] *Ibid.*, p. 392.
[28] *O negro brasileiro* (Rio, 1934), p. 22.

ture. It is a linguistic problem, a question of the influence of African dialects upon the Portuguese language. It is a sociological problem, a question of the influence of the Negro upon Brazilian social life.[29]

As here defined, then, the concern of Brazilian intellectuals interested in the Negro lies in problems other than those arising from racial maladjustment, with the possible exception implied by the phrase "questions of racial heredity and race mixture," and similarly suggested by the titles of the last-named three papers presented to the first Afro-Brazilian Congress. But, if the situation is analyzed more fully, one finds that each of these three papers *attacks* the positions that the Negro is racially inferior and that race mixture leads to degeneracy.

The thesis of Negro inferiority is today perhaps most forcefully defended by Oliveira Vianna, able sociologist and member of the National Academy of Letters. Well versed in the race literature of Europe and of the United States and impressed, like Nina Rodrigues, with the difficulties in the way of assimilating the African and his descendants, Vianna has written:

The pure Negroes never will be able, not even the most advanced representatives of the race, to be assimilated completely into the white culture; their capacity for civilization—their "civilizability," so to speak—does not extend beyond merely imitating, more or less imperfectly, the habits and customs of the whites. Between the Negro's mentality and that of the Caucasian lies a substantial and irreducible difference which no social or cultural pressure, no matter how long it may be continued, can possibly overcome.[30]

[29] *Ibid.*, p. 19.

[30] Oliveira Vianna, *Evolução do povo brasileiro* (2d ed.; São Paulo, 1933), p. 156. It is obvious from a careful reading of his books that this able scholar inadvertently fails to distinguish between the biological and the cultural determinants in mental functioning and personality and that he also confuses cultural achievement with racial potentiality.

Thus the Negro, being "insensible to those superior impulses which constitute the dominant force in the white's mentality," contributes to the superior classes, Vianna contends, "only when he loses his purity and mixes with the white."[31]

Recognizing, however, that there are in Brazil "both inferior and superior mixed-bloods," Vianna offers in explanation that "a fortunate crossing of a superior type of Negro (for the Negro is not a unit) .... with a white individual well gifted eugenically may produce a superior mulatto .... if, by chance, in the play of hereditary influences, the eugenic potentialities of the white predominate."

In another connection Vianna maintains that

the entire development of Brazilian collective mentality has in reality been nothing more than a continuous bringing-over .... of the racially inferior portions of our population to European mentality and morality: that is, to the mind and character of the white race. The superior mixed-bloods, those who during the long period of our national development have risen socially, did not rise nor establish themselves because of their mixed-blood mentality. Instead of preserving as they climbed the characteristics of their hybrid type, they on the contrary lost those very characteristics, left off being psychologically mixed; that is, they Aryanized themselves.[32]

To this latter passage the author of one of the three papers referred to above takes energetic exception.[33] Quoting this passage in full, he immediately disclaims any addiction to what he calls "the Aryan fetish of the illustrious sociologist." He maintains instead that "the greatness of Brazil comes from race mixture"; it has resulted in a better-adapted and more resistant individual, "the new variety, the mixed-blood *superior being.*"

[31] *Ibid.*, p. 161.

[32] *Populações meridionaes do Brasil* (3d ed.; São Paulo, 1933), p. 154.

[33] A. Austregesilo, "A mestiçagem no Brasil como factor eugenico," in *Novos estudos afro-brasileiros*, ed. Freyre *et al.*, pp. 325–33.

Sharply departing from Vianna, and also from Jorge de Lima and Euclydes da Cunha, to all of whom he refers as "devotees of Aryanism," and from "those foreign literary men and sociologists of little standing" who claim "that the Brazilian is a product of three melancholy, inferior, and indolent races: that is, that the Brazilian is racially inferior," this author asserts that "the notable intellectual capacity of the Brazilian people and the existence among us of geniuses to an extent greater than in any other Ibero-American country, prove that it is not Aryan descent but race mixture which has given birth to the intelligence and the creative capacity of the Brazilian people." Not racial inferiority or degeneracy, but illiteracy, malnutrition, and disrespect for labor are responsible for what deficiencies Brazil may possess. This author concludes:

> I am certain that in Brazil miscegenation has brought and will continue to bring more benefits than evils. The greater portion of our people, as well as of our talented invididuals,[34] in politics, in the sciences, and in the arts, were, or are, mixed-bloods. For instance, I can at once cite such men as Gonçalves Dias, Tobias Barreto, Barão de Cotegipe, Floriano Peixoto, Rebouças, José do Patrocinio, Nilo Peçanha, Machado de Assis, Juliano Moreira, Olava Bilac, Lima Barreto, and many others: scientists, painters, sculptors, musicians, poets, military men; in all of whom the blood of Africa is represented to a considerable degree.

A perhaps less extreme and more scholarly but nonetheless vigorous attack upon the theory of Negro inferiority is to be found in the second of the three papers referred to above.[35] Regretting that "our . . . . physical, moral and so-

[34] This is probably an exaggerated statement of an actual truth.

[35] See Senhora Juliano Moreira, "Juliano Moreira e o problema do negro e do mestiço no Brasil," in *Novos estudos afro-brasileiros*, ed. Freyre *et al.*, pp. 146–50. In this article the widow of the late colored alienist gathers together some of his writings upon the subject.

cial backwardness . . . . has been unjustly attributed to the single fact of miscegenation," the author of this paper, the able and widely known psychiatrist, Juliano Moreira, suggests that emphasis may more reasonably be laid upon the circumstances of colonization and slavery, the intemperate use of alcohol, and the debilitating effects of malnutrition.

It is much easier to analyze the psychology of a nation than the psychology of a race. The results of psychological tests indicate that there do not exist in Brazil profound differences between individuals of diverse ethnic origin. What variations I have encountered were due more to the degree of instruction of each individual examined than to the ethnic group from which he came. This explains the fact that individuals from supposedly inferior ethnic groups, when born and reared in large cities, present a better psychological profile than those even of Nordic descent who have been reared in the backward environment of the interior.

In the third paper[36] referred to above, the author concludes that "what we have [in Brazil] is not an unalterable racial inferiority or superiority . . . . but an invariable inequality in economic development." Similarly, Gilberto Freyre, who considers Oliveira Vianna "the greatest Aryan mystic who has yet risen among us,"[37] attacks with vigor the theory of racial inferiority;[38] as also does Arthur Ramos, with special reference to the views of Vianna, in a paper[39] given a few years ago before the Centro de Estudos Oswaldo Spengler in Rio de Janeiro.[40] An interesting fact in

[36] Edison Carneiro, "Situação do negro no Brasil," in *Novos estudos afro-brasileiros*, ed. Freyre *et al.*, pp. 237–41.

[37] *Casa grande e senzala* (2d ed.; Rio, 1936), p. 218; see also *ibid.*, pp. 155 and 156.

[38] *Ibid.*, pp. 208–12.

[39] Arthur Ramos, "O negro na evolução social brasileira," read November 25, 1933.

[40] In reply, Vianna wrote: "I do not know whether the Negro is actually inferior or whether he is equal, or even superior, to the other races; but, judg-

this connection, indicating the purely academic character of this question as conceived in Brazil, is that Vianna is himself a mixed-blood; while both Ramos and Freyre are whites.

That the position of Arthur Ramos, Gilberto Freyre, and the authors of the three papers referred to above represents in a general way the common attitude at Bahia is clearly indicated throughout a number of documents written by white Bahian students, each of whom, although aware of obvious mental and cultural differences between most of the Negroes, on the one hand, and most of the whites, on the other, consider this inequality to spring from the present inferior educational advantages of the Negro and consequently to be transitory in nature. One young lady wrote: "Although the blacks in Bahia are still on a rather inferior intellectual plane, and some people, especially outside Brazil, believe that they will never attain the level of the white man, I think that this class is continually preparing a foundation upon which one day it will rise illustrious." Another wrote: "Their former position as slaves gave to the Negroes a certain degree of inferiority which to some extent has continued down to the present time. However, this inequality is, day by day, disappearing. I believe that very early in the future the *pretos* in Bahia will have ability equal to anything in the white race."

We have already noted the pride in the "progressive whitening" of the population common to all classes in Brazil. A general tendency to absorb diverse ethnic groups has

---

ing by the testimony of the past and of the present, the only acceptable conclusion is that, up until now, civilization has been the dowry of races other than the black; and it has been necessary, if the Negro is to exercise any civilizing role whatsoever, that he be mixed with other races, especially with the Aryan and the Semitic: that is, he must lose his racial purity" (*Raça e assimilação* [2d ed.; São Paulo, 1934], p. 285).

been persistently characteristic of Brazilian society. Out of the traditional behavior which developed in response to the circumstances and conditions of colonial life emerged an informal racial policy, or racial ideology, which has served as a philosophy underlying and giving consistency to the mores, appearing only when they are challenged from without and individuals seek to rationalize and defend their customary conduct. A Bahian school girl of white parentage put this informal policy into words when she remarked: "Race mixture is an inevitable thing. We Brazilians are becoming one single people."

Thus in Bahia the black and the white do not stand over against each other as irreducible ethnic groups, differing not only in appearance, which is obvious, but also in kind, and fated ever to remain separate and distinct. Such inferiority as at present exists is not thought of as racial and permanent but rather as cultural and temporary, and already well on the way to extinction. Every citizen is considered first of all a Brazilian, and every Brazilian takes pride in all other nationals, irrespective of racial origin. Distinctions are secondary. In this connection one ought perhaps to point out that the widespread web of personal relationships in Bahia tends to make a man or woman not so much a member of a category (e.g., a Negro or a mulatto) as an individual (João or Maria).

Even for individuals beyond the range of intimate personal relationships racial terms are seldom used in Bahia. To call a colored man in his hearing a "Negro" or a "mulatto" is not "good form." These terms are used to a man's face only when one is enraged or otherwise desirous of giving offense. It is, as we have noted, like calling an Italian immigrant a "Wop" or a Mexican a "Greaser." These terms emphasize the alien character of the individual's origin. Thus, if a Bahian wishes to be particularly insulting, he will aggravate the sting of "Negro" by adding to it *de Africa* ("from Africa"). In this way he doubly accentuates his reference to the foreign origin of a black.

Although it is true that dark color, as we have seen, is ordinarily identified with lower status and white color with upper-class position, rising in class tends to take a man out of even the color category. For instance, a white Bahian remarked of an upper-class mulatto, "I would hesitate to call him a *pardo*, although he plainly is one; some of his friends might overhear me." For use in such cases, *moreno* is the term "mais elegante."

As early as the imperial period the title of *capitão-mor*, we are told, "whitened even dark mulattoes."[41] Thus, in the second decade of the nineteenth century, the Englishman, Henry Koster, on referring, in a conversation with a citizen of Pernambuco, to the fact that a mulatto was occupying the local office of *capitão-mor*, was told the man in question was not a mulatto. Insisting that he undoubtedly appeared to the eyes to be a mulatto, Koster received the rather unexpected reply, "He used to be a mulatto, but he is not now. For how can a *capitão-mor* be a mulatto?"[42]

Under such circumstances racial consciousness tends to be reduced to a minimum. For if the individual can with rela-

[41] Gilberto Freyre, *Sobrados e mucambos* (São Paulo, 1936), p. 318.

[42] "In conversing on one occasion with a man of color who was in my service, I asked if a certain Capitam-mor was not a mulatto man; he answered, 'he was, but is not now (era; porem já nam he).' I begged him to explain, when he added, 'Can a Capitam-mor be a mulatto man (pois Senhor Capitam-mor pode ser mulato)?'" (Henry Koster, *Travels in Brazil, 1809 to 1815* [Philadelphia, 1817], II, 175-76). Note reference to this incident in Vianna, *Evolução do povo brasileiro*, p. 153, and in Freyre, *Sobrados e mucambos*, p. 318.

tive ease escape identification with a group into which he has been born, not only so far as race is concerned but even to some extent color as well, and if there is little attempt on the part of other persons to treat him differently merely because some of his ancestors were of different ethnic origin, "we-group" and "others-group" will delay in arising as objects in his experience; or, having arisen, will tend to be vague and inchoate entities, not vivid, clear cut, and sharply defined.

Few colored intellectuals in Bahia are at all interested in studying and writing about the Negro; and, of those who are, such as the *preto* João da Silva Campos and the *pardos* Edison Carneiro and João Varella, their interest lies rather in the *Africano*, in his customs and traditions, and especially in those survivals of African culture still extant among descendants of imported slaves.

There is no tendency to dignify the term "Negro" as there is among race-conscious Negroes in the United States. In fact, as we have already seen, "Negro" is a term rarely used either by blacks or by whites. When on occasion it is employed, no Bahian colored man, unless by chance he has been in the United States or in communication with American Negroes, is at all concerned about spelling it with a capital *N*. Nor does he resent the word *ama* ("mammy").

This is not to say, however, that the blacks and the mixed-bloods are completely satisfied with their lot and that they utter no protest against the fate which has made the white man largely superordinate both economically and socially. On the contrary, the lower-class Negro often conceives of himself as mistreated and misunderstood.

There are, in this respect, two classes of blacks in Bahia: (1) those who are aware of, and articulate about, the race problem abroad and (2) those who are not. The former, a literate minority, are sensitive, for instance, to the situation in the United States and point to Brazil in favorable contrast. As one black remarked, "Here in Bahia whites and blacks are never at one another's throats as they are in the United States. A Negro is treated here as if he were no different from other men. So, while North Americans suffer more and more from internal strife, Brazil will every year become more and more one people, united in blood and sentiment."

A *preto* physician, of relatively unmixed African descent who possessed some command of English wrote the following in that idiom:

We have not such a thing here in Bahia as race segregation, as among our illustrious North American friends.

There is here only one constitution for all people without race or caste distinction.

There is not here either white or black; there are only Brazilian citizens and foreigners.

The Brazilian Negroes were born just like the whites and die the same way.

The blacks are brothers of the whites and they love each other in our country.

We are one nation and one people and not a conglomeration of peoples.

I think it would be well for North Americans to get acquainted with the great love which unites the whites and the blacks for the grandeur of our country and take with them the example to their country; which being at its elevation still lynches its Negro citizens, as if all men were not equal in the eyes of God and the law.

Is there one sun for the whites and another for the blacks, my good friends?

In Brazil we recognize *one* God, *one* nation, and *one* people.

Directing attention to a report in a Bahian newspaper of a lynching in Georgia, this man on another occasion said:

Look at that! We've never known anything like that in Brazil. Why do the whites in the United States do such a thing? [With a tone of unbelief] Is it just because he's black? I can't understand it. You just can't conceive of such a thing happening here. The black man is as much a Brazilian as any white.

On the other hand, there are Bahian blacks who, as we have noted, are dissatisfied with their lot. These individuals base their dissatisfaction, however, on an entirely different ground from that of Negroes in the United States; namely, upon class, rather than caste, differences. These blacks, who are all from the lower strata, feel very strongly that the classes occupying a superior social position are not giving the other classes what they deserve. The struggle for position in Brazil, therefore, takes on some of the character of a class struggle in the Marxian sense.

A reflection of this attitude is evident in one of the three last-named papers presented to the first Afro-Brazilian Congress. The author is a philanthropically minded young journalist. Under the influence of leftist ideology and earnestly impressed with the obviously low economic level of the Bahian lower classes, he writes, somewhat bitterly:

The black has been, and continues to be, a being apart, almost an animal, permitted by the authorities merely to have access to the streets and to labor for the whites. Nothing more. For this reason the black can never hope to improve himself, to raise very high his intellectual or moral level, the failure to do which is responsible for his continuing animism, his criminality, etc.[43]

Attitudes of dissatisfaction and protest are also evident in the following suggestions presented by a Bahian *preto* to the second Afro-Brazilian Congress:

[43] Edison Carneiro, *op. cit.*, p. 239.

The Afro-Brazilian Congress ought to point out how deplorable is the condition of the black man in Brazil.

The Afro-Brazilian Congress ought to say to the black man that social lynching is worse than physical lynching.

The Afro-Brazilian Congress ought to break the chains of oppression.

The Afro-Brazilian Congress ought to say to the black man that he is dying of tuberculosis, of the heavy labor of carrying weighty burdens, of passing up necessities,[44] and of sorrow.

The Afro-Brazilian Congress ought to remind the black man that he is selected for, and preferred in, the lower occupations.

The Afro-Brazilian Congress ought to ask the black man how long he wants to be a slave?

"What the black does not have here," admitted a Bahian white, "is economic equality. He ordinarily gets only the meanest of jobs. He may be a manual laborer, a *carregador*, a mason or other artisan, but he seldom gets much above this level." "The Bahian black is poor and oppressed," said a mulatto. "The best positions are usually difficult for him to attain, especially if he has no education. He has little chance of becoming an important intellectual, commercial, or political figure; the best jobs are ordinarily beyond his reach."

The feeling of being abused and unfairly treated by fate is quite evident in the following document written by a *preto* stevedore:

In the past the black man was the laborer, the slave, vilely treated by the owners of great wealth whose descendants today often fail to recognize in him the principal factor in the building of Brazil and continue to deny him what he rightly deserves as a reward and a recompense for his untiring services (and even sacrifices), and for his humility in making himself always acceptable to his masters.

Today the descendants of these slaveowners are the great indus-

[44] I.e., of going without midday meal while at work, without sufficient sleep, medical attention, etc.

trialists and capitalists. Although they are unable to do as their predecessors did, nevertheless they make use, in a disguised manner, of that same abuse of power. They give evidence of a feeling of superiority, which confirms the presence in them of remnants of the former sentiments; they deprive the black man of equality, if not in ability, at least in the opportunity to make use of it.[45]

If the black man were properly educated, he axiomatically would be equal to those who judge themselves superior. Only from men who have leisure to spend in study will there come descendants with lofty aspirations; not from men handicapped by excessive labor and deficient nourishment. This does not prove less intelligence but only less good fortune. For if the forebears of the blacks had been masters of the plantations, the slave huts, and the mines, their descendants would naturally have been capable of educating their children with the same diligence and care as do the whites.

Today, the blacks are employed only as simple laborers, such as masons, carpenters, tailors, mechanics, shoemakers, ironworkers, stevedores, *carregadores*, etc. The reason the blacks do not use their abilities as business agents, bookkeepers, custom-house clerks, exporters, importers, etc., is that they do not possess the requisite skill and training, a deficiency which is principally due to the whites themselves, who always hinder the entering of this element of the population into the above-indicated classes where they might exercise authority over the other element and then they call them "inferiors," "the poor," "low-class."

The black child may attend elementary school and learn a few indispensable things. But since his parents cannot send him to secondary and superior schools, directly thereafter he goes to work; which causes, or at least contributes to, his inability to enter pursuits other than those in which stevedores, *carregadores*, etc., work.

This is the reason why the black man cannot attain a position of economic security in the Bahian community.

In assessing the significance of this document, one must draw a distinction between the lower-class *pretos* and those other blacks who have climbed somewhat in the economic

[45] I.e., in opportunities to develop these abilities through education.

and social order and have attained a measure of security. If one takes account of class identification, the dissatisfaction and protest here illustrated may be interpreted—and in connection with the whole cultural situation in Brazil properly should be interpreted—as incidents of a class rather than of a racial struggle; of a competitive process which naturally takes on the seeming appearance of a racial struggle due to the coincidence, in general, of class and color identifications.

That this interpretation is tenable is borne out by the fact that from Negroes who have improved their social position one does not hear this note of dissatisfaction and protest. *Pretos* or dark *pardos* who have attained some standing in the community and some measure of recognition commonly defend the white man and laud the merits of Brazil, as did the Negro physician quoted above. Said he, on another occasion, somewhat exaggeratedly: "In Brazil there is no fear of color, no prejudice of race. A black man may enter any profession and draw his clients from any group. See, I was a member of the class of 1928 [proudly displaying a framed panel of photographs of graduates in that year of the Faculty of Medicine]. The greater part of my clients are white. And at the clinic, look at this! [showing a photograph of a large number of children, many of whom were white]. These came to me for professional advice."

A black of some social standing remarked with a show of pride, "Here we are all equal, black, white, and mixed-blood. No position is closed to the black man, and no profession. He can reach any level for which he shows himself fit."

If the presence of a limited degree of race consciousness in Bahia does not imply that the lower-class *preto* is completely satisfied with his lot, neither does it mean that the whites, as we have already seen, do not ordinarily look upon the mass of the blacks as, at least temporarily, socially and culturally inferior. This attitude is, however, more like that of an indulgent parent toward an immature but gradually developing child than like the attitude of one who feels himself superior because he belongs to a race which he believes to be endowed by nature with capacities superior to those of any other. As a white remarked, "At the present time the *pretos* are very backward in comparison with the whites. But I think that with social evolution they are becoming more and more intelligent and that eventually they will contribute equally with the whites to the forward march of Brazil."

If many of the lower-class blacks and darker mixed-bloods tend to feel themselves somewhat abused and misunderstood, the lighter, and to some extent the medium-dark, mixed-bloods are ordinarily jealous of their social advance, speak well of the whites and of treatment at their hands, and conceive of themselves as being, if not white, at least nearly white. At all events, they want to be white, and they ordinarily are, by their friends at least, so considered.

Pedro Calmon, thoroughly familiar with Bahian tradition, has stated:

The *pardos* very early in our history came to consider themselves equal to the whites. Usually they were free; and the free man always had contempt for the slave. This scorn, described by Ewbank, Kidder and Fletcher, Agassiz, and all the writers who left their testimony concerning the society of the nineteenth century, is quite characteristic of the time; even dark *pardos* were in their own estimation equal to the whites. The lighter ones did not permit their European character to be at all questioned.[46]

[46] In correspondence with the author.

While the mixed-bloods are consistently proud of their white lineage, they (at least the ambitious ones among them) tend, as we have noted, to be ashamed of black relatives and to hide, in so far as possible, the too obvious evidence of relation to them. This ordinarily occurs when the mixed-blood has achieved some economic competence or otherwise improved his standing in the social order.

Such an attitude is not greatly dissimilar to that of an upper-class resident of New York, for example, toward his relatives among the mountaineers of Tennessee. As with all individuals who within the span of a few years have climbed from one class to another, the self-confidence and sense of superiority of the Brazilian mixed-blood are to some extent intermittently, or even constantly, threatened by feelings of insecurity. João Varella has written of some of these individuals:

> Of his white father, whom he never saw,
> He has a picture in the parlor;
> But of the Negro woman who gave him birth
> He has no picture, nor does he even speak of her.[47]

Similarly, Gilberto Freyre has pointed out that many times in the past

there resulted from . . . . the fact that the mother or the grandmother of the house was a mulatto situations often dramatic which are reflected in certain Brazilian romances and other accounts. Fair individuals often sought to keep visitors from seeing the fat mulatto grandmother, or even mother, with her huge negroid buttocks; or kept out of sight the dark brother, or dark sister, the tira-teima"[48]

[47] From an unpublished manuscript entitled "O africano na Bahia."

[48] Elucidating this phrase, a Bahian said, "The *tira teima* is an individual who in himself constitutes a living negation of the family's claim to whiteness. Being darker, or otherwise revealing the presence of Negro blood, this individual destroys the illusion (*tira a teima*) of *fidalguia* [superior standing] which the family wishes to give out."

of the family, he or she whose color or features would inevitably reveal less noble or less Aryan origin.[49]

The black quite naturally resents this feeling of superiority on the part of the mixed-blood. His characteristic attitude is reflected in the common saying, "He who can't be a white man is a black." A Negro cook burst out one day, "Listen, wise one, you're just a dirty mulatto! You don't even belong to a pure race! I'd rather be black than yellow any day!" Another black, angry at a mixed-blood, blurted out, "All right! That's what you get from a mulatto. Mixing up the races always brings something like this."

"These mulattoes!" bitterly complained another *preto*, angered at the pretentious behavior of one of his mixed-blood relatives. "Dirty scum! Deny their grandparents, their uncles, and their aunts, even their own parents! They don't want to be blacks; they want to be whites!" "Mulattoes, when they get money," complained a black woman, "don't want to admit any longer that they are mulattoes." And, she added, somewhat bitterly, "the whites will accept them, too, if they have money."

[49] *Sobrados e mucambos*, p. 355. That, outside the ranks of the relatively small number of colored Bahians identified with the African culture, a desire to approximate as nearly as possible the whites in physical appearance is widespread is attested by numerous advertisements in the newspapers like that in *A Tarde* for November 30, 1936:

HAIR!!!

Wooly hair turned into a permanent!
Kinky hair unkinked!
Pomades Indiana, Americana, etc. [Japoneza, Fixa] correct defects no matter what they are!

Sung by mulattoes is the verse:

Sae azar	Go away!
Por aqui a fora!	Leave me alone!
Cabellos espixados	Only hair that's straightened
Estão na moda agora!	Is now in style!

Usually the whites acknowledge gratefully the blacks' contribution to the building of Brazil and prefer them to the *pardos* on the ground that they are less pretentious, more friendly, and more loyal and appreciative. "We like the blacks here," said a white Bahian. "And why not? Didn't they help build Brazil and aren't they still helping to create our country? We are not like the English and the North Americans. They are enemies of the Negro, but we are his brothers. We should all be kind to them, for it is not their fault that they are black."

A Bahian historian, in describing the colonial period, wrote:

The black was an agent of social regeneration by reason of his affective qualities which aided the interpenetration of . . . . diverse elements in the Brazilian population. The slave woman reared in her arms the children of her master; she brought into the white home not only African delicacies but also courteous manners and won protection and lasting friendship from the white family by her tractableness, her devotion, her kindly spirit.[50]

Another white Bahian remarked:

I like the blacks better than I do the mulattoes; in fact, much better! Do you know why? They're more honest, for one thing. They're more dependable. Why, I wouldn't hesitate to trust a fortune in the keeping of Francisco [his black servant]. They're more friendly, more considerate, more grateful. This is true not only of those who work for me [this man employs regularly sixteen laborers, has eighty-four Negro and dark mulatto hucksters whom he supplies with oranges from his *roça* for peddling in the streets], but it goes for black professional men as well. I know a black lawyer, for instance, a very fine man. I'd trust my legal affairs with him as soon as I would with any white lawyer I know.

I used occasionally to meet North American Negroes in France. I didn't like them. They were proud and haughty and very touchy.

50 Pedro Calmon, *Historia da Bahia* (2d ed.; Bahia, n.d.), p. 28.

And I used to tell them that the Brazilian Negro was much superior to them. That made them mad, and they used to say, "That's what you think, because the Brazilian Negro takes everything from you whites and is willing to live on an inferior plane." But I said, "I don't know about that. I'm a member of an organization in Bahia which has a black president."

The white acknowledges the mixed-blood's intelligence, but he often resents the characteristic aggressiveness which the mulatto, in the course of his ambitious struggle to climb the social ladder, has developed, as well as other distinguishing personality traits which have appeared in the course of this competitive struggle. As one man put it: "I resent their forwardness, their enviousness, their jealousy, their 'lack of respect,' their pretentiousness, their inconstancy and unreliability, their arrogance and (upon gaining some measure of improved social position) their overweening pride, their boastfulness, cocksureness, 'cheekiness,' and general manner of showing off." This attitude is also reflected in the common saying, "A mulatto *pernostico* is a redundant expression," a statement which a Bahian elucidated in the following words:

The mulatto who characteristically desires to be white and who for this reason looks down on the pure black, tends to exaggerate the qualities which he observes in the whites and to emulate them to such an extent that a word, *pernostico*, has been coined to describe him. He is always trying to be what he isn't.

Even the word *mestiço* ("mixed-blood") has come to be, to some extent at least, a term of *desprezo*, connoting, as a local citizen expressed it, "someone who is desirous of supplanting his father, exceedingly ambitious to get ahead, and gain prestige." Another reflection of this aversion is the common saying, "He who sees a mulatto and does not run, has oozing joints."

Said, somewhat exaggeratedly perhaps, a prominent white:

I'm going to get out of Bahia and go to São Paulo. This town is too full of mulattoes and of mulatto traits. Bahia has become a *pau de sebo* ["greased pole"]. No one wants to get the prizes, but they all want to pull down everyone who tries to get them. This place is full of envy, of ill will and egotism, all mulatto characteristics. The mulatto is not like the black; he is a person without character. He has no honor. He's always envious, he's jealous, he's so busy "maintaining himself," pushing himself in where he isn't wanted, that he can't tend to his business or to his job; he can't do anything except make of himself a general nuisance.

"I always find black servants preferable to mulattoes," another white Bahian said. "They're more faithful, more respectful, even if less intelligent perhaps. The mulattoes are always trying to be 'whiter' than they are."

A student wrote:

The *pardo* has one quality which the *preto* does not have. He is more *pernostico*, probably because he has the strong conviction that, even if one parent *is* black, the other is white. He ordinarily is not as accomplished as the whites, but he wants to appear in public better than he is. The *pretos*, no; they are more pleasant and have the natural gentleness of a race which has suffered much and has been made a martyr by the *senzalas*. I do not mean by this that there are no *pretos* who are ill-bred and stupid; but I do mean to say that such *pretos* are more rare than those *pardos* who, when they attain some position of importance in our public life, act as if they no longer tread upon the earth.

The attitudes engendered between the various ethnic groups at Bahia tend to be those ordinarily arising out of a struggle for position in any class order. The newly arrived, as well as those engaged in elbowing their way up, are everywhere resented. These attitudes focus upon color for the reason that, within limits, color is still identified with social position. But the fact that these attitudes tend to disappear in cases where the colored man's claim to advanced standing rests on grounds of demonstrated competence and obvious personal worth is highly significant. It identifies the Bahian social order as a class society wherein competition takes the form of a struggle between classes (which by reason of historic accident happen to coincide to a considerable degree with color) rather than a struggle between races or colors as such.

Said a white Bahian: "We like a person to be modest. One who is aggressive and self-assertive we tend to shove back a little. That's one reason why the black, Raul Caloge-ras, is so well regarded. He never presumes, never pushes himself forward. Whites respect him for what he is, especially for his great intellectual ability."

Another white Bahian, acquainted with the United States, said:

As I think of it, the feeling toward the Negro here is somewhat like the feeling toward the Jew in the United States. As long as he remains a Jew, it is not the thing to marry him, but occasionally it is done with more or less comment. Your dealings with the Jew depend a great deal on the kind of a Jew he is. If he's a low type, you leave him to himself. If he's overly ambitious, aggressive, and always pushing himself forward, you resent his behavior. If he's educated and capable, but still modest, and at the same time willing to give up his Jewish separatism, you are apt to share more or less your experiences with him. The less he is like a Jew, the more he tries to be like other Americans, the more you have to do with him. In a similar way, the more the Negro repudiates his African connections, the more he comes to be like Europeans, but in a modest, inoffensive way, the more we have to do with him.

A white Bahian wrote: "Naturally those persons who have ethnic characteristics more like those of the white race enjoy somewhat greater prestige. But this does not prevent a man who has real worth from attaining a superior position just because he is colored. Absolutely not."

"Especially in Bahia, where there is much prejudice regarding 'quality,' " wrote a black, "a *pardo* or a *preto* is, in the presence of whites, never well thought of except he be a person of intellectual capacity or of some means; for in Bahia these two characteristics are very important."

A white student wrote:

> Race for me changes nothing in an individual. I think the *preto*, the *pardo*, and the *branco* should all be treated alike. Distinctions open to the whites ought to be equally open to the blacks and to the mulattoes. It is not they who made themselves black; it is not they who are responsible for their dark color. I have seen or known of *pretos* and *pardos* who on every occasion could readily replace certain *brancos*. Such men as these, in my opinion, are at least equal to the whites. I repeat, not race but personality influences me; a man who has a good character and is intelligent and competent merits distinction, be he white, black, or *pardo*.

Among "the ten most important Bahians" selected by a hundred and twenty-two students in the Escola Normal were three mulattoes and two *brancos da Bahia*. Sixty-seven students in the Law School chose six whites, two *brancos da Bahia*, a mulatto, and a *preto* among the ten most prominent local citizens. Sixteen girls in a mission school conducted by North American missionaries listed two *brancos da Bahia*, a mulatto, and two *pretos* among those who, in their judgment, were "the ten most important Bahians."

V

THE AFRICAN HERITAGE

CHAPTER IX

OS AFRICANOS

THE connection between Africa and Bahia is perhaps more intimate and has been maintained over a longer period of time than any similar connection elsewhere in the New World. Although assimilation of the Africans and their descendants has been proceeding at a gradually accelerating rate and has now reached an advanced stage, identification with Africa and with African cultural forms still marks off rather noticeably a portion of the darker population. Differences in dress, in food and food habits, in forms of religious expression, in sacred specialists, in attempts to exercise control over personal destiny and over other human beings, in credulity in folklore, and, to a limited extent, in language describe different worlds which still coexist at Bahia: one largely African in derivation, the other European.

The mental world of the Bahian upper class, which, as we have seen, includes a considerable number of the lighter mixed-bloods, is not greatly dissimilar to that of the same stratum in predominantly Catholic areas of Europe, especially in Portugal, Spain, and France, the latter of which has for a long time been the "intellectual motherland" of Brazil.

But the superior, educated class is relatively small. Most of the people in the city, as well as in the state of Bahia, are illiterate and would be included in what is ordinarily conceived of as the folk. Of this group, the Africans and their descendants obviously constituted in the past, and still constitute today, a large element.

This division in cultural identification, however, is not always sharply defined. Adherence to African cultural forms, for instance, the *candomblé*, often varies not only from family to family but also from individual to individual in the same family group; and, occasionally, in the same individual with reference to different cultural elements, to different periods in his life, and even to varying moods in his experience. In other words, African cultural forms at Bahia are disintegrating at a comparatively rapid rate.

Nor should one assume that the body of customs and traditions which marks off to some extent this lower-class world is entirely of African origin. While it undoubtedly is composed in considerable part of elements originating in Africa, certain native Indian customs and traditions, together with ideas and practices common to the lower classes of Europe, as well as other customary behavior which has arisen in response to the circumstances of life in Brazil, contribute to it. The disentanglement of these diverse strands is, in some instances, a difficult and exceedingly laborious task.

It should be emphasized that these distinctions follow cultural and not necessarily racial lines. The lower class, as we have seen, includes a number of Europeans, and these have in numerous cases taken over sentiments and attitudes of African origin. Moreover, as the blacks and the mixed-bloods rise in class, they tend to slough off all identification with Africa and with African cultural forms.

Bahian Negroes long maintained direct contact with the West Coast. Even after the extinction of the slave traffic, vessels regularly plied between Bahia and Lagos, repatriating nostalgic emancipated Negroes and returning with West

Coast products much prized by Africans and their descendants in Brazil.[1] An elderly Bahian Negro recently brought out from among his treasured possessions a faded photograph of blacks aboard a ship on their way to Africa and pointed out an *atabaque*, or sacred drum, and a woman in *saia grande*.[2] He recalls having been many times with his father at the docks in Bahia when vessels came in from Africa and sailors brought news of Lagos.

Trade with the West Coast, however, gradually decreased until, by 1905, it had almost entirely disappeared. Today, only a few important articles employed in the fetish ritual, such as cowries, *obis* and *orobôs* (sacred fruits), *pimenta* (pepper) *da costa*, *palha* (straw) *da costa*, *sabão* (soap) *da costa*, and strips of *pano* (cloth) *da costa*, are occasionally imported from Africa.

Numerous Africans, their interest in Brazil stirred by Brazilian Negroes returning to the West Coast, are said to have emigrated to Bahia as recently as thirty years ago. Considerable areas in and about the city—for example, Caminho do São Gonçalo, Caminho do Cruz, and a portion of the Terreiro—were once owned, it is said, by *Africanos*.

Today, native-born Africans as a population element are

[1] Pedro Calmon, *Historia social do Brasil* (3 vols.; São Paulo, 1937–39), I, 182. It is also reported that on at least two occasions representatives of African chiefs arrived in Bahia from Ajudá, with which port Bahian officials were maintaining direct commercial relations. One arrived during the administration of the Vice-rei Conde de Athouguia; two others "and an interpreter," on May 26, 1795. See João Varella, *Da Bahia que eu vi* (Bahia, 1935), pp. 153–57; J. B. de Sá e Oliveira, "Dois embaixadores africanos mandados a Bahia pelo Rei do Dahomé," *Revista do Instituto Historico e Geographico Brasileiro*, LVI, Part I (1895), 413.

[2] The large skirt still worn *bouffant* by many Bahian black women. The date was approximately 1895.

virtually extinct.[3] Only an occasional individual of African
birth may be found, like, for instance, a certain elderly black
once prominent in the fetish cults not only of Bahia but also
of Rio de Janeiro who was born in Lagos, his father having
purchased his mother out of slavery in Brazil shortly before
his birth and taken her to Africa. He knows four *Africanos*
still living in Rio. In 1936 he met in Brotas (a subdivision of
Bahia) an elderly African woman with facial scarification
and almost no command of Portuguese. She has since died.

Thus, actual contact with Africa is today little more than
a memory in the minds of a few of the older blacks, who
recall stories told by their parents or by other Africans of
persons, places, and events in Africa; or who years ago visited in the home of African ancestors or were, perhaps, personally acquainted with blacks plying their small vessels between Bahia and the West Coast. However, certain individuals of the older generation still cherish sentimental attachment to Africa, as is indicated by the expression occasionally
heard on the lips of an elderly Negro, as he reverently turns
his eyes upward toward the sky, "Sou filho de dois Africanos,
graças a Deus!"[4] "If I had the money," remarked another
black, his eyes lighting up, "I'd go to Africa, to Abeokuta,
build me a house, and live like a man ought to."

An elderly Bahian Negro recalled:

My mother was just a young girl when she was captured by a
warrior in Africa. He wanted to sell her to a slave trader in Dahomey.

[3] Since lower-class Negroes who have difficulty in speaking correct Portuguese occasionally attempt to cover up their chagrin by saying that they are
Africanos, and others, participating in social circles where prestige attaches
to the native-born African, may deliberately misstate their origin, the in-
cautious observer may be led erroneously to think that there are a considerable number of Africans still living in Bahia.

[4] "My father and mother were both Africans, thank God!"

On that day two younger children were with her, a baby she was carrying on her back and a child she was leading by the hand.

She told me of a terrible thing which she saw on that day. Two warriors were running to catch a young girl. Each grabbed one of her arms, and they began to quarrel, pulling at her and shouting, "She's mine! She's mine!" But neither could jerk her away from the other. Finally one swung his big knife, and slash! He cut the girl in half and told the other man that now he could have his share.

My mother's name was Manjengbasa, which means, "Don't leave me alone." She was born after her mother had lost both of her first two children. She carried a scar on her cheek which meant that she was a Yoruba; for all Yorubas, both men and women, have this mark. She married my father here in Brazil, and when I was born they called me Ógeládê.

When I was thirteen years and eleven months old, my father took me to *Af-ri-ca;* to Lagos, *West-Coast-of-Af-ri-ca*, Nigeria. Ige-sha is two days away. Oyó used to be the capital. And there is Akra on the coast; there is Ashanti, and Groweh, and Ifé, and Egba. My father was from Egba, and his father was from Abeokuta. And there is Efun and Dahomey.

My father was only on a visit. He soon came back to Bahia to take care of his business. He was at that time importing African things. But I stayed in Lagos eleven years and nine months. From 1875 until 1886 I was there. Later I went again to Africa and remained another year. And three years after that I again returned, to sell coral and fine and coarse wool. I bought *pano da costa* to sell here.

My grandfather was a great warrior. He had a large plot of ground, but he was more of a warrior than a farmer. One day while fighting he got an arrow in his arm. He jerked it out and the blood covered him. When, years later, my grandfather died, I was a child of six years.

My uncle also was a great warrior. He was younger than my father. When they brought my father to Brazil, my uncle was left there in Africa.

My grandfather had forty wives. He lived in an *atalaia*,⁵ a house

⁵ Composed of many dwellings placed side by side and having a common roof.

as long as from here to the entrance of the fort,[6] just for the family of my grandfather. He was buried in a room. A *quartinha* of water which is always kept full still stands there today.

When my father was born, my grandmother was already an old woman. But she was still very strong. When my grandfather died, she walked all by herself up to the place where they buried him. When I went to Africa, she was in Ibadum. She never saw my father again. When he took me to Africa, she did not get to see him because the Africans were fighting fiercely. No one could travel as far as from here to Rio Vermelho.[7] So my father did not get to see his mother. But when she found out that he had been in Lagos and had left a son there, she never left off speaking of me. She wished to have me stolen, but the men who came to carry me to my grandmother never found me alone. They brought me presents. My grandmother had made me an African food which lasts two or three months and does not spoil. It is made with *fubá* of maize, crushed. All is seasoned with fragrant and savory seasonings, with onions and shrimps, and put in a large pan. It is like a cake they call here *bom bocado*. In the African language it is called *adúm*. Rolled up in leaves they gave it to me. My tutor ate part of it too.[8] For fifteen days we ate *adúm*. When I came back to Bahia and told my father I had eaten *adúm*, he lost almost the whole day crying, because he had not seen his mother for almost fifty years, let alone eaten her cooking. He looked up at me, and said 'You, my son; *you* ate *adúm!* ' "

Some contact with Africa is still maintained through family connections, although these are now rare; by means of African visitors, principally individuals from the crews of English ships recruited in Lagos; and by way of occasional newspapers published on the East or West Coast in Portuguese, English, or even African languages.

Thus, one will occasionally find in the possession of Bahian Negroes a copy of the *Nigerian Daily Times*, published

[6] About one hundred yards.

[7] About three miles.

[8] The boy had been placed in a mission school.

in Lagos.[9] In this journal for December, 1932, a Bahian black recently pointed out photos of Cleonice de Assumpção Alakija, "the youngest daughter of Dr. Maxwell P. de Assumpção Alakija, a lawyer of Bahia, Brazil," who "recently graduated as a throat and ear specialist from the Faculty of Medicine at Bahia"; of Dally Assumpção Alakija, youngest son of Dr. Maxwell, "recently graduated in Bahia as a civil engineer"; and of Adeyemo Alakija, their cousin, in the royal robes of an African chief from Abeokuta. The caption of the accompanying article was "A Notable Egba, Adeyemo Alakija."

This African cousin of Bahian blacks had been "honored by His Highness, the *Alaké* of Abeokuta," at a festival celebrating the one hundredth anniversary of the settlement of the Egbas at Abeokuta following severe internecine warfare and had subsequently been installed as "The Barujun of Aké." According to the account, Adeyemo Alakija belongs to a "distinguished family." His father was Marculino Assumpção, "Chief Akigbotum, known also as Elemeji, one of the first men to own a cotton gin in Abeokuta"; and his mother, Maxmilliana Assumpção Alakija, was the daughter of the late Alfa Cyprian Akinosho Tairu, native of Oyó, "a chief of Abeokuta with the title of Morope of Aké," for whom Tairu Lane in Lagos is named. Both of Adeyemo Alakija's parents were born in Brazil, the eldest living member of the family being the Bahian lawyer, Dr. Maxwell Porphyrio Assumpção Alakija, "father-in-law of His Worship, Olumuyiwa Jibouwu, our Police Magistrate."

[9] One *Africano* also possesses copies of *Wasu* ("Preach"), a missionary pamphlet used in Nigeria; the English prayer-book and the Bible, both in Yoruba; the *Nigerian Catholic Almanac* for 1933; a life of Marcus Garvey; and a copy of the *Negro World* for April 19, 1930, the latter given him by a Negro fireman on an English ship which occasionally puts in at Bahia.

Although it is exceedingly doubtful if there is in Bahia today anyone of African descent who does not speak Portuguese, a few individuals can and on occasion do converse in Nagô. One may also hear Gêge spoken, as well as those languages known locally as "Angola" and "Congo." However, the use of these tongues is very largely confined to the ritual of the *candomblé*, although at times one hears in the homes of blacks the Nagô greeting, "Ô-kú á-sán!" and the parting salutation, "Ôdî-ôlá-ô!" and even conversations in Nagô. Many African words are to be found in the predominantly Portuguese speech of the lower class, a limited number of which have become common to all Bahia and, to some extent, to all Brazil. Approximately three hundred of the latter were noted.

Certain gestures are to be observed among the lower-class blacks which are not common to the general population; for example, the *legua de beiço*, or slight extension of the lower lip when indicating distance (the words accompanying may be "one league," but the sense is much farther); and the *muxôxô*, or pursing of the lips as the lower portion of the face is pushed forward and upward, signifying disdain. Approbation is indicated by touching the tips of the fingers to pursed lips and withdrawing them while making a kissing sound. Silence is compelled by grasping the upper lip with the tips of the fingers. The act of eating is indicated by closing and opening the right hand before the mouth, and the act of drinking by raising the right hand before the face, flexing the three middle digits, and, with thumb and little finger extended, raising and lowering the hand at the wrist. The height of a human being is demonstrated by extending the palm flat in horizontal position in contrast to a vertical placement for indicating the height of a lower animal.[10]

Although one is not likely to find any Bahian black who has not been given at baptism a "Christian name," nicknames are very common, and many individuals are much better known by them than by their given names. Among such *apelidos* one will occasionally discover terms of probable African derivation; for instance, Okê, Bábá Cumdê, Cobê, Oum, Tau-édê, and Au-weh, all nicknames of members of a local labor union; or, among personages in the fetish world, such names as: Manoelzinho de Oxóssi, Lourenço Lemba, Maria de Tempo, Senhora de Yemanjá, João de Zázé, and Flaviano Cavungo, each of which recalls the African *orixá* to which the individual in question is dedicated.

Exercising considerable prestige among a portion of the Bahian population is the *babalaô*, or *olhador*, whose primary function, it seems, is to foretell the future; the *curandeiro*, who by means of herbs, prayers, and other magical manipulations seeks both to treat and to prevent disease; and the *feiticeiro*, or "witch doctor," who, for a price, works black magic. The office of the *babalaô* is occasionally exercised by the *pae de santo*, or priest of the fetish cult, although his function is more particularly that of supervising the rituals and public ceremonies of the cult and overseeing the sacred properties. To some extent he also exercises the function of a *curandeiro*.

[10] A form of greeting recalled by older blacks but rarely used today is as follows: If the individuals are social equals, each lifts his hands, palms outward, and grasps the hands of the other in such a way that the fingers of the one are interlaced with the fingers of the other, after which the "*ogan* grip" is exchanged; if not social equals, the individual of greater prestige places his right hand over the closed hands of the other.

Paris fashions largely dictate the nature of female attire among the upper classes at Bahia, but many black women still wear the *vestimenta bahiana*. This costume is composed of a *saia*, or very full skirt, of varying combinations of colors, which ordinarily measures some twelve to fifteen feet in circumference at the hem and is worn *bouffant*, spread by a heavily starched underskirt; a *bátá*, or long, loose-flowing white blouse which is ordinarily of cotton cloth but occasionally of silk, trimmed, in most cases, with wide lace, sometimes worn very loose at the neck and allowed to slip off one shoulder; a *pano da costa*, or long, heavy, striped cotton cloth, at times worn slung over the shoulder and pinned under the opposite arm, at times wrapped once or twice in a wide fold about the waist and tied rather tightly; a *torso*, or turban, of cotton or silk, bound about the head; *chinelas*, or strapless leather sandals with low heels; numerous necklaces of coral, cowries, or glass beads, with an occasional metal chain, often of silver; earrings of turquoise, coral, silver, or gold; and numerous bracelets of cowries or of iron, copper, or other metal. The *balangandan*, formerly an important ornament, has disappeared.[11]

As an alternate to the *bátá* a white blouse is sometimes worn tucked inside the *saia*, and in place of the *pano da costa* a woolen or silken shawl is occasionally substituted. For

[11] The *balangandan* (also known as *berenguenden, balançançan, cambaio,* or *penca*) consisted of a gold or silver frame on which were hung gold or silver images of animals, birds, fowls, fish, flowers, parts of the human body, houses, household utensils, amulets (including gold or silver balls inclosing soil from a cemetery), bells, medallions with religious significance, angels, suns, moons, etc. It was worn on festive occasions, tied at the waist (see F. Marques dos Santos, "As balangandans," *Espelho*, April, 1936). Many impoverished families, attracted by recent high prices of gold and silver, have disposed of these relics of a former splendor. A limited number may still be seen among the heirlooms of wealthy Bahians.

A *BAHIANA* IN *BAHIANA* COSTUME SELLING *ACARAJE*, *ABEREM*, AND OTHER FOOD DELICACIES

festive occasions *sandalias*, or leather "mules," are regularly preferred to *chinelas*, and one often sees the common foot-wear of the lower class, the *tamancos*, simple sandals with wooden soles and leather toe straps; or, occasionally, cloth slippers. Some women go barefoot.

The *torso*, commonly said to be of Arabic origin, was probably brought to Brazil by the Haussás and other Negro followers of Mohammed who were imported from the areas immediately south of the Sahara. In *Globus* for April 28, 1910,[12] there is a photograph taken in Togoland which shows Negroes wearing *torsos*, *panos da costa*, and *saias* similar to those seen today in Bahia, except that the heavily starched petticoat usually worn with the latter is lacking.[13]

The typical wearer of this costume, or *vestimenta bahiana*, as it is called, is a tall, graceful black woman of remarkable physique, self-confident bearing, and intelligent, cheerful countenance. She is known as a *Bahiana*, the first of whom to emigrate from Bahia to Rio, during the disorders attendant on the struggle for independence, impressed the French visitor Debret as notably different from the black women of Rio, not only in dress, but also in general bearing.[14] "The *Bahiana* came to symbolize, by extension, a gracious (*graciosa*) and spirited creole woman."[15]

The *Bahianas* were worth seeing at our festivals, with their resplendent costumes; their arms half-covered with gold or silver bracelets; their diamond earrings; their gold necklaces from which hung . . . . crosses, *figas*, and medallions of the order of *Carmo*, all of gold. . . . . They completely dominated our religious festivals. . . . . They

[12] XCVII, No. 16, 245.

[13] The *saia* is commonly worn in Bahia, on days other than those of festival, without starching the underskirt.

[14] J. B. Debret, *Voyage pittoresque et historique au Brésil, 1816–1831* (3 vols.; Paris, 1835), II, 105.

[15] Calmon, *op. cit.*, p. 188.

filled the churches at Mass, at prayers, and at sermons, accompanied by little black urchins carrying small stools of *jacarandá*[16] with carved feet. They were women who tended small stalls in the markets, or who sold in the streets, proprietors of small eating-places, elderly slaves, and young *mulatas* who came to turn the heads of the "old conquerors."[17]

[16] A very heavy wood of rich coloring much prized for furniture.

[17] "Onde estão as *Bahianas?*" *A Tarde*, June 23, 1936. It was of these *Bahianas* that Carmen Miranda sang when she recently captivated Broadway with the staccato notes of the rollicking *samba* by Dorival Caymmi, "Que é que a Bahiana tem?"

O que é que a bahiana tem?	What is it that a *Bahiana* has?
O que é que a bahiana tem?	What is it that a *Bahiana* has?
Tem torço de seda, tem	She has a *torço* of silk, she has
Tem brinco de ouro, tem	She has ornaments of gold, she has
Corrente de ouro, tem	She has a golden necklace, she has
Tem pano da Costa, tem	She has a *pano da Costa*, she has
Tem bátá rendada, tem, ah!	She has a *bátá*, embroidered, she has—ah!
Pulseira de ouro, tem	Bracelets of gold, she has
Tem saia engomada, tem	She has a *saia*, starched, she has
Sandalia enfeitada, tem.	Decorated *sandalias*, she has.
Tem graça como ninguem	She has "oomph" like nobody else
Como ela requebra bem	How well she swings those hips!
Quando você se requebrar	When you swing those hips
Caia por cima de mim	Fall on top of me
Caia por cima de mim	Fall on top of me
Caia por cima de mim.	Fall on top of me.
O que é que a bahiana tem?	What is it that a *Bahiana* has?
O que é que a bahiana tem?	What is it that a *Bahiana* has?
Tem torço de seda, tem . . . . etc.	She has a *torço* of silk, she has . . . . etc.
Só vae no Bomfim quem tem	Only those go to Bomfim who have
Só vae no Bomfim quem tem	Only those go to Bomfim who have
Um rosario de ouro	A rosary of gold,
Uma bolota* assim	A little ball, thus,
Quem não tem balangandans	She who has no *balangandans*
Não vae no Bomfim	Can't go to Bomfim
Quem não tem balangandans	She who has no *balangandans*
Não vae no Bomfim	Can't go to Bomfim
Oi, não vae no Bomfim	Oi, can't go to Bomfim
Oi, não vae no Bomfim	Oi, can't go to Bomfim
Oi, não vae no Bomfim	Oi, can't go to Bomfim,
Oi, não vae no Bomfim.	Oi, can't go to Bomfim.

* Instead of a cross the Malês, or Mohammedan Negroes in Bahia, used a ball on the rosary.

Although the Bahian upper classes, owing to their Negro cooks, are not unacquainted with those dishes of African origin so commonly eaten in the homes of lower-class blacks, one does not ordinarily find on their tables African delicacies like *abará, aberém, acassá, acaragé, arroz de Aussá, bóbó de inhame, carurú, efó, xin-xin,* etc., each of which is seasoned according to recipes handed down from African forebears who also extensively made use of African seasonings like *azeite de dendê, ataré, irú, pejerecum, iêrê,* and *egussi.*[18] The eating habits of the upper classes are, in general, European in origin. But the poorer inhabitants extensively utilize banana leaves for plates and for packaging foods and replace forks with fingers as eating accessories.

The music and dances enjoyed by large numbers of the darker population further distinguish this portion of the Bahian community. For instance, the *samba,* or *samba batida,* a regional form of the old *batuque,* although it has now been taken over by the upper classes and in a modified form become not only one of the most characteristic musical forms but also one of the favorite dances of Brazil, is still enjoyed in its primitive simplicity by the Bahian lower classes. With them it is a dance in which first one and then another of the participants enters a circle, dances a shuffling step while singing, cantor-fashion, the first line of a stanza, the others responding as a chorus. A song very popular at Mar Grande on the island of Itaparica in the bay at Bahia recalls the

[18] *Azeite de dendê* is oil from the *dendê* palm; *ataré,* said to have been imported from Africa by Bahian Negroes, is a variety of pepper; *egussi* are gourd or melon pips; *iêrê* are seeds similar to those of the coriander; *irú* and *pejerecum* (or *bejerecum*) are varieties of small beans. For recipes of a number of these dishes see Manoel Raymundo Querino, *A arte culinaria na Bahia* (Bahia, 1928).

labor of Negro slaves in the cane fields of the *engenhos* of the Reconcavo. The *cantador*, or leader, sings:

> Olha a cana madura . . . .
> Ela é verde, é madura . . . .
> Para fazer "raspadura" . . . .

to which the chorus responds:

> No cannaviá![19]

In a second chorus the solo is: "Lá vem o padre," and the response: "Pra casar vocês dois!"[20] In a third, the solo, "Por mim não, barbulêta," is followed by the chorus, "Você póde avuá!"[21]

The principal steps of this primitive *samba* are known as the *corta-a-jaca* (cutting the *jaca*), the *separa-o-visgo* (parting the pulp), and the *apanha-o-bago* (taking out the *bago*, or edible portion).

Capoeira is often *jogado* (played) in out-of-the-way places, and at times, particularly during Carnival or at such festivals as Segunda Feira do Bomfim and Conceição da Praia, it even invades more public places. It is a highly complex form of personal combat, originally developed by fugitive slaves to enable them to compete more effectively with armed *capitães do matto* and now enjoyed as a sport set to music. The agility of the contestants is remarkable, as they strive for points in a struggle without actual physical contact, where unexpected thrusts of the feet or elbows, rapid pivot-

---

[19] "See the ripe cane,
It is green, it is ripe,
Ready to make *raspadura* [coarse brown sugar]
Chorus:
In the *cannaviá* [roadway through the cane field]!"

[20] "Here comes the priest,
To marry you both! . . . . "

[21] "As for me, no, butterfly,
You can fly away!"

ing, and sudden "cartwheels" alternate with other attempts to confuse and "cripple" an opponent.[22]

The musical instruments commonly employed among this portion of the population are the *atabaques*, the *agôgô*, the *caxixi*, the *canzá*, the *agê*, the *chocalho*, the *xaque-xaque*, the *cuica*, and the *berimbau*. All but the last three instruments are rarely seen outside the *candomblé*.

The *atabaques* (or *tambaques*) are wooden drums, each approximately twenty inches in diameter but varying in height, invariably used in sets of three. The largest, called *ilú*, or *rum*, is seldom less than two and one-half feet tall and occasionally attains seven feet, while the medium-sized drum, known as *rumpi*, ranges from two to four feet in height, and the smallest, or *lé*, from one and one-half to two and one-half feet. To produce a soft, muted sound, the drums are beaten with the hands. For the heavier tones, *baquetas*, or short wooden sticks, are employed. The huge *bâtá-côtó*, or war drum, which played a prominent role in the slave insurrections, has long since disappeared.

The *agôgô* is a bi-tonal instrument, consisting of two hollow iron cones joined together. It is beaten with an iron pin. The *agê*, or *piano de cuiá*, is a large calabash containing pebbles and covered with a small cotton net in whose meshes *buzios*, or cowries imported from Africa, are firmly secured. If the latter are not available, dry seeds known as *contas da Nossa Senhora* are employed instead, and pebbles are occasionally inserted in the calabash itself to augment the sound. The *caxixi* is a tiny reed or straw basket containing cowries or small pebbles. The *xaque-xaque* is a hollow metal instrument shaped like a dumbbell, each of whose enlarged extremities contains small pebbles. When shaken, it produces

[22] See Edison Carneiro, *Negros bantus* (Rio, 1937), pp. 147–60.

the sound from which its name is derived. The *chocalho* is a similar instrument, but with only one extremity enlarged. The *adjá* is a small metal bell used to invite members of the cult to the ritual *dar comido ao santo*.[23] The *canzá*, or *ganzá*, now is seldom seen.[24]

The *berimbau* is used primarily to accompany *capoeira*. It consists of a wire strung upon a stick to form a bow, with a dried gourd open at the top attached at the lower extremity. The instrument is beaten, to produce numerous complex rhythms, with a wooden stick held, together with a *caxixi*, in the right hand, while with the left a copper *vintem* (old Portuguese coin) is alternately pressed against the wire and released. The *cuica* is a drumlike instrument, open at one end. Sound is produced by drawing the hand along a resined stick appended to the center of the drumhead.

In the lower-class world health and morality are in many cases closely identified. The cause of disease or bodily harm is often believed to lie in the direct intervention of a deity who has become angered by the nonfulfilment of obligations prescribed in the sacred ritual or by the breaking of taboos. Evil forces may be invoked, it is believed, through the magical influence of the *feitiço* and bring illness, blindness, insanity, or death.[25] The *mau olhado*, or "evil eye,"

[23] See chap. x.

[24] For illustrations of these instruments see Arthur Ramos, *O negro brasileiro* (Rio, 1934), Figs. 24 and 25 (p. 162).

[25] Rituals vary. A portion of the clothing of the one to be harmed, a shoe or other article, may be submitted to magical manipulation and thrown into the sea. In this way the individual is presumed to be subjected to the ebb and flow of the tide. Or a few hairs from the head of the one to be harmed may be mixed with crushed herbs of supposed magical power. Presumably he is then likely "to hate someone whom he now esteems, drink to excess, become crippled or insane, or lose his life." A pigeon, chicken, sheep, or he-

a magical power presumed in many parts of the world, including Europe, to be possessed, often unwittingly, by certain individuals, is thought at Bahia to bring death to plants, birds, and even small children whom the person has coveted or, perhaps, merely admired. More natural forces are the *ar do vento*, or "air of the wind," a cold draught said to result in indigestion, deformity, insanity, or death; the *espinhela caida*, or "fallen breastbone," which presumably brings on an emaciated condition of the body; and *sangue nova*, or "new blood," thought to be responsible for the breaking-out of a rash. Dew must not be allowed to fall on the head. Certain diseases, like syphilis and leprosy, are considered defects common to all men.[26] However, the persistent efforts of agencies like the Rockefeller Foundation have widely disseminated the idea that malaria results from the bite of a mosquito.

The treatment or prevention of disease is the logical counterpart of a magical theory of causation. Thus, members of this section of the Bahian population attempt to control personal destiny through the use of charms or other magical means or through the direct intervention of a deity, whose favor is sought by the offering of gifts or the performance of prescribed rituals. Thus, to counteract the influence of the "evil eye," charms are worn, or pieces of the *Guiné*, *Arruda*, or *Vassourinha Doce* plants are passed, to the accompaniment of magical words, over and about the affected person's

---

goat may be killed, or a doll made and its neck pierced by a bit of wood. Either object is then placed in the doorway of the individual to be harmed or in any other place where he is likely to pass, the one depositing the *feitiço* calling out, as he drops it, the name of the person for whom harm is intended.

[26] "Syphilis," a black explained, "began with the world. Everyone has it, even horses, although it may never show up."

head. The wearing of *patuás*, or written prayers, is presumed to "close the body" (*fechar o corpo*) against disease or accident. The nut known as *chapeu de Napoleão* ("Napoleon's hat"), if worn on a string about the neck, similarly is reputed to possess magical power.[27] A cord of deerskin passed over the affected area is presumed to cure erysipelas; a string of white beads worn about the neck of a mother is thought to increase the flow of her milk; a cord tied tightly about the waist of a pregnant woman will, it is believed, "keep the baby from going to the head"; and a stone in the hair is thought to retard delivery. Considered particularly efficacious in all cases of illness is the *"itá* of Xangô."[28] "Prayers," or the use of magical words or phrases over an affected part of the body, are also extensively employed. A common belief is that the *pae de santo* can in this way cure snakebite.

The direct intervention of a deity may be invoked as when presents are made to the *mães d'agua* (female deities who are presumed to inhabit bodies of water) to remove illness or misfortune or to assure future success. Thus, fisher-

[27] At the children's clinic a black mother brought in a child very ill. About his neck was a cord suspending a *chapeu de Napoleão*. To the physician's query, the mother replied, "They said it would make him well. Everyone told me to use it, and I didn't know."

[28] *Itás* (Tupi equivalent of "rocks" or "stones") of Xangô, or, as they are also called, *pedras* of Santa Barbara, are thought to have fallen from heaven during thunderstorms. They are said to have penetrated into the earth seven *braças* (2.2 meters) and to have returned to the surface after seven years. The person so fortunate as to find one of these stones is considered a highly privileged individual. The *itá* is used by the *pae do santo* to crush the leaves of certain medicinal plants which are then put, together with the yolk of an egg, into a vessel and mixed, while an invocation in Nagô, known as *etutu*, is intoned. The stone is then covered with the crushed leaves and egg yolk and allowed to stand for a period of time. The liquid prepared in this way is considered to possess miraculous healing power.

men, anxious for a good year's catch, or individuals wishing to be rid of some illness, to obtain employment, or to secure a satisfactory resolution of unrequited love, will purchase foods, wearing apparel, toilet articles, jewelry, and other gifts pleasing to a lady and place them with appropriate ceremonies in a body of water presumed to be inhabited by one of the *mães d'agua*. Particularly sacred are the waters of Mar Grande, off the island of Itaparica, where, a few years ago, a saddle horse, it is said, was presented to Yemanjá; Mont'serrat and Cabeceiras da Ponte, on opposite sides of Itapagipe; Baiutê,[29] near the village of Itapoan; and Mariquita, near Rio Vermelho.[30] Parents of twins make regular food and drink offerings to the twin-deities, the Beji, or Cosme and Damião. Omolú, the "*orixá* of smallpox," is believed to protect not only against the ravishes of this disease

[29] A foreigner was swimming in Baiutê when a passer-by, seeing him, shouted excitedly, "What are you doing in there? Don't you know that that water is charmed (*encantado*)? You might even turn into a fish. Haven't you seen the white swans? They say that they are two people who once swam here." For accounts of public offerings to the *mães d'agua* see *Estado da Bahia* for June 19 and September 23, 1936; *A Tarde* (Bahia), February 3, 1938.

[30] A letter headed, "Every Vow Fulfilled up to the End of the Year, 1936," and addressed to "Our Lady of Mont'serrat, the Mistress of the Sea, Janaina," was found in the bay near Mont'serrat. It read:

To MY GODMOTHER:

I promise you, my Lady of Mont'serrat, that if you arrange it so that I can marry Domingos Portella, I will give you a present worth fifty milreis. And on the second of February I will put in another present according to my means. If possible, I will give you thirty milreis, and if not I will give you at least twenty. As large a present as I have I will give you on February 2, from twenty milreis up. My Godmother, I promise thee that the day of my marriage to Domingos Portella will be a happy day for you also; while I shall be having a *festa* here on land, you also will be having a *festa* there in the holy sea. I will fix dishes of all that we have in the house for this day, and send them to you, with greetings from me.

Your goddaughter,

YVONNE D. L. BRAGA

(Letter presented here by courtesy of Friar Tomás.)

but also against all skin ailments, including leprosy. Particularly approachable is the deity to whom a person is dedicated. "This bad cut on my foot," remarked a *mãe de santo* dedicated to Xangô, "would not heal. So I talked it over with Xangô. He agreed to heal it, and told me what to use. It's now getting well; it's much better already."

An individual troubled by continued ill-health, business difficulties, or even bad dreams may request of the fetish-cult priest the ritual of *lavagem das contas*, or "washing the beads." Divination is first resorted to in order to identify the *orixá* "responsible" for the difficulty. Then the beads sacred to this deity are immersed in water, a newly purchased basin being used for the purpose, and a handful of leaves also sacred to him are crushed and added. After a time, the beads are removed and washed with *sabão da costa* ("soap from the Coast"). Thus purified, they are given to the person suffering the ill fortune, who must subsequently keep them in a clay vessel and from time to time wear them about his neck.

Considered one of the most effective methods of "removing" a disease or misfortune is the *troca da cabeça*, or "changing of heads," whose purpose is to transfer the disturbing influence from the afflicted person to another individual. The ritual varies. The afflicted one may have his head rubbed with a chicken or a pigeon, which, having thus acquired the evil influence, is then killed. Or an *ebó*, or *bozó*, as it is more commonly called, may be prepared,[31] and the affliction purposely transferred to another individual by leav-

[31] The *bozó* almost always includes a dead hen, popcorn, manioc meal with *azeite de dendê*, pieces of clothing from the one to be benefited, nickel or copper coins, certain African foods like *acassá*, *aberêm*, and *acarajé*, and, if available, the African fruits, the *obi* and the *orobô*, of ritualistic significance.

ing the *bozó* in a place where the intended victim is likely to step on it or otherwise touch it.[32] An animal may be "prepared with the *ebó*" so that whoever subsequently touches the animal will catch the illness or inherit the misfortune. If, however, one wishes to avoid transferring the evil to another person, he may do so and still rid himself of his affliction by leaving the *ebó* in a cemetery.

If a *filha de santo* (ceremonial dancer of the fetish cult) would avoid illness or other misfortune, it is considered highly important that she observe all the taboos, especially those attaching to food and drink. A pregnant woman must avoid vegetables and all meats other than chicken; she must not join a funeral procession, since the spirit of the deceased might enter her child; and she must avoid a rose touching her bare breast, for otherwise the child, it is believed, will be born with a birthmark.[33]

Charms may be of a specific nature like the *figa*[34] or the

[32] The affliction may, however, be transferred to someone toward whom no harm was originally intended if the individual placing the *ebó*, either ignorantly or with intention, fails to leave it in the designated place. The first person coming in physical contact with it will be affected. So widespread is this fear of the *ebó* that chauffeurs, even at the risk of an accident, will not run a wheel over one.

[33] Current folk medicines include: for syphilis, whale oil; for a toothache, pig or burro dung smoked in a clay pipe; for a cough, sweetened tea prepared by boiling a termite nest; for sore throat, tea made by boiling a live lizard whose body is then removed from the vessel and buried with its head toward the new moon. Native herbs are extensively employed, particularly by *curandeiros*, or they may be administered at the hands of anyone "instructed" by a "manifesting" deity, a common occurrence in those *candomblés* known as *de caboclo* (a portion of whose ritual is probably of native Indian origin) and in spiritualist centers like that in Alto do Bom Gosto, in Calcada, one of whose directors remarked, "So many *caboclos* 'manifest themselves' because they know so well how to heal with herbs."

[34] The *figa* is an image, usually made from wood, of a closed fist with the thumb inserted between the index and middle fingers.

oxhorn, both of which are employed for protection against the *mau olhado*, or "evil eye." Or they may be of a more general nature like the letters *J M J* (Jesus, Maria, José), or the *signo de Salomão* ("sign of Solomon")[35] either or both of which may be painted or carved on the door of the house or even tattooed on an individual's arm, leg, or chest; or a small pouch worn around the neck and containing either a *patuá* (presumed to protect against evil, especially the machinations of an enemy or death in battle)[36] or a small piece of garlic, "Danda root," *mil homens*, or *arruda*, a clove, or merely some object sacred to the *orixá* to whom the individual is dedicated. Similarly employed are such magical practices as the sprinkling of sea water in the four corners of the house, the emptying through the front door of a basin of water left overnight in the center of the floor, or the burning regularly at six o'clock in the evening of incense to which, occasionally, sulphur and pieces of oxhorn are added until the house is filled with magically potent smoke.

In the fetish cult, divination is commonly resorted to for such purposes as the identification of an unknown *orixá* who has "manifested himself" in human form, the determination of such matters as the eligibility of a prospective *ogan*, or male functionary of the cult, the cause of a troubling illness, or the proper course to pursue in some contemplated action. Divination is also employed to foretell future events, particularly the outcome of business or amorous ventures, jour-

[35] A six-pointed star at whose apex appears a cross.

[36] During the insurrection of 1835, the Malês, as we have seen, wore *patuás* consisting either of prayers or of verses from the Koran, written or printed in Arabic characters. They were presumed to protect against death in any form. For photographs of some of these see Nina Rodrigues, *Os africanos no Brasil* (São Paulo, 1932), p. 98, Figs. 1, 2, 3, and 4.

SYMBOLS OF THE SOOTHSAYER'S ART PAINTED ON THE
WALL OF A NEGRO DWELLING IN MATATU

neys, etc.[37] Oracles are invoked by way of such magical intermediaries as the *obî* and the *orobô*, or the *opélé-ifá* (a chain of thin disks), or they may be obtained directly from an *orixá* who speaks during the "possession" of a *filha* or a *pae de santo* by way of the mouth of the one "possessed."[38]

Contact between the living and the dead is believed not only to be possible but to occur regularly. Hence, the prac-

[37] The serious character of a transaction of this sort puts it in a different category from certain other magical acts, common to all classes, which have the character of a game, being similar, for example, to practices attaching to our festival of Halloween. Thus, one may take a glass, "bless" it three times, put in it the white of an egg, and, holding it over a fire, again thrice "bless" it; or partially fill a basin with water and permit the tallow from a lighted candle to drip into it; or stick a knife up to the hilt in a banana tree and leave it until morning. The patterns formed on the glass, the water, and the knife, respectively, are presumed to indicate the initials of one's future spouse. A similar image is presumed to appear in the dreams of one under whose pillow has been left a freshly husked ear of corn.

[38] Other magical practices of this sort are: the placing of crushed charcoal under a rock to expedite the recovery of a lost article, the burying of the third of a rosary to stop rain; also, it is commonly believed that a hummingbird inside the house, or the singing of an *adivem-quevem*, announces the coming of guests; that the appearance of an owl, or of an *ouriço cacheiro*, foretells death; that a black butterfly is a sign of misfortune; that a katydid with dark eyes brings unpleasant news, while one with light eyes brings favorable news; that seeing the new moon for the first time between the branches of a tree or anywhere partially obscured is a sign of misfortune throughout the coming month; that the showing of money to the new moon when seen for the first time will assure no want of income for the next thirty days; that ill fortune will attend one who dwells in a house on the corner of a street, enters a house with the right foot, or opens an umbrella inside a house. Still other "signs" of misfortune are: the toad; the black cat (or the "ghost" of a cat); the *anum* perched in a tree near the house; the *jacumim;* the hummingbird, if black; the katydid, if it has a black mouth (if the katydid has a red mouth, happiness is in store for the observer). In the opinion of numerous people, mutton must not be eaten, since it is "the *lamb of God* who taketh away the sins of the world." Sheep are animals which Christians must not eat.

tice, now not so common as formerly but still occurring, of forsaking a dwelling-place in which some member of the family has died. "Visions" are commonly reported. A *preto* related:

Once as I was working, I suddenly noticed an old friend, together with another man, standing by me, both of them "out of the flesh." My friend spoke and asked me how I was. I told him I was "so-so." Then he said, "Did you know that Fernando was dead?" I didn't, but, sure enough, I found out the next day that he had died that very morning.

One finds in many individuals an absolute credulity in folk tale and folk myth. Thus to many a Bahian of the lower classes the *lobishomem*, the *caipora*, the *mula de padre*, and the *biatátá* are actual entities which he himself, or someone known to him, has supposedly seen or heard.

The *lobishomem* (werewolf), credulity in which is also common to large areas of Europe, is said at Bahia to roam about on moonlight nights, preferably on Fridays, with dogs following him. He takes the form of a man, very pallid, with an enormous shock of hair and long fingernails. Coming up behind a traveler or sneaking into the house after a child, he grasps his victim and sucks his blood. A person "very yellow" from malaria is thought to be in danger of turning into a *lobishomem*. If a family has seven sons and no daughters, the first-born is believed liable to develop into one of these creatures unless he is made co-padre with his parents at the baptism of the seventh child. The hour of such transformation is midnight sharp. A house servant remarked:

When I was a small boy, I knew a man who turned into a *lobishomem*. There in my country, near Joazeiro [state of Bahia]. He had killed his father and his mother. He always went around with his head down, very sad and very pale. The children called him *chico-bicho* and ran and hid from him. Every Friday night he turned into a beast and wandered about. We knew he did, for a man who was passing a dark spot on the road late one night saw him; but when he took out his knife and started after him, the beast fled. The *lobishomem* was covered all over with hair and looked horrible. Other people saw him too, running around on all fours. The dogs always barked on Friday nights something terrible. On Saturday morning this man appeared dusty and more pale than usual. He never caught any children because they were all careful to stay in the house during the hours when he was out. But he caught many dogs and cats. He merely sucked their blood; he did not eat them. People found the bodies later, with all the blood drained out.

Mulas de padre are reputedly the concubines of priests who, transformed into headless animals, run about at night, preferably on Fridays. Covered with noise-making instruments, such as bells, *chocalhos*, and kitchen utensils, they are said to make "an infernal racket" which can be heard as much as a mile away and "makes one's blood run cold."

The *caipora* and the *biatátá* are probably survivals of Indian lore. The former is a creature thought to inhabit timbered areas, where he is peculiarly fond of leading people astray. When a person is lost, the *caipora* "may make him pass right by the path and never see it." The *caipora* calls out to the unfortunate person and leads him further and further astray. Of female sex, an animal some say, a half-body cut perpendicularly from crown to crotch according to others, the *caipora* may be driven away if one smokes tobacco, takes snuff, or chews garlic.

A young *pardo* shoemaker, having become by reason of his schooling somewhat skeptical of tales of the *lobishomem* and of the *mula de padre*, insisted, however, that

the *caipora* is real. Just as a blow on your arm will leave a red mark, the *caipora* has left signs of himself. I know a Portuguese immigrant, a man upright and truthful, who was warned not to hunt on Fridays. He laughed at the warning, and went on into the timber in search of *jacús*, found one, and shot at it. The *jacú* flew at him with its claws extended and severely scratched him. He shot at it again. It flew back and clawed at his eyes. Then he heard a voice, saying "You know you must not hunt on Fridays." It was the *caipora*. The man staggered home, and fell senseless in the door of his house. I knew this man well.

The *biatátá* is said to be a woman who inhabits the sea, appearing above water only at night, gradually increasing in size until she assumes an enormous shape, and "casting a huge and frightening shadow."

Fear of the toad, probably also a survival of Indian belief, is common.[39] If a toad happens to hop into the door of a house, the occupant will immediately grab a broom and sweep it out, repeating over and over, "Creio em Deus Padre."[40] If a malicious person paints a toad on the wall of a dwelling, its occupants will at once desert the place.

The following account reveals in an intimate way the mental world of a considerable portion of the Bahian lower class. It was related by a young Negro woman in the form of a series of personal experiences and is presented here in as nearly as possible the exact phrasing in which it was originally given.

I was three years old. I was sitting with my mother when something hit me, and I fell over unconscious. She picked me up and took me to a doctor. He gave me medicine and said that it was congestion. Some thought it was the *ar do vento*.

I knew nothing of what was going on; it was as if I were dead. To

[39] "Montoya says ('Manuscripto guarani da Bibliotheca Nacional do Rio de Janeiro sobre a primitiva catechese dos Indios das Missões,' *Annaes da Bibliotheca National*, Vol. VI) that among Indians observed by him, the entrance of a toad into a gathering of people was a sign of the approaching death of one of those present" (Gilberto Freyre, *Casa grande e senzala* [2d ed.; Rio, 1936], p. 99).

[40] "I believe in God, the Father."

help me get better, they took me up off the ground.[41] Then my mother called in Mamêdê [the local *pae de santo*], to see what was the matter with me. He came, *abriu a mesa*[42] and said that this had been with me from my birth. My mother then asked him if he could cure it. He said he could. He made her buy plates, *moringues*,[43] beads, cups, coconuts, etc. Then he prepared all that.[44] They washed my head with water from the sacred leaves. My mother asked if he could take that thing away so that it would not come back again. He said he would not dare to do that, or I would die. He said it always came back.

When it returned, they washed my head again. I did not know what was going on. It was as if I had slept. When I awakened, I was all "prepared": dressed *de creola* with a *saia grande* and a *torso* on my head. Everything red. *Sandalias* too. Everything the same color.

When this happened I was still small. The *pae de santo* said that I was under a spell [*era encanto*]. He "did the work" once more, and I was all right again. But when I was seven years old, it took hold of me once more. My mother was afraid and begged the *pae de santo* to do something about it. She pleaded so earnestly that finally he said he would speak with the enchantment [*encanto*] so that it would not come down any more.

It didn't come back until I was fifteen years old. Then they arranged another dress *de creola*, and also handkerchiefs, strings of beads, bracelets, and *sandalias*. They ordered plates, small glasses, and *quartinhas* bought. When all this was ready, the *pae de santo* washed my head in sacred water. He said it was the "owner of my head" [*dono da minha cabeça*] who had done that to me. There in Cachoeira, across the river from São Felix,[45] is the *casa de Gêge*.[46] The *pae de santo* is the grandson of an African.

[41] That is, she was removed from the reed mat which, placed directly upon the floor of a hut, is extensively used among the poorer families for sleeping purposes.

[42] That is, he set up certain means of divination.

[43] Water pots made of red clay.

[44] That is, he submitted it to the proper ritual.

[45] Cachoeira and São Felix are twin cities, separated by the Paraguassú River, located across the Bay to the north of the city of Bahia.

[46] The *candomblé* of the Gêge cult in which she had now been inducted.

When I was sixteen years old I went across the river to live in São Felix. There was a man there who was crazy. We asked what was the matter with him, and they said that he had seven Exú's[47] in his body. They had given him a cigar and when he began to smoke, he became wild. He was nearly insane. He did not want to hear the word of God. When they talked of going to Mass, he wanted to run away. They took him and tied him up. He stayed this way two whole weeks. Once in a while his relatives came to see him. Finally, they decided to take him to a *candomblé*. They untied him and he went. For a long time he remained there and kept on acting the same way. Then the head of the *candomblé* took a hand in the matter. He ordered them to get black cloth, candles, *azeite de dendê*, incense, and several other things which he needed. After he had finished, he gave the man a bath to clean him up. When twelve o'clock came, he stretched him out in the middle of the floor. And there he lay all sprawled out. We saw a black Negro with red lips sitting on his knee. He was about this high [indicating approximately two and one-half feet], and as black as coal. His lips were as red as the lid of that can [indicating a *matte* container with bright red cover]. He had large ears that stuck out like this [indicating about a twelve-inch spread]. He was horrible. His horns were this long [indicating about six inches]. And his tail, about a meter. His eyes were big, like this [indicating an oval three inches in diameter]. They were the size of "three children."[48] His tongue looked like a snake's; it was really four separate tongues. And he was sitting there on the man's knee. We were all afraid. We wanted to run; but we dared not. He didn't stay long. Only about ten minutes. He left the man's knee and disappeared into the body of the man who had bought and brought the "things." The *pae de santo* filled up a basin, and Exú took himself away. We did not see him disappear. Ten minutes later the man got up, feeling better. He had been sitting there crying hard. They shaved off his hair, washed his head and painted it with a pencil, white, blue, pink, and lavender. Then they

[47] Exú (pronounced "Ā-shu") is an African deity who is often, although not always, thought of as possessing an evil nature. See chap. x.

[48] This expression was explained in the following manner: "A person looking into an ordinary eye sees the image of one child; in Exú's eyes the image was three times as big."

put many beads of O Senhor do Bomfim on him, and a *figa;* they covered him with ornaments.

The *figa* is to free one from the evil eye. For example: I have a dress. You think it is pretty, and you want it very much; something then happens to it. Or a *sabiá*[49] sings beautifully. You are visiting its owner; you want it, you want it very badly. You leave, and it dies or something else happens to it because you cannot have it. This is the evil eye. One needs to "pray it away" with *Guiné, Arruda,* or *Vassourinha Doce.* An oxhorn in the garden will keep it away from plants.

Then the man went around with hands folded, "taking the blessing" from everyone there. Seven children went out with lighted candles. Then he got up entirely well. Today he has a *casa de candomblé.* He is now very old. His *orixá* is Ogum de Gêge. The *pao de santo* who treated him is of Ogum de Mina.

My guardian angel [*anjo de guarda*] is Xangô. Ogum is a soldier, Xangô is of the thunder and also of the lightning. He is Santa Barbara of the Irmandade. All the *orixás* are equal. But Oxalá directs everything. Nanan is his wife. In the Gêge language she is called Odé.

My sister, she died, burned up. She caught all on fire. He who killed her is Oxóssi; it was he who killed her. My sister is buried in the Quinta dos Lazaros.[50] She burned to death because she disobeyed him. He sent a message and she paid no attention to it. Her husband had a *saveiro.*[51] Every trip which he made she went along in the boat. She had no children. Everywhere he went, she went too. When, one time, the *orixá* "arrived" and told her that she should not travel on the water, she didn't take his words very seriously; she laughed the matter off, "gave it a *muxôxô.*" But about a week afterward, she went with her husband in a *saveiro* across the Bay to Bahia. Between Itaparica and Salinas the *saveiro* caught afire. It had powder on it and the powder exploded. Parts of the *saveiro* were ripped off and hurled into the water. She was surrounded by fire. When they finally reached her, she was badly burned. They brought her to the Santa Isabel Hospital,

[49] A Brazilian bird which can be trained to sing tunes.

[50] A Bahian cemetery.

[51] A sturdy sailboat used on Todos os Santos Bay and its contributory rivers to transport light articles of commerce.

and the next day she died. But before she died, he "arrived" and said it was he who had set fire to the *saveiro*. It was Oxóssi. Her husband also died. When one doesn't carry out his obligations [*cumpre com os seus deveres*], the *orixá* takes his life.

Once I had a party at my house for some friends. But Xangô sent me a message that I should go to the *candomblé*. I said that I was not going because I was having a party. A little while later, while I was dancing with my friends, I suddenly got a stiffness in my legs. But I didn't pay much attention to it. Then I suddenly felt an "opening of the body" [*aperto no corpo*],[52] and I didn't know anything more. When I came to, I was dancing in the *candomblé*. When the *candomblé* was over, I went running clear to the top of Boeiros do Inferno ["Funnels of Hell"] without knowing anything about what I was doing. These are two hills called by that name because they are so high. I didn't feel anything. Afterward, Xangô beat me on the hands, and my hands swelled. When he "arrived" again, he said that I should pay more attention to him, or he would beat me some more. Once he struck me. On that day I was very tired, but I went to the *candomblé* and danced anyway.

I dance when there is a big ceremony; I dance for hours at a time without getting tired. The spell seizes me, and sometimes I dance more than three days without feeling the least bit tired. When the *orixá* "arrives in my head," I spend a week or more "sleeping."[53] I don't feel anything. I don't see anything. People talk to me, but I don't know anything about what is going on.

If one drinks water, the *orixá* doesn't "arrive." For instance, one feels cold. That cold is in the body. The *orixá* wants "to arrive." Then one drinks water. He who is of the *preceito* does not drink water. And whoever drinks, breaks the *preceito*. It is prayed ten times.[54]

[52] A "trembling of the body," signifying that the *orixá* wished to enter and to "manifest himself" in human form. See chap. x.

[53] That is, moving about, but unconscious of what is happening.

[54] That is, by taking a drink of water, one can presumably prevent the deity from entering the body. One must at the same time pray ten words and tap the ground ten times. In this way, the *preceito* (i.e., the control of the deity over one) is broken.

I stayed only seven days in the *casa*,[55] because my head was washed. Others spend three months there, lying down all the time. They lie awhile on one side, then on the other, and then face down. One takes a bath in water perfumed with sacred leaves. Every day. The bath is cold, very cold. You must change your clothes and the bed linen every day. It isn't in a real bed that one lies down. They put a mat on the floor, and you have only a pillow and a sheet. You can move, but only from one side to the other, never over on your back. During the time you are in the *camarinha*, you cannot see your relatives. You may see them only on the day you leave. But then you must go at four in the morning and return at four in the evening so that the dew will not fall on your head.

There may be others in the *camarinha*. Sometimes many others. All of them stay in the same room. They sleep with their heads together. If there are ten, there will be space for all ten. While they are in the *camarinha*, they do not attend ceremonies.

I did not go through all this because my head did not have to be shaved. I had my *orixá* from birth. When I came into this world, he already knew everything.[56] My *pae de santo* has "worked" with many people. Last week he was here in Fazenda Grande.

When my *orixá* took possession of me, I quit eating he-goat. Because of the taboo of the *orixá* one cannot eat certain things. During all my life I cannot eat he-goat, because of the taboo. Neither can I eat turtle. For he who is of Xangô does not eat either he-goat or turtle. He who is of Ogum must not eat sheep's meat. Some *filhas* must not eat fruit; others must not eat fish *de couro*, only those fish which have scales. Crabs cannot be eaten by some, nor the leaf of Ogum. Water may be drunk, but only that which is drawn at 4:00 A.M., before the sun rises.

White maize must be eaten by some, depending on the *orixá*. For every *orixá* of every nation[57] has his own food. There is the food of Odé. There is that of Xangô, which is mutton.

[55] The period during which the candidate is initiated into her new function is spent within the sacred room, or *camarinha*, of the *candomblé* center.

[56] That is, he "knew" that she would be consecrated to him.

[57] That is, of each type of *candomblé*: Gêge-Nagô, Congo, Angolo, *de caboclo*.

My *pae de santo* made an *ebó* for me last week. It is a *limpeza do corpo* ["cleansing of the body"]. I had an unclean body and dragged myself around, listless. I went to the "master" of the *candomblé* and he "opened the table" and looked to see if my body was unclean. He then asked me to bring toasted maize, a black cloth, popcorn, honey, and a candle. He passed them all over me,[58] and when he had finished, he took them and left them in a crossroads. Friday is the day for this.

Now if a person puts a *bruxaria*[59] in your doorway, with a doll stuck through with pins, that is of the *feiticeiro* and it is different from a "cleansing of the body." My *pae de santo* does not make *feitiço*. He says that he does not care to do harm to people, because he has a soul for which he is responsible to God. But any *pae de santo* who wishes to bring harm upon someone can do so. For example, if I arrive in his *casa* and say that I want to do something to someone he asks me: "What do you want to do to her?" I say that when she comes to my door I want her to go blind. He will "make a business" and the next day she will come to my door and go blind. Or else I say that I want her to be wounded by a knife. He arranges it so that this happens.[60]

"Opening the table" is a thing done with *buzios*. The *pae de santo* puts an *orixá* on top of the table, together with his little towel.[61] He takes up the *buzios* and sees if "the way is open." My *pae de santo* "opens the table" with beads.[62] He takes the beads and puts them alongside *palha* from the *pindoba*.[63] These beads come from the Coast.[64] His set cost 1:000$000.[65]

[58] That is, in front, to side, behind, above the head, etc.

[59] Any instrument of black magic.

[60] That is, she will be attacked in a lonely place by robbers, or accidentally stabbed. The action is always mediate.

[61] The table-covering which is placed over the *orixá* in the *pegi*, or sanctuary.

[62] Other means employed: a glass of water, a set of playing cards.

[63] Fronds from a variety of the coconut palm.

[64] That is, from the West Coast of Africa.

[65] One thousand milreis, or one conto, equivalent at that time to approximately $60.

My sister is preparing *carurú*. She has twin boys. When God gives you twins, you are obliged to present *carurú* to Cosme and Damião. If you fail to do this, someone in the house will die that year.

If one were now to set down an account of the personal experiences of an upper-class Bahian, it would reveal an entirely different mental world. In general content it would reflect a culture distinctly European. Dress, music, food and food habits, forms of religious expression, sacred specialists, means of exercising control over personal destiny, and the ideas, attitudes, sentiments, points of view, and philosophy of life associated with them would, in general, not vary from those commonly characteristic of individuals of European origin wherever found.

This variation at Bahia in cultural identification between the Europeans, on the one hand, and the *Africanos*, on the other—this difference in ideas, attitudes, and sentiments— obviously erects serious barriers to intercommunication and consequently retards the development of a body of common understandings upon which the moral solidarity of any society is built. Although most of the Bahian blacks have now to a considerable extent sloughed off their former cultural identity with Africa and have been more or less completely incorporated into the European world, a remnant of *Africanos* still live, in spite of contiguity in space with the Europeans, to a considerable extent culturally apart.

As will be evident in greater detail in the following chapter, the Europeans tend to look upon the beliefs and the practices of the *Africanos* as matters for ridicule, scorn, disparagement, and condemnation. They are thought of as queer, bizarre, unintelligible, inferior forms of behavior.

They represent, to this element of the Bahian population, another world.

The general disposition, however, is to tolerate these African practices so long as they are not too obviously indulged in, particularly in public places, and they in no way interfere with the European habits of the major portion of the population. The Europeans act in this respect with somewhat the same leniency which an adult exercises toward the immature conduct of a child, in the confident expectation that "time and education" will do away with these evidences of what one upper-class individual referred to as "cultural backwardness and barbarism." Thus, the behavior of the numerically small group of *Africanos*, although under continuous disapproval and disparagement, is ordinarily treated more as a matter for levity than as a cultural threat; it meets with little deliberate effort at eradication, and even such attempts as are made in this direction are sporadic and halfhearted. Partially for these very reasons, African cultural forms are rapidly disappearing at Bahia.

The *vestimenta bahiana*, for instance, although ordinarily regarded by representatives of the European culture as picturesque, rather romantic wearing apparel, tends today to be largely discarded, especially by the mixed-bloods, and to be withdrawn more and more into the relative privacy of the *candomblé*. Of 500 mulatto women noted on the streets, only 5 were wearing the full costume, and 14 others had on certain portions of it, while 481, or 96.2 per cent, appeared in modern European dress. Of 500 black women noted, 91, or 18.2 per cent, were wearing the full costume, 82 others, or 16.4 per cent, were wearing parts of the costume, while 327, or 65.4 per cent, had on modern European clothing.

The *Africanos* ordinarily look upon the Europeans as presumptuous and quite naturally resent all evidences of a feeling of cultural superiority. Particularly do they resent what they consider to be unfair comparisons with the Europeans, on the one hand, and with the native Indians (who are ordinarily romanticized in Brazil), on the other. Said an *Africano:*

These people think the Indian is worth so much! Look here! Brazil has been discovered for more than four hundred years, and there isn't a single book in Tupi like this [showing the English Prayer-book printed in Nagô], or a single magazine like this [pointing to a periodical published in English in Lagos and containing several articles by Africans]. These people here call us fetish worshipers and say, "Aw, that's African nonsense!" It just goes to show that they don't know anything about what we have in Africa.

This sentiment was echoed by another *Africano*, who complained:

These people here in Bahia think Africans are all barbarous and uncivilized. They won't believe we write our language and that books are printed in it. They say, "Why, these *Africanos*, they're just pagan fetish worshipers, ignorant, and without culture." They don't know that in Lagos there are good schools, better than they've got in Bahia. Look at this [showing a photograph of a school in Lagos]! Is there anything in Bahia as fine as that?

It is perhaps obvious that these complaints reflect a sense of inferiority and an unconscious acceptance of European cultural standards. The case of the *Africanos* in Bahia confirms the hypothesis that the transformation of inner experience characteristic of all cases of assimilation is, to a large extent, an unwitting process which may at times go on even in direct opposition to the individual's intention and resolution. The ordinarily patient and tolerant attitude of the Bahian descendants of Europeans, whether or not they are aware of the fact, has been an eminently successful policy.

This change is not ·difficult to understand. The children and grandchildren of the *Africanos* are in more direct contact with the schools and other instrumentalities of European cultural diffusion. To a considerable extent they are being weaned away from the beliefs and practices of their ancestors. In most cases they have now come to take toward their parents and grandparents the same attitudes which the European community takes toward them. Gradually, the behavior of these children and grandchildren is developing in the *Africanos* themselves an increasingly acute sense of cultural inferiority.

At the same time *Africanos* resent every evidence of another *Africano* breaking with the traditions of his ancestors and thus tending, even unwittingly, to undermine the solidarity of the group. Especially do they resent someone's currying favor with Europeans. As one man put it, "If I see an *Africano* talking to one of these whites, I won't look at the white man but I'll look the black fellow all over, this way [giving facial expression to indicate contempt, disdain], and after I'm down the street a ways I'll do this [sharply clearing his throat and spitting]." A white man was walking one day in Caminho da Cruz da Redenção in Brotas (a subdivision of Bahia) in company with two *Africanos*, an elderly *feiticeiro* ("witch doctor") and his son. A black suddenly shoved his head out of the window of a hut which they were passing and shouted, "Such Negroes! Worthless trash! Walking around with a white man!"

At first sight, one is likely to assume that these outbursts, reflecting as they obviously do antagonistic attitudes toward the whites, are evidences of race prejudice. The fact, however, that outside the *Africano* group, among the more or less assimilated blacks, these antagonistic attitudes tend to disappear, indicates that what we see reflected here is a cultural, and not necessarily a racial, conflict. Antagonism is directed not at the whites as such but at *Europeans;* it is directed at the bearers of a culture, a body of ideas, attitudes, and sentiments, in conflict with the ideas, attitudes, and sentiments of the *Africanos*.

CHAPTER X

THE *CANDOMBLE*

AMONG the last elements of African culture to disappear at Bahia are the customs and traditions associated with the expression of religious sentiment. The *candomblé*, or Afro-Brazilian fetish cult, is still a vigorous institution and numbers among its adherents some of the most widely known and respected members of the Bahian lower classes. Its leaders, in several conspicuous instances, are able and intelligent individuals, whose prestige extends even into the upper circles. Some *seitas*, or cult centers, have maintained the same temple of worship for generations. Their rituals and ceremonies are serious, dignified, and carried on according to definite, fixed, traditional forms.

This highly complex organization of ritual and belief is built around an order of *orixás*, or deities, each of whom apparently personifies some natural phenomenon. Thus, of the more important and more widely honored deities, Xangô is worshiped as the *orixá* of lightning and thunder; Ogun, of war and iron; Oxossi, of the hunt; Omolú, of pestilence; Nanan, of rain; Yemanjá, of salt water; Oxun, of fresh water; Yansan, of wind and storm; Oxun-manrê, of the rainbow; and Beji, of twin births.

The older and more respected *seitas* are commonly considered to be of Nagô (Yoruba) or Gêge (Ewe) origin or represent a fusion in Brazil of these two apparently closely related bodies of African ritual and belief.[1] In details of lan-

[1] Nina Rodrigues, *Os africanos no Brasil* (São Paulo, 1932), p. 320.

guage, ceremonial dress, dance, song and pantheon, these centers differ from the *candomblés* known as "Congo" or "Angola," in which Bantú dialects are spoken, Loanda and Benguela become sacred places, and Tempo and the Angolan chief Kissimbe are worshiped. They differ also from the apparently more recently organized *caboclo candomblés* whose ritual is, in varying degrees from *seita* to *seita*, a mixture of the rituals of the other cults, together with dances and a pantheon of Tupi origin, the latter of which includes Tupan, an important Tupi deity, and Tupinambá, apparently a personification of the cannibal tribe by that name which inhabited the Bahian coast at the coming of the Europeans. The *caboclo candomblés* carry on their ceremonies principally in Portuguese, with the addition of certain phrases of African origin, usually much corrupted, which have been picked up from Gêge-Nagô or Congo-Angola *seitas*, and a few words of Tupi derivation. Feathers, the bow and arrow, and other Indian cultural elements enter into their ritual.

This borrowing of ceremonial elements on the part of *caboclo* imitators, who in many, if not most, cases have not been reared in the African tradition, is bitterly resented by the more orthodox and scrupulous *Africanos*, particularly those of the Gêge-Nagô *seitas*. As a Negro once said, "Si seja mistura, é bobagem" ("If it's mixed, it's nonsense"). A leader of a Nagô cult once burst out:

This fellow João da Pedra Preta! What a disgraceful whelp! His forebears, what did they know? Were they brought up in the *seita*, and did they "deixaram o cargo" [will the office of priest] to him? No! He came here from the *sertão* and started a *candomblé*. Picked up a little Gêge, a little Nagô, a little Congo, a little Indian stuff, and so on. A disgraceful mixture!

A Nagô *mãe de santo* boasted of the ritual in her seita: "It's all pure Nagô; there's nothing in my *candomblé* of this abominable mixture which these upstart places practice today. They call this *caboclo* nonsense *candomblé!* Why, they know absolutely nothing about the way it's done in Africa!"

However, the borrowing of ritual back and forth from *seita* to *seita* sometimes takes place even in the case of Gêge-Nagô and Congo-Angola centers. Moreover, these *seitas* have not entirely escaped some Indian influence.

With reference, then, to cultural origin and identification, there are three principal types of *candomblés* at Bahia: the Gêge-Nagô, the Congo-Angola, and the *caboclo*.[2] The *seitas* of probably most pure Gêge-Nagô origin are those of Engenho Velho, reputed to be the oldest cult center in Bahia; Gantois, which split off from Engenho Velho approximately a century ago and was, during the time of the famed *mãe de santo* Pulcheria, the seat of the researches of Nina Rodrigues; and São Gonçalo, whose able and widely respected *mãe de santo* speaks a Yoruba dialect locally known as Queito. These three centers are probably largely Nagô in origin,[3] while that of Bogum is said to be with the possible exception

[2] The Malê, or Mohammedan cult, which at one time was vigorous and flourishing, seems to have been largely forsaken in favor of the fetish cults by the Negroes at Bahia. Although, in 1905, Nina Rodrigues estimated that one-third of the Africans still living in the city were Mohammedans, he at the same time pointed out that they were then making few, if any, converts among blacks born in Brazil and that Mohammedanism would in all probability die with them (*op. cit.*, pp. 93–94). Certain of the Malê ritual, however, has contributed to the general fusion so characteristic of present-day *candomblés*, and at least three Malê centers are still functioning.

[3] Also of Yoruba identification is Lingua da Vaca ("Cow's Tongue"), which was organized by Negroes of Ige-shá and Egbá origin.

of a *seita* in the city of Cachoeira across the bay, the most purely Gêge in the region. Of the Congo-Angola centers, the one reputed to be most influenced by Congo tradition is Bata Folha; that most influenced by Angola tradition, the *seita* of Maria Nenen. Of the *caboclo* centers, the more noted are perhaps those of the wealthy and widely feared *pae de santo* Jubiabá in Cruz do Cosme, of *mãe de santo* Sabina in Quintas da Barra, and of "Pae Joazinha," or João da Pedra Preta (John-of-the Black-Rock), in Gomea.

Out of the Afro-Brazilian Congress which met at Bahia in January, 1937, came a memorial addressed to the governor of the state asking for official recognition of the *candomblé* as a religious sect with rights and privileges equal, under the Brazilian constitution, to those of all other forms of religious expression. In order to act more effectively in demanding and securing these rights and in combating the sorcery and quackery which are perhaps the principal obstacles in the way of their attainment, an attempt was made, sponsored by the young mulatto journalist, Edison Carneiro, to organize all Bahian *seitas* into one body. The result was an organization known as the União das Seitas Afro-brasileiras da Bahia with a governing body, consisting of one representative from each *seita*, charged with the special responsibility of eliminating unorthodox practices.[4]

The *seitas* are located in sections of the city where the residents are almost exclusively blacks and dark mulattoes or in the outlying regions where dwellings are few. They number perhaps between a hundred and a hundred and fifty. Some say there are two to three hundred, but this estimate

[4] At the first session animosity between the more orthodox centers and the *caboclo seitas* was so great that any substantial agreement appeared to be quite difficult.

appears to be an overstatement. In the area surrounding the sacred lake, or the Dique, and lying between the streetcar lines known as Rio Vermelho de Cima and Rio Vermelho de Baixo are more than a score. A black who regularly attends the *seita* known as Engenho Velho is personally acquainted with eighteen *seitas*, can give the location of their sacred grounds, indicate their line of African descent, and repeat the names of their leaders. Of these eighteen *seitas*, he says that eleven are of Nagô origin, six of Angola, and one of Gêge. All are located in the outlying areas of the city in sections principally inhabited by the darker portion of the population or in the more or less open country. Of their leaders, nine are males and nine are females.[5]

Sacred places include the *terreiro*, or temple grounds; the *franquia*, or sacred groves; sacred springs like that called Milagre do São Bartholomeu ("Miracle of St. Bartholomew"), located in an isolated spot near Pirajá, bathing in whose waters on the part of a *filha de santo* dedicated to Oxun-manrê "immediately causes the *orixá* to arrive";[6] sacred lakes, like the Dique; and the sacred arms of the sea, such as Cabeceiras da Ponte, Mont'serrat, and Baiutê. In the *terreiro* are the *barracão*, or sacred dance pavilion; the *pegi*, or fetish sanctuary; the *camarinha*, or sacred room in which initiates are interned during the period of their preparation; special huts for those *orixás*, like Exú, who "prefer to dwell outside the *pegi*"; and the living-quarters for the priest and his retinue.

In one *seita* of Gêge-Nagô origin whose *pae de santo* is dedi-

[5] Of the eleven Nagô centers, four of the heads are males, seven are women; of the Angola centers, five are males, one a female. The leader of the Gêge *seita* is a woman.

[6] See below, p. 286.

cated to the *orixá* Ogun, the special ceremonial season begins
with the second week in September and concludes with the
first week in December. During this period ceremonies are
held every Sunday, each dedicated to one or more of the
orixás. The first ceremony is in honor of Oxalá; the second,
of Oxagian ("Oxalá the Younger"); and the following three,
of Ogun. Succeeding Sundays are dedicated, respectively, to
Xangô, Oxun, Oxóssi, Yemanjá, and Yansan. On the elev-
enth Sunday and the subsequent Monday special honor is
paid to Omolú, and on the following Sunday and Monday, to
all of the *mães d'agua*. On the final Sunday a *feijoada* (a
Brazilian food delicacy) is offered, with elaborate ritual, to
Ogun. In addition to this regular season, special ceremonies
are held from time to time throughout the year, with the
exception of the Lenten period, when all *candomblé* activity
is suspended.

The Gêge-Nagô and the Congo-Angola pantheons contain
about the same number of deities, or approximately a hundred *orixás* each. The *caboclo* pantheon has perhaps a score
less. Each *orixá* possesses his proper fetish, insignia, sacred
day, sacred foods, sacred colors, sacred dress (including
bracelets and beads peculiar to himself), and a distinguishing
cry. Today, only in rare instances are the fetishes carved
images; more often they are polished stones which have been
worn smooth by the waters of a river or of the sea. They are
carefully cared for in the *pegi*, or sanctuary, by a special
functionary who at regular intervals washes them and re-
plenishes the food and drink offerings placed before them.

In some *seitas* Oxalá is considered the most important of
the deities; in others, Xangô; and, in still others, Omolú or,
as he is sometimes called, Xapanan. Olorun, "the father of
the *orixás*," is almost forgotten today in Bahia, although

occasionally one meets an older *Africano* who thinks of Olorun as "the creator of all the other *orixás*." Each is thought to have his home in Africa, and when one inquires of a black how the *orixás* can come so far to eat and drink the offerings set out for them, the answer is always easy, "They are summoned, and they come at once."

Each *orixá* is presumed on occasion to "manifest himself" in human form and to speak his will. Such "manifestation" is accomplished by "arriving in the head" of an individual who has been dedicated to him. His "presence" is attested by an abnormal psychic state accompanied by violent, spasmodic muscular movements, particularly of the neck, shoulder, and back muscles. Seizure ordinarily takes place during ceremonial dances, but occasionally (quite rare today) it may occur spontaneously while the individual is alone and about his work. Subsequently, the one in whom the *orixá* has "arrived" and "manifested himself" is unaware of what has transpired.

The name, sex, personification, fetish, insignia, sacred foods, sacred dress, sacred ornaments, sacred day, and identifying call of the principal Gêge-Nagô *orixás* at Bahia are as given in Table 15.

Each *seita* is presided over by a priest or priestess known as the *pae de santo* or *mãe de santo* (literally, the "father" or "mother" of the *orixás*). His (or her) most important functions are to identify a "manifesting" deity, supervise the initiation of the ceremonial dancers in whom an initial "manifestation" has occurred, perform the sacred ritual designed to "fix" the *orixá* in the fetish, supervise the sacrifices, and preside at public ceremonies. He may also exercise, to some extent at least, the office of an *olhador*, or diviner, who "throws the Ifá" to determine in advance the

PRINCIPAL *Orixás* OF THE GÊGE-NAGÔ FETISH CULTS AT BAHIA

Name	Sex	Personification	Fetish	Insignia	Sacred Foods	Dress	Beads	Bracelet	Sacred Day	Call
Oxalá (Orixá-lá, Obatalá)*	M,F	(?)	Lead ring, cowries	Shepherd's staff with small bells	She-goat, pigeon	White	White	White beads, lead	Friday	Tremulous groan
Xangô	M	Lightning	Meteorite	Lance, hatchet	Cock, turtle, he-goat, *carurú*	Principal color: red	Red and white	Brass	Wednesday	*hay-ee-ee*
Ogun (Ogum)	M	War, iron	Iron: hoe, anvil, scythe, spade, shovel, sledge	Lance, sword	He-goat, cock, oxhead, guinea hen	All colors	All colors	Bronze	Tuesday	*guara-min-fô*
Oxóssi (Oso-osi, Ochossi)	M	The hunt	Bow and arrow, clay skillet, stone	Bow and arrow, hunting bag, powder horn, oxtail	Sheep, cock, maize	Green, yellow; trimmed with *palha da costa*	Green	Bronze	Thursday	Bark like that of a dog
Omolú (Hu-moulú, Omanlú, Xapanan)	M	Pestilence, especially smallpox	*Piassava* with *buzios*	Lance	He-goat, cock, *acassá*, popcorn, *orôbô*, maize with *azeite de dendê*	Red, black	Red and black, red and white	Cowries	Monday	*há*
Exú	M	Evil (?), mischievousness	Clay, iron, wood	?	"Eats everything that is edible"	Red, black	Red, black	Bronze	Monday†	?
Yemanjá (Iemanjá)‡	F	Salt water	Seashell	Fan, sword	Pigeon, maize, cock, castrated he-goat	Red, dark blue, rose	*pingos da agua* (transparent)	Aluminum	Saturday	*hin-hee-ye-min*

* Also known in Gêge as Oulissa; in Angola as Cassumbeca; in Tapa as Inacoude Jegum. (The *x* in Oxalá, etc., is pronounced like *sh* in English.)
† Also the first day of any extended ceremony.
‡ In the *candomblés de caboclo*, Yemanjá is called Rainha do Mar, Dona Janaina (or simply Janaina), Dona Maria, Sereia do Mar, Princeza do Mar.

TABLE 15—Continued

Name	Sex	Personification	Fetish	Insignia	Sacred Foods	Dress	Beads	Bracelet	Sacred Day	Call
Yansan (Iansan)	F	Wind, storm	Meteorite	Sword	Goat, hen, *amalá*,§ *acarajé*	Principal color: red ("avoids" violet)	Red, coral	Copper, brass	Wednesday	*hay-ee-ee* ("softer" than Xangô)
Orun (Orun, Osun)	F	Fresh water	Stone worn smooth by a river	*Abêbê* (fan), looking-glass, small bell	Fish (*tainha*), she-goat, hen, beans	?	Yellow, blue	Brass	Saturday	*hmm-hmm*
Anamburucú (Nanan, Nan-amburucú)‖	F	Rain	Stone	Sword, small straw broom with cowries	Goat, hen, *obì*	White, dark blue	White, red and blue	Aluminum	Wednesday	*bu-bu-bu-bu*
Orun-manrê (Ochu-marê)	F	Rainbow	Stone	?	Cock, he-goat	?	Orange	?	?	?
Lokô (Rôkô, Irôkô)	?	?	*gameleira* tree	?	Cock, tobacco, beer, white wine	All colors¶	All colors	?	Tuesday	Low whistle
Ifá	?	Future events	Fruit of the *dendê* palm	?	?	?	Green-yellow	?	?	?
Beji (Ibeji)	M	Twin births	Images of São Cosme and São Damião	?	*carurú, acassá, abará, acarajé, farofa* with *azeite de dendê*	?	?	?	?	?

§ *Amalá* is *carurú* served with rice or with gruel made from the manioc root.

‖ Also known in Gêge as Tobossi. She is "the oldest" of the *mães d'agua* (Yemanjá, Oxun, Yansan, Anamburucú, Oxun-manrê).

¶ Also a straw mat or a strip of white cloth, called *owja*, which is wrapped about the trunk of a *gameleira* tree.

outcome of some projected action; and also the office of a *curandeiro*, who diagnoses ailments and prescribes cures. He may minister to a clientele even outside the members of the *seita*, giving advice and counsel on matters of business, politics, love, etc.

Disputes between members of the *seita* are ordinarily submitted for adjudication to the *pae* or *mãe de santo*. Persuasion is at first employed. But if this proves unsuccessful, the priest orders each of the disputants to wash his particular fetish, upon which, with rare exceptions, acceptance of mediation is secured. The settling of the dispute is then celebrated by each party to the quarrel drinking from the water in which the other's fetish has been washed. Continuance of the altercation will break the implied promise to the *orixá* and render the offender liable to punishment, which is ordinarily death.

The *pae* or *mãe de santo* may also exercise the function of a *feiticeiro* and deal in black magic. But this occupation is disclaimed by several of the more prominent priests and priestesses, who refuse to countenance deeds designed to do harm to their fellow-men. It appears to be exercised more often by heads of the recently organized and "less careful" *caboclo seitas.*[7]

Age, number of years a member of the cult, intimate knowledge of the ritual, and, particularly, purity of African descent are important considerations in determining the prestige of a *pae* or *mãe de santo*.

For some reason male members of the *seita* rarely experi-

[7] A *pae de santo* of a *caboclo candomblé* who is widely feared for his success in working black magic possesses a considerable bank account, numerous properties in the city, and rich cocoa land near Ilhéos, all acquired, it is said, from the exercise of this profession. However, it is quite probable that his political activity contributed a goodly portion.

ence, as do the women members, the "manifestation" of an *orixá*. Consequently, very few males ever pass through the rigorous period of training which must always follow the initial "appearance" of a deity in a given individual. Moreover, the men, being more mobile than the women, are ordinarily brought into more extensive contact with the Europeans and their descendants and consequently tend to take over more readily the ideas and sentiments of the whites. The women, on the other hand, ordinarily remain more closely identified with the customs and traditions of their African ancestors. It is probably for this reason that several of the more prominent and influential *candomblés* in Bahia now have women leaders. For the head of a *seita*, upon his approaching death, ordinarily chooses the new priest (or priestess) from among those members of the cult who are most learned in the ritual and other tradition. When asked about the occasion for So-and-so's selection, cult members always say, "Ele [*or* ela] é muito sabido" ("He is very learned in the ritual").

Other sacred functionaries include the *ogans*, or male members of the *seita*, who assist the *pae* or *mãe de santo* with the ritual, particularly in invoking the presence of the *orixás* during ceremonial dances, help initiate new *ogans*, act as intermediaries between the *seita* and the legal authorities, and contribute toward the expenses of the cult; the *achôgun*, or "second *pae*" as he is often called, who performs the sacrifices; the *jibonam*, or *pequena mãe* ("little mother"), next in authority to the *mãe de santo*, who assists the ceremonial dancers in carrying out their *preceitos*, or ritualistic obligations, and who makes the *despacho*, or food offering, to Exú at the opening of each important ceremony; the musicians, who assist at certain secret rituals and all public ceremonies, together with their leader, the *alabê;* and the very important *filhas de santo* (literally "daughters of the *orixás*"), or ceremonial dancers, who serve as the so-called *cavalos* ("horses") for the deities who "manifest themselves" in their bodies and speak through them their will.

This "visitation" is known as the *estado de santo* ("state of the *orixá*") and is ordinarily induced by prolonged fasting, the pungent odors of certain sacred herbs, the monotonous and long-continued beating of the *atabaques*, the heat from a large number of human bodies densely packed together on a warm night, the fatigue attendant on long-sustained dancing, the imperative expectations of the group, and, often as a precipitating incident, when tensions have been built up to the point where they can no longer be sustained, a sudden, loud, and unexpected noise. Seizure is said to be avoidable, as we have noted, by drinking cold water.

On the first "visitation" of an *orixá* in the body of an individual she must submit to either of two initiatory rites. She may elect the complete initiation of *fazer santo* ("to make the *orixá*"), or the partial initiation of *dar comida a cabeça*" ("to give food to the head"). If she elects the former, as most do, she makes an initial food offering to Exú, following which a fetish is secured and "prepared" by being washed by the *pae de santo* and immersed in *azeite de dendê,* honey, or *acaça,* depending on the *orixá,* the entire ritual being accompanied by special invocations. The initiate, or *yauô,* as she is now called, then surrenders all her garments, which, in symbol of the new life upon which she is about to enter, will never be worn again, and submits to a ritualistic bath, at dusk, in water scented with sacred herbs of a pungent odor. The *yauô* is then received in the *pegi* by the dignitaries of the cult and seated in a chair never before used,

FILHA DE SANTO IN CEREMONIAL COSTUME READY
TO ASSIST IN *CANDOMBLE* RITUAL

In her hand is the symbol of Xangô, the *orixá* of lightning. (Photograph by Friar Tomaz.)

while the *orixás* "partake" of a special sacrifice offered to them. Her hair is cut off, her head shaved,[8] and dots and circles are painted in white upon the crown, forehead, and cheeks. The initiate then takes on *obî* in her hand, the *atabaques* begin to beat an invocation to her *orixá*, and she dances the special dance sacred to him until he "arrives in her head" and she experiences once more the *estado de santo*. The *yauô* is then escorted from the *pegi* to the *camarinha*, where she remains for sixteen days before participating in her first public ceremony, whence she returns to the *camarinha* for a period of six months to a year, to be taught the various rituals of the cult, the songs, and, to some extent at least, an African language. Meanwhile, she is subject to certain food and other taboos.

To verify her acceptance by the *orixá*, a *filha* may be required to undergo without evidence of bodily harm an ordeal, such as swallowing lighted candlewicks soaked in *azeite de dendê*, thrusting her hands into boiling palm oil, chewing the leaves of the *urtiga* (Brazilian thistle), or submitting, on bended knee, to being beaten about the neck and arms with a sprig of the thorny *cansanção*.

Throughout her life the new *filha de santo*, in addition to submitting to the "manifestations" of her *orixá*, must perform on occasion certain ritualistic acts, rigorously observe certain food, drink, and sex taboos, and wear a special costume on ceremonial occasions and "days of obligation" (Fridays especially). On her death this costume, together with the other objects of cult worship belonging to her, are taken and dropped into the sea, "to be carried by the waves back to Africa."

Upon being "made," the *filha de santo* acquires a *guia*

---

[8] Formerly, all hairy parts of the body were shaved.

("guide") and a protector who, if she obeys the prescribed rituals and taboos, may bring her, it is thought, much fortune and happiness. "Look at me!" exclaimed a newly "made" *filha*. "My *orixá* is the greatest of all the *orixás*. He's powerful. I'm a black woman and can't read or write. But I'm living with a man *formado* in the Faculdade de Medicina. See what Oxalá did for me!"

As has already been noted, the rituals and ceremonies of the cult are serious and dignified and carried on in accordance with fixed traditional forms. Among the essential elements of the Gêge-Nagô ceremonies is the rigid separation of spectators according to sex. The males always occupy the seats to the left of the drums, the females those to the right. No drunkenness or obscenity is permitted. Said a member of a Nagô *seita*, "If they drink *cachaça* in a *candomblé*, you may know it is not well organized." Once at a ceremony at Gantois an intoxicated man forced his way through the crowd into the *barracão*. Immediately, the *mãe de santo* who was presiding signaled to two *ogans* who, calling out of the crowd a police official, promptly ejected the intruder.[9]

The *filhas de santo* before beginning a ceremonial dance make obeisance to the *pae* or *mãe de santo* by dropping to their knees and bowing their heads to the ground before the leader of their cult. Similar obeisance is also made to visiting *paes* or *mães de santo* or other honored personages of the fetish world and, occasionally, to the *ogans*.

When, during the ceremonial dance an *orixá* "arrives in the head" of a *filha*, she must, after the first violent seizure

[9] Such romanticized accounts of fetish cult ceremonies as that given by Graça Aranha and uncritically quoted by Vera Kelsey (*Seven Keys to Brazil* [New York, 1940], pp. 27–28), if they have any basis in fact at all, owe it to the disintegration of formerly wholesome cultural forms now characteristic of certain *macumba* centers of Rio de Janeiro.

has passed, dance the dance sacred to her *orixá*, after which she is assisted from the *barracão* into the *pegi*, taking due care to withdraw with her face always toward the drums. In a special room she is then dressed in the ceremonial robes sacred to her *orixá* and, with his sacred insignia, returns to the *barracão* to dance for hours the dances sacred to him.

The sacrifices are performed according to the ritual peculiar to the occasion and include the offering of chickens, pigeons, sheep, and goats.

In the *candomblé* world certain gestures are obligatory. Thus, when saluting a high dignitary of the cult, a *filha*, if the *orixá* to whom she is dedicated is masculine, prostrates herself, face downward at the feet of the one so honored; if her *orixá* is feminine, she lies at full length first on one side, then on the other, and, on rising, touches her head to the ground. In taking leave of an *orixá* who has "visited" the ceremony, a member of the *seita* clasps tightly the left hand of the ceremonial dancer. *Ogans* have a special handshake used only between them. Following a discussion among members of a *seita*, agreement is signified by rising, beating the palms, and shaking hands.

Status in the *candomblé* depends not only on one's position in the hierarchy of functionaries but more particularly upon priority in being "made" or confirmed. Those whose years of service are less are known as "the younger" and must address "the older" with greater respect and, as an *ogan* remarked, "prefer him above one's self."

The musical instruments employed include the *atabaques*, or drums; the *agôgô*, with which the priest or priestess strikes the first notes of each invocation and later accompanies the drums; the *caxixi;* the *agê* (also known as the *cabaça*, or *piano de cuia*); the *adjá;* and, occasionally, the *xaque-xaque*.

The *atabaques*, or drums, are indispensable to every ceremony. The heavy sound of the larger drum is intersected by
the higher tones of the medium-sized and the small one.
The rhythm is characterized by one-tone, interrupted syn-
copation and varies with each *orixá* invoked. Among the
more frequent cadences noted by Arthur Ramos[10] are the
following:

For the occasions on which an invoked *orixá* "delays" in
manifesting himself, even after the tempo of his invocation is
greatly increased, there is a special rhythm—vibrant, rapid,
continuous, unsyncopated—known as *adarrum*, which the
followers of the cult say no *orixá* can possibly "resist." It is
the following monotonous rhythm:

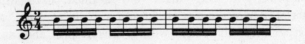

Although the instrumental music of the *candomblé* is quite
monotonous, as is also the hand-clapping which often accompanies it, the vocal accompaniment is polyphonic. The

[10] "Os instrumentos musicaes dos candomblés da Bahia," *Bahia Medica*,
III (July, 1932), 194.

songs are ordinarily composed of simple sentences in the minor key, and the scale, which on importation from Africa is said to have consisted of only five intervals, now has seven.

Among the invocations sung to the various *orixás* is that given by a former *ogan* of the *candomblé* of Gantois:

> Egbêji mori ô ri, okorin-kam
> Orolu mori ô ri, okorin-kam
> (Powerful One, I know thee as the first man)

> Ôkum-kum biri-biri
> Ajá lê mori ô korin-kam
> (Even in the dark I can see thou art powerful)

> A orêrê aiê, orixá loman,
> Iá, ochê Egbêji orêrê, aiê
> (In the whole world, nothing is hidden from the
> Great-One)[11]

At the burial of a cult member the songs and musical instruments of the *candomblé* ceremonies are now seldom used as, it is said, they formerly were. But the casket is carried by *ogans*, and the *filhas*, in *bahiana* costume, accompany the procession. Since it is still believed that the *orixá* of the departed may at this time seek a new *cavalo*, no pregnant woman attends. "Possession," however, may and does occur. Thus, at the burial of an elderly Negro woman, a *filha* of Ogun from the *candomblé* of Engenho Velho, who had been "made" for thirty-three years and was widely known and respected for her knowledge of African ritual, two *filhas de santo* were "seized" as the procession wound its way up the steep ascent to Quinta dos Lazaros Cemetery, and another later as the crypt was being sealed. In each case "possession" began with light weeping which soon increased to loud sobbing, the individual meanwhile pressing her hands

[11] Manoel Querino, *Costumes africanos no Brasil* (Rio, 1938), p. 108.

forcefully to her head, one in front and one in back, as if in great pain. Knees then gave way and shoulders and back muscles began to vibrate violently. In one case, the spine stiffened and, with the exception of the shoulder muscles which continued a rapid quivering, the entire body became rigid, with arms and legs stretched out at full length. Meanwhile, the *filha* whimpered, cried, or shrieked aloud.

To reach the *seita* of a well-known *mãe de santo*, one takes a Calçada car out of the city, past orange groves and fields of tall forage grass, to the Matadouro, where he alights and begins to climb a steep winding road lined with the *nativo* plant (said to be native to Africa) and *uricuri* and coconut palms, until, after more than a mile of trudging, he comes out onto a high ridge overlooking a green valley, where he can see, far in the distance, the houses of the city. A cool breeze blows in from the sea and tempers the heat of the tropical sun. In a grove of scattered palm trees nestle several houses, some of which are neatly whitewashed and others tinted pink, yellow, or blue.

The *mãe de santo* is called Anninha. She is a tall regal-appearing black, whose slightest gesture is immediately obeyed by members of her *seita*. She owns considerable property and is said to be otherwise quite well to do. She boasts, proudly, "Sou filha de dois Africanos, graças a Deus" ("I am the daughter of two Africans, thank God"). Queito she learned to speak, she says, from her parents; Nagô she acquired "in the *seita*." She is illiterate, but of her learning in the ritual and belief of the African cult an *ogan* says, with pride, "She knows African things better than anyone I know in Bahia." Intelligent, quick-witted, agile in debate, she is one of the most widely respected and

MÃE DE SANTO ANNINHA, COMPETENT AND HIGHLY
INTELLIGENT FETISH-CULT LEADER

revered leaders of the Afro-Brazilian world. When a priest argued with her that, since she had not been ordained by the pope, she had no "spiritual authority" to carry on religious rites, she quickly inquired if Moses, "that great prophet and leader of his people, was ordained by the pope?" The first man, she maintains, must not have been a white man but instead a colored man; "if not black, at least red. For do the scholars not say that man originated in Asia, and do white men ever come out of that continent?" Jesus also must have been an African, or at least a person quite dark. "For did not his parents once hide him in Egypt? And is not Egypt in Africa? If Jesus was not dark, how could they have hidden him among the people of Africa?"

This *mãe de santo* was "made" over fifty years ago in the *candomblé* of Engenho Velho. "My *seita* is pure Nagô, like Engenho Velho," she boasts. "But I have revived much of the African tradition which even Engenho Velho has forgotten. Do they have a ceremony for the twelve ministers of Xangô?[12] No! But I have." She is planning to rebuild her *barracão*, or sacred dance pavilion, to be paid for by tithes levied on the incomes of members of her *seita*. She owns a small store in the Terreiro where she sells the various articles used in the cult ritual and, since the members of the fetish world know that these articles must be, if she sells

[12] According to a well known Bahian *babalaô*, Xangô was a great African chief whose cruelties the people sought to do away with by setting fire one night to his dwelling. Everyone in it burned except Xangô, who walked unscathed through the flames. Astounded, the people prostrated themselves before him and begged his forgiveness. Xangô became a powerful king and subjected many neighboring tribes, twelve of whose chiefs subsequently became his royal advisers, or ministers. Even before his death, which occurred at an advanced age, Xangô was being worshiped. Cf. Martiniano do Bomfim, "Os ministros de Xangô," *Estado da Bahia*, May 5, 1937.

them, legitimate, the store does a thriving business. She says:

The *Africano* doesn't worship things made with human hands. He worships nature. What is the *pedra* [the fetish stone]? Is it not a mineral? No human hands have made it.

We are just as Christian as the Catholics. Only we follow the law of Moses. He commanded that sacrifices be made of sheep, goats, oxen, chickens, pigeons, and so forth. Is it not so? We merely obey his commandments.

There are two parts to the Bible, are there not? The Old Testament and the New. We follow the Old as well as the New. In the days before Christ, the people worshiped God with singing and dancing. Is it not so? David played his harp and sang psalms and danced before the Lord. We have our songs, too, and each has a special meaning. Just as the Catholics have something to remind them of their saints, so we have something to remind us of our *orixás*. But we do not worship images made with human hands like they do. We worship nature.

One of the assistants of the *mãe de santo*, an elderly Negro woman who "takes care of" the *terreiro*, is said to be over ninety years of age, is known by an African name, Bádá, and speaks Nagô as well as, or better than, she speaks Portuguese. No one in the fetish world at Bahia is said "to give her the blessing," because she is the "oldest" (that is, the longest "made" or "confirmed") in the city. She laments "the old days" before the Africans in Bahia all died.

A Negro man of seventy-seven years of age, Martiniano, one of two *babalaôs* in Bahia, known and thoroughly respected throughout the fetish world for his piety and sincerity and his knowledge of African customs and traditions, is, upon entering the connecting-room to the *pegi*, saluted by a rapid beat of muffled drums. He bows to the drummers, acknowledging their greeting, steps into the *pegi*, bows low before the altar, touches the ground with the tips of his fingers, and repeats a prayer in Nagô. So learned is he "in

BARRACÃO USED FOR FETISH-CULT CEREMONIES

Candomblé of Mãe Anninha, Centro Cruz Santa do Aché de Okô Afonjá

things African" that he is occasionally called to Pernambuco, four hundred miles up the Brazilian coast, to carry out
special rituals which cult members in that city are unable to
perform. Of the *candomblé*, he says, "The Nagô worships nature because he is realistic and wants to see what he worships. He can't see the Catholics' God."

The *barracão* here is about fifty feet by thirty, with roof
and one end thatched with palm fronds, and floor freshly
sanded. By nightfall it is gaily decorated with paper streamers, most of which are white; some, however, are red, blue,
green, or yellow. A large and neat placard, which one of the
ogans proudly says was painted by his daughter, a first-year
student at the Escola Normal, bears the inscription: "Centro Cruz Santa do Aché de Okô Afonjá," a combination of
Portuguese and Nagô which means "Sacred Cross Center of
the Brothers and Sisters of the Temple of Xangô." Chairs to
accommodate the priestess, the elderly Negro woman, and
the old Negro man have been placed on a dais to the left of
the musicians. The spectators are carefully excluded from
the dancing space in front of the drums by railings patrolled
by *ogans*. On the end wall hang three white pennants bearing respectively, the inscriptions, "Viva Oxalá," "Viva
Oxun," and "Viva Aryra," and one red pennant with the
words, "Viva Xangô."

The *filhas*, all of whom are escorted into the *barracão*
under a white sheet held by *ogans* who also light the procession with flaming torches, number seventeen, all of whom are
blacks, with the exception of two dark mulattoes. Of the
ogans, fourteen are blacks, eleven are mulattoes, six of whom
are dark mixed-bloods, and one is a Portuguese immigrant
who came to Brazil some thirty years ago and now owns a
small retail establishment in the Lower City.

Three of the dancers are *yauôs*, in process of being "made." Their heads have been shaved clean, and white spots and blue lines have been painted upon them. On their cheeks are white spots and white lines. Around the neck, or over the right shoulder and under the left arm, are long chains of large cowries imported from the West Coast.

In a special building with a cement floor is "the throne room of Xangô." At one side is an altar to him, which is lavishly decorated with candles and flowers, both fresh and artificial. Indicating the fusion of Catholic and fetish elements, one notes on the lower step an image of Santo Antonio, on the second, one of Nossa Senhora das Candeias, on the third, an image of the twins, Cosme and Damião, and, on the top level, one of São Jeronimo. The *mãe de santo* says that Santo Antonio is "just another name" for Ogun; as similarly is Nossa Senhora das Candeias, for the water deity, Oxun; Cosme and Damião, for Beji; and São Jeronimo, for Xangô.

On the other side of the room is "the throne of Xangô," a wooden chair, intricately carved, with a pillow for a headrest. Suspended on the walls are pictures of several Catholic saints.

In the center of an adjoining room is "the spring of the *mãe d'agua*," a huge basin built of cement and containing ten to twelve inches of water. On the wall is the Nagô inscription, "Ilé Awon Afonjá" ("House of Xangô").

The leader of another *seita* is a male black, known as Pae Procopio, sixty-six years of age, of Gêge descent, whose father, grandfather, and great-grandfather, he proudly boasts, were all Africans and *paes de santo*. His mother's sister was also "an *Africano*," but his mother was a Brazilian-born black, a *mãe de santo* who "deixou o cargo" (i.e., left the office of priest) to him. He is dedicated to the same *orixá*, Ogun, as was she, and speaks, he claims, "a little of six different African languages: Nagô, Gêge, Ige-chá, Queito, Egba, and Musurumi." He owns "a roomful" of ceremonial costumes, one of which is said to have cost six contos (approximately $360). He considers his task to be that of "doing good" and refuses to deal in black magic, an attitude which has cost him, it is said, "much money."[13] He is godfather to approximately a hundred and fifteen children and is soon to be godfather to nine others who are on the point of receiving the baptismal ceremony. He visits about the Reconcavo, particularly in Cachoeira, exercising his office of *pae de santo*, and is said to have paid similar visits to Rio de Janeiro, Pernambuco, Maranhão, and Pará, in each of which he has "made" several *filhas* and "confirmed" *ogans*.

The *achôgun*, or sacrificer, is an elderly black with a kindly face and snow-white hair. The leader of the drummers, or the *alabê*, a jolly black whose mother (now deceased) was a *mãe de santo* in Cidade de Palha, is very expert with the drums, speaks Nagô, and sings in a high-pitched but rather pleasant voice the African *cantigas*, or ritualistic songs. An *ogan* says of him, proudly, "He knows almost as much about African things as a *pae de santo*."

An elderly Negro woman, who walks haltingly with a cane, attends every ceremony. Younger friends carefully help her to a seat where she can see everything that goes on. Leaning forward on her cane, her intelligent eyes wide open, her face continually breaking into beaming smiles, she joins

[13] An *ogan* of this *seita* says that a *pae de santo* in Itapoan named Gregorio (now deceased) once declined twelve contos (approximately $720) "to make a man mad." This *ogan* knows, however, a *mãe de santo* who, as he says, became angered at the remarks of a young skeptic and "made a *negocio*" (literally a "business"; i.e., black magic) which "drove him mad in two days."

heartily in the songs, occasionally taps her cane on the
ground in time with the drums, and appears to enjoy thoroughly each part of the ritual. Every once in a while she
leans toward the drummers and shouts at the *alabê* in Nagô.
Sometimes, when the *pae de santo* is temporarily absent from
the *barracão*, she initiates the ritualistic songs. Her name is
Ismeira and she lives in an old house in a section of the city
which was once entirely inhabited, it is said, by Nagôs.

As the ceremony begins, 22 *filhas*, 1 *filho* (or male ceremonial dancer), and the *pae de santo* are in the circle which
has formed around the central post of the *barracão*. Seated
in the center of the circle is a visiting *pae de santo* named
Vidal. Twenty-one *ogans*, including visitors from other
seitas, are to the left of the drums. Into the other available
spaces are packed 208 spectators, of whom 136 are blacks, 68
are mulattoes (all dark mixed-bloods, except 6), and 4 are
brancos da Bahia. There are no whites. Approximately two
hundred other individuals mill about outside.

In this *seita* there are in all 34 *filhas de santo*, nearly 60 per
cent of whom are over forty years of age. The eldest are
seventy-two and seventy-one years, respectively, and 9 are
fifty or over. Ten are from forty to fifty, 7 are from thirty to
forty years of age; 6 are twenty to thirty, 1 is nineteen, and 1
is twelve. Two are married, 13 are *amaziada*, 2 are engaged
to be married, 15 are single, and 2 are widowed. All are from
the lower class. Thirteen are peddlers of African foods in the
streets, 7 are seamstresses, 5 are laundresses, 5 are domestic
servants, and 1 is a midwife. One, the next to the eldest, is
employed in looking after the *casa de candomblé*, 1 is the
zelador de santo,[14] and 1 an adolescent child. Thirteen, or

[14] It is the task of the *zelador de santo* to care for the *pegi*, wash the fetishes at regular intervals, and renew the food and drink offerings.

more than a third, live in the immediate vicinity of the *ter-reiro*, 16 live from one to four miles away in seven different sections of Bahia, 3 are from the neighboring villages of Armação and Pitúba, and 2 others, residents of Rio de Janeiro, are visiting relatives and friends in Bahia.

One *filha de santo* has been "made" fifty-eight years; another, fifty-seven. Three more have been functionaries of the cult thirty years or longer; ten, from twelve to twenty-one years; nine, from six to seven years; six, including the twelve-year-old girl, from one to two years; and two have been "made" only approximately one month. Six are dedicated to the *orixá* of lightning and thunder, Xangô; five to the *orixá* of pestilence, Omolú; four to the deity of the hunt, Oxóssi, and four to the deity of war and iron, Ogun. Two others are dedicated to Oxalá "the Elder," and two to Oxalá "the Younger," or Oxagian. Nine are sacred to the *mães d'agua*, or the water deities: four to Oxun, two each to Yansan and Nanan, and one to Yemanjá, "the *orixá* of the sea."

The sixteen *ogans* range in age from twenty to sixty years, with the exception of a five-year-old boy. The "eldest" in point of service to the cult has been *confirmado* ("confirmed") thirty-two years. Most are persons of relatively assured income from the lower class, there being among them hucksters, stevedores, day laborers, a *carroceiro*, a tinsmith, a painter, a baker, a tailor, and a typesetter. Only three, or less than one-fifth, live in the immediate vicinity of the *terreiro*, the residences of the others being scattered throughout the city in nine different sections.[15]

[15] This dispersion is perhaps indicative of the *candomblé's* gradual disintegration. An *ogan* remarked, "I would like to have all the *ogans* and the *filhas* living here near each other. It would be so much better. Years ago they used to live that way. But today everyone wants to live wherever he chooses anywhere in the city."

The dances continue unabated for hours, until the air of the *barracāo* becomes very warm and permeated with the odor of perspiring bodies. Seriously, with rapt attention, the closely packed crowd looks on, eager to see and hear the numerous *orixás* as they "arrive." During a period of the most intense excitement, when tensions have been built up almost to the breaking-point, a rocket suddenly bursts with a loud report outside the *barracāo*. A woman seated among the spectators who is not a *filha de santo* is immediately thrown into violent, convulsive muscular movements and bounces up and down with great force on the board seat, her head snapping back and forth in time to the now almost frenzied beat of the drums. The *pae de santo* rushes to support her in order to prevent imminent injury. Several visiting *filhas de santo* who do not want to dance in this strange place and are consequently "resisting" the imminent "arrival" of their *orixás*, call out with imploring voices, one after the other, "Dê-me agua, por amor de Deus" ("Give me water, for the love of God!"). The face of a servant girl named Joanna, a *filha* from a neighboring *seita*, is drawn, and she appears to be in pain. Afterward, she says that her *orixá*, Xangô, was beating and striking her to make her dance and that she felt more tired than if she had danced all night long. But other spectators remark, "How beautiful! I never saw Ogun dance like that before. And Oxóssi, and Yemanjá, they are wonderful, simply wonderful!"

The ceiling of another *barracāo* (at the *terreiro* called Gantois) is trimmed with paper streamers—red, white, blue, and yellow—each alternating with rows of white paper roses. The electric-light bulb suspended from the ceiling is shaded by red and white pieces of cellophane. On the walls are red and white paper shields, each bearing the words, "Louvores á

Xangou" ("Praises to Xangô") or "Louvores á Ogun" ("Praises to Ogun"). A small niche built in above the doorway which leads to the *pegi* is neatly decorated with red and white paper bows, and in it stands a crucifix about ten inches high, together with images of the Virgin Mary with the child Jesus in her arms, of Santo Antonio (St. Anthony), and of São Jorge (St. George).

In a circle in front of the drums are twenty-two women, the oldest of whom is about sixty years of age and the youngest eight. Fourteen are blacks, eight are mulattoes, none of whom is very light. All have serious expressions on their faces, especially the little girl, although none appear in the least bit self-conscious. Six are *yauôs*, or initiates, in the process of being "made," and range in age from fourteen to seventeen years. Two are dedicated to Omanlú (Omolú), and four to Oxun. The Omanlú initiates are dressed principally in shades of red. Strands of hemp died reddish-brown drop from the head to below the knee, completely obscuring the face. Above the head the strands rise vertically and are tied together in a cluster at the end. Below the hem of a dark-red skirt appear white pantalettes which fit tightly over the legs and extend to the ankle. Each girl wears four strands of cowries around each bare arm at the biceps and a long string of cowries over the right shoulder and under the left arm.

The Oxun initiates have their heads shaved, and three concentric circles have been painted in white around the crown. Smaller circles intercept the outer of these three. Large white spots have also been painted on the face, the neck, and the back of the head. Four feathers, one of which is red, one white, one black, and one brown, are held firmly upright at the forehead by à ribbon tied very tightly. Each girl carries in her hand the insignia of Oxun, a *leque* (fan) of brass decorated with a star.

All the other dancers, except one, are dressed in the *bahiana* costume, with wide-flowing skirts of bright-colored cotton prints, blouses trimmed in handmade lace, and a *pano da Costa* two feet in width tied tightly around the small of the back and over the breasts. One woman about thirty-five years of age is dressed in an ordinary street costume of tailored blouse and skirt. Many of the dancers wear bracelets of copper, brass, bronze, lead, or glass beads, often on both wrists and occasionally three to four to the arm. One dancer has five strands of cowries about her neck.

The priestess of the *seita*, Mãe Mennininha, is a large black woman, forty-one years of age, who has officiated in this *seita* for twenty-four years. She proudly speaks of herself as "uma neta d'um Africano" ("the granddaughter of an African").

Every dance begins with the salutation of the *mãe de santo*, which is accomplished by striking decisively the *agôgô*. Immediately the drums take up the rhythm. The *filhas* begin to dance, the circle turning like the rim of a wheel, counterclockwise. The women have their hands clasped behind their backs, their shoulders are hunching backward and forward, their bodies bending at the waist from side to side. One of the Oxun initiates moves with a halting, jerking movement, then suddenly pivots a complete turn. All the dancers are singing a refrain which sounds like, "Ô-mî-á, bá-tû-lê." After some twenty minutes of continuous dancing, one of the *filhas* suddenly becomes "possessed," her eyes close, her expression becomes listless, while her neck and shoulder muscles work convulsively back and forth "in time to the music." Voluntary control is apparently gone, and she is helped around the circle by the next in line. When the music temporarily ceases, she relaxes, staggers, and appears in imminent danger of falling. Several *filhas* rush to catch and support her.

Again the *mãe de santo* strikes the *agôgô*, the leader of the drummers takes up the rhythm and sings out a refrain in which all the dancers join, beating their palms in time with the music. The tempo increases. The dancers as they pass round the circle alternately bow their heads, flex their knees, and touch the right hand to the floor, then snap erect, all in perfect time with the music. An elderly black woman emerges from a connecting-room and, shaking vigorously a *caxixi*, joins in the dance. With loud reports, rockets go off outside the *barracão*. Popcorn is then brought in and thrown over the dancers. The eyes of the initiates, who have also made part of the circle of dancers, are closed and remain closed throughout the ceremony. The shoulders of one *yauô* jerk spasmodically, her head hangs limp and must be supported by other dancers.

Again the circle forms, and the *filhas*, singing at the top of their voices, shuffle forward in a half-stumbling movement, arms flexed at elbows and flapping up and down. An *ogan* says this dance is called *opanigê*. Sometime later, a *filha*, about forty-five years of age, suddenly sprawls stiff-legged on her hands and the tips of her toes, rapidly touches her forehead to the ground in front of the drums and shouts, "Hay-ee-ee," then leaps erect, jerks herself forward spasmodically, then repeats the performance. A girl joins the circle, wearing a pink and gold turban and carrying in her right hand a brass dagger eighteen inches long. Closing her eyes, she begins a wild dance, thrashing about with the dagger to right and to left. The tempo of the drums is accelerating. Another *filha*, a large but agile Negro woman, strikes out at the girl with her bare hands, and the two dance about, fighting a mock fight, while the beat of the drums becomes even more rapid and tumultuous until, just as the dancers close in upon one another where, it seems, harm might result, other *filhas* swing quickly in, catch each woman around the waist, and draw them apart, while the music slackens its tempo.

All the *filhas* begin to dance again, their arms swinging from side to side, the index finger of the right hand held closely pressing against the thumb of the left. The dancing is very animated. Suddenly, one of the *filhas*, her shoulders heaving violently back and forth, begins to sink upon her knees and, gradually lowering her heaving shoulders to the floor, turns over on her back, all the while keeping the index finger of her right hand firmly in contact with the thumb of her left. She then slowly rises, gets to her feet, and again joins the other *filhas*. An *ogan* says this dance is known as *ecú*.

The dances continue, rockets burst outside, confetti and flower petals are thrown over the initiates, and, at the insistent invocations of the drums and the spirited singing of the *filhas*, many *orixás* "arrive" and "take possession" of their human intermediaries.

The primary social function which the *candomblé* appears to serve is that of reinforcing, by way of the collective experiences of ritual and ceremony, those attitudes and sentiments which distinguish the *Africanos* and their descendants from the European population and from the major portion of the mixed-bloods. By promoting a measure of solidarity and group consciousness, it tends to slow up the process of acculturation. At the same time cult experiences help to satisfy the basic human needs for recognition and response. The resolution of all sorts of personal problems by way of the advice and counsel of the priest, priestess, or "manifesting" *orixá*, relieves personal strain and tension. And the reassuring affirmations regarding personal destiny which the body of belief affords, particularly at such times of crisis as the death of an intimate friend or relative, contribute to the apparently universal need of a sense of security.

Moreover, cult experiences serve as cogent means of maintaining group morale and enforcing group sanctions. The genuinely wholesome character of the Bahian *Africanos*, with the exception perhaps of certain individuals connected with recently organized *caboclo* centers, stands in sharp contrast to the personal disorganization which, according to report, characterizes the Rio de Janeiro Negro, whose *candomblé* (known locally as the *macumba*) is now in such a state of disintegration that many unwholesome and even vicious practices have crept into its ritual.

The Catholic church at Bahia, by exercising almost infinite patience and tact, has now incorporated into its organization all members of the Bahian fetish cults. Even the leaders of the *seitas* regularly attend Mass and, on occasion, participate, together with their entire *candomblé* personnel, in functions of the church. Thus, each year at an appointed time, *mãe de santo* Anninha takes her *filhas de santo*, dressed in their *bahiana* costumes, and her *ogans*, and attends Mass in Bomfim Church; as similarly does the *caboclo mãe de santo*, Sabina, in the *igreja* of Santo Antonio da Barra. Anninha, like certain other cult officials, is a member of a Catholic order. So far has the identification of many elements of the fetish tradition with Catholic ideology and practice now gone that to the simple minds of cult members there is little distinction between them. The *pae de santo* of a prominent Congo *seita* recently remarked, "I do everything (i.e., I carry on all cult rituals and ceremonies) in the name of the church."[16]

On the fiftieth anniversary of the death of the father of a well-known and widely respected *babalaô*, a special commemorative Mass was arranged in one of the city's principal churches. During the ceremony, a circle of friars who were standing with lighted candles about the bier was joined by an outer circle of Negro men, each bearing a funeral torch. Although the friars were probably unaware of the fact, the blacks were all *ogans* from the *candomblé* of *mãe de santo* Anninha. In the audience were more than a hundred important personages from the fetish world, including *babalaôs*, *paes* and *mães de santo*, *ogans*, and *filhas*. Said the *babalaô* whose father was being thus honored, "Last night at the *terreiro* we danced all night the African funeral dances for my father."

In the minds of cult members several of the more important African *orixás*, as we have seen, have come to be identified with certain Catholic saints. Thus, Ogun, the *orixá* of war, is now identified with Santo Antonio; Oxóssi, the *orixá* of the hunt, with São Jorge; Oxalá, who to most members of the *candomblé* is "the greatest of the *orixás*," with O Senhor do Bomfim, who is, among the lower classes at least, the most important Catholic saint at Bahia;[17]

[16] This point of view obviously is not that of the Catholic church itself.

[17] In Bomfim Church, which, with two rows of royal palms dominating its approach, occupies majestically the crown of a hill in Itapagipe, is a special room whose walls and ceiling are completely covered with photographs or plaster casts of crippled or diseased limbs or other parts of the body which have been, it is thought, miraculously cured of disease or other infirmary by the direct intervention of the saint. So great is his reputation for healing that thousands of people from miles around visit this shrine every year.

Omolú, the *orixá* of pestilence, with São Roque, or, in some
cases, with São Bento; and Exú, with Satan. Of the *mães
d'agua* (water deities), Yemanjá is confused in some cases
with Nossa Senhora da Piedade (Our Lady of Compassion),
and in others with Nossa Senhora do Rosario (Our Lady of
the Rosary); Oxun, in some cases, with Nossa Senhora das
Candeias and, in others, with Nossa Senhora da Conceição
(Our Lady of the Immaculate Conception); Yansan, with
Santa Barbara; and Nanan (Anamburucú, Nanamburucú),
with Nossa Senhora de Sant'Ana. Beji, the twins, are identified with Cosme and Damião; Irôko (Rôko, Lôko), who is
presumed to dwell in the *gameleira* tree, with Poverello (São
Francisco) de Assis;[18] and Ifá, the *orixá* of divination, with
Santissimo Sacramento (the Most Holy Sacrament). Even
Xangô, the *orixá* of lightning and thunder, to whom Edison
Carneiro refers as "indisputably the most African of all the
orixás worshiped at Bahia,"[19] and who is still thought of by
some blacks as being distinct from any Catholic saint, is worshiped in several of the most representative Gêge-Nagô
seitas under the name of São Jeronimo and, occasionally, of
Santa Barbara.

The conditions which favor fusion in this last-named case
are not difficult to understand. In Portuguese folklore Santa
Barbara is thought of as a protector against lightning, a conception which probably led very easily to the identification
of Santa Barbara in the Negroes' minds with Xangô, who is,
in the African tradition, "the *orixá* of the thunderbolts."
Fusion in this case, as in others, would have been aided by
the common conception that each African deity is both a
protector and a destroyer; a kindly protector when offered

[18] Edison Carneiro, *Religiões negras* (Rio, 1936), p. 155.
[19] *Ibid.*, pp. 153–54.

the proper ritual, and a vengeful destroyer if rites and taboos are ignored.

Although this fusion is proceeding rapidly, it is still far from complete. A number of Gêge-Nagô and Congo-Angola *orixás*, and at least thirty *caboclo* deities, have not yet been in any way identified with Catholic equivalents.

Occasionally, the critical attitude of members of the fetish world toward unorthodox practices in other *seitas* extends also to the incorporation of Catholic ritual, ideas, and sentiments into fetish practice and belief. A *babalaô* and *feiticeiro*, born in Africa of repatriated Brazilian slaves, recently remarked, "These Bahian *candomblés* aren't African any more. Why, they all go to Mass, pray the rosary, and burn candles to the saints! It's all mixed up now."

The following story illustrates the fusion of European and African traditions. Related recently by a local black, it recounts some of the experiences of Obaluaiê (Abaláu-aiê) and Omolú, known also in Bahia as Xapanan (Xapanā), and is obviously confused with the biblical stories of the Prodigal Son and of Lazarus. It also refers to a European city.

XAPANĀ, FATHER AND SON

Xapanā was fifteen years old when his parents sent him out into the world to see what life was like. After he had walked a long way, he came to a city called Venice, where he went about looking for work. But no one offered him anything, and finally, becoming very hungry, he began to go up to houses and beg for something to eat. But everywhere he asked he was turned away.

Sad and disillusioned, Xapanā continued on his way. At last he came to a forest, where he remained for some time, living on fruits and insects.

When Xapanā was nineteen years of age, he began to think of returning to his father's house and at last made himself ready and set out on the way. Xapanā walked and walked, until one day just as night was falling, he, all covered with sores and bruises, began to approach his father's house.

But his father, who saw the traveler coming a long way off, did not recognize him and consequently did not go out to meet him. Xapanā's mother, however, knew her son and in pity at his misfortune, begged and pleaded with her husband to have compassion for him and to receive him like the legitimate son he was.

But the old man turned to her and said:

"This fellow is not my son, because I never had a son who was full of sores."

But, at last, due to the continued pleadings of his wife, the ancient one inquired of the traveler what his name was. Xapanā replied:

"I am called Lazarus."

"Who is Lazarus?" asked the father.

Then Xapanā said: "I am he whom God permitted to use this name."

But the old man persisted in knowing the reason why, if he was Xapanā, he was using the name of Lazarus.

The son turned to his father and replied very quietly:

"I am Xapanā, the lord over pestilence throughout the whole world." And he sang in Queito:

> "I say "Guedé,"
> I am Obaluaiê,
> I call out "Guedé,"
> I am Obaluaiê,
> Tôtô."

The old man Omolú then replied:

> "Ojé badô
> Dó lá."

And the young man sang:

> "Ojé di apá."

In this way the two came to know each other, and Xapanā "the Elder" recognized Xapanā "the Younger."

A few whites, even from the upper classes, visit the *pae de santo* to obtain advice on business, politics, and other matters or aid in the cure and prevention of disease. Numerous families *da boa sociedade* ("of social standing") "dão comida" (make the food offerings, especially of *carurú*) to Beji (Cosme and Damião) and celebrate the day sacred to their honor. A number of white individuals on occasion make offerings to the *mãe d'agua*. Cases like that of the wife of a former state senator and political chieftain who kept an altar to an African *orixá* in her house are, however, not numerous.

Of 66 students in the Escola Normal classifying themselves as *brancos* and responding to the query, "Do members of your family give presents to the *mãe d'agua?*" 7, or 10.6 per cent, answered in the affirmative. Of 36 *pardos*, the families of 9, or 25 per cent, similarly made offerings. Of 63 whites, 29, or 46 per cent, thought one ought to fear the *bozo* (black magic); as did 12, or 37 per cent of the *pardos*, and all 6 of the *pretos* who replied. Of 63 whites, only 1 thought the statement "A *pae de santo* is more useful in time of illness than a physician" was true, but 9, or 14 per cent, regarded it as "partially true"; of 32 *pardos*, 2 believed the statement true, and 7, or 22 per cent, thought it "partially true." Of 197 students in the Escola Normal and the Law School, the families of 25, or 13 per cent, "give *comida*" to Cosme and Damião.

Ordinarily the attitudes which the inhabitants of European descent take toward the *candomblé* vary from good-natured tolerance, which is the most characteristic, through indifference, which is common, to active opposition, which is comparatively rare, although from time to time complaints like the one below find their way into the newspapers.

In *A Tarde* for May 8, 1936, appeared an editorial under the title:

DANGEROUS *CANDOMBLES*

Education may perhaps be the most certain means of eradicating harmful customs. But when these customs are linked with the persistent beliefs of African fetichism and constitute outrageous attacks upon the moral and physical well-being of those who practice them, it becomes necessary to insist upon immediate and complete suppression. This can be done in no way except by police action, energetic and persistent.

And, in *A Tarde* for December 9, 1935, appeared the following complaint:

THE CITY THAT GOD FORGOT

Scenes which Degrade and Depress .... The Revived *Candomblés* .... *Despachos* Even in the Heart of the City ....

The above looks like a movie title. But it is not. Our capital really is a city forgotten by .... God. ....

Your reporter .... has set down in his notebook curious scenes which reflect discredit upon our civilization; things which .... continue on for the eyes not only of those who live here but also of those who visit us from foreign places.

Bahia already has the reputation of being the city of *candomblés*, the paradise of the *macumbas*. However, these used to be localized in fixed zones where the devotees of Oxalá and Yemanjá beat their drums and "fell into the *santo*." Now they begin to encroach upon the most frequented streets, and the African cult is to be seen even in the best residential areas.

Your reporter verified this fact last Sunday night in the *bairro* of Barra, an elegant and aristocratic suburb. Here is to be found Grenfeld Street, very close to the Avenida Oceanica. And on this very street is a *candomblé*.

Happily there is no noise of drums. But palms are used instead, which beat without ceasing until day dawns. And whenever anyone makes an inquiry, the *pae de santo* insists that he has a license, and continues. ....

One morning not long ago, your reporter was passing in front of the

State Treasury building, a spot very much frequented. A *bozó* had been left there and still remained exposed to the curiosity of all who passed.

A black hen, three copper coins, yellow *farofia*, a cloth doll stuck full of pins, a piece of a man's shirt, and other *bugigangas* [trinkets].

The thing was there until midday. This is no uncommon occurrence, but one which is frankly deplorable. That in the heart of our city, so close to the Rua Chile, *despachos* are made to Exú is, to say the least, disgusting.

In the same newspaper sometime later (June 10, 1937), under the title, "A Specialist in Sport *Bozós*, *Pae de santo* Manoelzinho Is the Worst Enemy of the Limpeza Publica [Street Cleaning Department]," this complaint appeared:

A short time ago the *macumbeiro* known as Manoelzinho took up his residence in a *roça* at No. 256 Cruz do Cosme, and since that time his *bozós* have led to continuous complaints from dwellers along that road and from those who chance to pass that way.

At the side of the road just below the *roça* is a *loco* tree, that species so much preferred for fetishistic practices. Here *bozós* accumulate from day to day until they constitute a veritable mountain of refuse in which may be found an increasing number of dead fowls.

We are informed that this Manoelzinho, who is a *pae de santo* with considerable prestige, is a specialist in sport *bozós*. For it is said that among those who consult him are certain members of the different soccer clubs. Recently a policeman, on the eve of a great game at Graça, noted in one of these *bozós* the initials "T. V." which are the same as those of a well-known athlete.

Since the Street Cleaners never pass along Cruz do Cosme, the *bozós* keep polluting the atmosphere and obliging those who pass by to cover their noses with handkerchiefs.

To whom shall we appeal? Who will do something about this?

However, more characteristically, the Bahian identified with European customs and traditions adopts toward the *candomblé* a tolerant attitude. While he looks upon it as "ignorant fetishism," he ordinarily accepts it as "an African institution," which, in the words of a student at the Faculty of Law, "will gradually disappear with social evolution." "Education will do away with it. Just give it time," remarked a student at the Faculty of Medicine. There are a few intellectuals, individuals who have broken with the Catholic church, who believe that the *candomblé* is entitled to the same rights and privileges as any other religion. One of these remarked, "We should see to it that the government gives the *candomblé* a square deal."

Indeed, of those Bahians identified with the European culture, the whites tend to be more tolerant of the *candomblé* than either the blacks or the mixed-bloods. These blacks and mixed-bloods are seeking to establish themselves in class and naturally make every effort to disassociate themselves from what are commonly considered to be lower-class cultural elements. Of 66 white students in the Escola Normal who responded to the query "Do you think the *candomblé* ought to be suppressed?" 22, or one-third, said, "No"; while, of 22 *pardos*, all but one replied in the affirmative. Of 5 blacks, 4 said, "Yes."

In the face of constant, although ordinarily tolerant, disparagement on the part of most prestige-bearing individuals in the European portion of the community and of such institutions as the church, the school, and the newspaper, most of the younger Negroes now tend to forsake the *candomblé* and the body of ideas and sentiments identified with it and to look upon these customs and traditions as evidence of "ignorance," "backwardness," and "retarded mental growth." Older leaders of the cult often complain, as did Maria Bádá on one occasion, that "the *candomblé* isn't what it used to be. The young people today don't learn Nagô; they don't know how to carry on any of the ritual; and, what is worse, they don't want to learn." *Māe de santo* Anninha once remarked, in much the same words as in recent years have often been heard, on the lips of older members of, particularly, Protestant churches in the United States, "These young people today are not like we used to be. It's a shame the way they stray away."

João is a young black about twenty years of age who has just completed a business course subsequent to graduation from the Ginasio da Bahia, the city's state-supported secondary school. One day, in the home of his uncle, who is a prominent figure in the fetish world, João was copying a page in Nagô. Possessed of a deep affection for his uncle and being characteristically obliging and courteous, he was attempting to learn a few words of this African language. But the impression João made on a visitor was that his efforts with Nagô arose rather from a desire to please his uncle than from any genuine interest in the language itself. João remarked, apologetically, "You know I would like to learn it, but I just don't have time when I'm working every day."

A young mulatto girl who had completed two years at a secondary school remarked, "I don't care much for the *candomblé*, except to watch the dances and to see the [ceremonial] costumes. I seldom go, and then only for some special reason. I like the movies better, especially the North American and the English films." She further remarked:

My uncle doesn't believe in this business of the *orixás*. One day his daughter—my cousin—said that she felt an *orixá* about to "arrive." She ran all the way to a *candomblé*, began to dance, and, sure enough, "she fell into the *estado de santo*." But my uncle wouldn't stand for it. He got a sprig of *urtiga* and whipped her and then went and whipped the *pae de santo* too. The next day, my cousin couldn't bear anyone's hand on her, she was so sore. But that was the end of the *orixá*. He never came back.

José is a young mixed-blood, twenty-two years of age, employed as a janitor in one of Bahia's public buildings. Although he knows of three *seitas* near his home—one each in Pau Miuda, Cidade da Palha, and Cruz do Cosme—he has no interest in them. However, he has a consuming interest in the cinema, keeps an elaborate scrapbook which now contains over a hundred and fifty individual photographs of actors and actresses, and can glibly name nearly all the films in which each has played during the last three or four years.[20]

The following account by a young mulatto student of secondary-school age who has developed a somewhat skeptical attitude toward the *candomblé* in spite of his father's being a prominent *ogan* in one of the *seitas* who occasionally, when the elderly *achôgun* is ill, officiates at the sacrificial ritual, illustrates the difficulty which *candomblé* leaders now experience in enforcing the sanctions of the cult:

Pedro [a young *ogan*] didn't show proper respect for my father when he suggested that there ought to be some repairs made at the *terreiro*. Pedro said it had been that way when he was "confirmed" and that it was all right now. He used "você" in speaking to my father, although he is much "younger." And he said my father lied. When I heard about this, I hunted up Pedro and told him that he hadn't treated my father right, and when he talked nonsense I hit him. Pae Procopio then hunted me up. I told him that I didn't believe in anything he did, that I wasn't afraid of any sorcery he might make, that Pedro had ill-treated my father, and that I wanted nothing to do with him and with all his accursed *candomblé*.

[20] For instance, José named five films in which Patricia Ellis had played. His favorite actress is Shirley Temple, after which come, in order, Lilian Harvey, Joe E. Brown, Maurice Chevalier, and Laurel and Hardy. In addition, he likes Raul Roulien, Dolores del Rio, James Cagney, Lyle Talbot, Kay Francis, Dick Powell, Eddie Cantor, Clara Bow, Jeanette MacDonald, George O'Brien, Fred Astaire, John Boles, George Brent, Richard Talmage, José Mojico, Jan Kiepura, Adolphe Menjou, Pat O'Brien, Chester Morris, Buster Crabbe, Charlie Chaplin, Lee Tracy, Gary Cooper, Ramon Navarro, George Bancroft, Johnny Mack Brown, Alice Faye, Olivia de Havilland, and Ken Maynard. José does not care for Buck Jones, although many of his friends do. Neither does he like Lionel Barrymore, Douglas Fairbanks, Jr., Richard Arlen, Ronald Colman, or Gordon Westcott. Paul Muni, he says, is "only fair."

As a Bahian white said, "When a black man puts on a tie
and shoes and learns to read and write, he loses interest in
the *candomblé*. There are really two civilizations at Bahia,
ours and the African. When a black begins seriously to take
on our customs, he seldom spends any more time at *candomblés*." A prominent mulatto educator remarked, "I've
never been to a fetish cult. I have no interest in them." A
Negro laborer admitted that he used to go to such ceremonies, "but no more; I've given all that up now." The young
nephew of a prominent *babalaô* said, "All this low stuff ought
to be done away with. It's a sign of a very backward people.
It has even disappeared in Africa. The English came into
Lagos and brought modern civilization. Only in Bahia do
these old customs hang on."

Indicative of the disintegrating state of the fetish world is
the continuous and, at times, acute jealousy among the
leaders and members of its more orthodox centers. In a
given *seita* one hears much critical gossip regarding the practices of some other center. It is accused of forsaking the
"true" African tradition and of inadequately interpreting
mystical experiences. As the number of *Africanos* decreases,
competition between the *seitas* for their allegiance is naturally increasing.

Among the Negroes who still identify themselves with the
cult, the past tends to be romanticized, and the prestige of
the "old Africans," like Bambuxê, Adeta, Iyalode Erelu, and
others, to be constantly enhanced. Similarly, the prestige of
the older cult figures who are still living—the *babalaô* Martiniano, *mãe de santo* Anninha,[21] and the aged Maria Bádá,

[21] Since this was written, *mãe de santo* Anninha has died. Of her funeral,
the *Estado da Bahia* (January 5, 1938) said: "The crowd of people who accompanied the body to Quinta dos Lazaros Cemetery was one of the largest
ever seen in Bahia and recalls the funeral for Pae Adão in Recife. More than

all of whom represent the African tradition in its "purest" form—is, throughout the fetish world, very great.[22]

two thousand persons were present, including members of the Irmandade of Rosario Church, dressed in their robes. The coffin, which was, in keeping with Anninha's request, quite modest, had over it the robe she had worn as a member of this Irmandade of which she was so proud, and was carried on the shoulders of the Brothers of Nossa Senhora do Rosario and of São Benedicto. The crowd of mourners blocked traffic in Rua Dr. Seabra for more than half an hour. Some *filhas de santo* wept unceasingly. Others related the virtues of the kind Anninha.

"When the coffin, carried by pious hands, entered the large gate of the cemetery, the *atabaques* broke out into African rhythms, while sad voices rose in the African songs of the *seita* to which the illustrious *mãe de santo* belonged.

"In the chapel of the cemetery, Canon Assis Curvello repeated the *encommendação*, and her body was laid away in a recently opened crypt.

"Then several orators spoke, among them Snr. Alvaro MacDowell de Oliveira in the name of the União das Seitas Afro-Brasileiras da Bahia, the journalist Edison Carneiro, and representatives of the Centro Cruz Santa do Aché de Okô Afonjá and of the Irmandade of Rosario Church. When the ceremony was over, two omnibuses carried a large number of the friends of Anninha to São Gonçalo do Retiro, where they took part in the preparatory ritual for the African funeral ceremony of Axêxê, to be held seven days after the death of the beloved leader of the *terreiro* of Aché de Okô Afonjá. This ceremony will consist of rites for the eternal peace of the dead *mãe de santo* and will be participated in by *ogans, filhas de santo, paes de santo,* and other friends of the deceased."

[22] This chapter is primarily based upon the author's personal experience as a visitor at numerous ceremonies in eighteen *seitas* at Bahia and as a participant over a period of several months as an *ogan* in the *candomblé* of Pae Procopio in Matatú. For further information see, in addition to the works of Nina Rodrigues, Arthur Ramos, Manoel Querino, and Edison Carneiro previously cited: Padre Étienne Ignace Brasil, "Le Fetichisme des negres du Brésil," *Anthropos*, III (1908), 881–904; Gonçalves Fernandes, *Xangôs do Nordeste* (Rio, 1937) and *O folklore magico do Nordeste* (Rio, 1938); João Varella, *Cosme e Damião* (Bahia, 1938); the novels *O feiticeiro* by Xavier Marques (Bahia, 1922) and *Jubiabá* by Jorge Amado (Rio, 1935); and newspaper accounts such as "Creado o conselho africano da Bahia," *Estado da Bahia*, August 4, 1937, and "No mundo cheio de mysterios dos espiritos e 'paes de santo,' " *ibid.*, May 14, 1936.

VI

THE BAHIAN RACIAL SITUATION

CHAPTER XI

BLACK AND WHITE AT BAHIA

THE foregoing chapters have dealt with some of the consequences, in one part of the New World, of what has been the greatest population movement in all history, namely, the series of migrations associated with the expansion of western Europe. The Portuguese, with whom we are here particularly concerned, were in the forefront of this outward movement which now for over five centuries has been bringing European peoples and European cultures into intimate contact with native peoples and native cultures all over the habitable world. Park,[1] McKenzie,[2] and other writers have pointed out in some detail the chain of circumstances occasioned by this expansion which, in fact, has ushered in all that is peculiarly characteristic of the modern world.

The expansion of Europe is a distinct historical process. It constitutes an era of world-history which had a definite beginning and which, as Park has pointed out,[3] is now at or quite near an end. It has, therefore, a unitary character which makes it a thing that can be studied like any other natural object. Moreover, it is subject to comparison; simi-

[1] Robert E. Park, "Race Relations and Certain Frontiers," in *Race and Culture Contacts*, ed. E. B. Reuter (New York, 1934), pp. 57-85; and in Andrew W. Lind, *An Island Community: Ecological Succession in Hawaii* (Chicago, 1938), Introduction.

[2] R. D. McKenzie, "Industrial Expansion and the Interrelations of Peoples," in *Race and Culture Contacts*, ed. E. B. Reuter, pp. 19-33.

[3] Lind, *op. cit.*, pp. x-xi.

lar movements have occurred during recorded history: the
Arab march across northern Africa and into the Iberian
peninsula, for example, as well as the Mohammedan migrations through the passes of the Himalayas onto the plains of
northern India, and the so-called "barbarian" invasions of
the Roman Empire. The expansion of Europe is not a phenomenon so unique that it cannot profitably be compared
with other similar incidents of human dispersion.

The foregoing chapters have been oriented with reference
to this general point of view, but they dealt specifically with
one locus of European settlement. They sought to explore a
particular instance of racial and cultural contact and to describe it in such terms as will perhaps make it comparable
with other cases of racial and cultural contact in other parts
of the world.

Peculiarly significant are the facts that, although probably more Africans were imported into Brazil as one of the consequences of Portuguese settlement than into any other
region of the New World, and they at one time constituted, in such centers of concentration as Bahia, a majority
of the population, the Negro as a racial unit, like the Brazilian Indian before him, is gradually, but to all appearances
inevitably, disappearing. The general tendency throughout
Brazilian history has been to absorb, gradually but eventually, all ethnic elements into the dominant European
stock.

It is true that the mixed-bloods are increasing, but their
increase appears to be at the expense of the African and
not of the European. Nor is there growing up in Bahia a
relatively permanent mixed racial stock, like the Macanese
in China or the "Cape Coloured" in South Africa. Instead,
the mixed-bloods appear to be gradually absorbing the

blacks, while they themselves are increasingly being incorporated into the predominantly European stock.

In the development of this general tendency to amalgamate and to assimilate all ethnic minorities, the circumstances and conditions of settlement played a significant role. In Brazil, unlike in the case of the English settlement of the United States, few women, as we have seen, emigrated from Europe during the first century of colonization. Until stable conditions and a normal distribution of the sexes were achieved, cohabitation with native Indian women commonly occurred. In this way a population large enough to colonize successfully the new frontier was assured, in spite of the fact that Portugal, because of the drain upon her slender resources to enable her to conquer and hold the vast empire in the East, was unable to provide it. When Thomé de Souza in 1549 set up the first permanent settlement at Bahia, he found already on the site a numerous body of mixed-blood descendants of Portuguese sailors and adventurers who for some years had been living with the Indians. As far as the limited number of females made it possible, Thomé de Souza's men took mates from among these mixed-bloods; others cohabited with pure Indian women. These interracial unions, as in Goa (India) and elsewhere throughout the Portuguese dominions in the East, were subsequently encouraged as a matter of policy by the Portuguese state. Moreover, the Catholic church "regularized them into Christian marriage," thereby lending its powerful sanction to interracial crossing and bringing parents and children within the control and discipline of the church. In other words, a tradition of intermarriage became firmly fixed in the colonial mores.

The considerable body of *mestiços* which grew up are said

to have been better adapted to a tropical climate than their Portuguese fathers and thus to have materially aided the survival of the European stock with which they, by reason of its prestige, came largely to identify themselves and into which they were gradually absorbed.

This case of interbreeding and intermarriage during the precarious days of settlement is not unique in the history of European expansion. In fact, in those instances in which the sex ratio was out of balance, it seems to have been universal. The settlement of the United States, at least in large part, was not one of these cases. But the settlement of South Africa by the Dutch, and of India by the English, as we have noted, were accomplished under similar circumstances. In each of these cases the mixed-bloods were at first accorded the treatment and the career usually falling to the progeny of fathers whose parental sentiments do not run counter to caste sentiments laid down in the local mores. On the frontier new societies are emerging, and the mores which grow up and crystallize into fixed customs and traditions are a result of the unwitting and unplanned responses of human beings to the needs of their time and circumstance.

The similarity, however, between these three cases of European settlement—in India, South Africa, and Brazil—gradually disappeared with the subsequent development of the respective colonies. In India circumstances altered the original situation until intermixture and intermarriage came seriously to be frowned upon and eventually to lose all moral sanction. The mixed-bloods came to be despised and finally to be outcast from both parental groups. In South Africa, when Cape Colony had become fairly established and the Dutch housewives coming in from Europe had succeeded to a considerable extent in getting rid of the native concubines, the attitude of this community also changed, until "at the present time there is probably nowhere a more grim determination to preserve the integrity of their racial stock than there is among the descendants of those first Dutch settlers and of the French Huguenot and German immigrants who followed and fused with them to form the Boer people."[4]

But in Brazil the attitudes toward intermixture and intermarriage which grew up during the colonial period in response to the exigencies of the frontier seem not to have been subsequently seriously altered. Instead, the tendency to absorb all diverse ethnic elements appears to have been a persistent character of Brazilian society throughout the four centuries of its existence and is characteristic of it today.

The reasons for this deviation in Brazil are not very clear, and it continues, therefore, to be a problem. One of the difficulties in the way of its solution is the comparatively meager amount of information available on the "social history" of Brazil. Until quite recently, when such intellectuals as Gilberto Freyre became interested in digging out of the voluminous record of the past some understanding of the human relations characteristic of the colonial and imperial periods, Brazilian historians had limited their attention largely to the political, and especially to the administrative, aspects of Brazilian history. There is extant, of course, a considerable literature from the pens of foreign visitors, among whom were several able scientists, artists, and scholars like, for example, J. B. von Spix, C. F. P. von Martius, J. B. Debret, Prince Maximilian Wied-Neuwied, Maurice Rugendas, Henry W. Bates, Louis Agassiz, Richard F. Burton, Prince Adalbert, and L. F. Tollenare, which often con-

---

[4] Park, "Race Relations and Certain Frontiers," *op. cit.*, pp. 67–68.

tains pertinent observation and comment. But, unfortunately, the work of these men is almost entirely limited to the nineteenth century. The accounts which deal with an earlier period—for instance, the *Cartas* of Vilhena and of Nobrega, and the works of such able historians as Robert Southey, Heinrich Handelmann, and Francisco A. de Varnhagen—do not furnish sufficient information to resolve our problem. Voluminous records in numerous public depositories still await the careful sifting of competent scholars.

It may be that, by the time European women had arrived in any considerable number in Bahia, miscegenation, aided by the decimation occasioned by the rigors of slavery and the introduction of European diseases, had already proceeded to the point where the Indian, as a minority group, had disappeared, or had almost disappeared, so that the problem of serious competition with Indian concubines did not present itself to the incoming Portuguese housewives.

Large numbers of Africans were, however, by this time coming in, and they continued for generations to arrive. There were at least some females among them. No intermarriage with African women, as far as we know, at first took place. Miscegenation, however, was extensive. And the mixed-bloods, as we have seen, were treated with tolerance and consideration. Numerous unions, especially with mulatto women, were subsequently entered into and were socially accepted.

It may have been that one circumstance favorable to a deviant termination of race relations in Brazil was the contact which the Portuguese, unlike the English and the Dutch, had with the Moors. From the customs and traditions of their conquerors, the Portuguese, during the several centuries of Moorish domination of the Iberian peninsula, took over at least three cultural elements whose presence in the mores of colonial Brazil may be significant for our problem: the practice of concubinage, the subordinate position of woman in the household, and the comparative absence of color consciousness.

It may be that the Portuguese, like the Moors and other Mohammedans, were, as several commentators have said, a "color-blind" people; that is, awareness of color and other racial differences was not so pronounced with them as with us. It is probably true that the *conceptions* laid down in the culture materially influence the *perceptions* which individuals have.

Perhaps one reason the Portuguese in the New Country and their descendants cohabited with individuals from other races and interbred so extensively was that such behavior had long been common in the Old Country, where their ancestors had taken over from the Moors oriental customs tolerant of plural marriage. Even when Orientals exclude the children of concubines from the legitimate family in an attempt to preserve its status, emphasis is upon preserving status rather than purity of race.

Concubinage, or *mancebia*, as it is known in Bahia, seems to have been quite common throughout the history of Brazil. It appears always to have been more or less socially sanctioned and accepted into the mores. Divorce is illegal, and many marriages are made for family convenience. It is not rare today in Bahia for a man with a legal wife and family to keep in separate establishments one or more *amantes*.[5] The

[5] In one reported instance there are five; in another, eight. Usually the man, owing to the expense involved, is well to do; the women are from the lower strata. For instance, a wealthy and prominent intellectual figure lives most of the time apart from his legal wife with a mulatto woman who is intelligent, "attractive," and has traveled (with him) in France, Belgium,

custom is to some extent recognized in law.[6] Usually the children take the mother's name, but occasionally the father "recognizes" and registers them, so that they legally bear his name. They are sometimes taken into the legitimate household, where they are usually accepted without serious question by the legal wife.[7]

Particularly among the lower classes, illegitimacy is not seriously prejudicial to the child. Personal qualities and individual ability largely determine his role and status; his parentage is rather naturally considered to be a matter beyond his control. A surname is not of great importance, the given name being infinitely more used, even among the upper classes. Prominent intellectual and political figures are known throughout the city by their given names. A stranger

---

and Portugal. Their eldest daughter is studying to be a pianist. There are three younger children. The man also supports another mulatto woman, said to be "very young and very pretty."

[6] A single extra-marital amorous experience makes a woman liable to prosecution for adultery, whereas for a man such conduct must not only be proved to be habitual but also to háve involved an established relationship with a *single* individual. For a wife to have cause for legal action, she must previously have been ignorant of the extra-legal affair of her husband. Otherwise, her implied acquiescence constitutes participation in guilt.

[7] One wife said of her husband's "natural" child, "He's a fine boy. I like him as much as, or more than, my own children." In 1911 an American consul at Pará wrote: "In Amazonia the father assumes all the responsibility and legally adopts his illegitimate children who, in a majority of cases, become a part of his own family, taking an equal place in social privileges with those children within the bounds of the church regulations. . . . . There is no disposition in the higher social circles to discriminate against the number of these illegitimate aristocrats who, in the matter of education, refinement and address, are often the superior of some of those born in wedlock in the same families . . . . [and are], in many prominent cases, the acknowledged leaders of society" (J. Orton Kerbey, *An American Consul in Amazonia* [New York, 1911], p. 119).

is often surprised to discover individuals whom he had not previously thought of as related turning out to be brothers or other close relatives.

The gradually improving status of women is today working against *mancebia*, and many of the "more scrupulous" families discourage it. In these, the wife, if she knows of her husband's affairs, may reprove him, as also may other members of the family and its friends. But usually, as an upper-class woman said, "the ladies talk very little about it, and then only with their most intimate friends. The subject is not generally discussed."

Although in recent years at least two feminists have become quite prominent, and one of these has been elected to the state legislature, the common family pattern at Bahia is still patriarchal. Tempered, of course, by the natural claims which primary relations always tend to set up, the role of the husband and father has, throughout Bahian history, been a decidedly dominant role. For instance, it is said to have formerly been the custom—at Bahia today in some instances a custom still observed—for the husband to select and purchase the materials for his wife's clothing and even indicate the manner in which the goods should be made up. Formerly, women, other than prostitutes, servants, and other individuals of inferior status, were rarely seen upon the streets or in public places, the home being considered their proper sphere. Even in the home, women seem to have rarely appeared in the presence of strangers. Tollenare, visiting Pernambuco in the early nineteenth century, wrote, "At my arrival [in the house of a merchant], the women disappeared, and only the head of the house remained in the *salão* to talk to me." In another connection he remarked: "During eight months of residence in Pernambuco I never once saw the high society of the city in spite of my letters of introduction and my efforts to enter several homes."[8]

Another important question to raise is, "Why did not the structure of Brazilian slave society, like that of the United States, pass over into caste?" The situation here is somewhat more clear. The function of caste appears to be that of preserving inviolate the racial integrity of a dominant group. Caste in India apparently arose in an attempt on the part of incoming Aryan peoples to preserve the status of their families against the consequences of intermixture with the conquered aboriginal tribes.[9] The prohibition of intermarriage excluded almost completely from the more intimate social contacts individuals from groups considered undesirable.

In Brazil the characteristic tendency has always been just the reverse: namely, to incorporate eventually all ethnic minorities into the dominant group. The contact of the Portuguese settlers with the imported Africans was, of course, originally that of master and slave. But out of the slave system which grew up there gradually emerged a moral order in which most whites and blacks, as we have seen, came to share a common life on an intimate, personal basis.

Men come together ordinarily because they are useful to one another. Under these circumstances they may regard each other for a long time as mere utilities. But human beings do not live for long, like plants, in relations that are merely symbiotic. For men, unlike plants, communicate. In this way they come to know one another's minds and to be responsive to one another's attitudes and sentiments. They find themselves, eventually, living as it were, each in the mind of all his neighbors. It is in this way that a moral order grows up in which,

[8] L. F. Tollenare, "Notas dominicais tomadas durante uma residencia no Brasil, 1816–1818" (portion relative to Pernambuco translated by Alfredo de Carvalho from the unpublished French manuscript), *Revista do Instituto Arqueologico e Geographico Pernambucano*, No. 61 (1905), pp. 129 and 250.

[9] Sir Herbert H. Risley, *The People of India* (2d ed.; Calcutta, 1915), pp. 264–65.

under the happiest circumstances, the individual feels himself constrained only by those obligations which he freely accepts or imposes upon himself.

It is characteristic of such a moral order that it is nonrational. That means that it is not devised to protect any special interest, to serve any policy, and has no ulterior purposes of any sort. On the contrary, it arises in response to the natural claims which one individual makes upon another, as soon as he recognizes that other individual as human like himself.[10]

Manumission, as we have seen, extensively occurred from the first. And final emancipation came about as the culmination of a widespread liberation movement which had for years dominated the public mind. The Brazilian Negro was thus released from a servile status gradually and under circumstances which favored the continuance of intimate personal ties. Final emancipation was not, as in the United States, brought about as an incident of civil strife, and the race relations which had normally grown up under slavery were never exacerbated by a program of reconstruction imposed from without by armed conquest. The rise of the black and of the mixed-blood in Brazil has always had in its favor those sentiments and personal attachments which primary relations tend to develop.

In Bahia there is probably little or no race prejudice in the sense in which that term is used in the United States. There are no castes based on race; there are only classes. This does not mean that there is nothing which might be properly called prejudice but that such prejudice as does exist is *class* rather than *caste* prejudice. It is the kind of prejudice which exists *inside* the ranks of the Negro in the United States, the amount and intensity of which is actually very great.

That race prejudice has not arisen in Brazil is perhaps due

[10] Park, Introduction to Bertram W. Doyle, *The Etiquette of Race Relations in the South* (Chicago, 1937), pp. xiv-xv.

to the fact that the Brazilian white has never at any time felt that the black or the mixed-blood offered any serious threat to his status. The past and present experiences of the ethnic groups have not been such as would call out in the whites feelings of fear, distrust, apprehension, dread, resentment, or envy, all of which probably enter into the attitude of race prejudice. Besides, there has not been in Brazil that obscure sense of guilt which men sometimes feel toward those they have wronged or toward those by whom they themselves have been wronged. There have been few or no incidents which the Europeans resent and tend to construe as affronts or unwarranted aggressions and attacks; no events, like those attendant on our Civil War and its aftermath, which would stir the Europeans, arouse their feelings, and give to their conception of the Negro a new meaning and content. There are in Brazil no memories over which the whites brood like those which have been so strikingly called to our attention in a recent novel:

Looking about her in that cold spring of 1866, Scarlett realized what was facing her and the whole South. . . . . The Yankees had the South prostrate. . . . . The South had been tilted as by a giant malicious hand, and those who had once ruled were now more helpless than their former slaves had ever been.

Georgia was heavily garrisoned with troops and Atlanta had more than its share. The commandants of the Yankee troops in the various cities had complete power, even the power of life and death over the civilian population. . . . . They could and did imprison citizens for any cause, or no cause, seize their property, hang them. They could and did harass and hamstring them with conflicting regulations about the operation of their business, the wages they must pay their servants, what they should say in public and private utterances and what they should write in newspapers. They regulated how, when and where they must dump their garbage and they decided what songs the daughters and wives of ex-Confederates could sing, so that the singing of "Dixie" or "Bonnie Blue Flag" became an offense only a little less serious than treason. They ruled that no one could get a letter out of the post office without taking the Iron Clad oath and, in some instances, they even prohibited the issuance of marriage licenses unless the couples had taken the hated oath.

The newspapers were so muzzled that no public protest could be raised against the injustices or depredations of the military, and individual protests were silenced with jail sentences. . . . . Trial by jury and the law of habeas corpus were practically suspended. The civil courts still functioned after a fashion but they functioned at the pleasure of the military, who could and did interfere with their verdicts. . . . .

The Negroes had not yet been given the right to vote but the North was determined that they should vote and equally determined that their vote should be friendly to the North. With this in mind, nothing was too good for the Negroes. The Yankee soldiers backed them up in anything they chose to do, and the surest way for a white person to get himself into trouble was to bring a complaint of any kind against a Negro.

The former slaves were now the lords of creation and, with the aid of the Yankees, the lowest and most ignorant ones were on top. . . . . Thousands of house servants, the highest caste in the slave population, remained with their white folks, doing manual labor which had been beneath them in the old days. Many loyal field hands also refused to avail themselves of the new freedom, but the hordes of "trashy free issue niggers," who were causing most of the trouble, were drawn largely from the field-hand class.

In slave days, these lowly blacks had been despised by the house Negroes and yard Negroes as creatures of small worth. . . . . And now this class, the lowest in the black social order, was making life a misery for the South.

. . . . The former field hands found themselves suddenly elevated to the seats of the mighty. . . . . Like . . . . small children turned loose among treasured objects whose value is beyond their comprehension, they ran wild. . . . .

To the credit of the Negroes, including the least intelligent of them, few were actuated by malice and those few had usually been "mean niggers" even in slave days. But they were, as a class, ... easily led and from long habit accustomed to taking orders. Formerly their white masters had given the orders. Now they had a new set of masters, the Bureau and the Carpetbaggers, and their orders were: "You're just as good as any white man, so act that way. Just as soon as you can vote the Republican ticket, you are going to have the white man's property. It's as good as yours now. Take it, if you can get it!"

Dazzled by these tales, freedom became a never-ending picnic, a barbecue every day of the week, a carnival of idleness and theft and insolence. Country Negroes flocked into the cities, leaving the rural districts without labor to make the crops. Atlanta was crowded with them and still they came by the hundreds, lazy and dangerous as a result of the new doctrines being taught them. . . . .

For the first time in their lives the Negroes were able to get all the whisky they might want. . . . . Outrages were inevitable. . . . . The white people, unprotected by law, were terrorized. Men were insulted on the streets by drunken blacks, houses and barns were burned at night, horses and cattle and chickens stolen in broad daylight, crimes of all varieties were committed and few of the perpetrators were brought to justice.

But these ignominies and dangers were as nothing compared with the peril of white women, many bereft by the war of male protection, who lived alone in the outlying districts and on lonely roads. It was the large number of outrages on women and the ever-present fear for the safety of their wives and daughters that drove Southern men to cold and trembling fury. . . . .

Here was the astonishing spectacle of half a nation attempting, at the point of bayonet, to force upon the other half the rule of Negroes, many of them scarcely one generation out of the African jungles. The vote must be given to them but it must be denied to most of their former owners. The South must be kept down and disfranchisement of the whites was one way to keep the South down. Most of those who had fought for the Confederacy, held office under it or given aid and comfort to it were not allowed to vote, had no choice in the selection of their public officials and were wholly under the power of an alien rule. . . . .

Through these anxious days and nights, Scarlett was torn with fear. The ever-present menace of lawless Negroes and Yankee soldiers preyed on her mind, the danger of confiscation was constantly with her, even in her dreams, and she dreaded worse terrors to come. Depressed by the helplessness of herself and her friends, of the whole South, it was not strange that she often remembered during these days the words which Tony Fontaine had spoken so passionately:

"By God, Scarlett, it isn't to be borne! And it won't be borne!"[11]

Brazilian society nowhere passed through a comparable period of social upheaval in which a threatened reversal of the status structure elicited such deep-seated fear and apprehension that generations later it is so vividly recalled by the descendants of those who lived through it. The rape of white women by colored men, either real or fancied, has been unknown in Brazil. There has not been anything remotely comparable to the conquest of our South by northern armies, the imposition, for years, of onerous political control from without, and the consequent development of feelings of resentment and bitterness which, lacking normal expression (by reason of the North's formidable power), in the form of effective aggression toward the actual offending object, became displaced upon the more or less helpless Negro when northern force was withdrawn. On the contrary, the relations between the races in Brazil have always been, to a considerable extent, intimate and cordial. The moral order of the Bahian *engenhos*, which, as we have seen, was organized largely on a familial and personal basis, has persisted relatively undisturbed down to the present day, and the members of the different races have, by way of personal feelings and sentiments, long identified themselves with each other, entered into each other's personal experiences, and come to appreciate their common human character. Instead of conceiving the Negro as an abstract object, the Bahian white tends to think of him as João or Maria and as being wholly human like himself.

[11] Margaret Mitchell, *Gone with the Wind* (New York, 1938), pp. 652–57.

It is true that the Europeans at Bahia, like all groups, are ethnocentric, and individual whites share a general feeling of the superiority of their group. Many of them are adverse to the (to them) strange and bizarre behavior represented by the *candomblé* ritual and other African cultural survivals. In some minds at least these acts have taken on a disgusting and even offensive character and may have evoked deeply rooted antipathies. However, these antagonisms are directed at *cultural* rather than at *racial* variations, and they tend to disappear when the Negro, as he is now rapidly doing, gives up his identification with African cultural forms and becomes assimilated into the European world. The antipathy does not extend, therefore, to the Negro as such but rather to the *Africano*, the foreigner, he who constitutes an alien cyst in the social organism. This attitude is not greatly different from that characteristic of descendants of the first English settlers in the United States toward recent immigrants from southern and eastern Europe who for a time continue to live much to themselves and to cling tenaciously to Old World customs and traditions.

One might note that the Brazilian case of racial contact definitely supports Faris' challenge of a popular assumption which, confusing the customary with the natural, maintains that race prejudice is instinctive and hereditary.[12] If race prejudice were organic, it obviously would appear in all cases of racial contact. If, then, we discover cases in which it does not appear, the hypothesis that race prejudice is instinctive is no longer valid.

What we find, then, in Bahia is a multiracial class society.

[12] Ellsworth Faris, "The Natural History of Race Prejudice," in *The Nature of Human Nature* (New York and London, 1937), chap. xxxii, pp. 357 ff.

There is no caste based upon race; there are only classes. These classes are still largely identified with color, it is true, but they are classes nonetheless and not castes. The most characteristic tendency of the Bahian social order is the gradual but persistent reduction of all distinguishing racial and cultural marks and the fusing, biologically and culturally, of the African and the European into one race and one common culture.

The actual situation in any case of race contact can perhaps be precisely defined by a diagram which distinguishes between caste and class relations.[13] In a caste system the racial lines may run thus:

Race lines

White
Mixed-blood
Black

In case the structure of society is organized on the basis of class, as in Brazil or Hawaii, the color lines run vertically, cutting across class lines:

Class lines — White | Mixed-blood | Black

Each race, including the mixed-bloods, is likely to be represented in all the occupational classes. The hierarchy of occupations will inevitably take the form of a pyramid, but the

[13] The author is indebted for this schematic arrangement to Dr. Robert E. Park.

percentage of each racial stock in each occupational class will indicate the occupational status of the different racial elements. And since the group with superior status will have proportionately larger numbers in the upper brackets, and the groups with inferior status will have larger numbers in the lower brackets, one may describe a racial situation statistically. Thus, on the basis of a sample census recently taken, the relation to the class structure of the respective ethnic elements in the population at Bahia may be described as shown in Table 16.

TABLE 16

RACIAL DISTRIBUTION IN THE CLASSES AT BAHIA, 1936

ETHNIC GROUPS	INTELLIGENTSIA		MARGINAL		LOWER CLASS	
	No.	Per Cent	No.	Per Cent	No.	Per Cent
Blacks.................	5	0.4	23	5.1	1,245	75.2
Mixed-bloods..........	222	15.7	255	56.3	386	23.3
Whites................	1,183	83.9	175	38.6	25	1.5
Total............	1,410	100.0	453	100.0	1,656	100.0

One might indicate graphically the vocational distribution of the various ethnic elements at Bahia by a series of pyramids, as illustrated on the facing page.

If now one were able to obtain statistics showing the extent of intermarriage between, on the one hand, members of the different racial stocks in the same occupational class and, on the other hand, between the different classes in the same racial stock, these facts should provide an accurate statistical description of what the racial situation actually is. If one finds that, as in the United States, marriages between

CLASS DISTRIBUTION OF THE RACES, BAHIA, 1936

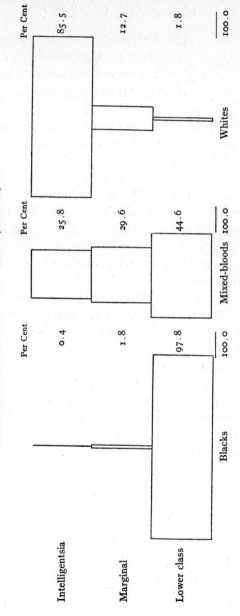

different occupational classes within each racial group are more frequent than intermarriage between members of the different racial groups in the same class, we should expect to find solidarity and co-operation for common ends organized along racial lines. The racial group would then assume more or less the character of a nationality or of a racial minority. On the other hand, if solidarity and co-operation were organized along class lines, then the struggle for status would take more or less the form of a class struggle.

Statistical data to resolve this problem are unfortunately not available in any depository in Bahia. Such information as it was possible to secure in the course of this study indicated that marriages cross race lines more often than class lines and that solidarity and co-operation tend to be organized along class lines.

Since, then, the blacks, mixed-bloods, and whites in Bahia do not constitute endogamous occupational groupings, the social structure is not that of caste. Although the hierarchy of occupations still takes a decidedly pyramidal form, and the white race, occupying superior status, has predominantly larger numbers in the upper brackets, and the black race, representing inferior status, is overwhelmingly dominant in the lower brackets, each race and the mixed-bloods are represented in all the occupational classes.

To the extent that the blacks, mixed-bloods, and whites fall into endogamous but not necessarily occupational groupings, one might say that the structure here takes the form of a racial minority, or a nationality, in free association with, but not accepted on a basis of social equality by, a dominant racial majority. Such is the relation of the Jew in Europe and, increasingly now, of the Negro in the United States. Of the latter, Park has said:

Although caste still persists and serves in a way to regulate race relations, many things—education, the rise within the Negro community of a professional class (teachers, ministers, and physicians) and of an intelligentsia, seeking to organize and direct the Negro's rising race consciousness—have conspired not merely to undermine the traditional caste system but to render it obsolete.

Meanwhile, the slow but steady advance of the Negro, as a result of a competition within and without the group, and the gradual rise of a Negro society within the limits of the white man's world have changed the whole structure of race relations in the United States, both in the North and in the South.

The restrictions on intermarriage still persist and continue to make of the Negro an endogamous social group, in much the same sense that the Jews, the Mennonites, and any of the more primitive religious sects are endogamous. On the other hand, in view of the fact that he has developed a society in which all the professions and many, if not most, occupations are represented, the Negro has an opportunity now, which he did not have earlier, to rise within the limits of the Negro world. Under those circumstances the Negro group has gradually ceased to exhibit the characteristics of a caste and has assumed rather the character of a racial or national minority.[14]

With the Negro in Brazil endogamy is far from absolute, breaking down particularly along the biological borders of the race, probably increasingly, with the passage of time and the continued rise of individuals from the inferior status group. The scale of race distinctions, including the Negro at the bottom and the white at the top, seems to correspond in a general way to the scale of color distinctions *within the Negro minority* in the United States.

Although color and negroid features are still indicative of slave origin and still tend to be closely identified with low status and hence to constitute a considerable handicap to marriage into the upper classes, these characteristics lose their limiting and restrictive character in proportion as the

[14] Introduction to Doyle, *op. cit.*, pp. xxi–xxii.

degree of European intermixture increases or their symbolic reference is called into question by evidence of status-enhancing qualities in a given individual. Similarly, personal competence or individual achievement admit persons possessing considerable color into such status-symbolizing institutions as exclusive clubs. Race consciousness is at a minimum, "passing" has no point, and the circumstances are not ordinarily conducive to the appearance of the "marginal man." The organization of society tends to take the form of a competitive order in which the individual finds his place on the basis of personal competence rather than of racial descent.

The racial situation at Bahia probably is, in a general way, typical of all Brazil. At the same time a considerable immigration of Europeans during the past century into the southern Brazilian states, especially São Paulo, Santa Catharina, and Rio Grande do Sul, and the gradual development of an industrial society in São Paulo, may have modified somewhat the attitudes formerly prevailing in these areas. A Bahian mixed-blood recently returned from Rio Grande do Sul with the statement that he had there been referred to as a "Negro" and had otherwise felt uncomfortable distinctions to which in Bahia he had been unaccustomed. That there is some prejudice in the cosmopolitan city of Rio de Janeiro is attested by the organization in 1935 of O Movimento Brasileiro Contra o Preconceito Racial ("The Brazilian Movement against Race Prejudice"), sponsored by the prominent intellectuals, Arthur Ramos and Roquette Pinto. In São Paulo, the organization in 1924 of a Negro journal, O Clarim d'Alvorada, and later of others like A Chibata, Cultura, O Clarim, and A Voz da Raça ("The Voice of the Race"); of several Negro clubs for recreational and

literary purposes like the Club 15 de Novembro, Club 13 de
Maio, Gremio Dramatus e Recreativo Kosmos, and the Gremio União da Mocidade; of the Negro women's organization,
Centro Civico Palmares; and, in 1931, of the Frente Negra
Brasileira[15] ("Brazilian Negro Front") with the aim of
"bringing together the Negroes of all Brazil," clearly indicates at least some race consciousness on the part of the
Negroes of São Paulo and consequently reflects feelings of
exclusion and discrimination; as also do the subsequently
organized Associação dos Brasileiros de Côr in Santos and
the Frente Negra Pelotense in Pelotas, Rio Grande do Sul.[16]
However, these indications of a measure of race consciousness are probably exceptions to the general Brazilian
cultural pattern and not typical of it. Organizers for the
Frente Negra do Brasil, after several weeks of fruitless effort, gave up an attempt to organize a chapter at Bahia.
The fact that noted intellectuals band together to resist attitudes prejudicial to racial minorities is in itself an evidence
of the racial ideology which we have noted. That these intellectuals are not atypical persons is attested by the general
tenor of the spontaneous utterances, as well as formal remarks, of numerous Brazilians. It may be that Bahia, by
reason of long being a passive cultural area in comparison
to the more active cultural areas of the South, is more characteristically representative of the original Brazilian mores
than São Paulo and certain other southern zones. But even
in São Paulo the journals referred to above have one by one
suspended publication, a fact which would seem to indicate

[15] With the advent of the new regime in November, 1937, the political
activities of the Frente Negra Brasileira were suppressed. Its social and educational program, however, was continued and the name changed to União
Negra Brasileira.

[16] See Arthur Ramos, *The Negro in Brazil* (Washington, 1939), pp. 168–74.

no great amount of race consciousness. The study of inter-marriage made in São Paulo by Dr. Lowrie[17] would appear merely to confirm the fact that in Brazil still today the Negro in most cases lacks class. At least it is true that several individuals with some colored blood occupy important positions in the Paulista community or have married into white families.

The race problem in Brazil, in so far as there is a race problem, tends rather to be a consequence of the resistance which an ethnic group offers, or is thought to offer, to absorption. Recent opposition to Japanese immigration into São Paulo apparently has been largely motivated by apprehension that the Japanese would constitute a group difficult to assimilate.[18] In an attempt to refute this imputation, the Japanese embassy in Rio published a pamphlet entitled *Intermixture among the Japanese: The Myth That They Do Not Interbreed with Other Races*,[19] to which were appended several photographs of mixed Japanese-Brazilian families.

Of the Negroes, Brazilians ordinarily say there is no Negro problem, because the Negroes are in process of absorption and eventually will be completely incorporated. To individuals from all classes of the population this eventual amalgamation and assimilation of diverse ethnic units is a matter of pride and self-commendation.

In summary, one might set down in the form of hypothe-

[17] Samuel H. Lowrie, "Racial and National Intermarriage in a Brazilian City," *American Journal of Sociology*, XLIV, No. 5 (March, 1939), 684–707.

[18] See, e.g., "O cruzamento de japonezes com brasileiros," *Jornal do Commercio* (Rio), September 17, 1935; "A infiltração japoneza," *ibid.*, October 16 and 22, 1935; "Oliveira Vianna e a immigração japoneza," *ibid.*, September 13, 1935; "Contra a imigração amarela," *ibid.*, August 11, 1935.

[19] *Cruzamento da ethnia japoneza: hypothese de que o japonez não se cruza com outra ethnia* (São Paulo, 1934).

ses for further testing what appear to be the more significant facts about the racial situation in Brazil, especially as it is related to the career of the African and his descendants.

1. Although probably more Africans were imported into Brazil than into the United States, or into any other region of the New World, the Brazilian Negro, as a racial unit, like the Brazilian Indian before him, is gradually but to all appearances inevitably disappearing, being biologically absorbed into the predominantly European population. Race mixture has gone on in an unobtrusive way over a long period of time. In few places in the world, perhaps, has the interpenetration of diverse races proceeded so continuously and on so extensive a scale.

2. There is not growing up a relatively permanent mixed racial stock, like the "Cape Coloured" of South Africa, the Macanese in China, or the Goanese in India. The Brazilian mixed-bloods are absorbing the blacks and are themselves in turn being absorbed by the predominantly European population.

3. In answer to the normal needs of a racial and cultural frontier a tradition of intermarriage arose and became firmly fixed in the colonial mores. This appears to be the natural response in all cases of racial contact where the sex ratio is out of balance.

4. Miscegenation, particularly when linked with intermarriage, resulted in bonds of sentiment between parents and offspring which hindered the arising of attitudes of prejudice and at the same time placed the mixed-bloods in a favorable position for social advancement.

5. With rise in class, intermarriage between mixed-bloods (especially those of the lighter shades) and whites became increasingly common. Thus, endogamy has for some time

been breaking down, particularly along the biological borders of the races, and, with the continued rise of individuals
from the inferior status group, this tendency is evidently increasing. Although color and negroid features are still symbolic of slave origin, still tend to be closely identified with
low status and hence to constitute an undeniable handicap to
marriage into the upper classes, these physical marks lose
their restraining character in proportion to the degree white
intermixture increases or—what is even more important—in
proportion to the degree their symbolic reference is called
into question by evidence of other qualities of a status-
enhancing character in a given individual.

6. In general, slavery in Brazil, as also in the United
States, was characterized by the continuous growth of intimate, personal relations between master and slave which
tended gradually to humanize the institution and undermine
its formal character. The Brazilian moral order became organized, to a considerable extent, on a familial and personal
basis.

7. The custom of manumission became firmly intrenched
in the Brazilian mores, constituting, under certain circumstances, universally expected behavior. Brazilian Negroes were thus released from a servile status gradually and
under circumstances which favored the continuance of those
intimate personal ties already built up.

8. Emancipation sentiment in Brazil never suffered from
a wave of fear like that which swept our South after the
Negro uprising in Haiti and the disorders attendant on the
subsequent annihilation of the Haitian whites.

9. Abolition sentiment and agitation was not limited to
any one section of Brazil but, on the contrary, penetrated
every community, even that of Bahia, where the institution

of slavery was apparently very firmly intrenched. Thus, the "struggle for consistency" in the Brazilian mores went on *inside* each local community, where it had in its favor the intimate and personal relations of individuals who not only lived in close proximity to each other but were also bound together by ties of family, religion, and friendship.

10. Final emancipation came about as the culmination of a widespread liberation movement which for years had dominated the public mind. The release of the last slaves in bondage did not, as in the United States, occur as an incident of civil strife, nor were the race relations which have normally grown up under slavery ever exacerbated by a program of "reconstruction" imposed by armed conquest from without.

11. The Brazilian white has never at any time felt that the black or the mixed-blood offered any serious threat to his own status. No feelings of fear, distrust, apprehension, dread, resentment, or envy have been stirred up, as in our South during and following the Civil War, no sense of unwarranted aggressions or attacks.

12. Today, the blacks and the mixed-bloods are represented throughout the entire occupational scale, although, as is to be expected, considering the original slave status of the Negro, his relatively disadvantaged position upon receiving his liberty, and the comparatively brief time he has enjoyed a freely competitive status, the darker portion of the population is still concentrated in the low-pay, low-status employments. However, the blacks, ordinarily but not always paced by the mixed-bloods, are gradually rising in the occupational scale.

13. This rise in class of the blacks and the mixed-bloods is recognized not merely in a Negro world, as is largely true of

similar advancement in the United States, but by all members of the Brazilian community.

14. Since, then, the blacks, the mixed-bloods, and the whites do not constitute endogamous occupational groupings, the social structure is not that of caste.

15. Nor does the Negro in Brazil appear to be, as he is in the United States, developing into a self-conscious racial minority in free association with, but not accepted by, a dominant racial majority.

16. Instead, the entire organization of society tends to take the form of a competitive order in which the individual finds his place on the basis of personal competence and individual achievement more than upon the basis of racial descent. This fact is perhaps best reflected in the common saying: "A rich Negro is a white man, and a poor white man is a Negro."

17. The Brazilian racial situation is, then, sufficiently distinct from that in India, for example, where the social order is organized on the principle of caste, and from those in many parts of the world where a national or racial minority (or minorities) is in free association with, but not accepted by, a dominant national or racial majority, to constitute, along with the Hawaiian racial situation and certain others, a distinct type: *a multiracial class society*.

18. There is no deliberate segregation as one finds where races have been embittered for a long time; spatial distribution is largely the consequence of economic sifting. Such isolation as exists is largely due to varying educational levels or to identification with elements of African culture, particularly the fetish cult.

19. For the assimilation of the *Africanos* at Bahia, while now far advanced, is not yet complete. African survivals still

persist, setting apart to some extent a (comparatively small) portion of the black population.

20. Lynching and the rape of white women by colored men are both unknown, "passing" has no point, and circumstances are not ordinarily conducive to the appearance of the "marginal man."

21. One drop of African blood does not, as in the United States (if known), class a mixed-blood as a Negro. Instead, many individuals are listed in the official statistics as whites, and are similarly known in the community, who not only have African ancestors but actually give some evidence of this descent in their color and features.

22. Prejudice exists in Brazil; but it is *class* rather than *race* prejudice. It is the kind of prejudice which one finds inside the ranks of the Negro in the United States.

23. It is possible that the Brazilian blacks and mixed-bloods, lacking as they do in most cases the sense of inferiority long characteristic of the Negro in the United States, particularly of the mixed-blood, have been less activated by personal ambition. Feeling themselves less under the necessity of demonstrating to a hostile white world their individual talents and abilities, they have not had the same incentive for social advancement and, consequently, have not, perhaps, as a group, risen in class as rapidly as has the Negro in the United States.

24. Although Brazil seems never to have had a formal racial policy, the traditional behavior which originally grew up and took shape under the influence of the immediate and unreflecting responses to the circumstances and conditions of colonial life gave rise to an *informal* racial policy, or racial ideology, which underlies and gives consistency to the mores, appearing only when they are challenged from without and

individuals seek to rationalize and to defend their customary conduct. This ideology is perhaps best summarized in the commonly heard phrase, "We Brazilians are becoming one people."

25. Thus, the race problem in Brazil, in so far as there is a race problem, tends to be identified with the resistance which an ethnic group offers, or is thought to offer, to absorption and assimilation.

This is not to say that there are no social distinctions in Brazil; for such are obviously common to all societies, one thing or another serving as a basis. Neither does it mean that there is no discrimination or that the blacks and mixed-bloods are completely satisfied with their lot. But it does mean (a) that a man of color may, by reason of individual merit or favorable circumstance, improve his status and even achieve position in the upper levels of society and (b) that this position will then be with reference not merely to the darker group whose color he shares but to the total community.

APPENDIXES

APPENDIX A

AN AUTOBIOGRAPHICAL SKETCH
OF A COLORED CITIZEN

The following autobiographical sketch was written by a man who is one of Bahia's leading colored citizens, a very dark mulatto referred to in Bahia as a *preto* or, literally, a "black":

I was born of modest parents. My father was a white man, an educated gentleman from a family of agriculturists, or "Senhores de Engenho," in the Reconcavo near Santo Amaro. My mother was a black woman, a person of notable beauty among her race. Domingas was her name.

Until I was ten years of age, I lived in Santo Amaro and its vicinity, at that time the richest area of sugar-cane cultivation in the state of Bahia. In 1865, when I was ten years old—for I was born on January 7, 1855—my father took me to Rio de Janeiro, where I finished my elementary education and prepared myself for secondary schooling in the Collegio de São Salvador, which was at that time under the direction of Monsenhor José Joaquim da Fonseca Lima, an illustrious priest, later *reitor* of the Collegio Dom Pedro II, the foremost secondary school in Brazil.

I owe what I know of the Humanities to my dear Masters at the Collegio de São Salvador, whom I later joined as teacher when, in 1871, at seventeen years of age, I entered the Escola Politecnica (then Escola Central) to take a course in Civil Engineering. I had among my teachers in the Escola Central the most eminent intellectual and scientific men of that time in Brazil, including Manoel da Cunha Galvão, Americo Monteiro de Barros, João Eugenia de Lossie e Seylbits, Carneiro, Saldanha da Gama, Villa Nova Machado, André Rebouças, Joaquim Murtinho, Visconde do Rio Branco, Borgia Castro, Sousa Pitanga, and Holanda Cavalcanti, all of whom were men of great importance in the field of science and some of whom were prominent in national politics.

In 1876, at twenty-one years of age, I finished my studies at the Escola Politecnica. While a student I had collaborated at the Museu Nacional (directed by Ladislau Netto, an illustrious botanist) with Orville Derby, Lacerda e Almeida, Pirarro, Rodrigues Peixoto, and Schwacke, in the scientific discussions held there and constantly attended by Emperor Dom Pedro II.

I then dedicated myself to the task of teaching in the principal *collegios* of Rio de Janeiro where I had pupils who today in the highest offices of the Brazilian government honor me with their learning and ability.

In 1878 I began my career as an engineer by serving as a member of the Comissão Hidraulica, organized at the instance of the government of Conselheiro Sinimbu for the study of ports and inland navigation and directed by the famed American engineer, Mr. W. Milnor Roberts, especially engaged for this purpose. The Commission was a large body, composed of chosen men destined to direct the future work of this nature in our country. I was invited to join the group by Senator Veriato de Medeiros. I positively did not solicit the position. The invitation was entirely spontaneous, a fact which made me feel somewhat flattered.

I will touch here upon an incident which occurred at that time because it makes plain one of the few cases of race prejudice which are now very rare in our country. The Commission on a certain day presented itself to the Minister to hear him explain the point of view of the government in creating the Commission. I was present, as were all of my colleagues. On the following day the *Diario Official* published a report in which all the engineers were presumably mentioned. However, my name, for some reason of which I was then ignorant, did not appear with the others. I was apparently omitted from a Commission which I had been invited to join. The omission was due, I later discovered, to the fact that I was the only *homen de côr* in that brilliant group and, to the mind of the official involved, this appeared very shocking (*chocante*); especially since I was to be working with American technicians who, it was said, did not appreciate the company of colored men. Hence I was excluded, and experienced for the first time the sting of prejudice. But to Senator Veriato de

Medeiros, whom I sought out that night to thank for his spontaneous gesture of invitation, my elimination was not official, and he immediately took the necessary steps so that on the following day everything was straightened out. I owe to the fine courtesy of this illustrious Senator the manner in which the incident was handled, although I did not find this out until much later through a mutual friend.

Meanwhile, the charge of prejudice, which the official had sought to bring against the Americans, completely disappeared, and I had the honor of winning their friendship and esteem. This proved with the passing of the years to be very beneficial and served me well in the profession which I adopted. After two years spent studying the ports of Santos and Maceió, and investigating the navigability of the São Francisco River, we all returned to Rio de Janeiro. Mr. Roberts, our illustrious chief, on presenting his report to the Minister, thought it proper to name me among his assistants, all of whom were distinguished men, and to present, in a special chapter, a description of the work with which I had been especially charged, calling it to the attention of the Minister under the title, "The Report of Snr. Calogeras."[1] The fact was that, in addition to the routine work with which we were each charged on the Commission, I was detailed by Mr. Roberts to explore the territory between the São Francisco River and the Atlantic coast across the Chapada Diamantina, and to collect geographic and geological data, together with information on the productive capacity, population, and commerce of the region. These data were later brought together in a book and published under the title, *O Rio São Francisco e a Chapada Diamantina*.

From my American colleagues on the Commission I received such proof of consideration and esteem that it captivated me. Rudolf Wiezer, Roberts' assistant who had accompanied him from the United States, in writing to a friend about me, used these words of extreme flattery: ". . . . the best Brazilian engineer on Roberts' staff." Orville Derby, the eminent geologist, who in his time was considered the greatest authority in the science of geology, took me for his collaborator in the work with which we were later intrusted by the governor of the state of São Paulo.

[1] The name is, of course, fictitious.

In 1882, the Roberts' Commission having been disbanded, I helped extend the rail line from Bahia to the São Francisco River, it being my job to draw up plans and specifications for the steel bridges of the railway.

In 1883 I was invited by Antonio Placido Peixoto de Amarante to be his First Engineer on the Comissão de Desobstrução do Rio de São Francisco, a project which we had studied together under the direction of Roberts three years before and which it had now fallen to his lot to execute as Chief Engineer. We removed the obstruction due to the celebrated Sobradinho Falls, the greatest obstacle to navigation in the upper part of the river, and shipping was soon established between the city of Joazeiro and the Falls of Pirapora, where the navigable section of the river ends.

For a little more than three years, or until 1886, I continued with this work. Orville Derby, who had been named head of the Geographic and Geological Commission of São Paulo, then invited me to be his First Engineer, charged especially with the geodetic survey.

The province of São Paulo was at that time governed by Senator João Alfredo Correa de Oliveira, an eminent man, who had always borne in mind the problem of communication with the interior and had just turned his attention to inland navigation and especially to the possibilities of connecting São Paulo with the faraway province of Matto Grosso. With this object in mind, we began the exploration of the Paranapanema, from its source in the Serra do Mar, in Itapetininga, to its junction with the Paraná River above Sete Quedas (Seven Falls). Studying the river from the point of view of its navigability, a labor which we carried out during the dry season of 1886, we found that more than two-thirds of its course was impracticable for navigation. This river failed to afford the solution for which we were searching. The Paranapanema is a great reservoir of hydroelectric energy rather than a passage between the Paraná-Paraguay and the Atlantic coast of southern Brazil.

On returning from these studies, which had also included an investigation of the geological character of the valley by the notable geologist, Francisco de Paula Oliveira, as well as an examination of those natural conditions bearing upon the productivity of the soil, and, in addition, ethnographic and ethnological studies of the Indians still dominating the woods and the plains of the Lower Paranapanema, we went to Campo Largo, setting up our camp near the iron foundry of Ipanema, a location which we had chosen by reason of its natural advantages to be our first base from which to survey the province of São Paulo.

We were proceeding with this measuring when a communication arrived from Colonel Mursa, director of the foundry, which surprised us greatly. His Majesty, the Emperor Dom Pedro II, the Colonel told us, had arrived there yesterday and had commanded the engineers of the Geographic and Geological Commission to present themselves before him without further delay and to bring with them their field notes and all data gathered during the exploration of the Paranapanema River, since His Majesty wished to see this information before its re-writing in the office. The order was urgent, and the Colonel advised us to go just as we were, in our field attire, since this was the wish of the Emperor.

All morning in Ipanema, Dom Pedro II examined our blueprints, measurements, notes, calculations, and drawings and inquired about the practical results of our work. He raised still other questions and objections on certain technical points, since he was a professional in this field. At luncheon he invited us all to join him at the same table, and I was given the honor of sitting in the chair at his right. During the luncheon we talked only of the studies carried out during our exploration, of the incidents of the trip, of the Indians, their customs and language. I state these details so that you may see how great was the interest of the Brazilian monarch in scientific studies, his vast erudition, his thirst for knowledge, his manifest desire for justice, and his utter lack of class or color prejudice. For Dom Pedro II was of all Brazilians most exempt from the prejudices of his time.

On taking leave of us, His Majesty desired that the studies of the Paranapanema River should be published as soon as possible.

Our investigation of the valley of the Paranapanema, a region which in former times was under the dominion of the Tupís and Guaranís, afforded me an opportunity of studying more closely this indigenous element so important in the history of the Brazilian people and in the formation of their national character. I gathered valuable data to contribute to the body of information regarding this race and the *lingua geral* which for nearly three centuries was the language spoken in this part of Brazil.

While working with the Geographic and Geological Commission, with which I remained for about four years, associated with such able and renowned colleagues as Orville Derby, Gonsaga do Campos, Francisco de Paula Oliveira, Washington de Aguiar, Alberto Loefgren, and other capable assistants, I had the opportunity of surveying nearly a third of the province, from Ipanema and Campo Largo along the ridge of the Serra do Mar, or the Paranapiacaba, and the peaks of the Mantigueira and their foothills from Santos and São Paulo inland as far as the banks of the Mogy-guassu River, which flows from the highlands of Minas Geraes. Owing to the time-consuming nature of this topographic work, we were not able to map completely such a large area. However, by 1890, we had made and published several geographical charts, when I left the Commission and accepted the invitation of the illustrious Dr. Vicente de Carvalho, then *Secretario de Estado dos Negocios do Interior*, to act as Sanitary Engineer for the city of São Paulo, and to carry out a sanitation project for which I, years before, at the instance of the provincial government following the proclamation of the Republic in 1889, had drawn up plans.

We were at that time in an era of social and political transformation, actually the greatest period of change through which the country has passed since independence. Following the war with Paraguay in 1870, Brazil had entered a notable epoch of reform and progress. This was especially evident during the ministry of Visconde do Rio Branco which brought us the law of civil marriage, the law of free birth, direct elections, as well as teaching reforms, and an extended development of the railway system of the country. Propaganda in favor of the emancipation of slaves was increasing. Those of sixty years and over were shortly freed by law, and, after a few more years of agitation, a most notable victory was achieved with the abolition of slavery without indemnification on the thirteenth of May, 1888. Eminent figures like Joaquim Nabuco, José do Patrocinio, and André Rebouças dominated the emancipation movement. The Emperor and the Princess Regent who signed the abolition decree, their ministers, João Alfredo Correa de Oliveira, and Antonio Ferreira Vianna, were the greatest figures in that glorious crusade which had gripped all Brazil.

The proclaiming of the Republic on November 15, 1889, a few months after the abolition of slavery, was facilitated by the illness of the emperor and by the fact that abolition had been decreed *without* indemnification. The republican propaganda, which had been active since the convention of Itú, gained its victory without great effort since, as it is only fair to remember, the tolerant spirit of the Emperor and the simplicity of his living had contributed greatly to the development of democratic ideas.

During this era of great transformation, in which the intellectuals and the youth of Brazil threw themselves with enthusiasm, we were all swept by the reform wave. I would not have made the Republic just as it was made; but I accepted it as a logical result of its historical antecedents and the democratic atmosphere then dominant in America.

The province of São Paulo soon took the lead in the extensive reforms which the country was experiencing. Political administration, agricultural development, immigration, all were stimulated by the new regime. I collaborated in all this as a citizen and as a public servant in proportion to my ability. In 1896 I was Chief Engineer of Sanitation for the state of São Paulo, a service which I directed for some years. With General Jardim and Salles de Oliveira I served on the Commission which organized the Escola Politecnica of São Paulo during the governorship of Bernardino de Campos. With Antonio Pisa, Cezario Motta, Horacio de Carvalho, Conselheiro Manoel Antonio Duarte de Azevedo, and others, we founded the Instituto Historico e Geographico of São Paulo, and I directed the construction of the building which still houses it. During the celebration of the three hundredth anniversary of Padre José de Anchieta's birth, which, through the initiative of Eduardo Prado, one of our most illustrious journalists and authors, launched a literary movement, I collaborated in the famed "Conferencias Anchietanas," which were to mark an epoch in the literary life of Brazil. My liking for historical studies then led me into the examination of documents from the first years of Brazilian colonization and the publication of the results of such research as monographs or articles in magazines of a scientific character. In this way I made a modest contribution.

It was during this period that I gave my leisure time over to the study of our indigenous races. I wrote and published some observations concerning the language of the Cayuas of the Lower Paranapanema and some data on the Guayanas of São Paulo. I published

O tupi na geographia nacional, in which I indicated the extent to which this Indian language had influenced the place names of Brazil. I studied the Krahos of the Upper São Francisco and their linguistic connection with the Krans tribes of the valley of the Tocantins and the Araguaya.

Discontinuing, in 1903, my work with the Sanitation Service of São Paulo, I returned to Bahia the following year to make a study of the possibilities of, and to bid for, a sanitation system for the city of Bahia; and on May 19, 1905, I signed a contract to put in these improvements for the *municipio.* Four years later I had completed the portion relative to the water supply, but only a third part of the sewage system. The failure of funds then paralyzed the work, and it remained suspended for several years, until in 1929 the contract was renewed by common consent of the parties concerned. With the completion of this task, my professional activity ended. As a young man, while still a student in the *curso superior,* I had been a teacher, lecturing in Latin, English, Mathematics, History, and Philosophy; and as a civil engineer, I had now worked without interruption for forty-eight years. I was never unemployed, and I early attained the highest rank in my profession.

Among literary and scientific studies which I have published, I might note: [Here follows a list of nineteen books or articles published in Brazilian literary and scientific publications, followed by the statement: "Various articles and lectures published in the *Revistas* of the Instituto Historico e Geographico de São Paulo, the Instituto Geographico e Historico da Bahia, and the Instituto Historico e Geographico Brasileiro de Rio de Janeiro."]

I had the honor of being chosen by my fellow-citizens of Bahia as their representative in the federal *camara* to replace Dr. Octavio Mangabeira, who had been named minister of foreign relations in the government of President Washington Luis. Not having been a militant politician, I was surprised at this choice which honored me so greatly. I continued in this office until the end of the session in 1929.

From the scientific and literary institutions of the country I have received the following spontaneous proofs of their appreciation: I am a member *effectivo de honra* of the Instituto Historico e Geographico Brasileiro; an active member of the Instituto Historico of São Paulo; president of the Instituto Historico of Bahia; corresponding member of the Instituto Historico of Minas Geraes; corresponding member of the Instituto Archeologico e Geographico Pernambucano; corresponding member of the Instituto Historico of Rio Grande do Norte; corresponding member of the Instituto of Ceará; member of the Instituto Historico of Sergipe; member of the Clube de Engenharia of Rio de Janeiro; charter member of the Sociedade Capistrano de Abreu; active member of the Academia de Letras da Bahia; active member of the Instituto Politecnico da Bahia.

I here end these autobiographical notes which are, I realize, somewhat deficient, since at my age [eight-one years] memory cannot be very faithful, and I fear it has failed me many times. These lapses of memory, however, have led me rather to understate than to exaggerate the honors which have been paid my modest talents and achievements.

APPENDIX B

COMMON SAYINGS REGARDING THE NEGRO

The following common sayings regarding the Negro probably date from the early years of the slave epoch. They are employed today more as interesting anecdotes of a former time than as characterizations of living individuals. They thus possess more the character of cultural survivals which are gradually disappearing than of racial myths actively functioning to maintain current racial inequalities or a caste order. Ordinarily, they are not thought of when individuals from the different races meet face to face. They are always uttered with a smile which seems to give them a character similar, for instance, to jokes about the Ford car which were so current in the United States in the 1920's or to humorous comments on the Irish, Scotch, or Swedes. Some of them are:

Negroes aren't born; they just appear.
Negroes don't marry; they just live together.
Negroes don't sleep; they just take naps.
Negroes don't eat; they bolt their food.
Negroes don't look at you; they only glance at you out of the corners of their eyes.
Negroes don't dance; they "samba."
Negroes don't take a bath; they just wet themselves.
Negroes don't dry themselves; they just shake the water off.
Negroes don't comb their hair; they curry it.
A Negro woman doesn't give birth to a child; she just "pops it out."
A Negro with gloves on is a sign of rain.
A Negro dressed in white is a fly in milk.[1]

[1] That is, "he looks out of place," a *parda* explained.

A Negro dressed in black is a black vulture with a cape.

A Negro is a *pau de fumo*.[2]

The Negro if he doesn't soil things on entering, soils them before he leaves.

Negro, *onça*'s food.

The following verses of a similar character also are recalled:

> The Negro has hair
> Which lard will not flatten;
> The more he combs it,
> The more it kinks.

> A Nagô Negro when he dies
> Is carried off in a banguê;[3]
> His relatives say,
> "The vultures have to eat."

> An old Negro when he dies
> Smells like a skunk;
> Our Lady, don't let
> That Negro into Heaven!

> A Negro when he dies
> Is laid out in a shirttail;
> His relatives say,
> "A poor man has no need of luxury."

> The odor of a Negro woman
> Comes from two places:
> The armpit
> And the heel.

> If the priest is white, he says Mass;
> But if he is a Negro, he only pre-
> tends to be saying it.[4]

[2] A piece of wood around which raw tobacco is wrapped for transport. It subsequently turns very black.

[3] A crude litter used in colonial Brazil to carry the bodies of dead slaves, to transport building materials, etc.

[4] An informant explained this line thus: "If he acted as if he was saying Mass, he was merely pretending, for he had not learned how to say it."

The Negro was born to be a dog
And to spend his life barking.

The Negro will not go to heaven,
Even though he prays,
Because his hair is kinky,
And it might stick Our Lord.

I have a pain in my chest
That goes to my heart
When I see a Negro with shoes on
And a mulatto barefoot.

Every white man comes from God,
Every mulatto is a *pimpão*,[5]
Every caboclo is a thief,
Every Negro a *feiticeiro*.

The white man is a son of God,
The mulatto is a foster-child,
The *cabra* has no relatives,
The Negro is a son of Satan.

The white man goes to heaven,
The mulatto stays on earth,
The *caboclo* goes to purgatory,
The Negro goes to hell.

The white man is a gold chain, the mulatto fine silver,
The *cabra* is a *relicario*, the Negro a leather cord.

It seems probable that the following sayings and verses arose as a form of protest from the Negro group itself:

The Negro was born just to be a lackey of the whites.
In the white's fishing, it's the Negro who pulls the net.
If the Negro doesn't want gruel, they give him gruel.
If the Negro doesn't want beans, they give him beans.
An insane white man is said to be only nervous; but an insane Negro is called a "drunk."

[5] A *pimpão* is one who is "sassy," provoking, "goes about with a chip on his shoulder."

The white man eats out of a plate, the mulatto where he likes, the *cabra* from a *cuia*,[6] the Negro out of an *aribe*.[7]

> The white man sleeps in a bed,
> The mulatto in the hall,
> The *caboclo* in the parlor,
> The Negro in the "privy."

> Whites sleep in beds,
> Mulattoes in the kitchen,
> *Caboclos* on the *terreiro*,[8]
> Negroes under the henroost.

> The white man drinks champagne,
> The mulatto Port wine,
> The *caboclo* beer,
> The Negro pig's urine.

> The *chique-chique* is a thorny wood,
> The *umburana* a bee's tree,
> The oxen's necktie is a yoke,
> The Negro's coat a beating.

> The mulatto, the *cabrinha*,[9] and the Negro
> Used to be able to drink;
> But today only whites and mulattoes
> Can swill it down all day.

> You call me ugly;
> I am ugly, but I am also affectionate.
> The seasoning is ugly too,
> But it makes a dish taste good.

[6] A *cuia* is a bowl made from half a gourd.

[7] An *aribe* is a crude clay dish.

[8] The space between the house and the servant quarters is called the *terreiro*. It may be paved with brick, or cement, but more often it is only of bare ground.

[9] Diminutive of *cabra*.

APPENDIX C

THE BOMFIM FESTIVAL

Certain popular festivals, like the Sabado and Segunda Feira do Bomfim, are largely taken over and even dominated by the lower classes. Individuals from the upper circles, both white and colored, attend only in their automobiles, driving slowly back and forth along the principal streets and through the crowds, or watch the festivities from the windows and doorways of near-by houses. In the words of a local citizen, the festival of Bomfim "springs from the people themselves, who regard O Senhor do Bomfim as their patron saint. It belongs to them more than Carnival does; Carnival is more refined (*mais elevado*), more under the control of the educated, 'cultured' Bahians."

Preceded by exclusively religious ceremonies, the celebration begins on the third Saturday in January and continues through the following Sunday and Monday. A large part of the population attends. Formerly, it is said, all business houses closed for the festival, and a few still do, while others take only a half-holiday on Monday. The celebration opens at the Church of Bomfim, which crowns a gently sloping hill on the peninsula of Itapagipe which juts out into Todos os Santos Bay to the north of the port. Black women in *bahiana* costume sit around the edges of the crowd selling such wares as *cocada*,[1] cakes, and other confections, mangoes, peanuts, *umbús*, and *cajús*.[2] In the *adro*, or open space, in

[1] *Cocada* is a confection made of coconut and sugar.

[2] *Cajús* are the fruit of the cashew tree. *Umbús* are a green, smooth-skinned fruit, about the size of a small lime.

front of the Church of Bomfim, booths are erected, each of which has been named for the patron saint of the proprietor or bears an inscription like *Fé em Deus* ("Faith in God"), *Salve a Nova Aurora* ("Hail to the Dawn"), or *A Bahianinha* ("Dear Little *Bahiana*"). At these booths one may purchase such famous Bahian dishes of African origin as *aberêm*, *carurú*, *vatapá*, *efó*, and *acarajé*, as well as drinks and other refreshments. *Kermesses*, or small booths given over to games of chance similar to those of traveling "carnivals" in the United States, bear such names as *Lua Cheia* ("Full Moon") or *Abrigo dos Filhos do Povo* ("Shelter for the Children of the People"). A brass band, composed of blacks from the fire department in uniform, plays intermittently from a raised platform in the center of the square.

At night the entire front of the church is ablaze with electric lights. Fireworks almost constantly sputter and bang in the air. An immense crowd mills about the *adro*, while other people sit at tables, eating, drinking, talking, and watching the festivities. About two hours after midnight, the *terno* of *Os Ciganos* ("the Gypsies") appears. It is a band of approximately thirty people, marching two abreast, ten musicians with brass instruments in the lead, followed by a dozen young men each of whom holds aloft a wooden staff branched at the top and lavishly decorated with paper flowers and Japanese lanterns, and an equal number of girls twelve to fourteen years old, dressed in gypsy costumes and shaking castanets and tambourines. After parading around the square, the *terno* halts in front of the church, greets the patron saint, then turns and ascends the platform vacated for this purpose by the band. The girls dance, sing, and play their instruments while one of the men performs a frenzied dance, twirling round and round a standard bearing the name and insignia of the *terno*. Before sunrise, the *ternos of Batutu* from the outlying area of the city known as Alto dos Pombos, of *Gata Abafa a Banca* ("the Cat 'Steals the Show' ") from Plataforma, of *Bacalhau* ("Codfish") from Estrada da Rainha, and *Filho do Arigofe* ("Son of Arigofe") from São Miguel, also appear and perform in a similar manner. Most of the black women venders and many of the celebrants will not return to their homes during the entire three days and nights of the *festa*.

On Monday the locale of the celebration shifts to Ribeiro on the opposite side of Itapagipe. Here in a large open space along the beach people crowd in by the thousands to compose informal groups of dancers, singers, and musicians, or merely promenade. People enjoy themselves for hours at a time, groups of singers and dancers dissolving only to form into new groups composed of different individuals, amid great hilarity and constant *sambas*. *Capoeira* groups form and draw their circles of onlookers. Almost all the actual participants are blacks or mixed-bloods; relatively few are of undiluted European blood.

SELECTED BIBLIOGRAPHY

SELECTED BIBLIOGRAPHY[1]

BAHIA

AMADO, JORGE. *Cacau.* Rio de Janeiro, 1933.

——. *Jubiabá.* Rio de Janeiro, 1935.

——. "Literatura dos negros e mulatos da Baía," *Revista do Arquivo Municipal* (São Paulo), XLVIII (June, 1938), 179–82.

——. *Suor.* 2d ed. Rio de Janeiro, 1936.

AMARAL, ALVARES DO. *Resumo chronologico da Bahia.* Bahia, n.d.

Annuario estatistico da Bahia. Published by the State of Bahia, 1934, 1936.

BOMFIM, MARTINIANO DO. "Os ministros de Xangô," *Estado da Bahia,* May 5, 1937.

BRASIL, PADRE ÉTIENNE IGNACE. "Le Fetichisme des négres du Brésil," *Anthropos,* III (1908), 881–904.

——. "Os Malês," *Revista do Instituto Historico e Geographico Brasileiro,* LXII, Part II (1909), 73–126.

BRITTO, EDUARDO A. DE CALDAS. "Levantes de pretos na Bahia," *Revista do Instituto Geographico e Historico da Bahia,* Vol. XXIX (1903).

CALMON, PEDRO. *Historia da Bahia.* 2d ed. São Paulo, n.d.

——. *Os Malês, a insurreição das senzalas.* Rio de Janeiro, 1933.

CARNEIRO, EDISON. *Negros Bantus.* Rio de Janeiro, 1937.

——. *Religiões negras.* Rio de Janeiro, 1936.

CARVALHO, CARLOS ALBERTO DE. *Tradições e milagres do Bomfim.* Bahia, 1915.

"A cidade que Deus esqueceu," *A Tarde* (Bahia), December 9, 1935.

Compromisso da Irmandade do Senhor Bom Jesus das Necessidades e Redempção. Bahia, 1929.

COSTA, JOVENTINO SILVINO DA. *Relatorio da Sociedade Protectora dos Desvalidos, 1832–1932.* Bahia, 1934.

"Creado o Conselho Africano da Bahia," *Estado da Bahia,* August 4, 1937.

[1] The system of listing Brazilian names here employed is that adopted by the Bibliotheca Municipal of São Paulo.

CUNHA, EUCLYDES DA. *Os sertões.* 12th ed. Rio de Janeiro, 1933.

CUNNINGHAME-GRAHAM, R. B. *A Brazilian Mystic.* New York, 1925.

DARWIN, CHARLES. *The Voyage of the Beagle.* "Harvard Classics," Vol. XXIX. New York, 1909.

"Era a mais popular 'Mãe de Santo' da Bahia," *Estado da Bahia,* January 5, 1938.

FERREIRA, JOSÉ CARLOS. "As insurreições dos africanos na Bahia," *Revista do Instituto Geographico e Historico da Bahia,* Vol. XXIX (1903).

FONSECA, LUIZ ANSELMO DA. *A escravidão, o clero e o abolicionismo.* Bahia, 1887.

MARQUES, CORYPHEU DE AZEVEDO. "No mundo cheio de mysterios dos espiritos e 'paes de santos,'" *Estado da Bahia,* May 11 and 14, 1936.

MARQUES, XAVIER. *O feiticeiro.* Bahia, 1922.

OLIVEIRA, J. B. DE SÁ E. "Dois embaixadores africanos mandados a Bahia pelo Rei do Dahomé," *Revista do Instituto Historico e Geographico Brasileiro,* LVI, Part I (1895), 413.

PEREIRA, A. PACIFICO. *A tuberculose na Bahia.* Bahia, 1904.

PINHO, WANDERLEY DE A. "O ultimo desembarque de escravos na Bahia," *Espelho,* September, 1936.

QUERINO, MANOEL RAYMUNDO. *A arte culinaria na Bahia.* Bahia, 1928. Republished in *Costumes africanos no Brasil.* Rio de Janeiro, 1938.

———. *A Bahia de outrora.* Bahia, 1922.

———. "A raça africana e os seus costumes na Bahia," *Annaes do Quinto Congresso Brasileiro da Geographia.* Rio de Janeiro, 1916. Republished in *Costumes africanos no Brasil.* Rio de Janeiro, 1938.

REIS, ANTONIO ALEXANDRE BORGES DOS. *Chorographia e historia do Brasil, especialmente do Estado da Bahia.* Bahia, 1894.

RODRIGUES, NINA. *Os africanos no Brasil.* São Paulo, 1932.

———. *L'Animisme fetichiste des nègres de Bahia.* Bahia, 1900. Reprinted from the original Portuguese text, with preface and notes by ARTHUR RAMOS, under the title, *O animismo fetichista dos negros bahianos.* Rio de Janeiro, 1935.

SANTOS, F. MARQUES DOS. "As balangandans," *Espelho,* April, 1936.

SILVA, IGNACIO ACCIOLI DE CERQUEIRA E. *Memorias historicas e politicas da Provincia da Bahia.* 4 vols. Bahia, 1919–33.

TAUNAY, AFFONSO DE E. *Na Bahia colonial, 1610-1774.* Rio de Janeiro, 1925.

———. *Na Bahia de Dom João VI.* Bahia, 1928.

VARELLA, JOÃO. *Na Bahia do Senhor do Bomfim.* Bahia, 1936.

———. *Da Bahia que eu vi.* Bahia, 1935.

———. *Cosme e Damião.* Bahia, 1938.

VILHENA, LUIZ DOS SANTOS. *Cartas.* Edited and annotated by BRAZ DO AMARAL. 2 vols. Bahia, 1922.

BRAZIL

ABREU, J. CAPISTRANO DE. *Capitulos de historia colonial.* 3d ed. Rio de Janeiro, 1934.

ADALBERT, PRINCE. *Travels of Prince Adalbert of Prussia.* Translated from *Aus meinem Tagebuche, 1842-1843* (Berlin, 1847), by ROBERT H. SCHOMBURGK and JOHN EDWARD TAYLOR. 2 vols. London, 1849.

AGASSIZ, PROFESSOR and MRS. LOUIS. *A Journey in Brazil.* Boston and New York, 1888.

AMARAL, BRAZ DO. "Os grandes mercados de escravos africanos. As tribus importadas. Sua distribuição regional," *Revista do Instituto Historico e Geographico Brasileiro* (Rio de Janeiro). Tomo especial do Congresso Internacional de Historia da America, V (1927), 437-96.

ANDRADE, MARIO DE. "Os Congos," *Lanterna Verde,* No. 2 (February, 1935), pp. 36-53.

———. "O samba rural paulista," *Revista do Arquivo Municipal* (São Paulo), XLI, 37-114.

ANDREWS, C. C. *Brazil, Its Condition and Prospects.* 2d ed. New York, 1889.

AZEVEDO, ALUIZIO DE. *O mulato.* 3d ed. Rio de Janeiro, 1889.

BARROS, F. BORGES DE. *Novos documentos para a historia colonial* Bahia, 1931.

BATES, HENRY W. *The Naturalist on the River Amazons.* Reprint. London, 1892.

BENNETT, FRANK. *Forty Years in Brazil.* London, 1914.

BILDEN, RÜDIGER. "Brazil, Laboratory of Civilization," *Nation,* CXXVIII (January 16, 1929), 73.

BLAKE, AUGUSTO VICTORINO ALVES SACRAMENTO. *Dicionario bibliographico brasileiro*. Rio de Janeiro, 1893.

BOMFIM, MANOEL. *O Brasil*. São Paulo, 1935.

BRYCE, JAMES. *South America*. New York, 1912.

BURTON, SIR RICHARD F. *Explorations of the Highlands of the Brazil*. 2 vols. London, 1869.

CALMON, PEDRO. *Historia social do Brasil*. 3 vols. 2d ed. São Paulo, 1937-39.

CALOGERAS, JOÃO PANDIÁ. *Formação historica do Brasil*. 3d ed. São Paulo, 1938.

————. "A politica exterior do imperio—as origens," *Revista do Instituto Historico e Geographico Brasileiro*. Tomo especial do Congresso Internacional de Historia da America (1927), pp. 1-471.

CENTRO NIPPONICO DE CULTURA. *Cruzamento da ethnia japoneza*. São Paulo, 1934.

CLAUDIO, AFFONSO. "As tribus negras importadas." *Revista do Instituto Historico e Geographico Brasileiro*. Tomo Especial, Part II (1914), pp. 597-655.

CODMAN, JOHN. *Ten Months in Brazil*. Boston, 1867.

COOPER, CLAYTON S. *The Brazilians and Their Country*. New York, 1917.

CORVO, J. DE A. *Estudos sobre as provincias ultramarinas*. 4 vols. London, 1883-87.

COSTA, FRANCISCO AUGUSTO PEREIRA DA. "Rei do Congo," *Jornal do Brasil* (Rio de Janeiro), August 25, 1901.

COUTINHO, JOSÉ JOAQUIM DA CUNHA DE AZEVEDO. *A analyse sobre a justiça do commercio do resgate dos escravos da costa d'Africa*. Lisboa, 1791.

COUTY, LOUIS. *L'Esclavage au Brésil*. Paris, 1881.

"O cruzamento de japonezes com brasileiros," *Jornal do Commercio* (Rio de Janeiro), September 17, 1935.

DEBRET, J. B. *Voyage pittoresque et historique au Brésil, 1816-1831*. 3 vols. Paris, 1835.

DENIS, PIERRE. *Brazil*. Translated from the French by BERNARD MIALL. New York, 1911.

DENT, HASTINGS CHARLES. *A Year in Brazil*. London, 1886.

DORNAS FILHO, JOÃO. *A escravidão no Brasil*. Rio de Janeiro, 1939.

EDSCHMID, KASIMIR. *South America.* New York, 1932.

ELLIOTT, L. E. *Brazil, Today and Tomorrow.* New York, 1917.

EWBANK, THOMAS. *Life in Brazil.* New York, 1856.

FERNANDES, GONÇALVES. *O folclore magico do Nordeste.* Rio de Janeiro, 1938.

——. *Xangôs do Nordeste.* Rio de Janeiro, 1937.

FIGUEIREDO, FIDELINO DE. *Estudos de historia americana.* São Paulo, n.d.

FREITAS, OCTAVIO DE. *Doenças africanas no Brasil.* São Paulo, 1935.

FREYRE, GILBERTO. *Casa grande e senzala.* 2d ed. Rio de Janeiro, 1936.

——. (ed.). *Novos estudos afro-brasileiros.* Rio de Janeiro, 1937.

——. *Sobrados e mucambos.* São Paulo, 1936.

——. "Social Life in Brazil in the Middle of the Nineteenth Century," *Hispanic American Historical Review*, Vol. V, No. 4 (November, 1922).

FRÉZIER, M. *Relation d'un voyage à la mer du sud.* Paris, 1716.

GALLET, LUCIANO. *Estudos de folclore.* Rio de Janeiro, 1934.

GARCIA, RODOLFO (ed.). *Dialogos das grandezas do Brasil.* Rio de Janeiro, 1930.

GARDINER, GEORGE. *Travels in the Interior of Brazil, 1836–1841.* London, 1849.

GRAHAM, MARIA. *Journal of a Voyage to Brazil, 1821–1823.* London, 1824.

GRANT, ANDREW. *History of Brazil.* London, 1809.

HANDELMANN, GOTTFRIED HEINRICH. *Historia do Brasil.* Translation of *Geschichte von Brasilien* (Berlin, 1860) by the INSTITUTO HISTORICO E GEOGRAPHICO BRASILEIRO. 2 vols. Rio de Janeiro, 1931.

HILL, LAWRENCE F. "The Abolition of the African Slave Trade to Brazil," *Hispanic American Historical Review*, Vol. XI, No. 2 (1931).

"A infiltração japoneza," *Jornal do Commercio* (Rio de Janeiro), October 16 and 22, 1935.

JOHNSTON, SIR HARRY H. "Slavery under the Portuguese," in *The Negro in the New World*, chap. v, pp. 77–109. London, 1910.

KELLER, ALBERT G. "The Portuguese in Brazil," in *Colonization*, chap. iv, pp. 131–67. Boston, 1908.

KERBEY, J. ORTON. *An American Consul in Amazonia.* New York, 1911.

KIDDER, DANIEL P. *Sketches of Residence and Travels in Brazil.* 2 vols. London, 1845.

KIDDER, DANIEL P., and FLETCHER, JAMES C. *Brazil and the Brazilians.* Philadelphia, 1857.

KOSTER, HENRY. *Travels in Brazil, 1809 to 1815.* 2 vols. Philadelphia, 1817.

LACERDA, JEAN BAPTISTE DE. "The *Metis*, or Half-Breeds, of Brazil," in *Papers on Inter-racial Problems*, edited by G. SPILLER. London, 1911.

LANE-POOLE, STANLEY. *The Story of the Moors in Spain.* New York and London, 1886.

LAYTANO, DANTE DE. *Os africanismos do dialeto gaucho.* Porto Alegre, 1936.

LIMA, MANOEL DE OLIVEIRA. *The Evolution of Brazil Compared with that of Spanish and Anglo-Saxon America.* Edited by PERCY A. MARTIN. Stanford University, Calif., 1914.

LINDLEY, THOMAS. *Narrative of a Voyage to Brazil.* London, 1805.

LOWRIE, SAMUEL H. "Racial and National Intermarriage in a Brazilian City," *American Journal of Sociology*, XLIV, No. 5 (March, 1939), 684–707.

MALHEIRO, AGOSTINHO MARQUES PERDIGÃO. *A escravidão no Brasil.* 3 vols. Rio de Janeiro, 1867.

MANCHESTER, ALAN K. "The Rise of the Brazilian Aristocracy," *Hispanic American Historical Review*, XI, No. 2 (May, 1931), 145–68.

MARROQUIM, MARIO. *A lingua do Nordeste.* São Paulo, 1934.

MARTIN, PERCY A. "Brazil." *Argentina, Brazil and Chile since Independence*, Part III: Washington, 1935.

———. "Slavery and Abolition in Brazil," *Hispanic American Historical Review*, Vol. XIII, No. 2 (May, 1933).

MATHISON, GILBERT FARQUHAR. *Narrative of a Visit to Brazil, Chile, Peru and the Sandwich Islands, 1821–1822.* London, 1825.

MAWE, JOHN. *Travels in the Interior of Brazil.* Philadelphia, 1816.

MENDONÇA, RENATO. *A influencia africana no português do Brasil.* 2d ed. São Paulo, 1935.

MORAES, EVARISTO DE. *A escravidão africana no Brasil.* São Paulo, 1933.

MORAES FILHO, ALEXANDRE JOSÉ DE MELLO. *Festas e tradições populares.* Rio de Janeiro, 1888.

NABUCO, JOAQUIM. *O abolicionismo.* London, 1883.

NOBREGA, MANOEL DE. *Cartas do Brasil, 1549–1560.* Rio de Janeiro, 1886.

NORTON, HENRY K. *The Coming of South America.* New York, 1932.

"Oliveira Vianna e a immigração japoneza," *Jornal do Commercio* (Rio de Janeiro), September 13, 1935.

D'ORBIGNY, ALCIDE. *Voyage dans les deux Amériques.* Paris, 1836.

PRADO, J. F. DE ALMEIDA. *Pernambuco e as capitanias do norte do Brasil, 1530–1630.* 2 vols. São Paulo, 1939–41.

QUERINO, MANOEL RAYMUNDO. "Os homens de côr preta na historia," *Revista do Instituto Geographico e Historico da Bahia,* XLVIII (1923), 353–63.

RAYMUNDO, JACQUES. *O elemento afro-negro na lingua portuguesa.* Rio de Janeiro, 1933.

RAMOS, ARTHUR. "Castigos de escravos," *Revista do Arquivo Municipal* (São Paulo), XLVII (May, 1938), 79–104.

———. "As culturas negras na America do Sul: Brasil," *As culturas negras no novo mundo.* Part V, pp. 281–371. Rio de Janeiro, 1937.

———. *O folk-lore negro do Brasil.* Rio de Janeiro, 1935.

———. *O negro brasileiro.* Rio de Janeiro, 1934.

———. "The Negro in Brazil." Manuscript especially prepared for publication in the United States and translated by RICHARD PATTEE. Washington, 1939.

REBOUÇAS, ANTONIO PEREIRA. *Recordações da vida parlamentar.* Rio de Janeiro, 1870.

Recenseamento do Brasil: 1920, Vol. IV: *População,* Bóok I. Rio de Janeiro, 1922.

REGO, JOSÉ LINS DO. *Banguê.* Rio de Janeiro, 1934.

———. *Doidinho.* Rio de Janeiro, n.d.

———. *Historias da velha Totonia.* Rio de Janeiro, 1936.

———. *Menino de engenho.* 2d ed. Rio de Janeiro, 1934.

———. *Pedra Bonita.* Rio de Janeiro, 1938.

———. *Pureza.* Rio de Janeiro, 1937.

———. *Usina.* Rio de Janeiro, 1936.

RIBEIRO, JOÃO. *Historia do Brasil*. 9th ed. Rio de Janeiro, 1920.

———. *A lingua nacional*. São Paulo, 1921.

ROCHA, PADRE M. RIBEIRO DA. *Ethiope resgatado, empenhado, susten-tado, corrigido, instruido e libertado*. Lisboa, 1758.

ROMERO, SYLVIO. "O Brasil social," *Revista do Instituto Historico e Geographico Brasileiro*, LXIX (1906), 105–79.

ROOSEVELT, Theodore. "Brazil and the Negro," *Outlook*, CVI (February 21, 1914), 409 ff.

ROQUETTE-PINTO, E. (ed.). *Estudos afro-brasileiros*. Papers presented to the First Afro-Brazilian Congress (Recife, 1934). Rio de Janeiro, 1935.

RUGENDAS, MAURICE. *Voyage pittoresque dans le Brésil*. Translated from the German by de Colbery. 3 vols. Paris, 1835.

SCOTT, S. P. *History of the Moorish Empire in Europe*. Philadelphia, 1904.

SETTE, MARIO. *Maxambombas e maracatús*. São Paulo, n.d.

SILVA, ARTUR LOBO DA. "Anthropologia do exercito brasileiro," *Archivos do Museu Nacional*, Vol. XXX. Rio de Janeiro, 1928.

SIMONSEN, ROBERTO C. "As consequencias economicas da abolição," *Jornal do Commercio* (Rio de Janeiro), May 8, 1938.

SOUTHEY, ROBERT. *History of Brazil*. 3 vols. London, 1810.

SPIX, J. B. VON, and MARTIUS, C. F. P. VON. *Travels in Brazil, 1817–1820*. Translation of *Reise in Brasilien* (3 vols.; München, 1823–31) by H. E. LLOYD. 2 vols. London, 1824.

STEPHENS, H. MORSE. *Portugal*. New York, 1903.

STEWART, C. S. *Brazil and La Plata*. New York, 1856.

TAUNAY, AFFONSO DE E. "Notas sobre as ultimas décadas do trafico," *Jornal do Commercio* (Rio de Janeiro), July 24 and 31, August 7, 1938.

———. "Numeros do trafico," *Jornal do Commercio* (Rio de Janeiro), September 30, 1936.

TAUNAY, VISCONDE DE. *Homens e cousas do imperio*. São Paulo, 1924.

TOLLENARE, L. F. "Notas dominicais tomadas durante uma residencia no Brasil, 1816–1818" (portion relative to Pernambuco; translated by ALFREDO DE CARVALHO from the unpublished French manuscript), *Revista do Instituto Arqueologico e Geographico Pernambucano*, No. 61, 1905.

VALLE, FLAUSINO RODRIGUES. *Elementos de folk-lore musical brasileiro*. São Paulo, 1936.

VARIOS AUTORES. *O negro no Brasil*. Papers presented to the Second Afro-Brazilian Congress (Bahia, 1937). Rio de Janeiro, 1940.

VARNHAGEN, FRANCISCO A. DE, VISCONDE DE PORTO SEGURO. *Historia geral do Brasil*. 3d complete ed. 4 vols. São Paulo, n.d.

VASCONCELLOS, SALOMÃO DE. "A escravatura africana em Minas Geraes," *Jornal do Commercio* (Rio de Janeiro), November 20, 1938.

VIANNA, F. J. OLIVEIRA. *Evolução do povo brasileiro*. 2d ed. São Paulo, 1933.

———. *Populações meridionaes do Brasil*. 3d ed. São Paulo, 1933.

———. *Raça e assimilação*. 2d ed. São Paulo, 1934.

VIEIRA, PADRE ANTONIO. *Sermões*. 15 vols. Lisboa, 1679–1748.

WALSH, R. *Notices of Brazil in 1828 and 1829*. 2 vols. London, 1830.

WELLS, JAMES W. *Three Thousand Miles through Brazil*. 2 vols. London and Philadelphia, 1886.

WIED-NEUWIED, PRINCE MAXIMILIAN. *Viagens ao Brasil, 1815–1817*. Translation of *Reise nach Brasilien in den Jahren 1815 bis 1817* (2 vols.; Frankfurt, 1820), by EDGAR SUSSEKIND DE MENDONÇA and FLÁVIO POPPE DE FIGUEIREDO. São Paulo, 1940.

WILLIAMS, MARY W. "The Treatment of Brazilian Slaves in the Brazilian Empire," *Journal of Negro History*, Vol. XV (July, 1930).

WYNDHAM, H. A. "Brazil," *The Atlantic and Slavery*, Part II, Sec. II. London: Oxford University Press, 1935.

INDEX TO NAMES

SUBJECT INDEX